C000104381

The History of the Euro Union

This book radically re-conceptualises the origins of the European Union as a trans- and supranational polity as it emerged between the Schuman Plan of May 1950 and the first enlargement of the European Communities at the start of 1973.

Drawing upon social science theories and debates as well as recent historical research, Wolfram Kaiser and Morten Rasmussen in their introductory chapters discuss innovative ways of narrating the history of the EU as the emergence of a transnational political society and supranational political system. Building on these insights, eight chapters based on multilateral and multi-archival research follow each with case studies of transnational networks, public sphere and institutional cultures and policy-making which illustrate systematically related aspects of the early history of the EU. In the concluding chapter, leading political scientist Alex Warleigh-Lack demonstrates how greater interdisciplinary cooperation, especially between contemporary history and political studies, can significantly advance our knowledge of the EU as a complex polity.

This book will be of interest to students and scholars of Politics, European Studies and History.

Wolfram Kaiser is Professor of European Studies at the University of Portsmouth, UK and Visiting Professor at the College of Europe, Belgium.

Brigitte Leucht lectures in European Studies at the University of Portsmouth, UK and is a Visiting Lecturer at the Graduate Institute of International and Development Studies in Geneva, Switzerland.

Morten Rasmussen is Assistant Professor of Contemporary European History at the University of Copenhagen, Denmark.

UACES Contemporary European Studies Series

Edited by Tanja Börzel, *Free University of Berlin,* Michelle Cini, *University of Bristol and* Roger Scully, *University of Wales, Aberystwyth,* on behalf of the University Association for Contemporary European Studies

The primary objective of the new Contemporary European Studies series is to provide a research outlet for scholars of European Studies from all disciplines. The series publishes important scholarly works and aims to forge for itself an international reputation.

1. **The EU and Conflict Resolution**
   Promoting peace in the backyard
   Nathalie Tocci

2. **Central Banking Governance in the European Union**
   A comparative analysis
   Lucia Quaglia

3. **New Security Issues in Northern Europe**
   The Nordic and Baltic states and the ESDP
   Edited by Clive Archer

4. **The European Union and International Development**
   The politics of foreign aid
   Maurizio Carbone

5. **The End of European Integration**
   Anti-Europeanism examined
   Paul Taylor

6. **The European Union and the Asia-Pacific**
   Media, public and elite perceptions of the EU
   Edited by Natalia Chaban and Martin Holland

7. **The History of the European Union**
   Origins of a trans- and supranational polity 1950–72
   Edited by Wolfram Kaiser, Brigitte Leucht and Morten Rasmussen

The History of the European Union

Origins of a trans- and supranational polity 1950–72

Edited by Wolfram Kaiser, Brigitte Leucht and Morten Rasmussen

Routledge
Taylor & Francis Group

LONDON AND NEW YORK

First published 2009 by Routledge
2 Park Square, Milton Park, Abingdon, Oxon OX14 4RN

Simultaneously published in the USA and Canada
by Routledge
270 Madison Avenue, New York, NY 10016

*Routledge is an imprint of the Taylor & Francis Group,
an informa business*

First issued in paperback 2011

© 2009 Editorial selection and matter Wolfram Kaiser, Brigitte Leucht
and Morten Rasmussen; individual contributors, their contributions

Typeset in Times New Roman by Keyword Group Ltd

British Library Cataloguing in Publication Data
A Catalogue record for this book is available from the British Library

Library of Congress Cataloging in Publication Data
A catalog record for this book has been requested.

ISBN 10: 0-415-46393-9 (hbk)
ISBN 10: 0-415-66402-0 (pbk)
ISBN 10: 0-203-92648-X (ebk)

ISBN 13: 978-0-415-46393-5 (hbk)
ISBN 13: 978-0-415-66402-8 (pbk)
ISBN 13: 978-0-203-92648-2 (ebk)

Contents

Notes on Contributors

Wolfram Kaiser is Professor of European Studies at the University of Portsmouth and Visiting Professor at the College of Europe in Bruges.

Ann-Christina L. Knudsen is Associate Professor of European Studies at the University of Aarhus.

Brigitte Leucht received her PhD from the University of Portsmouth where she lectures in European Studies. She is a Visiting Lecturer at the Graduate Insitute of International and Development Studies in Geneva, Switzerland.

N. Piers Ludlow is Senior Lecturer in the Department of International History at the London School of Economics and Political Science.

Jan-Henrik Meyer has submitted his PhD thesis at the Free University of Berlin. He is a Marie Curie Fellow at the University of Portsmouth.

Sigfrido M. Ramírez Pérez received his PhD from the European University Institute in Florence. He is a member of the French steering committee of the Permanent Group for the Study of the Automobile Industry and its Employees in Paris.

Morten Rasmussen is Assistant Professor at the Saxo Institute, History Section, University of Copenhagen.

Lise Rye is Postdoctoral Fellow in European Studies at the Norwegian University of Science and Technology, Trondheim.

Katja Seidel is Research Assistant at the University of Cardiff and has submitted her PhD thesis at the University of Portsmouth.

Kristian Steinnes is Associate Professor of European Studies at the Norwegian University of Science and Technology, Trondheim.

Alex Warleigh-Lack is Professor of Politics and International Relations at Brunel University and Chair of the University Association for Contemporary European Studies.

Preface

As editors and authors of this book we are united in our belief that the history of the European Union (EU) is in great need of conceptual innovation. We advocate theoretically informed, source-rich multi-national and multi-archival historical narratives, which retain their disciplinary distinctiveness, but are also suitable for interdisciplinary communication and co-operation. The desirable combination of conceptual sophistication and time-intensive archival research also means, however, that such historical narratives, which span longer periods of time and cover a multitude of institutional and political actors and different policy fields, require greater joint effort in the reconstruction of the history of the EU. Conscious of our limitations as individual scholars, we have from the beginning conceived of this book as a highly integrated collective endeavour. All of us have profited tremendously from working together so closely with each other and commenting on earlier drafts of our chapters during a workshop at the University of Trondheim and on subsequent occasions including the annual conferences of the University Association for Contemporary European Studies in Limerick and Portsmouth. Suffering from various new public management 'quality assurance' schemes, which increase our administrative burden and tend to stifle innovative research, we have enjoyed co-operating closely on this project. We hope that this will encourage other scholars, not merely contemporary historians, to work towards greater interdisciplinarity in the study of the EU as a trans- and supranational polity.

Acknowledgments

We are grateful to the University of Trondheim for funding a workshop which allowed us to discuss first drafts of our chapters. We would also like to thank the series editors for their continued encouragement and constructive criticism in the course of the preparation of this book, and Heidi Bagtazo, our Routledge editor, and her team for their professional management of the editorial and production process.

List of Abbreviations

ACEA	European Automobile Manufacturers Association
APEC	Asia-Pacific Economic Cooperation
CAP	Common Agricultural Policy
CCMC	Committee of Common Market Automobile Constructors
CED	Committee for Economic Development (United States)
CEO	Chief Executive Officer
CEPES	Comité Européen pour le Progrès Économique et Sociale
CIA	Central Intelligence Agency
CLMC	Liaison Committee of the European Producers of the Common Market
CNPF	Conseil National du Patronat Français
Cocor	Coordinating Committee
Coreper	Committee of Permanent Representatives
DG	Directorate-General
DG III	Directorate-General for Industrial Affairs
DG IV	Directorate-General for Competition
DNA	Det norske Arbeiderparti (Norway)
EC	European Communities
ECA	European Co-operation Administration
ECJ	European Court of Justice
ECSC	European Coal and Steel Community
EEA	European Economic Area
EEC	European Economic Community
EFTA	European Free Trade Association
EIB	European Investment Bank
ELEC	European League for Economic Co-operation
EP	European Parliament
EPC	European Political Community
ERP	European Recovery Program
ERT	European Round Table of Industrialists
EU	European Union
Euratom	European Atomic Energy Community
GATT	General Agreement on Tariffs and Trade

IAR	International Authority on the Ruhr
ICC	International Chamber of Commerce
IGC	Intergovernmental Conference
IR	International Relations
ISC	International Steel Cartel
LI	Liberal Intergovernmentalism
MEP	Member of the European Parliament
MRP	Mouvement Républicain Populaire
NATO	North Atlantic Treaty Organization
NEC	Labour Party National Executive Committee (United Kingdom)
OEEC	Organization for European Economic Cooperation
SAP	Socialdemokratiska Arbetarparti
SCA	Special Committee for Agriculture
SD	Socialdemokratiet (Denmark)
SEA	Single European Act
SER	Sociaal-Economische Raad (Netherlands)
SFIO	Section Française de l'Internationale Ouvrière (France)
SGCI	Secrétariat Général du Comité Interministériel pour les Questions de Coopération Économique Européenne
SI	Socialist International
SPD	Sozialdemokratische Partei Deutschlands (Germany)
SPÖ	Sozialistische Partei Österreichs (Austria)
TBV	Technical Bureau for Vehicles
UK	United Kingdom
UN	United Nations
UNICE	Union of Industrial and Employers' Confederation of Europe
US	United States
USHICOG	US High Commission for Germany
VAT	Value Added Tax
VW	Volkswagen
WP 29	Working Party 29 of the European Commission for Europe of the UN
WP 3	Working Party 3 co-ordinated by DG III

1 Origins of a European polity

A new research agenda for European Union history

Wolfram Kaiser, Brigitte Leucht and Morten Rasmussen

This book sets out to re-conceptualize the history of the present-day European Union (EU) as the gradual emergence over time of a European-level polity: a supranational political system with a complex institutional set-up and policy-making structures embedded in what could be called an incipient transnational political society of intense networking and informal political co-ordination and governance. With their predominant focus on current Community politics, political scientists have characterized the EU as a supranational political system of multilevel governance.[1] Crucially, however, its historical origins are in the formative phase of core Europe integration in the European Coal and Steel Community (ECSC) founded in 1951–52, and the European Economic Community (EEC) created in 1957–58, before its first enlargement by Britain, Denmark and Ireland in 1972–73. Integration in this formative phase created a broad corridor for institutional and policy options and developments up to the present. This book recasts the way we conceive of these historical origins of the present-day European polity. It does so by combining two chapters on network analysis and institutionalist theories as recent theoretical and conceptual approaches to understanding the EU as heuristic devices for developing sophisticated historical narratives of European integration with eight source-based transnational and supranational case studies followed by a concluding chapter on the scope for cross-disciplinary co-operation between a new history of the EU and social science research.

Starting in earnest with the creation of an industrial customs union after 1957–58, European integration has encroached so much upon the member-states and affected EU citizens in manifold ways that it should be inconceivable that historians of the economic, social and political history of postwar (Western) Europe and its nation-states should write about their specialized topics without sophisticated reference to this transnational and supranational context. Yet, much historical work on contemporary Europe more generally is as ill-informed about the history of the EU[2] as even many of those social scientists who actually argue from different theoretical perspectives that its historical origins and evolution are crucial for understanding contemporary issues of EU politics at the start of the twenty-first century. In large measure, this sorry state of affairs is due to the fact that much of the historiography of European integration has been conceptually underdeveloped and methodologically weak, reconstructing the history of the EU as merely one long series of national policy decisions and inter-state treaty negotiations.

From the 1960s through to the early 1980s, much early historiography was driven by a strong normative desire to write the history of European integration in a Hegelian perspective as the unstoppable ascendancy of federalist idealism over the nation-states and their internecine wars. Walter Lipgens, the first holder of the Chair in European Integration History at the European University Institute between 1976 and 1979, was the leading scholar to write in this historiographical tradition.[3] As a Catholic historian, an active member of the European Movement and a fervent supporter of German Chancellor Konrad Adenauer's policy of Western integration, he saw the formation of core Europe as a desirable attempt to overcome the nation-state: forward to the past of a new medieval order of 'unity'. In a revealing passage in an article published in 1983 in the German ped-agogical history journal *Geschichte in Wissenschaft und Unterricht*, Lipgens insisted that schools should teach European integration as 'the most successful peace movement to date', and that they must make clear that 'all deficiencies and weaknesses, the talk of Brussels bureaucrats and crises, . . . result almost without exception from areas where integration has not gone far enough'.[4] Academically, Lipgens was mainly interested in the contributions of the resistance movements and the European Movement to the European 'idea'.[5] He amassed fascinating sources from many European countries, but crucially, failed to establish causal links between these movements' ideas and proposals and the actual process of core Europe integration after 1950–51. The lack of methodological sophistication combined with the normative overdrive of Lipgens and other, especially Italian and some British researchers with close links to the European Movement,[6] subse-quently led contemporary historians to abandon attempts to trace transnational dimensions of European integration altogether.

The accelerated opening-up of member-state archives induced other historians to redirect their attention towards government records. In his revisionist account, the British economic historian Alan S. Milward analyzed the origins of European integration after 1945 as the result of intergovernmental bargaining of 'national interests'. He replaced Lipgens' transnational movements with states as the only relevant, and allegedly cohesive actors, and ideas with material interests. In his first book, *The Reconstruction of Western Europe 1945–51*,[7] Milward reinter-preted the origins of the Schuman Plan as having resulted from a search of European governments for an economic peace settlement through integration to control Germany. In his second book, *The European Rescue of the Nation-State*,[8] he sharpened his thesis by arguing more provocatively that the overriding moti-vation behind the integration process was not to overcome the nation-state, but to strengthen it. According to Milward, the creation of the ECSC/EEC stabilized the nation-states through the selective Europeanization of domestic welfare policies that each member state alone could not have sustained in the longer run, as in the case of agriculture, for example. His research design was perhaps somewhat unsystematically multilateral and comparative, but it went decisively beyond more limited attempts to explain the European policies of individual states. Especially by bringing states back in, and by emphasizing the socio-economic motivations of government policy on 'Europe', Milward made a fundamental contribution to the debate about the origins of the EU. His analysis of 'national interests', or what he has recently termed 'national strategies',[9] still has profoundly realist connotations, however. Milward has insisted that 'the process of integration is not separable from the evolution of domestic politics'.[10] He has sought to explain national governmental policy-making as embedded in parliamentary politics and reflecting electoral strategies. Some would argue, however, that his interpretation does not take sufficient account of the contested political nature of national European policy in the more pluralistic postwar democracies. In any case, Milward also wrote transnational actors out of the history of the origins of the EU altogether. Concentrating on the overriding importance in his view of material interests for national preference formation, moreover, he also tends to confuse policy ideas with idealism as in his brief discussion of the European policies of leading 'saints' like Robert Schuman, Konrad Adenauer and Paul-Henri-Spaak.[11] Yet, as Morten Rasmussen has recently demonstrated for the interesting Danish case, norms and ideas as well as material factors have shaped national preference formation.[12]

Whereas Lipgens failed to establish links between transnational movements, their ideas and governmental decision-making, Milward also does not demonstrate conclusively causal links between either the interests of particular domestic economic pressure groups or the musings of bureaucrats in economic ministries, who feature prominently in his studies, and the evolution of the external economic and integration policy of European states. Both Lipgens and Milward have transgressed the national perspective in reconstructing the origins of the present-day EU, however. This is more than can be said about most contemporary historians who have written about national policy 'towards Europe' based on government sources only. Milward in particular inspired more conceptually sophisticated attempts at explaining national European policies, especially in the Scandinavian context. On the whole, however, this dominant approach from the 1980s through to the early 2000s has been implicitly steeped in 'realist' assumptions about the autonomy of foreign policy-making elites in determining and bargaining 'national interests'. In this perspective, interests are mainly of a foreign and security policy (not economic) kind. Much of this historiography, which has also dominated the publications of the European Community Liaison Committee of Historians,[13] shares a kind of Gaullist conception of European policy-making as controlled by political leaders and foreign ministries with fixed preferences. It makes no sustained attempt even to reconstruct governmental policy-making as embedded in domestic political contestation of aims and objectives by political parties, socio-economic interest groups and other democratic actors, let alone as a segment of the emerging European political space of high institutionalization and legal penetration. Even Charles de Gaulle could not conduct foreign policy like the Austrian Count Clemens von Metternich in the first half of the nineteenth century, however. In the early postwar period, the politics of European integration was clearly qualitatively very different from the 'concert' of the Great Powers.

It is vital to move decisively beyond 'realist' state-centric approaches to understanding EU history. By reconceptualizing the history of European integration as the slow emergence of a European-level polity, we propose two new integrated fields of research that will not only broaden and improve our understanding of EU history, but also promise fundamentally to transform the way we conceive of national history and European policy-making. We advocate first, to analyze in a more conceptually sophisticated manner than Lipgens, and without his normative prejudices, the growth and character of the transnational political society in the making: the formation of formalized and highly informal networks of political parties, interest groups, policy experts, journalists and other actors with an interest, and a stake in, utilizing the new supranational political space for advancing their ideas and material interests, influencing European policy-making or transferring institutional rules and practices between member-states, below the supranational level. Networks have played a crucial role in shaping what Keith Middlemas first called the 'informal politics' of European integration:[14] from establishing recruitment methods for supranational institutions, to forming guiding integration ideas, influencing policy-making cultures and developing socialization patterns. Paradoxically, contemporary historians of European integration have largely ignored this transnational dimension of the emerging Community polity precisely at a time when modern historians have begun to rediscover this same dimension in an attempt to conceptualize cross-border networks, communication and cultural and policy transfer during national integration and proto-globalization in the second half of the nineteenth century.[15] Transnational networking and communication were in fact much more intense in Western Europe after 1945 compared to the nineteenth century, however, when it took place under more difficult conditions of transport and communication technology and was also regarded with great suspicion by nationalists everywhere.

We propose second, to conceptualize the early EU as an incipient political system. For contemporary historians, the main challenge is not to ascertain whether the EU already is, or will become, a continent-wide federal state of sorts, or whether it remains a legal system 'sui generis': neither an international organization nor a state by traditional legal definitions. It is clearly, and has been from its inception, a political system in the making with horizontal and vertical institutional structures and complex European-level policy-making involving member-states, supranational institutions and societal actors, as Piers Ludlow has also argued recently in the first multilateral study of the EEC in the mid-1960s.[16] Not least due to the traditional nation-state focus of modern historians of politics, however, which has been an endemic intellectual disease from the origins of history as a professional discipline in the nineteenth century, they have so far largely failed to explain convincingly the character of this new European political system.

We do not suggest that these two new integrated fields of research should replace the study of national history and policy-making as a core dimension of

EU historiography. Clearly, understanding the domestic socio-economic and political dynamics that shape national European policies remains essential for the analysis of EU history. Writing the history of the member-states and their policy-making requires a refined understanding of how national preference formation has increasingly taken place within an incipient European political system with more and more supranational competences characterized by ever closer network-type cross-border connections, however. Analyzing political processes in the national arena as isolated from supranational and transnational context and influences, as most contemporary historians still do, leads to a very distorted understanding of nation-states within the present-day EU, and of EU history. It also fails to conceptualize crucial long-term structural changes in the reduced capacity of member-states to act independently.

With the aim of upgrading the conceptual sophistication of empirical source-based research on EU history we propose that contemporary historians engage more effectively with the work of social scientists, especially political scientists, some of whom have for more than a decade analyzed the present-day EU as multilevel governance with strong transnational and supranational dimensions. We advocate such a dialogue with specific objectives in mind. Methodologically, social science theories and concepts can be used by historians as heuristic tools to clarify and discuss the often too implicit epistemological assumptions underlying their more empirically-driven research; enhance the scope and precision of their research agendas and more concretely, their guiding research questions; identify and show causal links in a more analytical and less descriptive research mode; and finally, prioritize in a more refined way factors and causes instead of merely listing different 'influences' that may have played a role in the integration process. Substantially, the theoretical and empirical state of the art of social science research on the EU as a political system and transnational society formation constitutes a natural point of departure for a new EU historiography that aspires to conceptualize the historical evolution of these two dimensions. We suggest that two sets of social science theories and concepts are especially useful for reconstructing the evolution of the core Europe polity: network-focussed approaches and institutionalist theories. We understand that social science 'meta'-theories like constructivism and other tools for understanding governance might also be beneficial for analyzing core Europe integration. The role of transnational networks in shaping institutional designs and policy solutions as well as the early development of the European institutions and their relationships with the member-states were especially crucial in this phase of integration until 1972–73, however.[17] Thus, in the first conceptual chapter, Wolfram Kaiser takes core concepts such as networks from social science debates on EU governance to show how they could assist contemporary historians in conceptualizing the process of European integration as the formation of increasingly dense political and social links and bonds across borders. In the second conceptual chapter, Morten Rasmussen discusses different institutionalist theories and how contemporary historians might apply them fruitfully to research on supranational aspects of the ECSC/EEC as an emerging political system.

The eight empirical chapters flesh out, and assess provisionally, the heuristic usefulness of the conceptual ideas and arguments in these two introductory chapters in source-based historical narratives. We have compiled them with a view to addressing first, the need to conceptualize the informal politics and political culture of, and within, the new supranational institutions, as in the chapters by Katja Seidel on the European Commission's strategy and objectives for a common competition policy and by Lise Rye on the origins and evolution of a Community information policy; second, the need for a sophisticated analysis of member-state interaction with supranational institutions, as in the chapters by Piers Ludlow on co-operation between the European Commission and the Committee of Permanent Representatives (Coreper) – member-state co-operation at ambassadorial level – and by Ann-Christina Knudsen on the origins of the Community's 'own resources' budgetary competences; third, the role of political and business networks in setting policy agendas and influencing institutional dynamics and supranational and transgovernmental policy-making in Western Europe as in the chapters by Kristian Steinnes on the debate and co-ordination of European policy within transnational Nordic-British socialist party networks and by Sigfrido Ramirez on business networks in the automobile industry; and finally, how supranational policy-making and transnational political networking have been embedded within an emerging European public sphere, as discussed by Jan-Henrik Meyer in his chapter on the summit of The Hague in 1969, as well as within the much larger political space of the Atlantic world, as in Brigitte Leucht's chapter on the role of transatlantic policy networks in the formation of the ECSC in 1950–51. Her contribution also suggests that it would be highly desirable for more contemporary historians to re-visit the origins of core Europe before 1957–58 through this book's conceptual lens.

At the same time, we advocate a strictly pragmatic approach to using social science theories and concepts. We use them in this book to improve the deductive dimension of our research, equipping the toolbox of historians with heuristic ideas and hypotheses for refining their historical narrative. As the international historian John Lewis Gaddis has recently argued in an acerbic critique of theory-driven social science studies of the Cold War, reductionist context-independent theory constitutes a fundamentally flawed approach to explaining social reality.[18] Such form of theorizing appears to be especially endemic in American social science research generally and also regarding the EU. As historians, we contend that human behaviour can only be understood as part of particular social, cultural and temporal contexts, which must be described in detail and traced over time to be well understood and explained.[19] From this perspective, no academic discipline that seeks to analyze the social world can, or will, ever develop what Thomas Kuhn termed a scientific paradigm, characteristic of the hard sciences.[20] In fact, rational choice research programmes have failed to produce convincing law like statements that apply to a broad range of cases and across time.[21] This is also true for the study of the history and contemporary politics of the EU. Historians have not found much explanatory value in Andrew Moravcsik's radical rational choice based claim, for example,[22] that the French President de Gaulle's EEC policy was almost exclusively driven by economic calculations of material advantage (especially in agriculture) and domestic political gains in the form of support from the agricultural community and not by his strong belief in the resilience of the (French) nation-state and the desirability of a more independent Western European world role under French leadership in competition with the 'Anglo-Saxon' powers. The present-day EU is, and always has been, a complex institutional, political and cultural space that does not lend itself to theory-driven mono-causal explanations of this kind.

Instead of grand theory, we advocate the superior qualities of sophisticated historical narrative as a multifaceted model anchored in context by means of an inductive research process that focuses on the careful documentation, description and explanation of historical processes. In our view, the strengths of the historical narrative derive directly from these attributes. First, historians appreciate the singular and accidental, offering empirically grounded indications of the limits to meaningfully generalizing social patterns. Second, the focus on context also leads most historians to emphasize the complexities of the social world and to point out multiple causes when explaining historical processes. On the whole, they rephrase classic ontological dichotomies in the social sciences such as agent versus structure, or ideational versus material factors and their role for motivating individual or collective actors, as empirical questions to which only concrete historical answers can usefully be provided. Third, historians in their source-rich studies tend to emphasize the importance of contingency in historical processes, which allows a more fine-grained interpretation of change over time. In contrast, political scientists – even of long-term processes such as socialization – tend to take 'snap-shots' for process tracing, with clear limitations, as Frank Schimmelfennig has also argued in his plea for a substantial contribution by historians to a debate about the emergence of the European polity which transcends disciplinary boundaries.[23] To advance the proposed utilization of social science theories and concepts as heuristic tools for historical research and to facilitate the reception of our historical research by social scientists we use some social science terminology. We emphatically reject the wholesale adoption of social science 'insider' terminology for historical research on the European polity, however, as we believe that it often inhibits communicating across disciplinary divides and reaching out to a wider community of interested readers more than contributing to clarifying concepts and assumptions.

Our advocacy of a theoretically informed historical narrative may well strike some social scientists of the EU as lacking theoretical ambition. Historical narratives according to this view suffer from similar problems to those of social science case studies. They produce particularistic knowledge on the basis of which the scope for generalization is limited; they cannot be used systematically to test such generalizations; and the inductive methodology used has a tendency to create a bias towards the preconceived views of the researcher. To some extent, such criticism reflects a misplaced trust in context independent theory. Although the insights derived from historical cases remain grounded in a particular temporal context, we contend that they have the potential to yield more meaningful guidance for understanding contemporary political choices than context independent theory that cannot be empirically sustained. We argue that historians can and should in fact make generalizations that are well grounded in their empirical research, and that they need to do this much more boldly than they have done in the past, with a few notable exceptions like Milward. Moreover, historical narratives are in fact very useful for testing theory because of the rigorous requirements of empirical documentation. Finally, there is no evidence that non-inductive research methods are less prone towards bias. In fact, the inductive methodology and the careful documentation and description of context may well have a greater potential for more thorough falsification than attempts by social scientists to illustrate a context independent theory with a large number of often badly documented cases.

We believe that sophisticated historical narratives have transdisciplinary value, too. Thus, this book is also intended as an invitation to social scientists in turn to engage in a dialogue with contemporary historians. In the concluding chapter, Alex Warleigh-Lack discusses from the perspective of a leading political scientist of the EU, and in relation to the conceptual and empirical historical chapters in this book, how social scientists might profit from such a dialogue, as well as contributing in important ways to the proposed transformation of EU historiography. Recent theoretical developments in comparative politics and International Relations in particular,[24] like historical and sociological institutionalism and constructivism, have made many social scientists of the EU much more interested once more in the temporal dimension of the integration process. Historical institutionalism, with its particular focus on how institutions develop over time and structure political choices, has developed various strands. As in the case of Paul Pierson's interesting application of this theoretical perspective to studying EU history,[25] they share the notion that detailed historical research is necessary for tracing and documenting the various types of 'path dependency' that historical institutionalists conceptualize.

Overall, however, the treatment of EU history by social scientists remains profoundly deficient in important ways. They often cite source-based historical literature arbitrarily to 'prove' their preferred theoretical approach. As historians and political scientists have shown in the prominent case of Moravcsik's study of 'grand bargains',[26] moreover, his theory-driven utilization of empirical evidence is not only highly selective, but also methodologically flawed.[27] Complex historical processes become condensed in this way into a neat theory that tells us a lot about theory formation in the social sciences, but little about the history of the EU. In another example, although coming from a diametrically opposed theoretical position, Craig Parsons has argued in a fascinating long-term study that pro-integration politicians have controlled French European policy by exercising 'entrepreneurial leadership' in domestic politics. Parsons has emphasized the role of purposeful actors who – according to this view – are at least in part motivated by guiding integration ideas and interact across party divides to advance their European agenda.[28] Yet, he, too, has ignored much of the more recent historical research, especially on European politics under the Fourth Republic until 1958, which leads him to exaggerate the intra-party divisions within the Mouvement Républicain Populaire (MRP), for example, on which his thesis crucially depends for his explanation of core Europe formation in the ECSC. Moreover, as Wolfram Kaiser has demonstrated, entrepreneurial leadership in the political battle over European integration crucially transcended national boundaries.[29] It had, and still has, strong transnational connotations, something that the domestic politics approach to understanding national European policy completely fails to take into account.

In view of these weaknesses of theory-driven social science research on the history and politics of the EU, we believe that there is ample room for fruitful interdisciplinary dialogue between historians developing a more sophisticated historiography of the present-day EU and social scientists who explore its temporal dimension without entertaining ambitions to construct reductionist context-independent theory.[30] With the qualitative transformation of EU historiography proposed in this book with two integrated research fields that have been central to the study of the contemporary EU in the last decade, we hope to make a significant contribution to this dialogue.[31] A conceptually strong historiography of European integration promises a wealth of fascinating empirical studies of crucial social, economic and political processes that have shaped the present-day EU and the wider Europe. They will hopefully yield insights into EU history that social scientists would neglect at their own peril.

Notes

1 For a recent overview of 'governance' research on the EU see Beate Kohler-Koch and Berthold Rittberger, 'Review Article: The "Governance Turn" in EU Studies', *Journal of Common Market Studies*, vol. 44 (supplement) (2006), pp. 27–49.
2 On the isolation of EU history in the historiography of Europe see Wolfram Kaiser, 'Bringing People and Ideas Back in: Historical Research on the European Union', in David Phinnemore and Alex Warleigh (eds.), *Reflections on European Integration*, Basingstoke: Palgrave 2008 – forthcoming.
3 See in greater detail Wilfried Loth, 'Walter Lipgens (1925–84)', in Heinz Duchardt *et al.* (eds.), *Europa-Historiker. Ein biographisches Handbuch*, vol. 1, Göttingen: Vandenhoeck & Ruprecht, 2006, pp. 317–36; Wolfram Kaiser, '"Überzeugter Katholik und CDU-Wähler": Zur Historiographie der Integrationsgeschichte am Beispiel Walter Lipgens', *Journal of European Integration History*, vol. 8, no. 2 (2002), pp. 119–28.
4 Walter Lipgens, 'Der Zusammenschluß Westeuropas. Leitlinien für den historischen Unterricht', *Geschichte in Wissenschaft und Unterricht*, vol. 34 (1983), pp. 345–72.
5 Walter Lipgens, *A History of European Integration, vol. 1: 1945–1947*, Oxford: Clarendon Press, 1982 [German 1977]; idem., *Europa-Föderationspläne der Widerstandsbewegungen, 1940–1945: eine Dokumentation*, Munich: Oldenbourg, 1968; idem. (ed. with Wilfried Loth), *Documents on the History of European Integration*, 4 vols, Berlin: De Gruyter, 1984–91.
6 See, for example, many contributions in Ariane Landuyt and Daniele Preda (eds.), *I movimenti per l'unità europea 1970–1986*, Bologna: Mulino, 2000; Sergio Pistone (ed.), *I movimenti per l'unità europea dal 1945 al 1954*, Milan: Jaca, 1992; Richard Mayne and John Pinder, *Federal Union, the Pioneers. A History of Federal Union*, Basingstoke: Macmillan, 1992.

7 Alan S. Milward, *The Reconstruction of Western Europe 1945–1961*, London: Methuen, 1984.
8 Idem., *The European Rescue of the Nation-State*, London: Routledge, 1992.
9 Idem., *The Rise and the Fall of a National Strategy 1945–1963 (The United Kingdom and the European Community, vol. 1)*, London: Frank Cass, 2002, p. 6.
10 Idem., 'Conclusion: the Value of History', in idem. *et al.*, *The Frontier of National Sovereignty. History and Theory 1945–1992*, London: Routledge, 1993, pp. 182–201, here p. 187.
11 Ibid. chapter 6.
12 Morten Rasmussen, 'The Hesitant European – History of Denmark's Accession to the European Communities 1970–73', *Journal of European Integration History*, vol. 11, no. 2 (2005), pp. 47–74.
13 Starting with Raymond Poidevin (ed.), *Histoire des débuts de la construction européenne (mars 1948 – mai 1950)*, Brussels: Bruylant, 1986. The most recent volume Antonio Varsori (ed.), *Inside the European Community. Actors and Policies in the European Integration 1957–1972*, Baden-Baden: Nomos, 2006 is a partial exception to the rule.
14 Keith Middlemas, *Orchestrating Europe. The Informal Politics of European Union 1973–1995*, London: Fontana, 1995.
15 By way of introduction see Wolfram Kaiser, 'Transnational Mobilization and Cultural Representation: Political Transfer in an Age of Proto-Globalization, Democratization and Nationalism 1848–1914', *European Review of History*, vol. 12, no. 2 (2005), pp. 403–24.
16 Piers Ludlow, *The European Community and the Crises of the 1960s: Negotiating the Gaullist Challenge*, London: Routledge, 2006.
17 As we also argue in succinct form in Wolfram Kaiser and Brigitte Leucht, 'Informal Politics of Integration: Christian Democratic and Transatlantic Networks in the Creation of ECSC core Europe', *Journal of European Integration History* vol. 14, no. 1 (2008) pp. 35–49; Ann-Christina Knudsen and Morten Rasmussen, 'A European Political System in the Making 1958–70: The Relevance of Emerging Committee Structures', *Journal of European Integration History*, vol. 14, no. 1 (2008) pp. 51–67.
18 John Lewis Gaddis, 'History, Science, and the Study of International Relations', in Ngaire Woods (ed.), *Explaining International Relations since 1945*, Oxford: Oxford University Press, 1996, pp. 32–48.
19 See also Bent Flyvbjerg, *Rationality and Power: Democracy in Practice*, Chicago: University of Chicago Press, 1998 [Danish 1996].
20 Thomas S. Kuhn, *The Structure of Scientific Revolutions*, Chicago: Chicago University Press, 1962.
21 James Mahoney and Dietrich Rueschemeyer, 'Comparative Historical Analysis: Achievements and Agendas', in idem. (eds.), *Comparative Historical Analysis in the Social Sciences*, Cambridge: Cambridge University Press, 2003, pp. 3–40, here p. 20.
22 Andrew Moravcsik, 'De Gaulle Between Grain and Grandeur: The Political Economy of French EC Policy 1958–70 (Part 1)', *Journal of Cold War Studies*, vol. 2, no. 2 (2000), pp. 3–43; idem., 'De Gaulle Between Grain and Grandeur: The Political Economy of French EC Policy 1958–70 (Part 2)', *Journal of Cold War Studies*, vol. 2, no. 3 (2000), pp. 4–68.
23 Cf. Frank Schimmelfennig, 'Transnational Socialization. Community-Building in an Integrated Europe, in Wolfram Kaiser and Peter Starie (eds.), *Transnational European Union. Towards a Common Political Space*, London: Routledge, 2005, pp. 60–82.
24 As an excellent introduction to current concepts and debates in political science research on the EU see Angela Bourne and Michelle Cini (eds.), *Palgrave Advances in European Union Studies*, Basingstoke: Palgrave, 2006.

25 Paul Pierson, 'The Path to European Integration: A Historical Institutional Analysis', *Comparative Political Studies*, vol. 29, no. 2 (1996), pp. 123–63; idem., *Politics in Time. History, Institutions, and Social Analysis*, Princeton: Princeton University Press, 2004.

26 Andrew Moravcsik, *The Choice for Europe. Social Purpose and State Power from Messina to Maastricht*, London: University College London Press, 1998.

27 For a detailed competent critique of Moravcsik's interpretation of de Gaulle's European policy, see Robert H. Lieshout, Mathieu L.L. Segers and Anna M. van der Vleuten, 'De Gaulle, Moravcsik, and *The Choice for Europe*. Soft Sources, Weak Evidence', *Journal of Cold War Studies*, vol. 6, no. 4 (2004), pp. 89–139.

28 Craig Parsons, *A Certain Idea of Europe*, Ithaca: Cornell University Press, 2003.

29 Wolfram Kaiser, *Christian Democracy and the Origins of European Union*, Cambridge: Cambridge University Press, 2007.

30 See also Wolfram Kaiser, 'History meets Politics: Overcoming the Interdisciplinary Volapük in Research on the EU', *Journal of European Public Policy*, vol. 15, no. 2 (2008), pp. 300–313.

31 See also some of the contributions by younger EU historians in Ann-Christina Lauring Knudsen, Jens Runge Poulsen and Morten Rasmussen (eds.), *The Road to a United Europe. Interpretations of the Process of European Integration*, Brussels: Peter Lang – forthcoming.

2 Transnational networks in European governance

The informal politics of integration

Wolfram Kaiser

Controlled by economic and political elites in institutionally complex and in-transparent forms of policy-making, the European Union (EU) seems to lack popular legitimacy. Institutional crises such as the demise of the Santer Commission in 1999 and the failed referendums about the Constitution in France and the Netherlands in 2005 have led to calls for more participatory supranational democracy. Greater interest and more active involvement of citizens in the politics of the EU, it is argued, could strengthen a collective European identity and lead to the greater transfer of loyalties to the supranational level within the complex EU system of multilevel governance.[1] The European Commission has even devised strategies for citizens' input into the legislative process by email communication.

In a long-term historical perspective, however, such ambitions to transform nationals of member-states into actively engaged European citizens who take a keen interest in, and even contribute directly to, EU policy-making appears both over-ambitious and less essential for successful state-building than the often heated debate about a 'democratic deficit' suggests. National integration and nation-state formation in the nineteenth century were as much driven by elites with shared economic interests and – importantly – political objectives as the process of European integration after 1945. At least by the time of the negotiation and ratification of the treaty establishing the European Economic Community (EEC) in 1956–57, the formation of an integrated core Europe of the six founding member-states encountered little societal opposition and could build on a growing permissive consensus. In fact, this process was much less hotly contested within the original member-states than forms of national integration and nation-state formation were almost anywhere in nineteenth century Europe. The declared long-term federal ambition in the preamble of the EEC Treaty to create 'an ever closer union among the peoples of Europe'[2] met with little hostility at the time.

In the nineteenth century, national integration and nation-state formation arguably did not require the prior integration of societies with politically conscious and active citizens, but trans-regionally connected elites with shared agendas and objectives. This experience suggests two hypotheses for the analysis of the transnational dimension of European integration history. First, social integration is an important dimension of, but not necessarily a pre-requisite for, the formation of a partly supranational multilevel polity. Second, transnational elites can play, and have played, a crucial controlling role in the process of European integration and (proto-) state formation, to be followed by subsequent attempts to create greater public allegiance. Such allegiance in turn may make the active political engagement of European citizens desirable from a normative perspective, but it does not necessarily require it on a large scale.

This crucial role of transnationally networked elites was recognized, although not deeply reflected, by the early historiography of European integration. Thus, Walter Lipgens studied the origins and evolution of guiding ideas for postwar European integration among European resistance movements during the Second World War and the federalist movements after 1945.[3] His and similar source-based historical works built in a general way on early neo-functionalist studies by Ernst B. Haas and others who also emphasized the importance of transnational functional elites – especially business and political parties. In his book, *The Uniting of Europe*, first published in 1958,[4] Haas argued that these elites with shared strategic interests worked closely with the new supranational institutions such as the High Authority of the European Coal and Steel Community (ECSC) under the leadership of Jean Monnet, to drive the integration process forward. Allegedly, this resulted in 'spill-over' from vertical (sectoral) to broader horizontal economic, from economic to political integration, and geographically from the newly created core Europe to other parts of Western Europe. Crucially, these early attempts to conceptualize the origins of supranational European integration after 1945 had major defects. Thus, Lipgens insinuated, but never attempted to demonstrate, a causal link between the ideas of the resistance and federalist movements and postwar policy-making by national governments. At the same time, Haas analyzed the formal policy-making and proposals of newly formed transnational organizations. At least in part due to a lack of access to suitable government sources, however, he did not establish convincingly their influence on the initiatives of the supranational institutions and on inter-state negotiations and policy-making in the Council of Ministers. Moreover, the neo-functionalists naturally focussed on the emerging supranational level, which they sought to explain, but largely failed to conceptualize or describe empirically the vertical interconnectedness of different levels of what Morten Rasmussen in his contribution to this book, calls the incipient 'political system' of the EEC.

These and other deficiencies of early research on European integration – especially its normative overdrive – largely account for the subsequent virtual extermination of the transnational politico-societal dimension from its analysis by contemporary historians. With the opening up of government records, diplomatic historians steeped in realist traditions usurped the study of European integration as intergovernmental bargaining of 'national interests'. Alan S. Milward also derided early normative 'teleological' research by Lipgens and others.[5] His revisionist thesis of integration as the 'European rescue of the nation-state'[6] does attempt to integrate domestic factors of interest group and national parliamentary politics. Regarding supranational policy-making, however, it is in essence as state-centric as diplomatic historical accounts in its focus on intergovernmental bargaining and based exclusively on the analysis of national government records and quantitative economic data. Paradoxically, the historiography of European integration ignored the transnational politico-societal dimension precisely at a time when modern historians began to rediscover this same dimension in an attempt to conceptualize cross-border networks, communication and cultural and policy transfer during national integration and proto-globalization in the nineteenth century.[7] At the same time, attempts to write the social history of Western Europe after 1945 as by Hartmut Kaelble, for example,[8] initially got bogged down in the mostly quantitative analysis of convergence processes compared to other world regions, without analyzing whether, to what extent, and how such Europeanization may have been induced by Community policies or transnational links within the new institutional and policy framework.

Against this background, this chapter will first explore how social science concepts that have recently guided much research on the EU, may be effectively utilized for conceptualizing the informal politics of European integration after 1945. Concepts such as networks, socialization and public sphere in particular can inform innovative ways of writing about transnational networks in European governance in historical perspective, as well as present-day EU politics. Building on recent attempts to bring the transnational politico-societal dimension back into the study of EU history, the second part of the chapter will discuss some major aspects of the historical evolution of what Keith Middlemas first called in the title of his book, the 'informal politics' of European integration.[9] It will focus in particular on the different functions of cross-border networks and how they might have contributed to the evolution of the ECSC/EEC as an incipient multilevel polity, and to policy-making within it.

Social science concepts: networks, socialization and public sphere

In his book, *The Rise of the Network Society*, Manuel Castells has claimed from a sociological perspective that modern society is characterized by intense long-distance communication and the informal exercise of power by networked social elites with control over crucial resources, especially knowledge.[10] Political scientists have increasingly recognized that much the same is true for the EU. They insist that EU governance – unlike traditional forms of nation-state governance – 'is not based on hierarchical coordination by government-like structures or on a strong authoritative basis'.[11] Instead, it links different vertical levels – the supranational, national and regional/local – and horizontally structured institutions involved in supranational policy-making – mainly the Commission, the Council and the Parliament. As a political system, the present-day EU requires constant communication and negotiation within a complex institutional setting, in which the informal control by networks that link public and private actors and are capable of locking the different levels and institutions into informally prepared policy solutions, plays a crucial role: from treaty changes to directives and, below the supranational level, co-operation between member-states and policy transfer.

Similarly, economic sociologists have analyzed (market) institutions as embedded in systems of social relations. From a different social science perspective this approach, too, has utilized the network concept for understanding the mobilization of transnational resources for collective action and relations between business actors and political institutions.[12]

Policy networks could be defined as entities 'consisting of public, quasi-public, or private actors who are dependent on each other and (. . .) maintain relations with each other'.[13] The role of such policy networks was first studied by researchers of public policy in the national context who were struck by the increasing reliance of government upon non-state actors such as interest groups, think tanks and multinational companies for providing policy solutions, and by the blurring of boundaries between the public and the private. More recently, the network concept has been applied to the study of the supranational EU level, which is even more characterized by informal exchanges of knowledge and policy ideas, something on which an under-resourced Commission in particular crucially depends. One school of network analysis has a more empirical approach to studying the role of networks in the generation of policy ideas, their further development and legislative or administrative implementation.[14] Other writers have taken the increasing role of networks in policy-making as reflecting a new form of non-state-centric informal governance in which formal institutions and authority matter much less for policy outcomes than in the ideal-type centralized modern nation-state. To some extent informed by their analytical experience of a complex federal political system, several German authors have decisively shaped the network governance agenda.[15]

Political scientists have disaggregated policy networks into a number of ideal types that have varying characteristics and fulfil different functions. According to Rod Rhodes and David Marsh,[16] one type would be the policy community whose members normally share a policy paradigm; in other words, they have similar compatible values and world views and broadly agree on desirable policy developments for a particular organization or sector. Such a policy community would be highly integrated with restricted membership and substantial resources to invest in co-operation and influence on policy-making processes. In contrast, an issue network would be more loosely organized around a particular concrete agenda, more temporary and latently unstable.

Related to policy networks are two other analytical concepts, namely epistemic communities and advocacy coalitions that could also inform historical research on important aspects of the integration process. Peter Haas has defined an epistemic community as 'a professional group that believes in the same cause and effect relationships, truth tests to assess them, and shares common values'.[17] They are 'channels through which new ideas circulate from societies to governments as well as from country to country'.[18] In essence, epistemic communities are networks of experts who share expert knowledge and have a common understanding of the technical, scientific and political nature of an issue. Such expert communities may develop out of, and be influenced by, the activities of professional associations, scientific collaboration and joint policy advice, especially at the supranational and international levels where their regionally or globally shared views of a particular issue may be influential.

In contrast, advocacy coalitions link different types of organized groups who share some deep core beliefs with similar related policy goals, without necessarily being interested in co-operation on unrelated issues.[19] The analysis of such advocacy coalitions starts from the assumption that in the complex political system of the EU, no single actor or group can impose their policy ideas. Instead, they need to identify partners to pool resources and to achieve hegemony in a particular policy domain. Crucially, such advocacy coalitions will normally unite groups from different sectors of the polity, such as political parties, more traditional socio-economic interest groups, non-governmental organizations and epistemic communities, for example, as well as state actors sympathetic to their ideas, who may in turn need support in intra- and inter-institutional bargaining processes, as is especially true of the European Commission. In principle, this concept also recognizes the importance of the temporal dimension of policy-making, as it can take such advocacy coalitions years or even decades, to make their policy ideas hegemonic and reach the stage where they can successfully implement them.

For contemporary historians analyzing European integration since 1945, the network approach with its origins in public policy and comparative politics has distinct heuristic advantages over other social science attempts (especially those originating in International Relations theory) to conceptualize the EU. First, it is not a rigid theory and better able to accommodate conflicting empirical historical evidence, for example regarding the relative control by the member-states over policy-making after the creation of the ECSC/EEC. The network approach can account for the fact that member-state control may vary significantly between different policy sectors, for example. The creation of the Common Agricultural Policy (CAP) in the 1960s may have come about as the result of intergovernmental bargaining of mainly domestic agricultural interests with a large influence of the farmers' organizations, although these were also increasingly transnationally organized and began to exercise influence at the supranational, not just national level. In contrast, as Frans van Waarden and Michaela Drahos have argued, but not demonstrated historically,[20] the 'low politics' competition policy of the 1960s may have been decisively shaped by an emerging epistemic community of specialized lawyers and liberal economists who formed an advocacy coalition with the responsible Directorate-General (DG) IV in the Commission and select liberal competition-oriented national ministries. They also influenced the judgements of the European Court of Justice (ECJ) formulated by lawyers who have largely come from this same epistemic community, thus locking in their structural preference for a competition-oriented customs union and internal market in a kind of informal policy *coup d'état*.

A second major heuristic advantage of the network approach is its intimate link with the governance agenda for understanding the EU as a polity.[21] Although networks can fulfil a variety of functions, the focus has been on explaining public policy-making in national or supranational and international frameworks as a markedly informal process of continuous communication and negotiation between various types of mostly transnationally organized or at least, oriented actors. The analysis of the historical evolution of the EU as a political system, as advocated by Morten Rasmussen in his chapter, crucially requires a sophisticated understanding not only of the formal legal-institutional framework for decision-making and its change over time as a result of treaty revisions and ECJ decisions, but of the political flesh on this constitutional skeleton; in other words, how formal rules have been shaped, reshaped, and at times, replaced with informal rules in the form of transnational and inter-institutional patterns of co-operation and decision-making practiced after all by human actors integrated in transnational social networks. Thus, the transnational politico-societal dimension is of paramount importance for the analysis of the informal politics of the EU in historical perspective.

The network approach has a third major heuristic advantage. It cannot only contribute to understanding policy-making in an existing polity, although this is of course the dominant interest of social scientists studying the contemporary EU. Crucially, it has the potential to help explain the formation of European organizations in the first place. Strangely, political scientists like Markus Jachtenfuchs,[22] Craig Parsons[23] and Berthold Rittberger[24] have recently shown a greater interest in the early period of integration than most contemporary historians, albeit as part of a long-term continuum and without consulting additional historical sources. In contrast, too many historians define and adjust their research interests in line with the opening up of government sources, and as a result, have neglected European constitutionalization between 1945 and 1957. Yet, Lipgens' idealist explanation with its exclusive focus on the resistance and postwar federalist movements and Milward's state-centred rational choice economic interpretation both lack a sophisticated understanding of domestic and transnational political processes. In particular, they have failed to demonstrate convincingly what groups of actors succeeded in accumulating sufficient resources in what kinds of domestic and transnational alliances to achieve core Europe institutionalization with supranational dimensions and excluding the United Kingdom. In this particular form, this outcome was after all highly contested in Western Europe during 1949–51.

Although networks usually form for influencing policy-making from guiding ideas for major treaty revisions to technical advice on a piece of legislation, they also have other functions. The analysis of these other functions could facilitate an enlarged understanding by contemporary historians of what actually constitutes Europeanization as induced by European integration: a process of economic, political and societal convergence and integration, with the potential for reverses and disintegration. In particular, networks have increasingly contributed to the transfer of ideas and policy solutions between national and sub-national actors below the supranational level.[25] In the diverse cultural space of the original core Europe and even more so, in the present-day EU with twenty-seven member-states, this function is not limited to the mere exchange of information on what policies may function well under what conditions, and what may therefore (in modern public policy slang) constitute 'best practice'. Crucially, this knowledge needs to be 'translated' by what historians have called transnationally networked 'cultural brokers' who are culturally and linguistically versatile. Networks have traditionally fulfilled this function of translation between different socio-economic, political and cultural contexts. In postwar Western Europe, however, market integration, supranational institutionalization and intense inter-state co-operation have massively increased socio-economic and institutional competition and led to more intense cross-border communication. This in turn has facilitated greater political transfer within the emerging polity compared to other world regions.

The other major function of networks is to facilitate cross-border communication not only with the objective of influencing or transferring policies, but to socialize actors into existing behavioural patterns, policy ideas and preferences. Transnational socialization actually played an important role in Karl Deutsch's transactionalism, although this was applied to NATO as a 'security community',[26] not the ECSC/EEC, and in neo-functionalist theory. Haas even expected socialization to lead to 'a new national consciousness of the new political community'.[27] His prediction was perhaps not so much premature as misguided in that it did not consider the option of multiple identities (including regional, confessional, gender and others) and allegiances, which has been typical of Europe in a long-term perspective. Since then, however, social scientists have developed a more sophisticated understanding of transnational socialization processes that are no longer assumed to have fixed outcomes. Socialization can of course be induced by state actors. From the creation of the EEC and the first agreement with Greece in 1961, Community-induced socialization has been a constant feature in the processes of association and enlargement. The EU has defined increasingly detailed pre-accession conditions for domestic reform and progressive adaptation to the growing legal acquis communautaire. The Commission especially has accompanied the adjustment process with structured advice to governments and non-governmental actors as well as financial support with a view to securing their large-scale adoption of Community rules and behavioural norms before the actual accession. In the process of enlargement in particular, however, societal networks can play, and have played, an important role, too.

Both constructivist and rational choice-based conceptualizations of Europeanization processes have addressed the role of socialization processes. Although in this general way, socialization transcends the main ontological divide within the social sciences, it is core only to constructivist understandings of international (and European) relations. Based on James G. March's and Johan P. Olsen's distinction of social action as guided by either the logic of consequentiality or the logic of appropriateness,[28] Frank Schimmelfennig has developed a typology of socialization mechanisms.[29] According to this typology, 'imitation' and 'social learning' involve processes of habitualization, that is, the mechanical adoption of appropriate behaviour as demonstrated by the socialization agency, or internalization as a result of processes of social learning in which recipients are actively persuaded by the claims of the socialization agency. In contrast, rational choice approaches conceptualize socialization as the result of social influence or bargaining based on either social or material incentives. Such incentives can induce 'appropriate' behaviour that can then become habitual over time. Not surprisingly, constructivists have shown a greater interest in the role of non-state actors in socialization processes because cross-border societal contacts tend to be less shaped by power differentials. Thus, Jeffrey Checkel has defined a catalogue of conditions under which social learning might occur as the result of arguing and internalization.[30] According to this catalogue, it is particularly propitious for social learning processes if first, new actors find themselves in an uncertain environment (like the EU); second, the socialization agency is an 'authoritative member of the in-group to which the persuadee belongs or wants to belong'; third, the rules of engagement are seen as legitimate; fourth, the process of arguing and persuasion takes place in non-coercive and non-politicized, private settings; and fifth, the rules resonate well with the actor's domestic political culture and traditions.

These forms of conceptualising transnational socialization could help contemporary historians to reflect in a more abstract form what role different factors may play in influencing communication and learning processes in transnational network-type contexts. At the same time, the deep ontological divide in the social sciences between constructivist and rational choice-based interpretations of individual and collective human behaviour is profoundly alien to historical research. Most historians will agree that human behaviour is usually informed by factors such as historical experience, cultural traditions and practices and norms and values as well as calculations of social and material advantages. Empirical research on individual actors – especially in the form of biography – provides overwhelming evidence of the influence of ideational as well as material factors for opinion formation and policy outcomes. It is the crucial task for contemporary historians to demonstrate empirically the interplay and relative weight of constructivist and rational choice dimensions of social communication, opinion formation and policy-making, not to contribute to often sterile theoretical social science debates over the nature of human behaviour.

As the process of transnationalization has been most advanced among elites in Western Europe since 1945, one would also expect any socialization effects of cross-border networking and the orientation towards Europe to be most pronounced among them. In fact, this is what Thomas Risse has recently found in a study of contemporary identity change within the EU.[31] Not least due to insufficient data, contemporary historians will be unable quantitatively to measure such socialization effects for the earlier postwar period. By conducting interviews with eyewitnesses and analyzing private papers and autobiographies, however, they can conceptualize and assess conversion to 'European' causes among these elites, and the reasons for it. These reasons may well be a combination of socialization effects of cross-border networking with partly shared experience of, for example, totalitarian government, collaboration and the Second World War or the Cold War rivalry with the Soviet Union and communism. In this context, historians could also re-conceptualize the possibly fundamental impact of collective experiences that have the potential of uniting people of the same generation, class, confession or political beliefs across borders – an important dimension of postwar core Europe integration that has been largely ignored after the academic rebellion against normatively driven research in the tradition of Lipgens.

Transnational socialization has taken place beyond the elites, however, even if its effects on European citizens have been less pronounced. The consequences of societal transnationalization more generally potentially include the growth of supranational political activism, identity change and the evolution of a European public sphere. As Doug Imig and Sidney Tarrow have found, however, Europeans have turned their political claims to the European level to a very limited extent even today.[32] Their claims continue to be channelled via interest groups and their influence on supranational policy-making, not popular activism. At the same time, collective identity change has occurred in the form of a significant rise in the number of EU citizens who feel attachment to Europe and to their nation-state – and in many cases, their region, too.[33] Such identity change may result from what Risse calls the EU's growing 'entitativity', that is, its tangible impact on the daily lives of European citizens. At the same time, it could also have been influenced from attempts by European elites to instigate long-term identity change with a view to strengthening allegiance to the supranational level, especially through new strategies of political representation and communication.

Finally, such elite strategies may well have contributed to the creation of a European public sphere of sorts with a degree of public and partially transnationally connected (or at least similar) deliberation of European-level issues. Hans-Jörg Trenz has found that the current EU is still predominately characterized by short-lived and partial publics constituted by specific events.[34] In fact, such transnational European events have influenced European politics since the acceleration of communication and the development of mass (print) media in the second half of the nineteenth century, from the Vatican Council in 1870 to the murder of the Austrian Archduke Franz Ferdinand in Sarajevo in 1914. In postwar Western Europe they include the demise of the EDC Treaty in the French Assemblée Nationale in 1954 or Charles de Gaulle's triggering of the 'empty chair' crisis in 1965, for example. Together with the other dimensions of European transnationalization outlined above, contemporary historical research on the formation of such (temporary) European publics could potentially make a significant contribution to the study of the integration process as long-term Europeanization.

Transnational networks in European governance

The incipient contemporary historical research on transnational Europe in the early postwar period up to 1973 shows that network co-operation fulfilled a number of important internal functions and may have had significant effects in structuring the emerging integrated core Europe and its relations with other parts of Western Europe and the United States. In my own archive-based study of transnational Christian democracy and European integration, I have identified five core internal functions of transnational networking which had important direct and indirect repercussions for European integration policy-making.[35] This is by no means a comprehensive list. Moreover, the five functions will not have been equally important in other types of networks. They provide an empirically based introduction to considering the role of networks in the process of early European integration, however.

First, the Christian democrats' formal and informal co-operation contributed to the lasting creation of transnational social capital. Compared to interwar Europe, when Catholic party co-operation was still dominated by domestic nationalist claims and inter-state rivalry, the Christian democrats accumulated not instrumental trust directed at securing specific interests, but social trust in the form of normative-emotional bonds between party elites. Their regular party-level meetings in mostly non-politicized private contexts allowed the Christian democrats to communicate their congruent political beliefs and preferences, especially for the creation of an economically integrated core Europe with supranational institutional dimensions and without British participation, over longer periods. In this way, their decision-making as governing political elites in power in all founding member-states of the ECSC in 1950–51 became mutually reliable and calculable despite of conflicting domestic pressures from coalition partners, public opinion and economic pressure groups.

In the immediate postwar period, the greatest contribution to the formation of social trust of this (and other such political and socio-economic networks) was arguably the swift integration of German partners despite the experience of the Second World War and occupation. Especially French elites greatly mistrusted the Germans and hesitated to opt for Western integration at the expense of an understanding with the Soviet Union over the German question. In the case of the Christian democrats, however, Konrad Adenauer became their dominant German interlocutor through a series of private meetings involving Georges Bidault, Robert Schuman and other leading politicians of the Mouvement Républicain Populaire (MRP). Although Bidault once claimed never to have 'eaten a German',[36] his public rhetoric as French foreign minister during the first postwar years initially did seem to suggest that he had at least one German grilled *à point* for dinner every evening. Yet, Bidault was extremely impressed with Adenauer's stoical personality and his strong preference for Franco-German reconciliation at almost any price.[37] Adenauer seemed to fear the Germans even more than Bidault did, urging his French partners repeatedly to bind them into integrated supranational economic and political structures. In one conversation with Pierre-Henri Teitgen in 1949, for example, Adenauer insisted that many young Germans would still join any column of men defiling past their house.[38]

Second, their network communication also allowed the Christian democratic elites to define common policy objectives. Embedded in broadly similar ideological traditions, they developed what Markus Jachtenfuchs has called a shared social system for interpreting the world as it was evolving in the early Cold War.[39] This convergence of worldviews was a precondition for developing common ideas for European constitutionalization including in particular, functional integration in specified economic sectors, mixed institutional solutions with a strong supranational dimension and the long-term goal of a federal Europe, and inducing British non-participation in core Europe integration to achieve a breakthrough for this basic concept. These ideas in turn defined a corridor within which national governments (largely controlled by the same elites and individual politicians) negotiated the detailed rules for the ECSC. The shared broad policy commitments also made it easier for the Christian democrat-led governments to control domestic influences and lobbying and to override domestic pressures as in the case of Adenauer and the thorny issue of deconcentration of the steel industry as a precondition for the successful conclusion of the Schuman Plan negotiations in early 1951.[40]

Other transnational networks introduced much more specific ideas and proposals into the process of European integration. As Brigitte Leucht demonstrates in her chapter in this book, a transatlantic policy community of academics, civil servants and politicians helped to construct an alliance for a competition and consumer-friendly anti-trust policy for the ECSC, and even influenced the interstate negotiations of the relevant treaty clauses. With the creation of the EEC in 1957–58, epistemic communities also began to explore the options within this much enlarged treaty framework to instil policy ideas into the evolving core Europe. Incipient historical research on the origins of EEC competition policy appears to confirm the hypothesis, for example, that a network of academics, lawyers and officials in the Commission and some national ministries did play a crucial role in shaping this policy domain decisively for decades.[41] In her chapter, Katja Seidel shows clearly how dominated the DG IV for competition policy was by lawyers and economists with ordo-liberal training, and how keen they were on cultivating contacts with competition policy experts from outside their institution to enhance the technical quality and political legitimacy of their policy-making. As Sigfrido Ramirez demonstrates in his contribution, the business network of European automobile companies – a precursor of sorts to the European Round Table of Industrialists officially formed in 1983 – played a crucial role in the attempted development of an EC level industrial policy in the early 1970s.

Transnational networks, third, mattered for early European integration because they were able to develop mechanisms for socializing uncommitted individuals and younger generations into their policy consensus. The numerous examples of Christian democrats who became converted to the core Europe option from their former more strongly transatlantic orientation include the Italian Prime Minister Alcide De Gasperi and Bidault. Bidault had doubts about the Schuman Plan's proposed degree of supranationalism. His inclusion in the core Europe consensus through the informal Geneva Circle meetings guaranteed, however, that as Prime Minister, he nevertheless supported Schuman in the crucial ministerial meeting and in the MRP executive. Together with the negative British reaction, this was essential for swinging the French government behind the Schuman Plan which might otherwise have disappeared in a binder.[42] Similarly, the European Movement and in particular, the Jean Monnet Action Committee founded in 1955, appear to have played an important role in converting the leadership of the German Social Democratic Party (SPD) to the core Europe option, something that was crucial for the evolution of a bipartisan 'pro-European' consensus in one of the two most important ECSC/EEC states.[43] Such socialization mechanisms operated at the level of civil servants, too. As cited by Seidel, an Italian A official new to DG IV found that in order to be taken seriously in the competition policy community, he first had to familiarize himself with the works of ordo-liberals like Walter Eucken and Franz Böhm, for example, whose works had played no role in his own university education.

At the same time, networks also employed mechanisms for excluding non-compliant members of their national political or socio-economic group from European resources in the form of access to information and knowledge, and the ability to form cross-border alliances for their dissenting views. Once core Europe organizations were formed, the High Authority and the European Commission in particular worked with networked elites to minimize core Europe-critical dissent in the collaboration between European institutions and transnational networks. In the case of the Christian democrats, for example, Adenauer and other strong supporters of core Europe integration utilized their collaboration with French, Belgian, Dutch and Italian Christian democrats to exclude politicians like Jacob Kaiser, Friedrich Holzapfel and Josef Müller, who either favoured initiatives to secure German unification or had a more pro-British and Atlantic orientation, from transnational co-operation and national European policy-making.[44] In the case of the MRP, the Christian socialist Léo Hamon recollected later how the small and shrinking anti-supranationalist Left was aggressively marginalized in the face of a 'frenzied European fury'.[45] In these two important ways, 'pro-European' elites utilized their networking to enhance their domestic as well as transnational bargaining power which was at times out of proportion to their relative strength within their respective national political or socio-economic group.

Transnational networking, fourth, created useful platforms for identifying suitable domestic and transnationally constituted partners for implementing European policy ideas and objectives. Multilateral bargaining of treaties and treaty revisions and policy-making within the new European organizations made it necessary that purposeful actors acquired knowledge of the domestic politics of other member-states if they wanted to forge effective transnational advocacy coalitions. This was a crucial characteristic of the new institutionalized core Europe as a slowly emerging political system with horizontal and vertical power structures. In 1950, for example, the German and Italian Christian democrats were tempted to use the Schuman Plan issue to polarize domestic opinion and slander the socialists, who agitated – like the German SPD leader Kurt Schumacher – against the creation of a conservative and clerical 'Vatican Europe', as 'anti-European'. Through their transnational co-operation, however, the Christian democrats learned that a strategy of aggressive polarization could be counterproductive, as the French MRP within the centrist 'Third Force' government depended on close co-operation with the socialist Section Française de l'Internationale Ouvrière (SFIO). To gain the support of SFIO and of leading trade unions like the Deutscher Gewerkschaftsbund, the German trades union congress, the Christian democrats coupled the Schuman Plan proposal with the supranational design, which attracted socialist federalists, and the rejection of the cartel solution for coal and steel – the interwar policy option that most industry leaders from this sector still preferred by 1950. This combination eventually assured the Christian democrats sufficient transnational support for their proposal, and the ratification of the ECSC in all six member-states.[46]

The fifth function of political networks in particular was to support intergovernmental relations over European integration. In the case of the Christian democrats, this function consisted of informal strategic interventions to secure national governmental policy-making and the conduct of inter-state negotiations consistent with their main objectives. National bureaucracies could throw spanners in the wheels of smooth intergovernmental co-operation. They tended to be attached to national policy traditions and administrative detail, and they were often under the influence of domestic lobbying. The French state administration in particular was initially a stronghold of resistance to the supranational core Europe of integrated markets.[47] The economic ministries were steeped in the tradition of protectionism and the foreign ministry attached to the Gaullist conception of national power. Within this hostile administrative environment, Monnet built personal networks that helped him to devise his plan and to garner crucial internal support.[48] The Christian democrats also parachuted reliable transnationally networked politicians into core government posts. This happened, for example, when De Gasperi made Emilio Taviani – the main Italian representative in party co-operation – state secretary in the Palazzo Chigi, his foreign policy adviser and chief Italian negotiator of the ECSC and EDC treaties during 1951–53. Taviani's leading role with the backing of the Prime Minister accelerated the Europeanization of the Italian foreign ministry and its political orientation.[49] More generally, transnational networks furnished political entrepreneurs, who suffered from an overload of often conflicting information and mainly domestic responsibilities, with crucial insider information on suitable governmental strategies for achieving their strategic objectives for European politics. Networks thus helped to reduce political uncertainties and minimized risks, thus widening the scope for ambitious policy initiatives like the Schuman Plan.

In these different ways transnational networks clearly played a crucial role after 1945 in creating favourable political conditions for the successful negotiation of the ECSC and EEC treaties. Once the new institutions were operating, and their core objectives embedded in, and defended by them, the Christian democrats relaxed their transnational co-operation until 'their' Europe came under threat from Gaullism and the prospective strengthening of socialism as a result of the first enlargement of the European Communities (EC) of 1972–73.[50] In contrast, it seems that transnational socio-economic interest group actors as well as expert communities became energized into developing their activities by the Europeanization of policy domains like agriculture and competition, for example, which were now open to influence at the supranational as well as the national levels. The crucial role of political networks in facilitating core Europe formation in the 1950s also suggests that historical institutionalist accounts of European integration need to search in transnational network activities shortly after 1945 for the roots of the first major European bargain and any path-dependency of institutional patterns and policy designs. Long-term corridors for institutional and policy developments became defined already before the first formal institutions were set up and began to exert influence on European policy-making. Contemporary historians have increasingly discovered the importance of transnational networks – not just political party networks – for European integration and policy-making. Thus, Anne-Myriam Dutrieue and Michel Dumoulin have demonstrated that the influence of the European League for Economic Cooperation (ELEC) lay not so much in its liberal policy declarations for a unified European market, but overlap with other political and socio-economic networks.[51] Rather than taking policy declarations by the European Movement as explaining policy developments, as Lipgens still did, research on these and other societal actors has concentrated more on the concrete links between different networks and European institutions to assess their role.

Although historical research on European networks and their role in policy-making and socialization processes has expanded, much remains to be done. So far, four important research themes have been largely neglected. First, the formation, identity and influence of interest groups on European level policy-making. Haas and other neo-functionalists mainly studied their formal institutionalization and policy statements. We need to know more about what could be called the political culture of European interest group politics, however. To what extent did leading national interest group representatives become engaged in EEC level coordination and bargaining, or was this left to brokers with cultural competence, but no substantial material resources or influence? Did interest groups primarily use the national channel for influencing intergovernmental bargaining, or did they switch to a European multilevel lobbying mode, and did their strategies vary from one policy domain to another, and why? The most crucial empirical question in this context is how the European farmers' associations succeeded in establishing a controlling influence over the CAP as it developed throughout the 1960s. Although contemporary historians have increasingly analyzed intergovernmental bargaining of agricultural questions in the Council of Ministers,[52] as well as the lobbying of member-state governments by national groups,[53] we know very little about the European-level activities of the Committee of Professional Agricultural Organisations, the EEC level farmers' organization.

Second, most research on political and socio-economic networks has focussed on core Europe and the transatlantic world. The first focus has been induced by interest in the formation of the present-day EU and the second by research on the 'Americanization' or 'Westernization' (or not) of Western Europe after 1945. The latter literature has only recently become more multilateral and comparative. Volker Berghahn has demonstrated how all-pervasive the financial support of the Central Intelligence Agency (CIA) and American philanthropic institutions like the Ford Foundation was after 1945 for almost all non-communist 'pro-European' transnational organizations, for example.[54] Yet, transnational networks also formed and were active on the Western European political periphery. Postwar international organizations like the Nordic Council and the European Free Trade Association (EFTA) encouraged transnational activities by political and socio-economic actors.

As Kristian Steinnes demonstrates in his chapter, northern European socialist parties from Scandinavia and Britain cultivated close links that up to a point, influenced their perception of the EEC as the 'Other' in European politics and informed their strategies of semi-detachment, conditional accession, or association with the EEC/EC. EFTA business associations and trade unions also forged especially close links from 1957–59 onwards, which remain largely unexplored.[55] The EFTA Council and its secretariat supported elite contacts with the objective of forging an EFTA identity of sorts.[56] In January 1961, politicians, industrialists and trade unionists including, for example, Maurice Macmillan, a member of Parliament and son of the British Prime Minister Harold Macmillan, founded the International EFTA Action Committee with national branches to promote the new organization.[57] The analysis of such networking activities is not merely relevant for the countries concerned. Instead, these activities may well have impacted in the long-run on the attitudes and policies towards core Europe integration and the present-day EU of both political and socio-economic elites and what the EFTA Secretariat called 'the average newspaper reader'.[58] We could hypothesize, for example, that elite attitudes to the EU in Austria may be more positive than in Denmark because Austrian elites – like the leadership of the Austrian People's Party and business associations – actually cultivated very close network contacts with core Europe throughout the postwar period which could have offset any socialization effects of the much earlier Danish EC membership.

Related to the geographical coverage of research on transnational networks in the process of European integration is, third, their role in the process of enlargement and shaping of the EU's external relations more generally. In many cases, political and socio-economic networks may have played a crucial role in convincing new members of the material advantages and the political desirability of EU membership. Such transnationally networked societal actors could have played a crucial role in swinging governments or popular opinion to support the membership option. It is clear, for example, that the German Christian democrats invested a lot of resources from the 1960s onwards into bringing more conservative and protestant-confessional parties into the core Europe consensus.[59] It would be interesting to analyze the domestic and transnational factors, which decided why such socialization strategies worked in some cases – e.g., the Spanish Partido Popular – but not in others like the British Conservative Party. In one country case study, Pilar Ortuño Anaya has recently demonstrated how important the ideational and material support of European networks of socialist parties and trade unions was during the transition process in the 1970s for transforming the Spanish socialists into a mainstream social-democratic reform party that became strongly in favour of Spanish EC (and even NATO) membership.[60]

Finally, contemporary historians of the present-day EU have to address the popular dimension of transnational societal integration. The strong focus on elites is justified in view of the nature of early European integration, but not entirely satisfactory. Aggravated by the deep intra-disciplinary divide between economic and political history on the one hand, and social history on the other, which has so far shown almost no interest in European integration as Europeanization, contemporary historians have largely failed to evaluate networks and socialization processes beyond the elites. Attempts such as by Jan-Henrik Meyer in his contribution to this book, to conceptualize and analyze the slow emergence of a European public sphere mark a useful beginning. Apart from media communication, however, transnational societal integration was facilitated by numerous cross-border exchanges such as the European Youth Campaign funded by the American Committee for a United Europe, with 1,900 workshops during 1951–58, congresses and other activities to win over the non-communist youth to the idea of supranational integration,[61] Franco-German youth exchanges and town twinning as well as worker migration and tourism. Not all of these transnational contacts were the direct result of European integration or, indeed, induced by the EEC. Taken together, however, they may have made a significant contribution to the long-term affective and identity change that political scientists have identified for the present-day EU. Research on such transnational exchanges needs to move beyond the policy level, however, and develop a more bottom-up approach to capture any socialization processes.

Conclusions

Research on the transnational dimension of European integration after 1945 can make major contributions to re-conceptualizing this process as the slow emergence of a multilevel polity.[62] Two points stand out concerning the formation and operation of core Europe organizations, but also of EFTA, for example. First, the evidence from the role of transnational Christian democracy suggests that networks can play a crucial role in shaping constitutionalization processes by defining guiding ideas and principles and closing off alternative options such as – in this case – more intergovernmental co-operation involving Britain in 1949–51. Powerful networks – especially policy communities and advocacy coalitions with significant political resources – can 'lock in' governmental actors (with whom they are either identical or at least closely allied) and minimize undesirable trade-offs or compromises in intergovernmental bargaining leading to the signing of treaties or their revision. In the concrete case of transnational Christian democracy, this policy community continued tenaciously to defend the federal vocation and to exercise crucial influence over important constitutional revisions such as the major institutional changes of the Maastricht Treaty negotiations, when the British Prime Minister Margaret Thatcher found herself outmanoeuvred by a coalition of federalist Christian democrats led by the German Chancellor Helmut Kohl, and socialist leaders like François Mitterrand.[63] The available historical evidence seems to corroborate that political networks can exercize especially powerful influence over non-economic dimensions of constitutionalization such as the principle of supranationality in the ECSC treaty. Importantly, however, these matter for economic integration outcomes, too. Without the purposeful exclusion of Britain (and self-exclusion by the Labour government) from core Europe integration in 1950, the CAP would never have developed in this form in the 1960s, for example.

The historical study of transnational networks and their activities can also provide valuable insights into the informal politics of the ECSC/EEC in the core Europe phase as well as for later periods after the first enlargement of 1972–73. State-centric historical accounts have failed to conceptualize this crucial characteristic of the emerging European polity because they are implicitly informed by an understanding of centralized nation-state governments as largely autonomous purposeful actors taking decisions under hierarchical and institutionally transparent conditions. Although member-state governments probably were both more autonomous and more purposeful in the 1960s than under the currently prevailing conditions of pluralistic media democracies, their intergovernmental bargaining and decision-making in the Council of Ministers took the form of complex time-consuming multilateral negotiations with at times strong domestic and transnational influences on their evolving positions and involving many issue linkages, and all of this under the conditions of secrecy and a lack of public scrutiny. More importantly, however, contemporary historians of the early EEC until the summit of The Hague in 1969 have too often taken the rather abstract Gaullist idea of leadership and control by a popular ruler at face value. In fact, even de Gaulle's France was sufficiently democratic, pluralistic and multi-centric to allow a large number of dissenting individuals and political and socio-economic groups to use their transnational activities to undermine de Gaulle's intergovernmental vision of core Europe run from the Elysée Palace. Federalists combined in the European Parliament (EP) to advance the constitutional debate and to strengthen claims for the institution's direct election. Directly elected mayors like the leading Christian democrat Pierre Pflimlin from Strasbourg used their networking to challenge de Gaulle's policies. French economists and lawyers colluded with epistemic communities and DG IV to help introduce an ordo-liberal competition policy that largely contradicted French protectionist economic policy traditions.

At the same time, informal policy-making with low intensity involvement of member-state governments was in some ways more important even in the 1960s than formal decision-making in the Council of Ministers. Ironically, Regulation 17 on competition passed by the Council in 1962, but developed by the Commission and an epistemic community of ordo-liberal economists and lawyers with important input from experts in the EP, may have had a much greater long-term impact on the EU than the so-called Luxembourg Compromise of January 1966 at the end of the empty chair crisis – a gentlemen's agreement of no legal relevance and very limited legitimacy outside of Gaullist France which soon fell into disrepute. Nevertheless, contemporary historians of European integration have paid much attention to the public confrontation of the empty chair crisis[64] while ignoring until very recently the informal politics of the origins of competition policy.

More generally, the study of transnational dimensions of European integration has the potential to elucidate the reasons for, and to define more precisely the character of, spatial differentiation in the process of European integration, concretely between the ECSC/EEC core Europe and EFTA within Western Europe in the first 25 years after the Second World War and more generally, between the centre and periphery in Europe. With a view to the more recent history of

European integration, the transnational dimension may help to explain centre-periphery differentiation within the enlarged EC/EU, too. The comparison of Sweden and Finland in the EU provides an interesting recent example. Both states joined the EU at the same time, in 1995, and operate under the same legal conditions of membership, with no so-called opt-outs. Nevertheless, Finland has adopted the Euro and appears to have played a much more active role in EU politics, despite its smaller population and GDP and even more peripheral geographical location compared to Sweden, and to have succeeded better at inserting its priorities into EU political agendas. To explain this or similar historical phenomena (such as the continued British semi-detachment within the EU) necessitates a sophisticated understanding of the interplay of domestic cultural and political factors and transnational elite interaction and socialization. While domestic cultural and political factors can erect barriers to effective transnational engagement, elite interaction in turn can provide important resources for influencing the informal politics of the EU – resources that can possibly compensate for smaller formal decision-making powers such as fewer votes in the Council of Ministers.

Finally, research on transnational networks and socialization could also contribute to a better understanding of the temporal dimension of European integration. Combining their political function of facilitating the formation of stable policy preferences with their social function of creating interpersonal and institutional trust, transnational networks and their activities help explain continuities in European integration such as the survival of the long-term federalist objective through various enlargements and treaty revisions. The role of networks in developing and lobbying for a particular repertoire of constitutional and policy options can also contribute to a better understanding of change in European politics under conditions of fast structural transformations. Transnational networks have played an important role in developing new integration agendas in suddenly insecure environments, for example by reorienting governments to functional economic integration after the collapse of the European Defence Community treaty in the French Parliament in 1954, by working for the direct election of the EP after de Gaulle's exit from French politics, and by pushing for monetary union after the breakdown of the Iron Curtain, and combining this indirectly with the issue of German reunification. Whereas social scientists (including those studying transnational networks and socialization) mostly take snap-shots of situations of deliberation and decision-making, contemporary historians are better placed to explore change over time. In a more general sense, this is also the most important contribution they can make to the study of the present-day EU as a product of the transnational informal negotiation in multiple institutional and societal contexts, of only partially nationally specific traditions, beliefs and preferences.[65]

Notes

1 By way of introduction, see Christopher Lord, *A Democratic Audit of the European Union*, Basingstoke: Palgrave, 2004.

2 EEC Treaty, extract printed in A.G. Harryvan and Jan van der Harst (eds.), *Documents on European Union*, Basingstoke: Macmillan, 1997, pp. 104–19, here p. 104.

3 Walter Lipgens, *Europa-Föderationspläne der Widerstandsbewegungen, 1940–1945: eine Dokumentation*, Munich: Oldenbourg, 1968; idem., *Die Anfänge der europäischen Einigungspolitik 1945–1950, Erster Teil: 1945–1947*, Stuttgart: Ernst Klett, 1977.

4 Ernst B. Haas, *The United of Europe. Political, Social, and Economic Forces 1950–57*, Notre Dame, IN: University of Notre Dame Press, 2004, [1958].

5 Alan S. Milward, 'Historical Teleologies', in Mary Farrell, Stefano Fella and Michael Newman (eds.), *European Integration in the 21st Century: Unity in Diversity?* London: Sage, 2002, pp. 15–28, here p. 18.

6 Alan S. Milward, *The European Rescue of the Nation-State*, London: Routledge, 1992.

7 By way of introduction see Wolfram Kaiser, 'Transnational Mobilization and Cultural Representation: Political Transfer in an Age of Proto-Globalization, Democratization and Nationalism 1848–1914', *European Review of History*, vol. 12, no. 2 (2005), pp. 403–24.

8 Hartmut Kaelble, *Auf dem Weg zur europäischen Gesellschaft. Eine Sozialgeschichte Westeuropas 1880–1980*, Munich: Beck, 1987.

9 Keith Middlemas, *Orchestrating Europe. The Informal Politics of European Union 1973–1995*, London: Fontana, 1995.

10 Manuel Castells, *The Rise of the Network Society*, Oxford: Blackwell, 1996.

11 Karen Heard-Lauréote, 'Transnational Networks: Informal Governance in the European Political Space', in Wolfram Kaiser and Peter Starie (eds.), *Transnational European Union: Towards a Common Political Space*, London: Routledge, pp. 36–60, here p. 37.

12 Cf. W.W. Powell and L. Smith Doerr, 'Networks and Economic Life', in Neil J. Smelser and Richard Swedberg (eds.), *The Handbook of Economic Sociology*, Princeton, NJ: Princeton University Press, 2005, pp. 379–403.

13 Johan A. De Bruijn and Ernst F. ten Heuvelhof, 'Policy Networks and Governance', in David L. Weimer (ed.), *Institutional Design*, Boston, MA: Kluwer, pp. 161–81, here p. 163.

14 See, for example, David Marsh and Rod Rhodes (eds.), *Policy Networks in British Government*, Oxford: Clarendon, 1992.

15 Cf. Tanja Börzel, 'Organising Babylon. On the Different Conceptions of Policy Networks', *Public Administration*, vol. 76, no. 2 (1998), pp. 253–73.

16 See Marsh and Rhodes, *Policy Networks*.

17 Peter Haas, *Saving the Mediterranean*, New York: Columbia University Press, 1990, p. 55.

18 Idem., 'Introduction: Epistemic Communities and International Policy Coordination', *International Organization*, vol. 46, no. 1 (1992), pp. 1–35, here p. 27.

19 Paul Sabatier, 'The Advocacy Coalition Framework: Revisions and Relevance for Europe', *Journal of European Public Policy*, vol. 5, no. 1 (1998), pp. 98–130.

20 Frans van Waarden and Michaela Drahos, 'Courts and (Epistemic) Communities in the Convergence of Competition Policies, *Journal of European Public Policy*, vol. 9, no. 6 (2002), pp. 913–34.

21 For a recent overview of 'governance' research on the EU see Beate Kohler-Koch and Berthold Rittberger, 'Review Article: The "Governance Turn" in EU Studies', *Journal of Common Market Studies*, vol. 44 (supplement) (2006), pp. 27–49.

22 Markus Jachtenfuchs, *Die Konstruktion Europas: Verfassungsideen und institutionelle Entwicklung*, Baden-Baden: Nomos, 2002.

23 Craig Parsons, *A Certain Idea of Europe*, Ithaca, NY: Cornell University Press, 2003.

24 Berthold Rittberger, *Building Europe's Parliament. Democratic Representation Beyond the Nation-State*, Oxford: Oxford University Press, 2005.

25 On this much neglected topic see for example Simon Bulmer, *et al.*, *Policy Transfer in European Union Governance. Regulating the Utilities*, London: Routledge, 2007.

26 Karl Deutsch, *Political Community and the North Atlantic Area. International Organization in the Light of Historical Experience*, Princeton, NJ: Princeton University Press, 1957.
27 Haas, *The Uniting*, p. 14.
28 James G. March and Johan P. Olsen, *Rediscovering Institutions. The Organizational Basis of Politics*, New York: Free Press, 1989, pp. 160–61.
29 Frank Schimmelfennig, 'Transnational Socialization. Community-Building in an Integrated Europe, in Kaiser and Starie (eds.), *Transnational European Union*, pp. 61–82, here p. 64f.
30 Jeffrey Checkel, 'Why Comply? Social Learning and European Identity Change', *International Organization*. vol. 55, no. 3 (2001), pp. 553–88, here p. 562f.
31 Thomas Risse, 'European Institutions and Identity Change: What Have we Learned?', in Richard Herrmann, Thomas Risse and Marilynn Brewer (eds.), *Transnational Identities. Becoming European in the EU*, Lanham, MD: Rowman & Littlefield, 2004, pp. 247–71.
32 Doug Imig and Sidney Tarrow, (eds.), *Contentious Europeans. Protest and Politics in an Emerging Polity* Lanham, MD: Rowman & Littlefield, 2001, pp. 3–26.
33 Risse, 'European institutions'.
34 Hans-Jörg Trenz, *Zur Konstitution politischer Öffentlichkeit in der Europäischen Union. Zivilgesellschaftliche Subpolitik oder schaupolitische Inszenierung?* Baden-Baden: Nomos, 2002.
35 Wolfram Kaiser, *Christian Democracy and the Origins of European Union*, Cambridge: Cambridge University Press, 2007, chapters 6 and 8.
36 Cited in Jacques Dalloz, *Georges Bidault. Biographie politique*, Paris: L'Harmattan, 1992, p. 189.
37 See also based on eyewitness interviews Georgette Elgey, *La République des illusions 1945–1951*, Paris: Fayard, 1965, p. 385.
38 Pierre-Henri Teitgen, *'Faites entrer le témoin suivant'. 1940–1958: de la Résistance à la Vème République*, Paris: Ouest-France, 1988, p. 476.
39 Jachtenfuchs, *Die Konstruktion Europas*, p. 262.
40 On this issue see also John Gillingham, *Coal, Steel and the Rebirth of Europe, 1945–1955. The Germans and French from Ruhr Conflict to Economic Community*, Cambridge: Cambridge University Press, 1991, pp. 266–83.
41 Although still state-centric, see in particular Sibylle Hambloch, *Europäische Integration am Beispiel der Wettbewerbspolitik in der Frühphase der Europäischen Wirtschaftsgemeinschaft*, Habilitation, Siegen: University of Siegen, 2007; Laurent Warlouzet, *Quelle Europe économique pour la France? La France et le Marché commun industriel, 1956–1969*, PhD, Paris: University of Paris-Sorbonne, 2007; idem., 'La France et la mise en place de la politique de la concurrence communautaire, 1957–64', in Eric Bussière, Michel Dumoulin and Sylvain Schirmann (eds.), *Europe organisée, Europe du libre-échange? Fin XIXe siècle-Années 1960*, Brussels: P.I.E.-Peter Lang, 2006, pp. 175–93.
42 Cf. Kaiser, *Christian Democracy*, chapter 6.
43 François Duchêne, *Jean Monnet: The First Statesman of Interdependence*, New York and London: W.W. Norton, 1994, 286–88.
44 See Kaiser, *Christian Democracy*, chapter 6; Hans-Peter Schwarz, *Adenauer. Der Aufstieg: 1876–1952*, Stuttgart: Deutsche Verlagsanstalt, 1986, pp. 648–50.
45 Cited in Jean-Claude Delbreil, 'Le MRP et la construction européenne: résultats, interprétation et conclusion d'une enquête écrite et orale', in Serge Berstein, Jean-Marie Mayeur and Pierre Milza (eds.), *Le MRP et la construction européenne*, Paris: Editions Complexe, 1993, pp. 309–63, here p. 356.
46 See about this transnational alliance in greater detail Kaiser, *Christian Democracy*, chapter 6.
47 See also Gérard Bossuat, 'La vraie nature de la politique européenne de la France (1950–57)', in Gilbert Trausch (ed.), *Die Europäische Integration vom Schuman-Plan*

bis zu den Verträgen von Rom / The European Integration from the Schuman-Plan to the Treaties of Rome, Baden-Baden: Nomos, 1993, pp. 191–230, here p. 206.

48   Jean Monnet, *Mémoires*, Paris: Fayard, 1976, pp. 342–55; see also Duchêne, *Jean Monnet*. For the crucial transatlantic connections of Monnet's domestic network see Brigitte Leucht, 'Transatlantische Politiknetzwerke: Kulturtransfer und Schuman-Plan 1950/51', *Comparativ*, vol. 16, no. 4 (2006), pp. 200–218, here pp. 208–14.

49   Ralf Magagnoli, *Italien und die Europäische Verteidigungsgemeinschaft. Zwischen europäischem Credo und nationaler Machtpolitik*, Frankfurt: Peter Lang, 1999, p. 99.

50   Cf. Kaiser, *Christian Democracy*, chapter 8.

51   Michel Dumoulin and Anne-Myriam Dutrieue, *La Ligue Européenne de Coopération Économique (1946–1981). Un group d'étude et de pression dans la construction européenne*, Bern: Peter Lang, 1993.

52   N. Piers Ludlow, 'The Making of the CAP: Towards a Historical Analysis of the EU's First Major Policy', *Contemporary European History* vol. 14, no. 3 (2005), pp. 347–71. See also idem., *The European Community and the Crises of the 1960s: Negotiating the Gaullist Challenge*, London: Routledge, 2006.

53   Ann-Christina Knudsen, *Defining the Policies of the Common Agricultural Policy. A Historical Study*, PhD, Florence: European University Institute, 2001. See also the case study with particular emphasis on the role of the German Bauernverband in influencing the Erhard government's negotiating stance in idem, 'Creating the Common Agricultural Policy. Story of Cereals Prices', in Wilfried Loth (ed.), *Crises and Compromises: The European Project 1963–1969*, Baden-Baden: Nomos, 2001, pp. 131–54.

54   Volker R. Berghahn, *America and the Intellectual Cold Wars in Europe: Shepard Stone between Philantrophy, Academy, and Diplomacy*, Princeton, NJ: Princeton University Press, 2001.

55   For the divide within the Western European trade union movement resulting from the creation of the ECSC/EEC see by way of introduction Patrick Pasture, 'Trade Unions as a Transnational Movement in the European Space 1955–65: Falling Short of Ambitions?', in Kaiser and Starie (eds.), *Transnational European Union*, pp. 109–30, here p. 113. The Trade Union Committee of EFTA Countries was created in Vienna in March 1960.

56   Cf. Wolfram Kaiser, 'A Better Europe? EFTA, the EFTA Secretariat, and the European Identities of the 'outer Seven', 1958–72', in Marie-Thérèse Bitsch, Wilfried Loth and Raymond Poidevin (eds.), *Institutions européennes et identities européennes*, Brussels: Bruylant, 1998, pp. 165–83.

57   Cf. Fritz Diwok, Bericht über die Zusammenkunft des International EFTA Action Committees am 6. Juni 1961, 9 June 1961, Stiftung Bundeskanzler Kreisky-Archiv, Vienna, Bestand VII.3, Box 3.

58   EFTA Information Policy, Note by the Information Department of the Secretariat, 23 January 1961, EFTA Archives, Geneva, EFTA 15/61.

59   Cf. Karl Magnus Johansson, *Transnational Party Alliances: Analysing the Hard-Won Alliance between Conservatives and Christian Democrats in the European Parliament*, Lund: Lund University Press, 1997.

60   Pilar Ortuño Anaya, *European Socialists and Spain: The Transition to Democracy*, Basingstoke: Palgrave, 2002.

61   Jean Marie Palayret, 'Eduquer les jeunes à l'Union: la campagne européenne de la jeunesse 1951–58', *Journal of European Integration History*, vol. 1, no. 2 (1995), pp. 47–60.

62   Michael Gehler has used the term 'Mehrebenensystem' (multilevel system) in his insightful advocacy of a contemporary European history beyond the nation-state: *Zeitgeschichte im dynamischen Mehrebenensystem. Zwischen Regionalisierung, Nationalstaat, Europäisierung, internationaler Arena und Globalisierung*, Bochum: Winkler, 2001.

63 Cf. Karl Magnus Johansson, 'Another Road to Maastricht: the Christian Democrat Coalition and the Quest for European Union', *Journal of Common Market Studies*, vol. 40, no. 5 (2002), pp. 871–93.
64 See in particular Ludlow, *The European Community*; Jean-Marie Palayret, Helen Wallace and Pascaline Winand (eds.), *Visions, Votes and Compromises. The Empty Chair Crisis and the Luxembourg Compromise Forty Years On*, Brussels: P.I.E.-Peter Lang, 2006.
65 On co-operation between contemporary historical and social science research in the study of the EU see also Wolfram Kaiser, 'History meets Politics: Overcoming the Interdisciplinary Volapük in Research on the EU', *Journal of European Public Policy*, vol. 15, no. 2 (2008), 300–313; idem., 'Bringing People and Ideas Back in: Historical Research on the European Union', in David Phinnemore and Alex Warleigh (eds.), *Reflections on European Integration*, Basingstoke: Palgrave, 2008 – forthcoming.

3   Supranational governance in the making

Towards a European political system

Morten Rasmussen

In 1994, British political scientist Simon Hix argued forcefully that the European Union (EU) was best conceptualized as a political system.[1] His article was a response to the rather sterile debate between a revitalized neo-functionalism and intergovernmentalism over how to interpret the new dynamism of the integration process since the Single European Act (SEA) of 1986. It also reflected how Comparative Politics scholars like Hix increasingly analyzed the EU as having its own internal political arena. According to the classic standards defined by Gabriel Almond[2] and David Easton,[3] the EU indeed qualifies as a political system. Thus, it has stable and clearly defined institutions for collective decision making which continuously interact with societal groups. Citizens and societal groups seek to achieve their political objectives at the EU level either directly or through intermediary organizations, such as interest groups or political parties. Finally, supranational legislation affects citizens across the EU by redistributing important economic resources and shaping social and political values.[4] At the same time, the EU in fundamental respects lacks features of classical statehood such as a single government, a coherent foreign policy and a standing army. Moreover, the EU still relies on the member-states to implement legislation and administer coercion. While the EU can be defined as a political system, this does not entail any teleological prediction of the development of a European state.

In this book we demonstrate how important cornerstones of the European political system were laid during the formative period of the EU from 1950 to 1972. Historians have tended to assume that states acted in a unitary manner in the European field and largely controlled the development of European institutions and policy-making. This is lamentable because these crude conceptualizations preclude a nuanced understanding of the relationship between the member-states and EU institutions, which arguably is fundamental to tracing the historical roots of the European political system. Political scientists, in contrast, perhaps because they have had to come to terms with the emerging European political system during the last two decades, apply much more refined theoretical and conceptual approaches to analyzing this system.

To overcome the theoretical and conceptual poverty of current historiography, this chapter will consequently explore recent institutional theory. The somewhat narrow focus on this body of theory is justified in this context because it particularly addresses the crucial relationship between the member-states and the European institutions. However, an analysis of the contemporary European political system cannot rely on institutionalist theory alone, but must also draw on the various approaches to transnational society formation dealt with in Wolfram Kaiser's conceptual chapter, approaches to governance and Europeanization.[5] The aim of this chapter is to establish an informed research agenda for historical research in this field. In the first section, various schools of institutional theory will be discussed. In the second section, existing source-based historical literature will be reviewed with regard to the major hypotheses and arguments of institutional theory and the development of an agenda for future research in this direction.

New institutionalism

Institutional analysis experienced a great revival during the 1980s and 1990s after having been largely absent in the social sciences, which were dominated for decades by the behavioural approach to the study of the social world. Institutional analysis emphasizes the explanatory value of context and has brought institutions back into the spotlight. At least three distinct schools of institutionalism can be identified within the social sciences, namely rational, historical, and sociological institutionalism.[6] All clearly differ at the ontological and epistemological levels; consequently, they define institutions differently. In the context of this chapter, in which I search for conceptual approaches to the institutions of the European Coal and Steel Community (ECSC) and the European Communities (EC), institutions are, unless otherwise specified, defined narrowly as formal organizations, rules and procedures that structure the conduct of political actors.

The first school, rational institutionalism, has strong roots in neoclassical economics. Starting with the behavioural assumptions that actors behave rationally, guided by the wish to maximize their preference, rational institutional theory aims to explain why institutions arise. The underlying notion is that institutions lower the transaction costs associated with interaction or co-operation to reduce uncertainty and provide stable structures for exchange.[7] This core of thought has been applied by political scientists to explain institutional choices in fields as far-ranging as United States (US) Congressional politics, public bureaucracy and international co-operation.[8]

The focus here is on delegation theory, which originally was developed by scholars studying US Congressional politics but has recently been applied to European integration by different scholars such as Andrew Moravcsik, Mark A. Pollack, Alec Stone Sweet and Giandomenico Majone.[9] The basic argument in this literature is that 'principals', for example US Congress or EU member-states, delegate authority to 'agents', for example international institutions, courts or agencies, for two major reasons. First, principals can lower the transaction costs and increase the efficiency of co-operation by delegating authority to an agent that provides policy-relevant information or technical expertise. Second, principals establish credible commitments by delegating authority to an agent that possibly sets the legislative agenda, monitors compliance, provides dispute resolution or runs a particular policy according to fixed guidelines. This might be particularly useful if the principals have engaged in a classic framework treaty such as the treaty establishing the European Economic Community (EEC), in which the policy details need to be filled out later. The discretion granted to agents varies. Greater discretion will be granted agents when information about a policy field is highly complex and technical, or similarly, when a credible commitment must be particularly firm.

Scholars differ regarding the nature of these two types of delegation. Pollack, for example, prefers the classic principal-agent model emphasizing how the inherent interests of agents in self-empowerment necessitate mechanisms of oversight and control by the principals. These control mechanisms vary from administrative procedures, i.e. control over appointments and budgetary control, to oversight procedures designed to identify and subsequently control possible independent behaviour by agents, for example through new legislation or even institutional reform. Control mechanisms involve costs, however. Narrow administrative control seriously hampers the ability of the agent to conduct business, while oversight procedures swallow resources. Finally, the extent to which control mechanisms align the agent effectively within the preferences of the principal remains an open question.[10]

In contrast to Pollack, Majone argues that the focus on the control of member-states over agents makes little sense when dealing with delegation to create credible commitments. To create such credible commitment, principals delegate very substantial powers to what Majone terms a 'fiduciary', or, in case they delegate the full powers, a 'trustee'. The discretion granted varies according to the different requirements of various policy fields. In a fiduciary relationship, principals may continue to attempt circumventing the 'fiduciary', but they cannot control the authority delegated to it in the same strict manner as would be possible with an agent. The main concern is therefore whether the 'fiduciary' perform satisfactorily and thereby attain legitimacy. If this is not the case, this type of delegation may inflict a serious cost on the principals by undermining the legitimacy of the policy choices in question. Indeed, Majone has recently argued that the Community method, characterized by the fiduciary relationships between the member-states, on the one hand, and the Commission and the European Court of Justice (ECJ), on the other hand, is in crisis exactly because it has never attained a sufficient level of legitimacy.[11]

A brief consideration of each supranational institution on the basis of these theoretical perspectives suggests different ideas as to the relationship between supranational institutions and member-states. The competences of the Commission, Pollack has argued, follow the prediction of the principal-agent model. The central powers of the Commission, such as setting the agenda for Council decision-making, monitoring member-state compliance with EU law and implementing regulations, are all typical agency functions. In general, the Commission enjoys most discretion in its monitoring-and-enforcement functions and less discretion in agenda setting and its regulatory function. Furthermore, the discretion granted to the Commission varies across policy fields. Member-state motives for delegating competences to the Commission were mainly to secure rapid and efficient decision-making and create credible commitments.[12] An array of mechanisms was established and applied by member-states to control the Commission. Among these mechanisms were budgetary controls, the appointment of commissioners, the establishment of the Committee of Permanent Representatives (Coreper), which introduced the permanent diplomatic representation of member-states in Brussels, and comitology, the committees which the member-states established to monitor and advise the Commission in its implementation of EU law.[13] In contrast, Sweet and Majone find that the principal-agent model cannot explain all of the features of the delegated powers enjoyed by the Commission. Several Commission functions, such as agenda setting and the anti-trust role in the field of competition, were designed in the EEC treaty to be independent of the member-states, and state control in these fields remains fragmented at best.[14]

According to Moravcsik and Pollack, the basic competences of the ECJ can also be explained using the principal-agent model.[15] Member-states wanted the court to monitor, enforce compliance and solve questions, which had been left unclear in the EEC treaty or Council legislation. Sweet has argued, however, that the ECJ resembles a trustee much more than an agency monitored and controlled by the member-states.[16] The ECJ was originally designed to be independent. The threshold for legislative overruling, not to speak of constitutional reform, is very high, requiring unanimity between the member-states. Attempts to maintain the functional assumption that the ECJ acts in accordance with the general preferences of at least the large member-states have failed to convince.[17] Instead, recent social science explorations of the role of the ECJ in the constitutionalization of the EEC treaty have demonstrated how this development proceeded significantly beyond the original mandate given by the member-states and, even more, despite the outright opposition of several member-states.[18]

With regard to the European Parliament (EP), Pollack accepts that the principal-agent model has limited relevance for explaining the competences of the EP. The fundamental reason for this is that member-states did not grant the EP powers merely to lower transactions costs, but rather as a means of addressing the democratic deficit and democratizing the Community.[19] Nevertheless, Pollack maintains that delegation to the EP has not been made irrespective of potential consequences. Instead, member-states have limited delegation to fields in which distributional implications are either unclear or unimportant, the budgetary powers of the EP constituting the prime example of this approach.[20]

The different conceptualizations of the relationship between supranational institutions and the member-states implicit in the principal-agent model and the notion of the fiduciary relationship, respectively, are important when rational institutionalist scholars discuss the extent to which institutional dynamics constitute an independent causal factor in the process of European integration. Moravcsik, for example, claims that governments control the discretion of agents and are able to shape the process of European integration according to their preferences. The grand bargains at intergovernmental conferences therefore have decided the political direction of the EC/EU. The periods in between these 'big bangs' are merely used to fill in the objectives set out by the governments.[21] Pollack argues that not only do supranational institutions, like agents, attempt to expand their own competences, but they also occasionally have an independent causal effect on political and constitutional outcomes. Pollack maintains the notion of state control, however: 'the Commission, the Court of Justice, and the European Parliament are . . . actors in an intergovernmental play written, and periodically rewritten, by the EU's member governments.'[22] In contrast, by conceptualizing how the ECJ and, in particular cases, also the Commission act as fiduciaries, Majone and Sweet Stone have developed precise predictions for when supranational institutions potentially have independent causal effects on European integration.

Rational institutionalism provides potent, yet somewhat restricted, explanations of why the European institutions were founded, what functions they perform, and which power structures define their relationship with the member-states. Several important weaknesses can be identified, however. First, the lack of the temporal dimension is highly problematic, because it does not allow us to trace the evolutionary dynamics of agency or a fiduciary relationship. Scholars using the principal-agent model in particular underestimate the causal effects of such dynamics, because they tend to assume that agents fulfil the functional needs of the principal.[23] Second, the assumption that states and institutions act according to the predictions of rational choice theory means that rational institutionalism is blind to potentially transformative effects, caused by European institutions, on norms, identities and social practises. Finally, the assumption that states and institutions behave in a unitary fashion and with fixed preferences represents an excessive simplification. Rational institutionalism offers no insights into the internal decision making processes of principals or agents and their political and administrative culture, which are decisive to the preferences pursued. However, reconsidering the assumptions of unitary behaviour and fixed preferences seriously undermines the theoretical logics of the principal-agent model.

Historical institutionalism essentially represents an effort to conceptualize the distinct impact of the passage of time on the social world. The fundamental idea is that certain types of formal and informal institutions create path-dependent processes that over time slowly reshape the context within which politics play out. This basic notion is familiar to historians who normally assume that different social processes develop along different time frames. When applied to European integration, this insight clearly demonstrates the limitations of rational institutionalism. While numerous scholars have recently emphasized the importance of the temporal dimension to the understanding of European integration,[24] Paul Pierson's explorations of the temporal dimension, which he also applies to European integration, are by far the most comprehensive and sophisticated.[25]

Pierson adopts the basic assumptions of rational institutionalism that governments and institutions behave in a rational and unitary manner in order to demonstrate more clearly the implications of adding the temporal dimension to the analysis of the process of European integration. His main conclusion is that the member-states did not fully control the evolution of the EU. The gradual evolution of European institutions and policies created path-dependent processes involving self-reinforcing mechanisms, i.e. so-called 'positive feedback'. Such processes would over time fundamentally reshape the context in which the member-states operate and consequently condition and change the nature of the political game. Pierson defines path-dependent processes as self-reinforcing in the sense that each step down a particular path increases the probability of further steps along the same path. According to Pierson, this type of path-dependent process is characterized by unpredictability, because there are multiple outcomes depending on the sequence in which events unfold. Path-dependent processes are also prone to contingency: small, even accidental events, early in the sequence have a disproportionate impact on the direction of a particular path. Finally, once established, paths will be relatively resistant to change.[26] Rittberger and Stacy have argued that the existence of path-dependent processes has had a fundamental effect on member-state decision making. A large part of the treaty rules does not come directly from member-state bargaining during the large intergovernmental conferences that revise treaties, they claim, but rather from the 'interregnum' or in between day-to-day bargaining that gradually determines institutional and policy paths.[27]

A central question is what type of self-reinforcing mechanisms help 'lock in' particular policy or institutional paths in the field of European integration. First, strong linkages develop among institutional arrangements over time. The European institutions gradually became part of an overall institutional infrastructure in which important common policies such as the Common Agricultural Policy (CAP) and the common market were based. Removing or reforming European institutions would inadvertently affect established policies. Second, institutions may create powerful incentives that strengthen their own stability. For example, European institutions facilitated the creation of additional institutions and norms that place pressure on actors to adjust to the new context. Finally, institutions may fundamentally affect the perceptions, incentives and preferences of state and societal actors. Political, social and economic actors develop investments in a particular institution or policy. These investments can range from the educational training necessary to participate in institutional decision making to the investment in particular modes of production to benefit from a specific policy. When investments in a particular institutional set up or policy are high, actors will resist reform.[28]

For several reasons, it is difficult for member-state governments to reverse paths, which are already locked in. Politicians are caught in the logic of electoral politics. Governments will therefore tend to make short-term decisions on the basis of electoral concerns, while the consequences of institutional choices and policy reform that often play out only in the long-term will be discarded.[29] Given the high costs of leaving the EU, member-states are forced to correct gaps either by adopting new policies or, in extreme cases, through institutional redesign. Treaty revision is very difficult because it requires unanimity and parliamentary ratification or even public referenda in certain member-states. But even policy revisions are not easily obtained. Many policy fields still require a unanimous vote of the Council, which is often internally divided. Even a qualified majority vote can be difficult to achieve.[30]

Historical institutionalism has recently been used to systematically structure empirical studies of institutional development.[31] That European law has been at the centre of recent historical institutionalist analyses is not a coincidence; it reflects the important role played by precedent in judicial decision making.[32] One example is Dorte Martinsen's empirical study of the development of Regulation 1408/71 on the free movement of labour from 1970 to 2002. Here, member-state control over policy making falters over time as gaps emerge caused by the legal activism of the ECJ and political entrepreneurship of the Commission. Member-state preferences at times converge sufficiently to overturn judicial developments. More often than not, however, member-states find themselves unable to alter legislation and must respond individually to the rulings of the court. Martinsen documents that even when member-states first ignore ECJ rulings, they over time gradually accept European jurisprudence.[33] Lisa Conant has recently argued that member-states accept ECJ rulings because the effects of European law can be weakened considerably through non-compliance or by containing compliance to the single court cases in question.[34] In the long term, however, such strategies are exhausted and member-states comply broadly with European law.

By conceptualizing the impact of the passage of time, historical institutionalism substantially complements and improves rational institutionalism. Nevertheless, because Pierson maintains that member-states and institutions behave in a rational and unitary manner, his version of historical institutionalism suffers from several of the weaknesses of rational institutionalism. Therefore, the question is whether both theories, by excluding norms, culture and ideas, ultimately offer a fundamentally restricted, if not outright distorted, understanding of European integration. The third variety of institutional theory, with intellectual roots in sociology, argues that this is indeed the case.

With roots in American organizational sociology, constructivist theories on International Relations (IR) and Pierre Bourdieu-inspired sociology of internationalization, the many different sociological approaches to analyzing the European political system cannot be captured with one headline.[35] However, these theories share a basic notion of the mutual constitutiveness of social structures and agents. In Thomas Risse's words: 'The social environment in which we find ourselves, defines ("constitutes") who we are, our identities as social beings. "We" are social beings, embedded in various relevant social communities. At the same time, human agency creates, reproduces, and changes culture through our daily practices.'[36] The three theoretical schools differ significantly in terms of how they explore this notion.

Organizational sociology and constructivism both pay much more attention to the effects of structures than the role of agency, arguably because they were formulated in opposition to rational choice. Both approaches have primarily focused on how institutions, very broadly defined as norms, identities, informal and formal rules, influence the behaviour of actors. The claim is that institutions structure the behaviour of actors and at the same time have constitutive effects.

For example, the norm of sovereignty not only regulates state behaviour in International Relations, but also defines what constitutes a state.[37] At the micro level of human behaviour, James G. March and Johan P. Olsen have introduced the logic of appropriateness: 'Human actors are imagined to follow rules that associate particular identities to particular situations, approaching individual opportunities for action by assessing similarities between current identities and choice dilemmas and more general concepts of self and situations.'[38] According to this, human behaviour is rule-based, i.e. guided by an effort to 'do the right thing' and deeply embedded in particular institutions and norms. Institutions in the broad sense cannot therefore be regarded as external to actors.[39] These insights fundamentally change the way scholars in this field approach and analyze the European political system.

In contrast to organizational institutionalism and constructivism, Bourdieu's sociology is much more firmly based upon the mutual constitutiveness of structure and agency. In an effort to historicize the institutions he explored and to avoid blindly legitimizing them, Bourdieu developed the notion of the 'field' as an analytical research tool. By mapping out fields of actors situated objectively vis-à-vis each other and analyzing the mechanisms actors use to reproduce the power relations between them, as well as the mechanisms causing change, he not only exposed the internal divisions of institutions but also placed these in a wider context of historical structures and processes.[40] Although Bourdieu's original work was not concerned with IR or Europe, Mikael Rask Madsen and Yves Dezalay have recently adopted his approach in order to explain the international-ization of law in a European context.[41] According to this sociology, European institutions and the European political system should not be studied in isolation, but as part of broader fields of actors operating both at the national and European level. In these fields, actors reproduce their positions of power in the national arena by promoting their particular know-how and self-interest, and as a result contribute to the establishment of new practises through the building of the European judicial and political orders. As an analytical approach the notion of the field overcomes the dichotomy between the national and the international, and thus captures the ongoing interplay between the national and the European levels, which in many respects has shaped the EU. By emphasizing the individual actors, although conceptualized as being positioned in a particular field, and in this sense contextualized, this approach points out how institutions, be it EU insti-tutions or national ministries, are less able to formulate coherent preferences than typically assumed by political scientists. Instead, institutional preferences are characterized by discontinuities and shaped by the interplay with other institutions. This does not mean that the approach ignores the degree to which the nation states remain centres of power, and how the tension between these and the new European centre of power has shaped the EU. However, Dezalay and Madsen conceptualize these power struggles not primarily as a battle between nation states and EU institutions, but rather as continuing battles between competing political, social, economic and judicial elites operating both at the national and European level. The incipient European political system in the postwar period was thus created by the emergence of a large number of fields of actors incorporating existing structures, but differentiating themselves vis-à-vis each other to promote their respective knowledge and values. The EU is a result of these multiple processes and thus reflects a high degree of differentiation of institutional and legal arrangements, a comprehensive import of state knowledge, a particular balance of market liberalization and protectionism and a fusion between national and European levels of administration. Together these processes have created ambiguous and indeterminate European judicial and political orders characterized by multiple interconnected social fields with different relations of power with the national arenas.

Various sociological approaches have resulted in a number of interesting empirical insights of importance to the study of the incipient European political system. Addressing the origins of institutions, for example, sociological institutionalism has argued that their design will reflect the cognitive and normative features and social practices of the political culture existing at that point in time.[42] The concept of 'diffusion' conceptualizes one central mechanism of how political culture influences institutional design. The concept refers to the use by institutional designers of already known and accepted institutional models, which are then applied to the new situation.[43] A similar conclusion is drawn by the sociology formulated by Dezalay and Madsen. Empirical research has demonstrated that a number of important personalities, politicians, jurists and economists pursued their careers through the development of the European political space. By exporting their particular 'state knowledge', these actors formulated and later to a large extent negotiated the construction of Europe. Thus, the particular shape of European institutions cannot be perceived merely as a functional expression of state interest, but must be understood in the context of the emergence of these broader European fields.[44]

Organizational sociology and constructivism also claim that the establishment of European institutions and the gradual development of a European political system not only constrain the choices available to member-states, as argued by historical institutionalism. In addition, the institutionalization of the European political space has fundamentally reconfigured the identities of member-states and consequently changed how they define their interests. Several important features of what it means to be an EU state have been explored. EU membership extends the economical, social, legal and political space available to national citizens for pursuing their preferences, for example.[45] Membership also implies the adoption of the acquis communautaire, i.e. the formal and informal rules of the EU, and consequently the adaptation of national legal and administrative practises to the requirements of membership.[46] Furthermore, the establishment of a European administration constituted by a large and complex committee system, has led to what has been termed a politico-administrative fusion between national and European administrative levels.[47] Together, these effects of the institutionalization of the European space have arguably transformed EU member-states and societies.

By focusing on the mutual constitutiveness between actors and structures, this body of research has also proved a useful approach to understanding the impact of institutional and administrative culture on actors inside and outside these institutions. Marcus Jachtenfuchs has argued that institutions create 'theories' or discourses about themselves that have consequences for the behaviour of employees and for the preferences pursued by the institutions.[48] In other words, institutions nurture certain values and a mission to legitimize the goals pursued, while their employees internalize these values through socialization.[49] Other empirical research suggests that Coreper, the Special Committee of Agriculture (SCA) and comitology cannot merely be considered control mechanisms with which the member-states control the Commission. Research on the agricultural administration suggests that national officials felt more in common with their European colleagues in this highly specialized environment, than with national officials from other ministries.[50] Christian Joerges and Jürgen Neyer have explored the EU foodstuff regulation and found that a scientific discourse dominated talks that consequently were deliberative in nature. The fact that the same national experts participated in the scientific advisory committee in the preparation of the Commission proposal, the working groups inside the Coreper and finally the advisory committee (comitology) dealing with the implementation of legislation offered the possibility of long-term socialization in European norms.[51] These are important insights considering how little rational institutional and historical institutional theory have to say about the effects of institutional and administrative culture on preferences of the European institutions and ultimately on policy outcomes.

Finally, Bourdieu-inspired analyses demonstrate how the supranational institutions placed in the European political space are continuously reproduced and at the same time slowly reconfigured through the interplay with national political arenas. By taking the approach of relational biographies to map out the European political space, this sociology completely breaks with the notion employed by rational and historical institutionalism that member-states and institutions act in a unitary manner. Exploring the genesis of the European legal 'field', scholars such as Antonin Cohen, Antoine Vauchez and Madsen have argued that the establishment of the ECJ was born out of the continued investments of jurists in the formulation of the European construction. They have shown, furthermore, how the powers and practises of the court were created through complex processes that involved lawyers employed in foreign ministries, national judges and advocates, private litigants, legal advisors of the High Authority and the Commission, and the Advocates General and judges of the ECJ.[52]

There is little doubt that sociological and constructivist approaches to the study of the European political system not only provide a necessary complement and corrective to rational and historical institutionalism, but in fact already constitute a serious alternative research agenda. As demonstrated above, important theoretical hypotheses have been formulated on the emergence of the European political system and the establishment and functioning of European institutions, and a number of recent empirical studies have started to demonstrate their usefulness. The various approaches have different weaknesses. Organizational institutionalism and constructivism often overemphasize the importance of structure over agency. Considering the central role of agency in historical change, this leads to theoretical and empirical contributions that merely complement the actor-oriented approaches based on rational choice. Bourdieu offered an escape from this trap by formulating a sociology, which explores fields of contextualized social actors and by focusing on how the practice of these actors structures fields. The main weakness of this approach, however, might be a tendency to overlook the extent to which institutional structures do determine the behaviour of individual actors. While the field as an analytical approach is useful in order to avoid simplistic assumptions of unitary behaviour of states or institutions and also help mapping out the context in which institutions exists, only empirical research can estimate the precise impact of fields of actors compared to the structuring logic of institutions.

All in all, social science institutional theory offers a valuable extension of the theoretical and methodological toolbox of historians studying the history of the EU. The three schools of institutional theory all contribute with important hypotheses and insights into why Western European nation states established supranational institutions in the 1950s and how these institutions developed over time. Potentially, future historiography also has much to offer the social sciences if historians apply and test the various theoretical propositions explored here in their empirical studies of the European institutions.

Towards a European political system 1950–72

Five broad empirical questions are raised by the theoretical discussion above. First, what originally motivated European states to pool their sovereignty and delegate competences to supranational European institutions? Second, to what extent can institutional delegation be interpreted as a means to obtain consolidated policy outcomes? Do member-states, third, try to control the supranational institutions and with which tools? Fourth, did supranational institutions consistently attempt to increase their own competences, or did administrative culture and policy ideas influence their preferences? And finally, how did the development of the European polity over time affect the member-states? By discussing these questions in relation to existing historiography, I attempt not only to provide nuanced empirical answers of interest to social scientists, but also to demonstrate which empirical questions historians must address with greater care.

The first question as to why Western European nation states chose to pool sovereignty and delegate competences to supranational institutions in the first place is central to any study of the foundation of the ECSC and the EEC. Moreover, this question concerns the continuous delegation of competences to supranational institutions in treaty revisions and day-to-day policy-making. Historical research on the foundations of the ECSC and the EEC is probably the most extensive of the entire EU historiography. While the first historical analyses were state-centred,[53] recent literature has demonstrated, as suggested by the sociological approaches treated above, that the shape and functions of the new European institutions were arguably the result of a process of the negotiated transfer of state knowledge by overlapping transnational networks of experts and politicians. Tracing these broad political processes, scholars have documented how transnational networks were closely associated with – and to a large extent had their activities financed by – American political and economic elites preoccupied with stabilizing Europe.[54] Three main types of networks have been analyzed. Focusing on the question of constitutionalization, Cohen has revealed how legal elites played a central role in formulating proposals on how to institutionalize the European political space after the Second World War. The influence of jurists was at the apogee during the negotiations on the doomed European Political Community (EPC). However, the failure to grant an overarching constitution to the different European institutions was not considered the ultimate defeat, because the ECSC Court of Justice had the potential to develop into a constitutional court.[55] Wolfram Kaiser has recently demonstrated how party networks between Christian democratic parties of the six founding members of the ECSC not only formulated a shared notion of how to establish a supranational Europe from the late 1940s onwards, but that this common outlook combined with the trust established between political leaders was instrumental to the successful conclusion of the negotiations on the ECSC treaty.[56] Finally, examinations of the origins of the Schuman Plan have shown that a nucleus of French civil servants and jurists around Jean Monnet was decisive when the French government adopted, and later during the negotiations on the ECSC treaty promoted, the principle of supranationality.[57] In this book, Brigitte Leucht documents that the same circle of French civil servants was also embedded in a wider transatlantic network of experts and policy-makers that had a direct impact on the negotiations of the ECSC treaty.

New research thus suggests that governments were influenced by transnational networks when conceptualizing and discussing the institutionalization of the European political space. The question arises, however, to what extent governments behaved along the lines of delegation theory during intergovernmental negotiations leading to the ECSC and the EEC/Euratom treaties. Historical research demonstrates that governments, on the one hand, were deeply concerned about the competences of the new European institutions but on the other hand also had to design a political system strong enough to carry through the common policy objectives. For this reason, supranational institutions became a mixture of agency and fiduciary functions depending on the role they had to perform. Furthermore, governments designed a political system of checks and balances to control the supranational institutions. For example, the High Authority of the ECSC, which Monnet and his staff had envisioned to be a trustee with sweeping powers, was gradually constrained during the negotiations by the establishment of an institutional system of checks and balances. The creation of a Council of Ministers, a ECJ and even the Common Assembly were all initially conceived as being control mechanisms to balance the High Authority.[58]

In the negotiations on the EEC and Euratom treaties, all governments with the exception of the Dutch merely wanted to establish the common institutions 'functionally necessary' for the attainment of the objectives of the common market and Euratom, respectively. Constitutional ideas that had dominated negotiations on the EPC were considered politically dangerous in so far as they would make the ratification of the treaties all but impossible in the French Parliament. Therefore, the Commission had less sweeping competences than the High Authority. The Council of Ministers became the new legislative organ, while the Commission maintained the right to initiate legislation despite strong French objections.[59] Despite the consensus between governments not to interpret the new treaties as a significant step towards a federal Europe, the *groupe de rédaction*, constituted by legal experts from the negotiating states and the ECSC and dealing merely with legal matters and the rules guiding the ECJ, managed by stealth to insert several articles and legal principles that the ECJ would later apply in the constitutionalization of the treaties. Most importantly, with article 177, these legal experts introduced the option for national courts to send preliminary references to the ECJ on questions concerning the interpretation of European law.[60] This mechanism, not well understood by the French delegation at the time, had the potential, and eventually was used, to turn the ECJ into a constitutional court.[61]

With regard to the second theme, institutional delegation as a means of consolidating policy outcomes, the historical literature has been less explicit. The number of studies on European policy-making in the 1950s and 1960s has steadily grown over the last decade, but many important policy fields remain unexplored. A preliminary conclusion drawn from existing empirical studies is that delegation theory and the notion of credible commitments constitute a useful starting point for empirical analysis. In general, member-states with an intense interest in a particular policy would be prone to delegate sovereignty, while governments sceptical or opposed to a policy would try to minimize the pooling of sovereignty and delegation. French European policy demonstrates that this mechanism was at work despite the fact that President Charles de Gaulle opposed the supranational element of the EC in his public rhetoric. In the CAP negotiations, the French government thus consistently and successfully supported proposals for institutional delegation to 'lock in' the various agreements. In contrast, in the field of competition policy, Katja Seidel demonstrates in her chapter that the French government preferred a relatively weak common policy. Consequently, France only reluctantly accepted the granting of wide powers to the Commission. Governments from other member-states such as Germany and the Netherlands, although officially supportive of supranational solutions, behaved in a similar manner, refusing to pool sovereignty and delegate powers when not intensely interested in a particular policy outcome.[62] The patterns of institutionalization emerging from this day-to-day policy making are an important contribution to the incremental evolvement of the European political system and arguably had a more lasting impact on the nature of the EC than the publicized institutional battle between de Gaulle and the Commission.

The third theme suited for empirical investigation concerns the institutional mechanisms that member-states use to control the discretion granted to the supranational institutions. Here the historical literature is limited and in most cases has not linked the question to wider debates about institutional dynamics. What emerges from the different empirical studies of European policy-making is that member-states have been very careful when delegating powers to supranational institutions. Delegation has been generally accompanied by control mechanisms. Studies of the Interim Committee, which from April 1957 to January 1958 set up the institutions of the EC, show how member-states established and gradually extended their permanent representation in Brussels in order to supervise and control the work of the Commission and the EC as a whole. The result of this process, the Coreper, constituted a major institutional development not clearly envisaged by the EEC treaty, but in fact already experienced in the ECSC.[63] Likewise, but largely unexplored in the historical literature, member-states devised three types of committees to oversee the implementation of policies by the Commission (comitology) and the SCA to regulate the CAP. In the case of the latter, Ann Christina Lauring Knudsen has argued that the close connections between the SCA, the comitology system and the national agricultural administrations, often through overlapping memberships of national agricultural experts, socialized experts in what gradually developed into an administrative community.[64] Piers Ludlow's chapter for the first time offers an empirically well-founded history of Coreper in the 1960s, which demonstrates that none of the current theoretical approaches capture the full complexity of this institutional mutation. According to Ludlow, the Coreper was not designed merely to control the Community, but was rather part of efforts by the member-states to improve the operations of an increasingly complex Community. At the same time, the permanent representatives were quickly socialized through participating in the European political system and therefore often shared the assumptions and views of the Commission. Ludlow maintains nevertheless that Coreper essentially provided the member-states with the general control of the Community.[65] Beyond the establishment of this institutional infrastructure to secure member-state control, it is quite clear that questions of competences and institutional delegation always played a central role in policy-making. In her chapter, Knudsen traces this question in the ongoing negotiations on one of the most contested policy question of the 1960s, namely how to devise a system of own resources for the Community.[66]

The fourth theme is the administrative, cultural and intellectual history of the supranational institutions. Did supranational institutions consistently, and acting in a unitary manner, attempt to increase their own competences and those of the Community as predicted by rational choice approaches? Alternatively, were the preferences of common institutions conditioned by a particular administrative culture or commonly held ideas, as argued by various sociological approaches? These questions are of central importance to understand the role of the common institutions in the European political system. There are several ways of approaching these questions empirically; one is to explore the broader history of the supranational institutions.[67] This has been carried out to some extent with regard to the High Authority and the Commission.[68] Important contributions have also traced the history of the Social and Economic Committee and the Monetary Committee.[69] The most important omission in the literature is the lack of an archive-based study of the ECJ.[70] While the broader history of a particular institution has its merits, most of these stories have been conceptualized in a traditional way and not addressed the questions raised here. An alternative approach is to study the cultural and intellectual history of the supranational institutions and their personnel. With regard to the latter, historiography has recently focused on important personalities of the Commission, such as Walter Hallstein and Sicco Mansholt.[71] However, with the exception of Francois Duchêne's excellent biography of Monnet, we are still short of serious biographies of the leading personalities of the European institutions.[72] Two smaller studies have dealt with the intellectual history of the Commission, namely Ivor Maes' exploration of the economic policy ideas of the Directorate-General for Economic and Financial Affairs and Jonathan P. J. White's analysis of the extent to which neofunctionalist scholars and theories influenced the Hallstein Commission during 1964–65.[73] Both studies argue that particular ideas and notions influenced policy-making in the Commission and thus shaped preferences. In this book Seidel's chapter on the administrative culture of Directorate-General for Competition (DG IV) demonstrates how Commission preferences in competition policy were determined by a predominantly German ordo-liberal outlook on how to devise an effective policy in the field. Lise Rye's chapter on the Commission's communication strategy offers new insights into the self-perception of the Commission. She also shows that before the fusion of the executives of the ECSC, the EEC and Euratom in 1967, information policy remained fragmented and incoherent.

The fifth and final theme concerns empirical strategies for exploring the development of the European political system over time and its effects on the member-states. Historians have been quick to assume that member-states control policy outcomes and supranational institutions. Only few have explored path-dependent effects of community policy-making or explored to what extent those undermined member-state control.[74] The notion that European institutions, once established, become part of the institutional infrastructure on which common policies are based and therefore are difficult to reform is confirmed by historical research. The highly contested compromises on the CAP in 1962 and 1964 and the own resource system in 1970 meant that any reform of the EEC treaty threatened to open Pandora's Box. Thus, the SEA was only negotiated and adopted after a compromise had been reached offering Britain a rebate on her contribution to the budget and placing a ceiling on expenses to the CAP at the Summit of Fontainebleau in 1984. The consequences of the inability to reform the EEC treaty from the early 1960s to the mid 1980s were numerous and important. First, it locked in the institutional set up of the Community. As demonstrated by the 'empty chair crisis' in 1965–66, unless a member-state was willing to leave the Community, even the hardest fought compromise did not lead to a treaty revision. Instead, the Luxembourg compromise explicitly stated that five member-states did not accept that the French assertion of the right to veto infringed upon the legal and institutional set up of the EEC.[75] Second, the wish to introduce new policy fields that were not covered by the treaties during the 1970s, such as environmental policy, could only be realized through an expansive legal reading of article 235 that allowed legislation to complement existing policies. As demonstrated by Joseph Weiler, however, this undermined the principle of enumerated powers opening wide access by the community to policy fields hitherto protected by national sovereignty.[76]

Another important topic is the extent to which supranational institutions culti-vated transnational networks to consolidate the European political system. For example, the ECJ and the Commission educated legal academic circles in the 1960s and financed new European journals in the member countries to further the understanding and adoption of European law.[77] A similar strategy was applied by DG IV to develop and consolidate the common competition policy, as demon-strated by Seidel.

Historical research has only recently begun to document how societal actors invested in the new European institutions and policies. Empirical research demonstrates that the establishment of a formal institution to host transnational associations of industry and labour, the Economic and Social Committee, only gradually managed to attract the attention of the national peak organizations during the 1960s. However, other studies of multinational firms have demonstrated how the foundation of the EEC and the European Free Trade Association influ-enced investment patterns and the geographical structuring of production.[78] In his chapter, Sigfrido Ramirez likewise documents how the European automobile industry chose a distinct European strategy in the late 1960s as an effort to respond to the challenges of new security requirements. Without a substantial improvement in our knowledge of whether societal groups invested in European policies and the European political system, EU historiography will find it difficult to determine the nature of societal constraints on governments.

In general, historians have not seriously explored whether member-states have been able to reverse the various path dependencies created by earlier institutional and policy choices. One of the reasons for this omission is the almost complete negligence of the ECJ and the legal dimension of the Community. As mentioned above, studies of European constitutionalization have not only documented how this development was driven by the ECJ in contradiction to the preferences of the member-states, but also that unsatisfied governments later have found it difficult to roll back unwanted legal developments.[79] What is needed in this essential field of research, are more studies structured on the basis of historical institutionalist assumptions, such as the above-cited work by Martinsen, to map out the extent to which member-states have lost control over the direction of European integration.

Conclusion

In order to trace the historical roots of the contemporary EU, historians must go beyond their traditionally exclusive focus on national history and embrace new fields of research. This chapter has argued for the establishment of a new historiography of the European institutions and the emerging European political system. To set up a research agenda in this field, recent social science theory on the origins and development of the European institutions can inform new historical research. Reflecting the keen interest of the social sciences over the last two decades in the emergence of a complex and multi-level European polity with an overwhelming impact on European and national politics, this body of theory offers a number of alternative conceptualizations of why European institutions were established and how they developed. To some historians, the different institutional theories might appear unnecessarily abstract, potentially distorting empirical research. By using them pragmatically as heuristic tools, however, this chapter has identified five general themes thus far only explored by historians in a rudimentary way, which promise to fundamentally change the manner with which we understand European integration history.

Writing this history solely by exploring the European policies of the member-states as if they were isolated from the emerging European political system and could fully control the direction of the integration process clearly creates a distorted understanding of the phenomenon under investigation. This does not imply that the socio-economic and political choices of the member-states, as conceptualized by Alan S. Milward, are not central to capture the momentum of the integration process. But it means that the gradually changing context in which member-states operate at the supranational level must be taken into account. Without a serious understanding of the nature of this European-level political system, historians cannot address what is possibly the most pertinent question of contemporary nation state history, namely how and to what extent long-term structural changes have reduced the capacity of member-states to act independently; or to paraphrase Milward's famous and provocative book title: what price did the nation-states have to pay for their 'European rescue'?[80]

Notes

1 Simon Hix, 'The Study of the European Community: The Challenges to Comparative Politics, *West European Politics*, vol. 17, no.1 (1994), pp. 1–30.
2 Gabriel A. Almond, 'Comparing Political Systems', *Journal of Politics*, vol. 18, no. 2 (1956), pp. 391–409.
3 David Easton, 'An Approach to the Study of Political Systems', *World Politics*, vol. 9, no. 5 (1957), pp. 383–400.
4 Simon Hix, *The Political System of the European Union*, London: Macmillan, 1999, pp. 2–5.
5 With regard to the latter two, see respectively Hix, *The Political System*, and Lisbet Hooghe and Gary Marks, *Multi-Level Governance and European Integration*, Lanham, MD: Rowman and Littlefield, 2001.
6 Mark A. Pollack, 'The New Institutionalisms and European Integration', in Antje Wiener and Thomas Diez (eds.), *European Integration Theory*, Oxford: Oxford University Press, 2004, pp. 137–58; Thomas Risse, 'Social Constructivism and European Integration', in ibid. pp. 159–76; Ben Rosamond, *Theories of European Integration*, London: Palgrave, 2000, pp. 113–23; Hans Arnum, *Ideas and Institutions in the European Union. The Case of Social Regulation and its Complex Decision-Making*, Copenhagen: Copenhagen Political Studies Press, 1999, pp. 9–89 and Peter A. Hall and Rosemary C. R. Taylor,

'Political Science and the Three Institutionalisms', *Political Studies*, vol. 44, no. 5 (1996), pp. 936–57.

7 Douglas C. North, *Institutions, Institutional Change and Economic Performance*, Cambridge: Cambridge University Press, 1990, pp. 3–61.

8 For central contributions within these three traditions, see respectively: Kenneth A. Shepsle, 'Institutional Arrangements and Equilibrium in Multidimensional Voting Models', *American Journal of Political Science*, vol. 23, no. 1 (1979), pp. 27–60; David Epstein and Sharyn O'Halloran, *Delegating Powers: A Transaction Cost Politics Approach to Policy Making under Separate Powers*, New York: Cambridge University Press, 1999 and Robert O. Keohane, *After Hegemony*, Princeton: Princeton University Press, 1984.

9 Andrew Moravcsik, *The Choice for Europe. Social Purposes & State Power from Messina to Maastricht*, Ithaca, New York: Cornell University Press, 1998; Mark A. Pollack, *The Engines of European Integration – Delegation, Agency, and Agenda Setting in the EU*, New York: Oxford University Press, 2003; Alec Stone Sweet, *The Judicial Construction of Europe*, New York: Oxford University Press, 2004 and Giandomenico Majone, *Dilemmas of European Integration – The Ambiguities and Pitfalls of Integration by Stealth*, New York: Oxford University Press, 2005.

10 Pollack, *The Engines*, pp. 19–56.

11 Majone, *Dilemmas*, pp. 64–82.

12 Pollack, *The Engines*, pp. 152–54.

13 Ibid., p. 379f.

14 Sweet, *The Judicial Construction*, p. 28f. and Majone, *Dilemmas*, p. 78f.

15 Andrew Moravcsik, 'Preferences and Power in the European Community: A Liberal Intergovernmentalist Approach', *Journal of Common Market Studies*, vol. 31, no. 4 (1993), pp. 471–524, here p. 514; Pollack, *The Engines*, pp. 200–202 and Pollack, 'The New Institutionalisms', p. 147.

16 Sweet, *The Judicial Construction*, pp. 27–30.

17 Geoffrey Garret, 'The Politics of Legal Integration in the European Union', *International Organisation*, vol. 49, no. 1 (1995), pp. 171–81 and Geoffrey Garret, R. Daniel Kelemen and Heiner Schulz, 'The European Court of Justice, National Governments and Legal Integration in the European Union', *International Organization*, vol. 52, no. 1 (1998), pp. 149–76.

18 Karen J. Alter, *Establishing the Supremacy of European Law – The Making of an International Rule of Law in Europe*, New York: Oxford University Press, 2001 and Sweet, *The Judicial Construction*.

19 Bertold Rittberger, *Building Europe's Parliament. Democratic Representation beyond the Nation-State*, Oxford: Oxford University Press, 2005, pp. 114–210.

20 Pollack, *The Engines*, pp. 56–59.

21 Moravcsik, 'Preferences and Power', pp. 509–14.

22 Pollack, *The Engines*, p. 391.

23 Sweet, *The Judicial Construction*, p. 29.

24 For example Jeffrey Stacey and Berthold Rittberger, 'Dynamics of Formal and Informal Institutional Change in the EU', *Journal of European Public Policy*, vol. 10, no. 6 (2003), pp. 858–83.

25 Paul Pierson, 'The Path to European Integration: A Historical Institutional Analysis', *Comparative Political Studies*, vol. 29, no. 2 (1996), pp. 123–63 and idem., *Politics in Time. History, Institutions, and Social Analysis*, Princeton and Oxford: Princeton University Press, 2004.

26 Path dependency is best defined and analyzed in Pierson, *Politics in Time*, pp. 18–21.

27 Stacey and Rittberger, 'Dynamics of Formal and Informal'.

28 Pierson, *Politics in Time*, pp. 34f., 49 and 147f.

29 Pierson, 'The Path to European Integration', p. 135f. and Pierson, *Politics in Time*, p. 41f.

30   Pierson, *Politics in Time*, pp. 42–44.
31   Alter, *Establishing the Supremacy*; Sweet, *The Judicial Construction*; Dorte S. Martinsen, *European Institutionalisation of Social Security Rights: A Two-layered process of Integration*, PhD, Florence: European University Institute, 2004 and idem., 'The Europeanization of Gender Equality – Who Controls the Scope of Non-discrimination?', *Journal of European Public Policy*, vol. 14, no. 4 (2007), pp. 544–62.
32   Sweet, *The Judicial Construction*, pp. 30–35.
33   Martinsen, *European Institutionalisation*, pp. 323–35.
34   Lisa Conant, *Justice Contained. Law and Politics in the European Union*, Ithaca and London: Cornell University Press, 2002, pp. 1–14.
35   See the following three key works from these different theoretical approaches: Woody Powell and Paul DiMaggio (eds.), *The New Institutionalism in Organizational Analysis*, Chicago: University of Chicago Press, 1991; Alexander Wendt, *Social Theory of International Politics*, Cambridge: Cambridge University Press, 1999 and Yves Dezaly and Bryant G. Garth, *Dealing in Virtue: International Commercial Arbitration and the Construction of a Transnational Legal Order*, Chicago: Chicago University Press, 1996.
36   Risse, 'Social Constructivism', p. 161.
37   Ibid. p. 162f.
38   James G. March and Johan P. Olsen, 'The Institutional Dynamics of International Political Orders', *International Organisation*, vol. 52, no. 4 (1998), pp. 943–69, here p. 951. Cited from Risse, 'Social Constructivism', p. 163.
39   Risse, 'Social Constructivism', p. 163.
40   See in particular Pierre Bourdieu, *The State Nobility: Elite Schools in the Field of Power*, Cambridge: Polity Press, 1996 and idem. and Loïc Wacquant, *An Invitation to Reflexive Sociology*, Chicago: Chicago University Press, 1992.
41   Yves Dezalay and Mikael Rask Madsen (eds.), 'The Power of the Legal Field: Pierre Bourdieu and the Law', in Reza Banakar and Max Travers (eds.), *An Introduction to Law and Social Theory*, Oxford: Hart Publishing, 2002, 189–204; idem., 'La construction européenne au Carrefour du national et de international', in Antonin Cohen, Bernard Lacroix and Philippe Riutort (eds.), *Les formes de l'activité politique: Eléments d'analyse sociologique XVIIIe – XXe siècle*, Paris: Presses Universitaires de France, 2006, pp. 277–96; Mikael Rask Madsen, 'Sociology of the Internationalisation of Law', *Retfærd-Nordisk juridisk tidsskrift*, vol. 3, no. 11 (2006), pp. 23–41 and idem., *Rethinking the International as Social Field: Bourdieuian Research Strategies for the Study of the 'International' in the Era of Globalization*, draft paper presented at the Millennium Journal of International Studies, 35th Anniversary Conference, London School of Economics, 21–22 October 2006.
42   Frank Dobbin, *Forging Industrial Policy. The United States, Britain, and France in the Railway Age*, Cambridge: Cambridge University Press, 1994, pp. 217–33.
43   Dobbin, *Forging Industrial Policy*, p. 227.
44   See for example Antonin Cohen, 'Constitutionalism without Constitution: Transnational Elites Between Political Mobilization and Legal Expertise in the Making of a Constitution for Europe (1940s-1960s)', *Law & Social Inquiry*, vol. 32, no 1 (2007), pp. 109–35 and Antoine Vauchez, 'Une élite d'intermédiaires. Les premiers juristes communautaires et la construction de l'autorité sociale du droit européen (1950–70)', *Actes de la recherche en science sociales*, vol. 166–67 (2007), pp. 54–65.
45   Risse, 'Social Constructivism', pp. 163. See the contributions of Brigid Laffan, Rory O'Donnell, and Michael Smith (eds.), *Europe's Experimental Union. Rethinking Integration*, London: Routledge, 2000 and Christer Jönsson, Sven Tägil and Gunnar Törnqvist (eds.), *Organising European Space*, London: Sage, 2000.
46   Morten Rasmussen, 'State Power and the Acquis Communautaire in the European Community of the early 1970s', in Jan van der Harst (ed.), *Beyond the customs union: the European Community's quest for deepening, widening and completion, 1969–1975*, Brussels: Bruylant, 2007, pp. 359–76.

47 Wolfgang Wessels, 'An Ever Closer Fusion? A Dynamic Macropolitical View on Integration Processes', *Journal of Common Market Studies*, vol. 2, no. 35 (1997), pp. 267–99.

48 Rosamond, *Theories of European Integration*, pp. 120. Markus Jachtenfuchs, 'Conceptualizing European Governance', in Knud E. Jørgensen (ed.), *Reflective Approaches to European Governance*, Basingstoke: Macmillan, 1997, pp. 39–50.

49 Jarle Trondal, 'Political Dynamics of the Parallel Administration of the European Commission', in Andy Smith (ed.), *Politics and the European Commission: Actors, Interdependence, Legitimacy*, London: Routledge, 2004, pp. 67–82.

50 Carsten Daugbjerg and Flemming Just, 'Internationalisering af landbrugsforvaltningen og nationale magtkonstellationer', in Marten Marcussen and Karsten Ronit (eds.), *Internationaliseringen af den offentlige forvaltning i Danmark – Forandring og kontinuitet*, Århus: Århus Universitetsforlag, 2004, pp. 128–55.

51 Pollack, 'The New Institutionalisms and European Integration', pp. 143–144. Christian Joerges and Jürgen Neyer, 'Transforming Strategic Interaction into Deliberative Political Process: European Comitology in the Foodstuffs Sector', *Journal of European Public Policy*, vol. 4, no. 4 (1997), pp. 609–25 and idem., 'From Intergovernmental Bargaining to Deliberative Political Process: The Constitutionalization of Comitology', *European Law Journal*, vol. 3, no. 3 (1997), pp. 273–99.

52 Cohen, 'Constitutionalism without Constitution' and Antoine Vauchez, 'European Constitutionalism at the Cradle: Law and Lawyers in the Construction of a European Political Order (1920–60)', in Alex Jettinghoff and Harm Schepel (eds.), *In Lawyers' Circles: Lawyers and European Legal Integration*, The Hague: Elsevier Reed, 2005, pp. 189–204.

53 The classics are: Hans Jürgen Küsters, *Die Gründung der Europäichen Wirtschaftgemeinchaft*, Baden-Baden: Nomos Verlagsgesellschaft, 1982 and Peter Weilemann, *Die Anfänge der Europäischen Atomgemeinschaft. Zur Gründungsgeschichte von Euratom 1955–1957*, Baden-Baden: Nomos Verlagsgesellschaft, 1983.

54 Richard J. Aldrich, 'CIA and European Unity: The American Committee on United Europe, 1948–60', *Diplomacy and Statecraft*, vol. 8, no. 1 (1997), pp. 184–227.

55 Antonin Cohen, *Histoire d'un groupe dans l'institution d'une "communauté" européenne (1940–1950)*, PhD, Paris: University of Paris I, 1999 and Cohen, 'Constitutionalism Without Constitution'.

56 Wolfram Kaiser, *Christian Democracy and the Origins of European Union*, Cambridge: Cambridge University Press, 2007.

57 Raymond Poidevin, *Robert Schuman. Homme d'État, 1886–1963*, Paris: Imprimerie nationale, 1986, pp. 244–63; Antonin Cohen, 'Le plan Schuman de Paul Reuter entre Communauté nationale et Fédération Européenne', *Revue francaise de science politique*, vol. 48, no. 5 (1998), pp. 645–63 and Jérôme Wilson, 'Aux origines de l' ordre juridique communautaire', in Christian Franck and Sandra Boldrini (eds.), *Une Constitution pour un projet et des valeurs. Annales d'Études Européennes de l'Université Catholique de Louvain*, vol. 7 (2003–4), Brussels: Bruylant, 2004, pp.11–33.

58 The most comprehensive and well documented work on the negotiations on the institutional system is Anne Boeger-De Smedt, *Aux origines de l'Union européenne: La genèse des institutions communautaires (C.E.C.A., C.E.D., E.E.E. et EURATOM). Un équilibre fragile entre l'idéal européen et les intérêts nationaux*, PhD, Liège: University of Liège, 1996, pp. 99–156. For two excellent general analyses of the negotiations see John Gillingham, *Coal, Steel and the Rebirth of Europe, 1945–1955. The German and French from Ruhr Conflict to Economic Community*, Cambridge: Cambridge University Press, 1991, 228–98 and Raymond Poidevin and Dirk Spierenburg, *The History of the High Authority of the European Coal and Steel*

Community. Supranationality in Operation, Weidenfeld and Nicolson: London, 1994, pp. 9–42.

59   Boeger-De Smedt, *Aux origines de l'Union européenne*, pp. 569–79.

60   Article 41 of the ECSC treaty also offered the ECJ to rule on preliminary references on the validity of acts. This was now widened crucially to include interpretation.

61   Morten Rasmussen, 'From Costa v. ENEL to the Treaties of Rome – A Brief History of a Legal Revolution', in Miguel Poiares Maduro and Loïc Azoulai (eds.), *The Future of European Law – Revisiting the Classics in the 50th Anniversary of the Rome Treaty*, Oxford: Hart Publishing, 2008, forthcoming.

62   Ann-Christina Lauring Knudsen, *Defining the Politics of the Common Agricultural Policy. A Historical Study*, PhD, Florence: European University Institute, 2001, pp. 225–77 and Laurent Warlouzet, 'La France et la mise en place de la politique de la concurrence communautaire, 1957–64', in Eric Bussière, Michel Dumoulin, Sylvain Schirmann, (eds.), *Europe organisée, Europe du libre échange?* Brussels: P.I.E.-Peter Lang, 2006, pp. 175–202.

63   Michel Dumoulin, 'Les travaux du Comité Intérimaire pour le Marché commun et Euratom (8 avril 1957 – janvier 1958)', in Antonio Varsori (ed.), *Inside the European Community. Actors and Policies in the European Integration 1957–1972*, Baden-Baden: Nomos Verlag, 2006, pp. 23–37 and N. Piers Ludlow, 'Mieux que six ambassadeurs. L'émergence du COREPER durant les premières années de la CEE', in Laurence Badel, Stanislas Jeannesson and N. Piers Ludlow (eds.), *Les administration nationales et la construction européenne. Une approche historique (1919–1975)*, Brussels: P.I.E.-Peter Lang, 2005, pp. 337–56.

64   Ann-Christina Lauring Knudsen, 'Danmarks-eller Europahistorie? Overvejelser omkring historisk metode, europæisering og jagten på den nationale interesse', in Lise Hedegaard Rasmussen and Kristine Midtgaard (eds.), *Omverdenen trænger sig på. Politik og ider i det 20. århundredes historie. Festskrift til Thorsten Borring Olesen*, Odense: Syddansk Universitetsforlag, 2006, pp. 107–21, here p. 115f.

65   For a different view see Ann-Christina Lauring Knudsen and Morten Rasmussen, 'A European Political System in the Making, 1958–70. The Relevance of Emerging Committee Structures', *Journal of European Integration History*, vol. 14, no. 1 (2008), pp. 51–67.

66   See another example concerning the case of social policy. Maria Eleonora Guasconi, 'Paving the Way for a European Social Dialogue', *Journal of European Integration History*, vol. 9, no. 1 (2003), pp. 87–111.

67   See in particular the contributions of *Die Anfänge der Verwaltung der Europäischen Gemeinschaft* (*Jahrbuch für Europäische Verwaltungsgeschichte*, vol. 4), Baden-Baden: Nomos Verlagsgesellschaft, 1992 and *Storia Amministrazione Costituzione. Annale dell'Istituto per la Scienza dell'Ammistrazione Publica*, Bologna: Il Mulino, 2000.

68   See for example Poidevin and Spierenburg, *The History of the High Authority* and Michel Dumoulin (ed.), *The European Commission, 1958–72. History and Memories*, Brussels: European Commission, 2007.

69   Antonio Varsori (ed.), *Il Comitato Economico e Sociale nella costruzione europa*, Venezia: Marsilio Editori, 2000; Age F. P. Bakker, *The Liberalization of Capital Movements in Europe. The Monetary Committee and Financial Integration, 1958–1994*, Dordrecht, Boston and London: Kluwer, 1996.

70   The author of this chapter is currently working on a project tracing the early history of the ECJ from 1950 to 1970. For the first results, see Rasmussen, 'From Costa v. ENEL'.

71   Wilfried Loth, William Wallace and Wolfgang Wessels (eds.), *Walter Hallstein-Der Vergessene Europäer?* Bonn: Europa Union Verlag, 1995 and Guido Thiemeyer 'Sicco Mansholt and European supranationalism', in Wilfried Loth (ed.), *La gouvernance supranationale dans la construction européenne*, Brussels: Bruylant, 2005, pp. 39–54.

72 Francois Duchêne, *Jean Monnet: The first Statesman of Interdependence*, New York: W.W. Norton & Company, 1994.
73 Ivo Maes, 'Macroeconomic and Monetary Policy-Making at the European Commission, from the Rome Treaties to the Hague Summit', *National Bank of Belgium Working Papers*, no. 58, (2004) and Jonathan P. J. White, 'Theory Guiding Practice: the Neofunctionalists and the Hallstein Commission', *Journal of European Integration History*, vol. 9, no. 1 (2003), pp. 111–32.
74 Rasmussen, 'State Power and the Acquis Communautaire'.
75 N. Piers Ludlow, *The European Community and the Crises of the 1960s. Negotiating the Gaullist Challenge*, London and New York: Routledge, 2006, pp. 71–125 and Jean-Marie Palayret, Helen Wallace and Pascaline Winand (eds.), *Visions, Votes and Vetoes. The Empty Chair Crisis and the Luxembourg Compromise Forty Years On*, Brussels: P.I.E.-Peter Lang, 2006.
76 Joseph H. H. Weiler, 'The Transformation of Europe', *The Yale Law Journal*, vol. 100 (1991), pp. 2403–83.
77 Vauchez, 'Une elite d'intermédiaires'.
78 Varsori, *Il Comitato Economico*, pp. 66–76 and several contributions in Varsori, *Inside the European Community*.
79 Hjalte Rasmussen, *On Law and Policy in the European Court of Justice. A Comparative Study in Judicial Policymaking*, Dordrecht, Boston and Lancaster: Mantinus Nijhoff Publishers, 1986, pp. 301–76 and Alter, *Establishing the Supremacy*, pp. 182–208.
80 Alan S. Milward, *The European Rescue of the Nation State*, London: Routledge, 1992.

4 Transatlantic policy networks in the creation of the first European anti-trust law

Mediating between American anti-trust and German ordo-liberalism

Brigitte Leucht

One crucial dimension of the formation of the first integrated core Europe organization of six member-states at the Schuman Plan conference was the creation of a supranational European anti-trust law. Following the initiative of the French government to pool the coal and steel industries first of all of France and Germany under a supranational 'joint high authority', the delegations of France, the Federal Republic of Germany, Italy and the Benelux countries from 20 June 1950 to 18 April 1951 held a multilateral conference in Paris. Adhering to their policy preference for an intergovernmental Europe, the British government in early June 1950 decided not to participate. The High Authority was created in 1952, after the six member-states had ratified the treaty establishing the European Coal and Steel Community (ECSC). The anti-trust provisions embodied in articles 65 and 66 of the treaty set a precedent for European Union competition policy. Next to mergers, state aids and public utility, anti-trust is one of the four separate areas constituting this key policy area. It comprises the scrutiny and control of cartels and restrictive practices and the abuse of a dominant market position.[1] In this chapter, I will show how informal transatlantic policy networks of academics, civil servants and politicians shaped the anti-trust provisions of the ECSC treaty during the inter-state negotiations on the Schuman Plan.

The historiography of early European integration and of postwar transatlantic relations has focused on the governmental level of the negotiations. It has portrayed the Schuman Plan negotiations as a process of a multilateral bargaining by national governments.[2] Domestically derived material and economic interests were driving the negotiation process among apparently cohesive state entities.[3] Implicitly accepting the thesis of American empire building after 1945, the historiography of transatlantic relations has also introduced the notion of American influence on the creation of core Europe.[4] Geir Lundestad in particular has made a strong case for the American empire, which he argues was an 'empire by invitation'. Accordingly, the United States (US) government in their fight against Soviet communism supported efforts at European integration as the formation of a democratic and capitalist Western Europe within an Atlantic framework.[5] Other works have highlighted the critical link between the Schuman Plan and the reorganization of the German heavy industries after the Second World War, which was a pre-requisite for the ECSC treaty.[6] On the whole, however, historical literature has focused on state actors and drawn almost exclusively on the national paradigm to explain policy outcomes. It has not given sufficient attention to the link between earlier co-operation patterns of actors working in US and European postwar administration agencies and the transatlantic co-operation of actors at the Schuman Plan conference.

Works that go beyond the intergovernmental approach acknowledge the role of two types of individual actors. First, they argue that policy entrepreneurs, i.e. transatlantic key figures such as Jean Monnet, the head of the French Planning Commission and US High Commissioner for Germany John J. McCloy influenced the negotiations.[7] Second, and in line with the theme of the American empire, they recognize US advisors who were affiliated with these policy entrepreneurs and brought into the conference as experts. An example of such a policy expert was Robert Bowie, General Counsel to the US High Commission for Germany (USHICOG) under McCloy. However, Bowie's contribution, just like that of other US advisors, has not sufficiently been contextualized within the larger framework of the post-Second World War transatlantic co-operation.[8] In short, historiography has not assessed systematically the role of individual actors who as part of transatlantic policy networks helped shape the anti-trust provisions of the ECSC treaty.

Together the insufficiency of the national paradigm to account for all policy outcomes and the necessity to assess systematically the role of actors and networks in policy-making provide a decisive motivation to utilize the network approach developed by the social sciences. I draw on the network concept primarily to refine the research questions for the analysis of archival sources. As Wolfram Kaiser suggests in his chapter, the concept of transnational networks first, has the potential to overcome the national paradigm as the exclusive explanation for policy outcomes and second, it can help systematize the transfer of ideas and policy solutions between actors from different national contexts. Like the policy network concept, the concept of cultural transfer emphasizes the link between actors and policies and focuses on the dynamic process that connects an original culture with a target culture through the mediation of individual and collective actors.[9] Privileging such categories as interchange, interaction, translation and dialogue over notions of influence or coercion, which characterize the contesting concept of Americanization, means that the very idea of original and target culture becomes blurred, however. In contrast to Americanization, which suggests a direct transfer of US anti-trust law into the European states signing the ECSC treaty, cultural transfer therefore highlights the significance of understanding the conditions of reception, in this case of alternative European domestic politico-legal concepts regarding anti-trust policy.[10]

Based on research from seven archives in France, Germany, Switzerland and the US, I will, in the initial section of this chapter, briefly present the networks involved in the negotiations, explain why they were constituted and sketch which types of actors and networks contributed to policy-making. The following sections outline the potential of the Schuman Plan to set up an international cartel and address significant external developments, which contributed in October 1950 to Monnet's request to integrate explicit anti-trust provisions in the draft treaty. The fourth section treats in detail the various draft articles introduced into the conference from October to December 1950. In the conclusion, I will analyze the impact of transatlantic policy networks at the inter-state negotiations.

Transatlantic policy networks

Transatlantic policy networks did not originate in 1945. The unique circumstances of the immediate postwar period gave rise to an especially increased density of contacts between American and European actors at a number of levels, however. Two factors accounted for this density. First, and most importantly, the US government committed itself to staying involved in Europe after the end of the Second World War. Second, because of the ongoing presence of US institutions and officials in Western Europe, previously existing relationships between individual American and European actors flourished. To democratize and 're-educate' European societies, in particular the society of defeated Germany,[11] the US government introduced and administered two major policies, which provided the structural backbone for the formation of transatlantic policy networks at the Schuman Plan negotiations: The European Recovery Program (ERP, Marshall Plan) and the US occupation policy for Germany. A detailed analysis of primary sources has shown that the most influential governmental organizations, which encompassed US institutions established specifically to realize these policies as well as their European partner organizations, were the European Co-operation Administration (ECA), set up in 1948 to manage the ERP on the American side; the USHICOG which was in charge of US occupation policy for Germany after the transition from military to civilian occupation government in 1949; and the French Planning Commission, which managed the French national programme for economic reconstruction and modernization and since 1948 was financed by capital made available to the French government under the Marshall Plan. In this setting, two informal transatlantic policy networks developed at the Schuman Plan conference: a working group that was attached to the US Embassy in Paris and a transatlantic university network, which to some extent overlapped with the West German delegation.[12]

An informal, but highly integrated policy network, the working group at the US Embassy in Paris was made up of individual US actors William Tomlinson (US Paris Embassy and ECA), Stanley Cleveland (US Paris Embassy), Bowie (USHICOG) and George Ball, a private citizen affiliated with the French delegation, and French actors Pierre Uri (French Planning Commission), Etienne Hirsch (French Planning Commission) and Paul Reuter (legal expert to the French Foreign Ministry). Actors became involved in the negotiations as a result of a variety of previously existing working relationships. American civil servants Tomlinson and Cleveland, for example, owed their role in the conference to the established working patterns between the ECA mission to France and the French Planning Commission. Next to the structural framework of post-Second World War US policy-making in Western Europe, the co-operation of the individual actors in the working group was facilitated by such actors as Monnet. In his varied professional occupation during the Second World War – with the Anglo-French Coordinating Committee in London, the British Supply Council in Washington and the French Supply Council – Monnet had previously co-operated with Ball[13] and Hirsch, among others. Moreover, he had worked together with Uri in the French Planning Commission. Particularly important to the formation of the working group was the professional relationship and friendship of Monnet and McCloy, whose association went back to the 1920s.[14] In the context of US policy in postwar Western Europe McCloy supported the involvement in the US Embassy working group of Bowie. A Harvard law professor with a background in anti-trust law, Bowie as General Counsel in the Federal Republic was responsible for the implementation of the de-cartelization and deconcentration programme for the German heavy industries. Hirsch and Uri in turn were not only high-ranking co-workers of Monnet in the French Planning Commission, but also members of the French delegation who played a vital role in the conference working groups.[15]

Also contributing to the inter-state negotiations was a transatlantic university network composed of legal experts with an academic affiliation including the German emigrant and law professor at Georgetown University Heinrich Kronstein;[16] German law professors Walter Hallstein and Hermann Mosler; civil servant and law professor Hans-Jürgen Schlochauer; and civil servant and honorary law professor Carl Friedrich Ophüls. While Hallstein was the head and Mosler, Schlochauer and Ophüls were experts of the German delegation, Kronstein had no institutional affiliation accounting for his role in the conference. Essential to initiating the transatlantic university network was the nomination of Hallstein, who taught law at Frankfurt University, as head of delegation. As a result of Hallstein's appointment, two sets of professional contacts became important in the conference. First, participation in an academic exchange programme between the University of Frankfurt and Georgetown University connected Hallstein, Kronstein and later Mosler. Second, Kronstein and Schlochauer were involved in 1950 on the American and the German side, respectively, of an ECA programme designed to promote in European countries the introduction of laws safeguarding competition.[17] While in the decisive period up to December 1950 the US Embassy working group helped to shape the anti-trust provisions, the transatlantic university network participated in the simultaneous negotiations on German deconcentration and a German anti-trust law. Both networks were involved in the final drafting period in February and March 1951.

A competitive market economy for the coal and steel pool

Incompatible with the US government's policy preference for a competitive free market economy, transnational collaboration in the European heavy industries often took the shape of cartels, most visibly in 1926 in the International Steel Cartel (ISC), founded by Germany, France, Belgium and Luxembourg. An industrial agreement, the ISC was established for political motives, namely to bridge national disputes in Western Europe.[18] As John Gillingham has demonstrated, moreover, from the 1920s to the 1940s a largely unbroken tradition of co-operation in the heavy industries co-existed with the ongoing Franco-German conflict.[19] However, cartels had not only shaped transnational collaboration in the heavy industries, but they were also deeply embedded within the national economic structures of Germany and France. During the Second World War cartels grew rapidly in both countries, while the representatives of the heavy industries collaborated with the German National Socialist and the French Vichy regimes, respectively.[20] Highlighting that cartels have the potential to facilitate the rise of autocratic and totalitarian systems, US foreign policy planners promoted the introduction of laws and regulations safeguarding free competition to guarantee the sustainability of democratic governments in Western Europe. In a nutshell, this was the politico-economic rationale informing the Marshall Plan as well as the American occupation policy for Germany.

When on 9 May 1950 French Foreign Minister Robert Schuman announced the proposal to pool the French and German coal and steel industries, two major political conditions had to be fulfilled to realize the plan. First, there was the acceptance of the proposition by the West German government. Despite the acrimonious Franco-German relationship and only five years after the end of the Second World War, Schuman trusted that West German Federal Chancellor Konrad Adenauer would react favourably to the initiative by the French government. As Kaiser has shown, high-ranking French politicians including Georges Bidault and Schuman had developed a functioning interpersonal relationship with Adenauer through the informal meetings of European Christian democrats since 1947.[21] In his memoirs, Adenauer described his immediate and positive response to the French government's scheme: 'Schuman's plan matched exactly the ideas of pooling the European key industries I had promoted for such a long time. I immediately communicated my whole-hearted support of the proposal to Robert Schuman'.[22] Adenauer had indeed declared his preference for fusing the Western European heavy industries on a number of occasions, going back to the interwar period.[23] More difficult to meet was the second major political precondition to fleshing out the Schuman Plan, namely the support of the US government.

Because of the US security guarantee and funding for Western Europe, the backing of the Truman administration was crucial to any initiative advancing European integration. The American government would support a proposal only as long as it matched their policy preference for a democratic and supranational Western Europe with a competitive free market economy, however. On 7 May 1950 US Secretary of State Dean Acheson arrived in Paris, en route to the Foreign Ministers' and NATO meetings in London. When later that day, Schuman introduced Acheson and US Ambassador David Bruce to the idea of pooling the German and French coal and steel industries,[24] the two Americans were not impressed. According to Acheson, '[a]ll sorts of questions at once arose. To begin with, was the plan cover for a gigantic European cartel?'[25] Against the backdrop of the US government policy preference, Acheson and Bruce feared the revival of traditional forms of transnational collaboration of the heavy industries. The two

Americans could only be won for the plan through 'the patient coaching of Monnet and McCloy'.[26] Vital to the eventually successful informal mediation of Monnet and McCloy in generating the favourable official reaction of the Truman government to the Schuman Plan, was the social trust between Acheson and McCloy, which had developed during the Second World War when the former worked for the State Department and the latter for the War Department. Alarmed by Acheson's initial reluctance to embrace the proposal, however, Monnet asked Uri to prepare a publishable statement to contradict the notion that the plan would form a cartel.

The Schuman Plan declaration itself contained merely a section broadly stating that the coal and steel pool would not establish a cartel: 'Unlike an international cartel whose purpose it is to divide up and exploit national markets through restrictive practices, and the maintenance of high profits, the projected organization will insure the fusion of markets and the expansion of production.'[27] Uri's anti-cartel note was more specific, contrasting the proposed supranational joint authority with an international cartel and establishing five criteria against which the politico-economic rationale of the Schuman Plan were to be measured: the projected organization's objective, mode of operation, means of action, management and scope.[28] As to the intellectual background of the anti-cartel note of 8 May 1950, several authors have emphasized Monnet's American socialization and his endorsement of the US political system. Gillingham therefore has acknowledged Monnet's admiration for the New Deal legislation.[29] Grounded in the Sherman Act of 1890, US anti-trust law was constantly developed through congressional and judicial action and had undergone major reforms in the New Deal era.[30] Matthias Kipping has shown that Monnet and his co-workers in the French Planning Commission had been involved in the ECA-promoted debate on a French national anti-trust law and in 1949 had drafted an anti-trust bill.[31] An American official who commented on the bill observed:

'Early in 1949 officials in the Monnet Plan, reportedly disturbed over the additional expenses that cartel agreements were imposing on the cost of the Plan's projects, prepared an anti-trust bill which was largely modelled after the United States laws on this subject in that it would have prohibited all agreements in restraint of trade.'[32]

Although the 1949 bill proved too far-reaching for business representatives and the French Ministry of Finance and was therefore unsuccessful, it is significant in the context of the Schuman Plan. Most importantly, the bill shows that Monnet and planning officials, who were key actors at the conference, were practiced in translating the American concept of a free market economy into French domestic politics and simultaneously experienced in reassuring doubtful ECA officials. Further, the comment suggests that the planning officials drew on US anti-trust law when they were realizing the damaging effects of cartel agreements on the revitalization and modernization of the French postwar economy. This supports Matthias Middell's notion that processes of cultural transfer are guided by the willingness to import rather than the intention to export and refutes the logic of Americanization.[33]

The need for specific anti-trust provisions

Even before Monnet triggered the debate on specific anti-trust articles in October 1950, the discussion on the competitive framework of the Schuman Plan and its potential to foster cartels continued. Among the mutually dependent issues shaping the discourse were varying notions of competition for the coal and steel pool; the problem of whether producers, workers or consumers would be the beneficiaries of the pool; various approaches to price policy; and the potential of the planned regional associations to operate like cartels. The need to integrate specific anti-trust provisions into the treaty, however, resulted from a blend of external pressures and developments at the conference. Although not linked to the Schuman Plan conference, the outbreak of the Korean War not only marked a key event in the early Cold War, but also caused the US Secretary of State, an important supporter of the Schuman Plan, to shift his attention from European integration to more pressing defence issues. As a result of the war, the American government was concerned that only with the participation of the Federal Republic in the defence of the West could the expected increase in the demand of steel coupled with the projected need for manpower be met. Finally, at the Foreign Ministers' conference in New York in September 1950 the Allies agreed to raise the limit of the German steel production. Furthermore, Acheson proposed to rearm the Federal Republic.

Acheson's request had at least two significant consequences for the negotiations. First, the prospect of a quickly rearmed Germany alarmed the French government, which felt pressurized into presenting the Pleven Plan for a European army. Developed by Monnet and his associates since the summer of 1950 and proposed on 24 October 1950 by French Prime Minister René Pleven, the plan eventually evolved into the concept for the European Defense Community.[34] Second, as rearmament and with it a greater degree of equality and independence for the Federal Republic seemed within reach, the German government pushed its preferences with fewer restraints. Accordingly, it displayed resistance to attempts in late September by Bowie, in his capacity as the General Counsel of the USHICOG, to enforce law 27, which specified the deconcentration and de-cartelization programme.[35] Moreover, the Adenauer government demanded the revision of the Occupation Statute and the dissolution of the International Authority for the Ruhr (IAR), established in 1949 to allocate the coal, coke and steel of the Ruhr region.[36] This hardened attitude of the government reflected the understanding that the Schuman Plan would meet considerably stronger resistance in German industrial circles now that a major tactical incentive for collaboration within a European supranational framework had diminished.[37]

Meeting with Monnet in Paris on 28 September 1950, German Economics Minister Ludwig Erhard complained about the High Commission's latest efforts to enforce deconcentration and de-cartelization without consulting the federal government. He argued this was contradictory to the spirit of the Schuman Plan and the agreements of the Foreign Ministers' conference in New York, which had stipulated that by the end of 1950 the German government would be responsible for carrying out deconcentration. Further, Erhard criticized the protectionist position the French delegation defended in the negotiations.[38] An ordo-liberal who became the face of the German 'economic miracle', Erhard in Germany promoted his policy preference for an ordo-liberal conception of competition law. Ordo-liberalism was developed at the University of Freiburg by a group of scholars including Franz Böhm, Walter Eucken and Hans Großmann-Doerth in response to the experiences during the Weimar Republic and the National Socialist regime. An intellectual movement promoting an interdisciplinary approach to integrate economic policy and law, ordo-liberalism also put forward a political and economic programme. Like earlier conceptions of liberalism it maintained that a free, equitable and affluent society was based on a competitive economy. To guarantee such a development of society ordo-liberalism emphasized the importance of embedding the competitive order in an 'economic constitution', however. While due to its foundations in the interwar years, ordo-liberalism was chiefly concerned with the problem of private economic power it did however share affinities with US anti-trust law in that competition was seen as providing the key to the dual goal of economic prosperity and political stability.[39] A former student of ordo-liberal Franz Oppenheimer, Erhard co-operated with US military government officials trying to implement a free competitive economy in postwar Germany, first as economic advisor to the military government and then as Bavarian economic minister and as head of the Verwaltung für Wirtschaft der Bizone, the Administration for the Economy of the Bi-zone, i.e. the joint occupied zones of the US and the British governments.[40]

In late September 1950, furthermore, US State Department and ECA officials jointly condemned the progress of the conference concerning the competitive framework, described in Annex IV to the Conference Interim Report (10 August) and the Memorandum on Institutions and Permanent Economic and Social Provisions (28 September).[41] A working paper of unidentified authorship that the French delegation had circulated in August 1950 equally indicated that cartel-like practices would creep back into the treaty.[42] Finally, on 4 October 1950, in a meeting of the heads of delegation and select delegation members, Monnet openly criticized the agreements between enterprises and the planned regional groups that were contained in the Memorandum of 28 September.[43] A memorandum of 5 October 1950 reflecting the concerns of US foreign policy officials, which Embassy staff had expressed to the French negotiators,[44] complemented Monnet's oral critique. At the core was the call to prohibit cartels and only allow concentrations and specialization agreements if they were previously authorized by the high authority.[45] While concerns of US foreign policy officials almost certainly triggered Monnet's call to integrate anti-trust provisions into the treaty, domestic considerations may also have enforced his move. In a diary entry about an informal lunch on 5 October with Monnet, 'two from the staff' and Albert Denis, responsible for the steel industry in the French Ministry of Industry and

Commerce, Clarence Randall, the President of US Inland Steel and a former ECA Steel Consultant (1948–50) recorded that while Monnet was '… in complete accord that for a vital economy [the] industry must be self-policed by actual and vigorous competition …, [t]he difficulty lies not with Monnet but with those around him here and in the other nations who seek to defeat him'.[46] While Randall, who was one of the most fervent American critics of the Schuman Plan, might have overstated the degree of Monnet's isolation, his observations draw attention to the difficulties Monnet faced in promoting free competition not only at the inter-state conference, but also in the domestic context. French steel producers, for example, resisted the plan while promoting the continuation of Allied policies vis-à-vis Germany and the IAR. However, the French steel industry was not unified in their opposition to the Schuman Plan with the Syndicat Général des Industries Mécaniques et Transformatrices des Métaux, the Metal Manufacturing Syndicate, initially endorsing the project as a promising solution to the problem of rising domestic steel prices.[47] Acting as a reliable ally for Monnet and Hirsch, Jean Constant, the president of the Metal Manufacturing Syndicate, promoted consumer protection as one crucial benefit of the coal and steel pool and even reinforced his contacts with ECA officials to advance the goals of consumers.[48] As the failure of the 1949 anti-trust bill of the French Planning Commission indicated, it would be difficult to find a coalition for European anti-trust provisions in France. Arguably therefore Monnet might have also considered safeguarding the essential domestic support, especially that of Constant, when he demanded anti-trust provisions for the Schuman Plan.

Drafting the anti-trust articles

Following the call for anti-trust provisions, the German and French delegations each prepared draft versions of treaty articles. A proposal of the German delegation, dated 21 October, which may however not even have been introduced into the inter-state negotiations, made agreements subject to the authorization of the high authority, but refrained from barring them.[49] In contrast, the draft the French delegation presented on 27 October banned cartels. It prohibited first, all agreements and practices that hindered free competition (including price fixing), entailed production quotas, and divided up markets, products, customers or material resources. The proposal made the high authority responsible for declaring and terminating such agreements or practices. To enforce its orders, the high authority was entitled to demand penalty fees from relevant enterprises. Second, the proposal addressed specifically those agreements and practices likely to secure a market-dominating position for one enterprise, including the concentration of enterprises.[50] Critical to the two-fold structure of the proposal, later incorporated into the first complete draft treaty of 9 November as articles 41 and 42, was the understanding that cartels or agreements between enterprises were made for a limited period of time and therefore maintained the competitive independence of the enterprises. Concentrations, in contrast, once they were completed, were virtually impossible to dissolve. Instead of outlawing transactions creating market-dominating enterprises, the proposal made them subject to previous authorization by the high authority and stipulated the precise conditions for authorization. Accordingly, transactions hampering the normal operation of competition or granting to an individual, an enterprise or a private group more than 20 per cent of the market share were forbidden. In sum, the proposal presented by the French delegation was a much more comprehensive anti-trust draft than that of the German delegation.

It is justifiable to assume that the US Embassy working group was already involved in sketching the 27 October proposal. At the very least, American officials were knowledgeable about draft versions even prior to the release of the proposal by the French delegation: in a telegram to the Paris Embassy Acheson considered the '[r]ecent French draft articles on cartels, [... transmitted to the Department on] October 24 . . . excellent'.[51] At the conference, the Italian and Dutch delegations supported the French delegation's proposal, while it was contested by the Belgian delegation, in particular. The West German delegation, too, in early November officially reaffirmed their initial position on authorizing agreements and rejected the proposition by the French delegation regarding market-dominating enterprises.[52] On 13 November therefore in a meeting with diplomat Ulrich von Marchtaler, the Secretary to the German delegation in Paris, Tomlinson expressed in the strongest possible terms his preference for a 'complete ban on cartels and cartel-like agreements'. To support this, he referred to his experiences within the Organization for European Economic Cooperation (OEEC), established in 1948 by 16 Western European states to assess and coordinate European requirements for Marshall Plan aid, and in negotiations with the French business representatives: 'the slightest exception to a comprehensive ban on cartels invites cartels back in'. Further, Tomlinson compared the draft article with the latest draft German anti-trust bill and emphasized that if USHICOG officials appeared more conciliatory on the German bill, this reflected their having to consider the preferences of their British and French colleagues. In contrast, the Schuman Plan, which represented a solution for Europe and applied to one economic sector only, required meeting stricter criteria, not least to satisfy the American public and guarantee their support for the project.[53]

In addition to evaluating the initial articles vis-à-vis the negotiating parties, the US Embassy working group directly contributed to the drafting process on two specific occasions, namely from 20 to 24 November and again in early December 1950. As to the first instance, American lawyer Ball, who was then officially advising the French delegation,[54] on 21 November recorded a lunch with Bowie and a conference at Tomlinson's office in his diary. Further, on 23 November, after having dinner with Hirsch, he worked on the 'revised draft',[55] without however specifying on which article. More particularly, the journal of Ulrich Sahm, the head of the Sekretariat für Fragen des Schuman Plans, the German Office for the Schuman Plan, suggests that the General Counsel of the USHICOG authored an 'American proposal'[56] for article 42, dated 23 November. Just like the French delegation's original proposal, the draft article prohibited concentrations not previously authorized by the high authority, but outlined different conditions for authorization.

In an inter-ministerial meeting in the German Federal chancellery on 24 November, in which Ophüls also participated, Hallstein discussed article 42 with Roland Risse, the head of the cartel division in the German economics ministry who was intimately involved in the deliberations on the German anti-trust law. Hallstein reportedly observed that 'Bowie's interim draft [was . . .] inadequate since it require[d] previous authorization'. In the debate on article 41, which implied the dissolution of the Deutscher Kohlenverkauf, the agency centralizing the sales of Ruhr coal, Risse related that Erhard intended to discuss the matter with USHICOG officials.[57] Consequently, Sahm's notes not only substantiate Bowie's input into the negotiations,[58] but they also confirm that the drafting of the German anti-trust law had become intimately connected to the debate on the anti-trust provisions of the Schuman Plan.[59]

Alongside Bowie and Grant Kelleher, the head of the USHICOG de-cartelization branch, Erhard and Risse from 10 to 19 October 1950 took part in the negotiations on a draft German anti-trust law between representatives of the German economics ministry and the Allied High Commission for Germany.[60] According to McCloy, '. . . Erhard and his group . . . provide[d the] main support for anti-cartel legislation'[61] in West Germany. In favour of a strict ban on cartels for the Federal Republic, Erhard was guided by his ordo-liberal ideas regarding the German law.[62] Risse in turn was less radical in his conception of a competitive framework for Germany. Crucially therefore when Erhard expressed his policy preferences in the national domain, he was faced not only with opposition from the industry and other federal ministries, but also with reservations from his own leading cartel official.[63] In the context of the Schuman Plan Erhard did not promote an ordo-liberal conception of competition law, however. According to Chancellor Adenauer and the Minister for the Marshall Plan, Franz Blücher, Erhard even compromised the good working relations with Allied officials when he defended the demands of the representatives of the heavy industries with regard to German deconcentration and the anti-trust provisions for the coal and steel treaty.[64] Volker Berghahn has pointed out that Erhard was first of all a pragmatic politician and not a dogmatic representative of the Freiburg school.[65] As economics minister, Erhard was politically accountable and was expected to represent the interests of the German industrialists. While domestically marginalized in promoting a strict ban on cartels, Erhard nevertheless could trust that a sufficient number of German academics and officials shared his general preference for advancing competition and that USHICOG officials would support this policy preference. Against this background, Erhard – unlike Monnet – might not have deemed it necessary to try to implement his ideas of a competitive order in the Schuman Plan treaty. Moreover, other multiple affiliations of individual actors validate that there was an interaction between American anti-trust law and German ordo-liberal ideas on competition. A case in point was Hallstein's correspondence in October 1950 with his friend Böhm, co-founder of the Freiburg school and a law professor at the University of Frankfurt, regarding deconcentration and the problem of cartels.[66] Böhm in summer 1950 headed the German commission of academic experts and practitioners from various ministries that travelled to the US to get a first-hand impression and deepen their knowledge of American anti-trust law. Funded by the ECA, the study trip served the preparation of the German anti-trust law. Among others, the commission met with Kronstein, a mutual friend of Hallstein and Böhm.[67] Not only had Kronstein advised US governmental agencies on anti-trust policy, but he also had previously contributed to the discussion on a public information programme explaining American anti-trust policy in Germany with Kelleher and his associate Sidney Willner.[68] Another member of the study group, Schlochauer, taught law at the University of Cologne and was an official in the justice ministry and a member to the German delegation at the Schuman Plan conference.

On 24 November, the French delegation presented another version of article 41, which was co-authored or drafted by Jacques Van Helmont, the Secretary to the Schuman Plan conference.[69] The article gave the high authority power to authorize temporary agreements concerning the specialization, the purchase or the sale of specific products if the high authority concluded at first that such agreements improved the production or distribution of products; were essential to cause these effects without implying any further restrictions; and did not entitle the enterprises involved to fix prices or to control or limit the production or distribution of products.[70] In essence, this draft version represented what was later discussed as article 60 and incorporated into the ECSC treaty as article 65. The US Embassy working group for a second time influenced directly the negotiations on the anti-trust provisions, more specifically on article 42, when Ball contributed to drafting a memorandum on cartels (28 November) and collaborated with Tomlinson and Bowie on several memoranda on the Schuman Plan (5 December).[71] On 6 December Ball provided Monnet with a revised 'Note regarding the French position on articles 41 and 42', which in its opening focussed on the politico-economic goals of the Schuman Plan: 'the establishment of a single market and the creation within that market of conditions which will serve to bring about maximum productivity, full employment and low cost'.[72] As I have argued elsewhere, the terminology reflected that of the domestic debate over the US Employment Act of 1946 (15 USC 1021, Sec. 2).[73] Linking the objective of full employment to the notion of creating the largest possible body of consumers, contemporary US political economy emphasized that consumption rather than production provided the key to a prosperous economy and consequently highlighted the need for consumer protection.[74] Ball's memorandum stressed that together, articles 41 and 42 contained the powers for the high authority to realize the politico-economic goals of the Schuman Plan. Article 41 would declare cartels invalid and article 42, in turn, would be ' . . . designed to prevent such mergers and consolidations which would result either in a horizontal development of single enterprises to a point where they would control an important part of the market or a vertical combination of enterprises which would result in discriminatory pricing'.[75]

It is impossible to show precisely how Ball's note informed the more comprehensive memorandum the French delegation presented to the other delegations together with a revised draft article 42.[76] Jointly, however, the two memoranda reflect the co-operation of the US Embassy working group on the anti-trust provisions. Both notes emphasized the intimate connection between articles 41 and 42.

Even more they argued that the prohibition of agreements under article 41 – to prevent price fixing, the control of production and technical progress and market-sharing agreements – would reinforce efforts at concentration to achieve precisely these effects. Specific horizontal and vertical concentrations therefore had to be considered as long as they did not create market-dominating enterprises or restrain competition. Minor modifications notwithstanding, this article would subsequently be discussed as article 61 and finally incorporated into the ECSC treaty as article 66.

In mid-December 1950, the German delegation expressed that they were not prepared to agree to the anti-trust provisions without having resolved the decon-centration of the Ruhr and thus caused the temporary breakdown of the Schuman Plan conference.[77] The talks on the anti-trust provisions only continued on 9 February 1951. According to Bernard Clappier, the director of Schuman's personal cabinet of advisors and a member of the French delegation, the West German delegation expressed that the separate discussions on the German econ-omy, in which Bowie and McCloy again played an important part, had proceeded sufficiently to reopen the talks on the said provisions.[78] An official agreement between the Adenauer government and the Allied High Commission on the reor-ganization of the German heavy industries was reached in March 1951 and paved the way to the signing of the ECSC treaty.

Conclusions

An analysis of the impact of transatlantic policy networks at the inter-state nego-tiations with regard to the anti-trust provisions reveals a number of findings. First, the legal traditions of US anti-trust law and German ordo-liberalism interacted with each other in the making of the anti-trust provisions for the ECSC treaty, albeit in the context of the negotiations on German deconcentration and the German anti-cartel law. A purely textual analysis falls short of attributing the articles fully to either American anitrust law or German ordo-liberalism. Ophüls in an article on the economic law of the ECSC treaty, published just after the conclusion of the conference, acknowledged that the anti-trust articles matched more or less the German Freiburg School and contemporary US anti-trust law.[79] An analysis of the final articles shows that the ban of agreements and practices hampering competition (art. 65) and of market-dominating enterprises (art. 66) resembled American anti-trust law. Treating differently an accumulation of power depending on whether it results from concentration or from an expansion of an existing enterprise, however, is an idea contrary to US anti-trust law.[80] At the same time, one could argue, the emergence of the anti-trust provisions highlights the significance for the history of European integration to broaden its scope of analysis and go beyond the geographical and chronological confines of core Europe formation at the Schuman Plan conference.

Second, the utilization of the network concept has been crucial in identifying the overlapping sets of negotiations on German deconcentration, the Schuman Plan anti-trust provisions and the German anti-cartel law. Empirical evidence has confirmed that transatlantic policy networks functioned as mediators between different politico-legal concepts and thus fulfilled a key function of policy networks. Moreover, the US Embassy working group directly influenced the negotiations on two occasions at least.

Third, transatlantic policy networks assumed another function in shaping the negotiation tactics of various stakeholders. Monnet and Erhard, for example, both shared a belief in the competitive principle and, on the surface, were both marginalized in their respective domestic context. Arguably, the very existence of transatlantic policy-making on the anti-trust provisions, allowed Monnet to transfer his efforts to break with French cartel traditions to the core European level. At the same time, it allowed Erhard to defend the position of the industrialists in the context of the Schuman Plan. Advancing his policy preference for a ban on cartels in the domestic setting instead, the German economics minister could rely on external pressure by USHICOG officials.

Fourth, key to the formation of the supranational European anti-trust law was a process of tying transatlantic policy-making to a wider process of transnational coalition building including Monnet and the Planning officials, Constant and his Syndicate and proponents of German ordo-liberalism. Triggered by Monnet, the process was successful because its goals matched the US government policy preference for a free market economy and for consumer protection in Western Europe.

Last, Paul Hirst has defined governance as 'new practices of coordinating activities through networks, partnerships and deliberative forums that have grown up on the ruins of the more centralized and hierarchical corporatist representation of the period up to the 1970s'.[81] Empirical evidence has demonstrated, however, that these practices were not as new and nation-states were not as cohesive as Hirst's reference suggests. Transatlantic policy networks co-ordinated their preferences and constrained the policy options of governmental actors at the inter-state negotiations on the Schuman Plan prior to the governance turn that designates the shift from state-centred government in a unitary state to governance in our present-day 'centre-less' society.

Notes

1 For an introduction see Michelle Cini and Lee McGowan, *Competition Policy in the European Union*, Basingstoke: Macmillan, 1998.
2 Dirk Spierenburg and Raymond Poidevin, *The History of the High Authority of the European Coal and Steel Community: Supranationality in Operation*, London: Weidenfeld & Nicholson, 1994.
3 Alan S. Milward, *The European Rescue of the Nation-State*, London: Routledge, 1994 [1992].
4 Klaus Schwabe, '"Ein Akt konstruktiver Staatskunst" – die USA und die Anfänge des Schuman Plans', in Klaus Schwabe (ed.), *Die Anfänge des Schuman Plans 1950/51. Beiträge des Kolloquiums in Aachen 28. bis 30. Mai 1986*, Baden-Baden: Nomos, 1988, pp. 211–39.
5 Geir Lundestad, *The United States and Western Europe since 1945. From 'Empire by Invitation' to 'Transatlantic Drift'*, Oxford: Oxford University Press, 2003 [1998].

6   Volker Berghahn, *The Americanization of West German Industry 1945–73*, Leamington Spa, New York: Berg, 1986; John Gillingham, *Coal, Steel, and the Rebirth of Europe, 1945–55. The Germans and the French from Ruhr Conflict to Economic Community*, New York: Cambridge University Press, 1991; Matthias Kipping, *Zwischen Kartellen und Konkurrenz. Der Schuman-Plan und die Ursprünge der europäischen Einigung 1944–1952*, Berlin: Duncker & Humblot, 1996; A.W. Lovett, 'The United States and the Schuman Plan. A Study in French Diplomacy', *Historical Journal*, vol. 39, no. 2 (1999), pp. 425–55.

7   François Duchêne, *Jean Monnet. The First Statesman of Interdependence*, New York, London: Norton, 1994; Clifford Hackett (ed.), *Monnet and the Americans. The Father of a United Europe and his U.S. Supporters*, Washington, DC: Jean Monnet Council, 1995; Kai Bird, *The Chairman: John J. McCloy. The Making of the American Establishment*, New York: Simon & Schuster, 1993; Thomas A. Schwartz, *America's Germany. John McCloy and the Federal Republic of Germany*, Cambridge, MA: Harvard University Press, 1991.

8   Schwabe, 'Ein Akt konstruktiver Staatskunst'; Kipping, *Zwischen Kartellen und Konkurrenz*; Lovett, 'The United States and the Schuman Plan'.

9   Helga Mitterbauer, 'Kulturtransfer – ein vielschichtiges Beziehungsgeflecht?', *newsletter Moderne*, vol. 2, no. 1 (1999), pp. 23–25.

10   For an introduction to Americanization see Philipp Gassert, 'Amerikanismus, Antiamerikanismus, Amerikanisierung. Neue Literatur zur Sozial-, Wirtschafts-und Kulturgeschichte des amerikanischen Einflusses in Deutschland und Europa', *Archiv für Sozialgeschichte*, vol. 39 (1999), pp. 531–61.

11   Tony Smith, *America's Mission. The United States and the Worldwide Struggle for Democracy in the Twentieth Century*, Princeton: Princeton University Press, 1994, pp. 146–76.

12   On the constitution of these networks see Brigitte Leucht, 'Netzwerke als Träger grenzüberschreitenden Kulturtransfers. Transatlantische Politiknetzwerke bei der Schuman-Plan-Konferenz 1950/51', *Comparativ*, vol. 16, no. 4 (2006), pp. 200–218.

13   David L. DiLeo, 'Catch the Night Plane for Paris: George Ball and Jean Monnet,' in Hackett (ed.), *Monnet and the Americans*, pp. 141–69.

14   Thomas Schwartz, 'The Transnational Partnership: Jean Monnet and Jack McCloy', in Hackett (ed.), *Monnet and the Americans*, pp. 171–95, here p. 172.

15   The working groups were set up on 4 July 1950. Conversations sur le plan Schuman: Séance restreinte du mardi apres-midi, Archives nationales (AN), Archives du Commissariat du Plan (81 AJ), 131, Folder 2.

16   Cf. Ernst C. Stiefel and Frank Mecklenburg, *Deutsche Juristen im amerikanischen Exil (1933–1950)*, Tübingen: J.C.B. Mohr, 1991, pp. 60–62.

17   Vorläufiger Bericht der deutschen Kommission zum Studium von Kartell-und Monopolfragen in den Vereinigten Staaten, Beilage zum Bundesanzeiger Nr. 250, 29 December 1950, Auswärtiges Amt Politisches Archiv (PA AA), Sekretariat für Fragen des Schuman Plans (B 15), Personal papers Hans-Jürgen Schlochauer (340), Fiche 3.

18   Gillingham, *Coal, Steel*, pp. 1–44, esp. pp. 26–28. See also Ulrich Nocken, 'International Cartels and Foreign Policy: the Formation of the International Steel Cartel 1924–26', in Clemens Wurm (ed.), *Internationale Kartelle und Aussenpolitik*, Stuttgart: Franz Steiner Verlag, 1989, pp. 33–82.

19   John Gillingham, 'Zur Vorgeschichte der Montan-Union. Westeuropas Kohle und Stahl in Depression und Krieg', *Vierteljahreshefte für Zeitgeschichte*, vol. 34, no. 3 (1986), pp. 381–405.

20   On the German industrialists and a critical assessment of cartelization before and after 1933 see for example Berghahn, *The Americanization*, pp. 19–26.

21   Wolfram Kaiser, *Christian Democracy and the Origins of European Union*, Cambridge: Cambridge University Press, 2007, chapter 6.

22   Konrad Adenauer, *Erinnerungen 1945–53*, Stuttgart: DVA, 1965, p. 328.

23 Hans-Peter Schwarz, *Konrad Adenauer. A German Politician and Statesman in a Period of War, Revolution and Reconstruction*, vol. 1: 1876–1952, Providence and Oxford: Berghahn Books, 1995 [German ed. 1986], pp. 177 and 189.

24 Telegramme Acheson to the President and Webb, 8 May 1950, 396.1 LO/5–1050, Foreign Relations of the United States (FRUS) 1950 III Western Europe, Washington: US Department of State, 1977, p. 694f.

25 Dean Acheson, *Present at the Creation. My Years in the State Department*, New York: W. W. Norton & Company, 1969, p. 383.

26 Ibid.

27 Déclaration officielle du gouvernement français, corrigée de la main de Robert Schuman, 9 May 1950, Grégoire Eldin, Pierre Fournié, Agnès Moinet-Le Menn and Georges-Henri Soutou, *L'Europe de Robert Schuman*, Paris: Presse de L'Université de Paris Sorbonne, 2001, XI-XIV. For the contemporary English translation see Bonbright to Acheson, 9 May 1950, 740.00/5–950, FRUS 1950 III, pp. 692–94.

28 London to Secretary of State: Text of anti-cartel note, 12 May 1950, 396.1 LO/5–1250, FRUS 1950 III, p. 700f.

29 Gillingham, *Coal, Steel*, p. 362.

30 Alan Brinkley, *The End of Reform. New Deal Liberalism in Recession and War*, New York: Vintage Books, 1996.

31 See Kipping, *Zwischen Kartellen und Konkurrenz*, pp. 156–64. Cf. also Kai Pedersen, 'Re-educating European Management: the Marshall Plan's Campaign against Restrictive Business Practices in France, 1949–53', *Business and Economic History*, vol. 25, no. 1 (1996), pp. 267–74, here p. 268–70.

32 US Embassy Paris to US Department of State, 2 February 1950, US National Archives and Records Administration (NARA), Record Group (RG) 59, Central Decimal Files 1950–54, 851.054/2–250. See also Matthias Kipping, 'Concurrence et compétitivité, les origines de la législation anti-trust française après 1945', *Études et documents*, vol. VI (1994), pp. 429–55, here p. 437f.

33 Matthias Middell, 'Kulturtransfer und Historische Komparatistik – Thesen zu ihrem Verhältnis', *Comparativ*, vol. 10, no. 1 (2000), pp. 7–41, here p. 20f.

34 For the drafting of the Pleven Plan before its publication see Holger Schröder, *Jean Monnet und die amerikanische Unterstützung für die europäische Integration 1950–1957*, Frankfurt am Main: Peter Lang, 1994, pp. 131–80.

35 Ulrich Lappenküper, 'Der Schuman Plan. Mühsamer Durchbruch zur deutsch-französischen Verständigung', *Vierteljahreshefte für Zeitgeschichte*, vol. 42, no. 3 (1994), pp. 403–45, here pp. 429–31.

36 Memorandum remis par M. Hallstein à M. Monnet. Communauté charbon-l'acier et droit d'occupation, 13 October 1950, Archive du Ministère des Affaires Etrangères (MAEF), Diréction des affaires économiques et financières Service de coopération économique 1945–66 (DE-CE), 507.

37 William Diebold, *The Schuman Plan. A Study in Economic Cooperation 1950–1959*, New York: Frederick A. Praeger, 1959, pp. 67–70.

38 Note Jean Monnet à Schuman pour rendre compte visite Erhard à Jean Monnet, 28 September 1950, AN 81 AJ 137, File 1; Kommuniques zur New Yorker Aussenministerkonferenz, 14, 19 September 1950, *Europa-Archiv*, vol. II (1950), pp. 3405–7.

39 By means of introduction see David Gerber, Law and Competition in *Twentieth Century Europe: Protecting Prometheus*, Oxford: Clarendon Press, 1998, pp. 232–65.

40 See Bernhard Löffler, *Soziale Marktwirtschaft und administrative Praxis. Das Bundeswirtschaftsministerium unter Ludwig Erhard*, Wiesbaden: Franz Steiner Verlag, 2002, p. 56f.; Alfred C. Mierzejewksi, *Ludwig Erhard: A Biography*, Chapel Hill: North Carolina Press, 2004, p. 51f.

41 Acheson to Bruce, 3 October 1950, 850.33/10–350, FRUS 1950 III, pp. 754–58.

42 Kipping, *Zwischen Kartellen und Konkurrenz*, pp. 212–14.

43 Kurzprotokoll über die Sitzung des Comité Restreint im Planungsamt, 4 October 1950, PA AA, B 15, 99.

44 Bruce to Acheson, 2 October 1950, 850.33/10–250, FRUS 1950 III, p. 753f.

45 Dokument 45: Observations sur le memorandum du 28.9.1950, exposées par M. Jean Monnet au cours de la réunion restreinte des chefs de délégation le 4.10.50, 5.10.50, in Reiner Schulze and Thomas Hoeren (eds.), *Dokumente zum Europäischen Recht*, vol. 1: *Gründungsverträge*, Berlin, Heidelberg: Springer, 1999, pp. 241–44.

46 Memo No. 7, 7 October 1950, Seeley G. Mudd Library, Princeton University, Princeton, Personal papers of Clarence B. Randall, Box 1, ECA Paris 1950.

47 Kipping, *Zwischen Kartellen und Konkurrenz*, pp. 182–87.

48 Bruce to Secretary of State, 20 June 1950, NARA 850.33/7–2050.

49 Dokument 8: Bestimmungen zum Schumanplan, 21.10.1950, in Reiner Schulze and Thomas Hoeren (eds.), *Dokumente zum Europäischen Recht*, vol. 3: *Kartellrecht (bis 1957)*, Berlin, Heidelberg: Springer, 2000, p. 23f. See also the introduction to this volume, here p. XXIIf.

50 Nr. 18, Propositions relatives à la mise en oeuvre du plan Schuman en ce qui concerne les accords et pratiques restrictives ou tendant à la constitution de monopoles, 27 October 1950, MAEF, DE-CE, 500. In the use of legal terminology, I have relied on Richard A. Hamburger, 'Inter-relationship of the cartel, monopoly and merger provisions of the European Coal and Steel Community Treaty', in International Conference on Restraints of Competition (ed.), *Cartel and Monopoly in Modern Law Reports on Supranational and National European and American law*, Karlsruhe: C.F.Müller, 1961, pp. 243–60, here p. 250.

51 27 October 1950, NARA, RG 469, Special Representative in Europe, Office of the General Counsel, Subject Files 1948–53, 1950–53, Box 30.

52 Dokument 12: Stellungnahme der deutschen Delegation zu den Vorschlägen über die Inkraftsetzung des Schumanplans, 10.11.1950, in Schulze and Hoeren (eds.), *Dokumente zum Europäischen Recht*, vol. 3, pp. 30–32.

53 Gesprächsaufzeichnung Marchtaler für Hallstein, 13 November 1950, PA AA, B 15, 114.

54 Letter Ball to Leo Gottlieb, 28 November 1950, Seeley G. Mudd Library, Personal papers of George W. Ball, Box 43.

55 23 November 1950, Diaries 1950, ibid.

56 Dokument 14: Entwurf zu den Artikeln 32a, 41, 42, 20./23.11.1950, in Schulze and Hoeren (eds.), *Dokumente zum Europäischen Recht*, vol. 3, pp. 34–38, here pp. 36–38.

57 Protokoll Ulrich Sahm, Deutsches Bundesarchiv (BA), Personal papers of Ulrich Sahm (N 1474), 41, p. 218f. Mierzejewski, *Ludwig Erhard*, p. 51 mentions Risse as a friend of Erhard's in 1945.

58 Acknowledged in telegramme McCloy to Acheson, 9 November 1950, NARA 850.33/12–950.

59 Cf. also Dokument 17: Vorschlag 1 des Bundeswirtschaftsministeriums zu Article 42 a-e, 29.11.1950, in Schulze and Hoeren (eds.), *Dokumente zum Europäischen Recht*, vol. 3, pp. 40–42.

60 Lisa Murach-Brand, *Antitrust auf Deutsch. Der Einfluß der Amerikanischen Alliierten auf das Gesetz gegen Wettbewerbsbeschränkungen (GWB) nach 1945*, Tübingen: Mohr, 2004, p. 157, footnotes 188 and 190.

61 Telegramme McCloy to Acheson, 9 December 1950, NARA, RG 59, 850.33/12–950.

62 Murach-Brand, *Antitrust auf Deutsch*, p. 148f.

63 Berghahn, *The Americanization*, p. 159f.

64 Löffler, *Soziale Marktwirtschaft*, p. 534f.

65 Berghahn, *The Americanization*, p. 158.

66 Letter Böhm to Hallstein, 12 October 1950, BA, Personal papers of Walter Hallstein (N 1266), 1853; Letter Ernst Steindorff to Sahm, 22 October 1950, PA AA, B 15, 2, Fiche 2, p. 129f.
67 Heinrich Kronstein, *Briefe an einen jungen Deutschen*, Munich: Beck, 1967, pp. 248 and 254.
68 Memorandum Buttles to Baker, 23 January 1950, NARA, RG 59, 862A.054/1–2350.
69 Note Van Helmont du 24 novembre 1950, Versions successives des articles 41 et 42 dont notes jointes, AN 81 AJ 138.
70 Draft given to the French delegation on 24 November 1950, Article 41, PA AA, B 15, 163, Fiche 2, p. 126f.
71 28 November and 5 December 1950, Diaries 1950, Ball papers, Box 43.
72 Fondation Jean Monnet pour l'Europe, Archives de Jean Monnet (AMG), Le plan Schuman (1950–52), 10/6/2bis.
73 Cf. Brigitte Leucht, 'Tracing European Mentalities: Free Competition in Post-WW II-Europe', in Marie-Thérèse Bitsch, Wilfried Loth, Charles Barthel (eds.), *Cultures politiques, opinions publiques et intégration européenne*, Brussels: Bruylant, 2007, pp. 337–53.
74 Brinkley, *The End of Reform*, pp. 227–64, esp. p. 229.
75 AMG 10/6/2bis.
76 Memorandum, 6 December 1950, PA AA, B 15, 163, Fiche 2, pp. 141–45; Article 42. Révisé, ibid., p.132f.
77 Memorandum Monnet to other heads of delegation, 16 December 1950, PA AA, B 15, 53.
78 Clappier to Harvey, 9 February 1951, Historical Archives of the European Union, Foreign Office Files for Post-War Europe Series One: The Schuman Plan and the European Coal and Steel Community, 1950–55, Part I, 1950–53, Microfilm, 371/93826.
79 Carl Friedrich Ophüls. 'Das Wirtschaftsrecht des Schumanplans', *Neue Juristische Wochenschrift*, vol. 4, no. 10 (1951), pp. 381–84, here p. 382.
80 Hamburger, 'Inter-relationship', pp. 254 and 256.
81 Paul Hirst, 'Democracy and Governance', in Jon Pierre (ed.), *Debating Governance*, Oxford: Oxford University Press, 2000, pp. 13–35, here p. 19f.

5 Transnational business networks propagating EC industrial policy

The role of the Committee of Common Market Automobile Constructors

Sigfrido M. Ramírez Pérez

Research on business networks in European integration in historical perspective[1] lags behind that by political scientists and sociologists.[2] The neo-functionalist work of Ernst B. Haas[3] encouraged social scientists to focus on spill-over from sectoral to horizontal and from economic to political integration. Transnational business actors and interest groups were regarded as prominent drivers of such spill-over. More recently, sociologists and political scientists have modified the earlier neo-functionalist view of the role of transnational business actors in integration, which appears too determinist and teleological.[4] In contrast, historians of European integration have traditionally focused on national political elites and governmental actors, with at the most a secondary role for interest group politics in interpretations, which have remained very state-centric. Searching for the domestic roots of European integration policies, they have paid little attention to transnational networks. Instead, they have privileged the study of national business actors within member-states, especially general business associations such as the French Conseil National du Patronat Français (CNPF),[5] the German Bundesverband der Deutschen Industrie,[6] the Italian Confindustria,[7] the Belgian Fédération des Industries de Belgique,[8] the Dutch Hoofdgroep Industrie,[9] the Federation of British Industries,[10] and the business confederations of Nordic countries.[11]

At a general level we can differentiate between several types of business networks in the history of European integration: national, international, transnational and multinational. Different types of business networks are often nested with each other. Transnational business networks consist mainly or entirely of companies or businessmen who are directly affiliated with the networks without intermediary organizations. In contrast, international business networks have national or sectoral associations, not individual businesses, as affiliated members. Lastly, the term multinational business networks connotes organizations created by multinational corporations with cultural or political objectives (like foundations and research institutes), but without direct business objectives. Alternatively, such networks have purely economic aims as commodity-chain networks, business groups or joint ventures with a multinational scope.

In European integration, significant international business networks include the little studied sectoral and horizontal business associations. The European confederations of national confederations have received more attention, especially the precursor to the present-day Business Europe, the Union of Industrial and Employers' Confederation of Europe (UNICE).[12] As to transnational business networks, some of them were exclusively European and others European sections of larger global networks. Of the exclusively European transnational business networks, two were most important in the early phase of European integration: the European League for Economic Co-operation (ELEC) created in 1948[13] and the Comité Européen pour le Progrès Économique et Sociale (CEPES) formed in 1952.[14] ELEC had its origins in the Ligue Indépendante de Coopération Européenne formed in 1946 by Christian social and liberal politicians: the former Belgian Prime Minister Paul Van Zeeland, the Polish Secretary-General of the European Movement, Joseph Retinger,[15] and the Dutch Senator Pieter Kersten, later joined by the French think-tank Comité d'Action Économique et Douanière led by Edmond Giscard d'Estaing, colonial businessman and father of the later French President Valéry Giscard d'Estaing.[16] ELEC quickly created other national organizations in the Netherlands, France, Britain, Luxembourg, Austria, Germany and Italy.[17] Intimately linked to the European Movement through its long-serving president, the Belgian industrialist from the chemical multinational Solvay, Baron René Boël, ELEC included an international central committee made up of politicians, trade unionists, economists and businessmen from Western Europe, including Franco's Spain. This committee and the national ELEC organizations met regularly adopting policy positions on European integration matters, which they transmitted to the governments and European institutions.

In contrast, CEPES was created as an exclusive think-tank of businessmen and bankers from the six founding member-states of the European Coal and Steel Community (ECSC) only. Its origins go back to an initiative of the Ford Foundation and the American Committee for Economic Development (CED), whose members Milton Katz and Paul Hoffman sought to create a European counterpart of their own American business network.[18] Headed by Vittorio Valletta, president of the Italian automobile producer Fiat, CEPES brought together the most important business leaders in Italy and Germany, but weak in France, Belgium and the Netherlands, where the ELEC dominated. In 1959, CEPES reached its peak with the creation of a Joint Committee with the CED, the British think-tank Political and Economic Planning and the Swedish business network, Studieförbundet Näringslivet och Samhället.[19] A strong rivalry developed between both transnational European networks which failed to merge on several occasions until the replacement in June 1966 of Valletta as Fiat chairman by Giovanni Agnelli, who decided to merge CEPES with ELEC.

Of those transnational networks that were not composed only of European businessmen, the most prominent were the Bilderberg Group and the International Chamber of Commerce (ICC).[20] Initiated by Retinger, Van Zeeland and the President of the Anglo-Dutch chemical multinational Unilever, Paul Rykens, the Bilderberg Group was an Atlantic network founded in 1952 under the patronage of Prince Bernhard from the Netherlands. Unlike the European

Movement or the American Committee for a United Europe, the Bilderberg Group was not financed by the Central Intelligence Agency. Its major financial support came from private companies from both sides of the Atlantic,[21] especially the American Committee for a National Trade Policy, which included John McCloy, president of the Chase National Bank, and the companies Heinz, Burroughs, McGhee and Rockefeller. This informal network brought together not just business leaders, but also left-wing politicians like the French socialist leader Guy Mollet and intellectuals like Shephard Stone from the Ford Foundation.[22]

Founded in 1919 to stimulate international exchanges, the ICC, which had a secretariat in Paris, brought together the most prominent businessmen from large companies and banks from all over the world. Its presidents had often been Europeans business leaders.[23] Apart from its national sections, the ICC had a Committee for European Affairs and a series of working groups where European members played prominent roles such as the Committee on International Business Agreements Affecting Competition. It was through the Committee for European Affairs that Fiat owner Agnelli unsuccessfully attempted to influence the drafting of the regulations for competition policy of the European Economic Community (EEC) in the early 1960s.[24]

In contrast to research on some of the international and transnational business networks, very little is known about the role of multinational companies in creating and sustaining business networks and influencing the politics of integration.[25] One European company, which did play a prominent role, was Fiat. It actively contributed through institutions like the Agnelli Foundation and different policy initiatives to the creation of networks engaged in European politics.[26] Later, Fiat also became a founding member of the most influential transnational European business network in the current European Union, the European Round Table of Industrialists (ERT).[27] Agnelli was also a prominent member of the Association for European Monetary Union, the transnational business group campaigning for the Euro.

This chapter will explore the role of Fiat and other large automobile corporations in the creation and political activities of another transnational European business network, the Committee of Common Market Automobile Constructors (CCMC). It included the chairmen and chief executive officers (CEOs) of the largest EEC-based multinationals of the automobile sector, but excluded the European subsidiaries of American and Japanese multinationals. The CCMC survived until 1990 when it was replaced with the European Automobile Manufacturers Association (ACEA) as a result of a conflict between Peugeot and the other members over changing two central elements of the CCMC's statutes, namely abandoning the unanimity rule for decision-making and accepting the European subsidiaries of American corporations.[28] The first section will outline the historical evolution of network-type contacts in the automobile industry and analyze the reasons for the formation of the CCMC as well as the role of state-owned corporations and of the European Commission in this process. The second section addresses factors that determined which actors were insiders and outsiders. The third section analyzes the way in which the CCMC attempted to influence European Community (EC) policy-making in the early 1970s to achieve the creation of a common industrial policy, a measure of positive integration proposed by the European Commission. This will be followed by some general conclusions about the role of transnational business networks in the history of European integration.

The French initiative for a European Safety Agency

In Geneva in 1969, the CEOs of the European automobile industry issued a public statement expressing their common objective to obtain from the EC common technical regulations for their sector. These business leaders had already instructed the existing European organization, the Liaison Committee of the European Producers of the Common Market (CLMC), to lobby for this goal, but it had not been successful. This was not because the CLMC lacked direct access to political decision-makers or competence in dealing with issues of technical regulation. It resulted from the clear political incapacity of European institutions to respond to some of the fundamental consequences of the realization of a customs union for creating a real common market, in particular the necessary harmonization of technical standards to abolish non-tariff as well as tariff barriers to trade. The European Commission had attempted to address such problems from 1961 in its Working Group (WP3), set up by its Directorate-General for the Internal Market to deal with 'barriers to automobile trade'. Co-ordinated by what eventually, in 1967, emerged as the Directorate-General for Industrial Affairs (DG III), WP3 completely failed to harmonize technical standards and in particular, did not achieve the mutual recognition of safety standards. By 1966, it had only reached a consensus on minor questions. Delegating approving powers for technical regulations from the Council of Ministers to the Commission could have solved the problem, but the French government was unwilling to do so as it opposed a greater role of supranational institutions in policy-making.

Soon after the French President Charles de Gaulle's retirement from politics, in the spring of 1969, the Council of Ministers approved the Commission's *General Programme for the Removal of Obstacles to Trade*, which eliminated the structural political barrier to progress in this field. A European solution favoured by the carmakers did not materialize quickly, however, because of the historical opposition between French and German automobile producers, which were the largest car manufactures in the EC. While the German manufacturers had important exports to the United States (US), this did not apply to French and other EC producers like Fiat. This difference was extremely important because the Germans were keen on achieving a convergence between the safety and other standards of the US and the EC. Against this background in 1970 the most important European carmakers including Renault, Peugeot, Fiat, Volkswagen (VW), Daimler-Benz and British Leyland Motors Corporation, formed an informal technical network called X Group, which brought together the technical directors in charge of research and development within these companies. It was in this group that the first contacts were established with a view to creating the CCMC.[29]

The formation of the CCMC was initiated by Renault's president, Pierre Dreyfus, and Marc Ouin, his secretary-general. They closely followed instructions of Robert Toulemon, the French director-general of industrial affairs in the European Commission, who had often assisted Renault informally. Toulemon had worked for a long time in the personal cabinet of the long-serving French Commissioner, Robert Marjolin. He also drafted the influential 1970 *Colonna Memorandum on Industrial Policy*,[30] the first Commission communication on positive integration in the field of industrial affairs.[31] This document was not adopted by the member-states, not least due to the opposition of Germany, Belgium and the Netherlands to the proposed control of non-EC foreign direct investments, a French preference that Dreyfus and Marjolin first unsuccessfully attempted to introduce during the negotiations of the EEC treaty in the mid-1950s.[32] In April 1972, Toulemon organized a conference in Venice to collect the views of organized business in order to draft the first Commission's *Action Programme in the Field of Technology and Industrial Policy* submitted by the federalist Italian Commissioner Altiero Spinelli to the Council of Ministers in 1973, which became known as the Spinelli report. The historical context of a directorate-general in search of an ambitious European industrial policy under Spinelli's strong political leadership was particularly relevant to the creation of the CCMC. Toulemon needed a platform for getting the support of large European multinationals for his project of deepening integration through more common European policies.

In a meeting with Ouin in January 1972, Toulemon suggested the most appropriate strategy to follow in order to create a new transnational business network of automobile multinationals, which could back the creation of common European regulations on vehicle safety. In view of the continued resistance by some member-states to giving more powers to the Commission in common market issues, Toulemon believed that the initiative had to come either from a member-state or from the automobile producers themselves. With regard to a member-state initiative, he suggested that the French government make a declaration asking for the quick development of a new EC regulation on vehicle safety. The French were best suited for such a proposal given that they had already initiated a Commission on Safety Affairs, whose objectives included the elaboration of a European strategy. The X Group members would have to lobby their own governments to support any French proposal. Alternatively, the automobile producers from the X Group would issue a public statement signed by all CEOs. Thus, Toulemon clearly encouraged Ouin to go beyond the strictly technical tasks of the X Group, even if this did not imply the creation of a stable network of companies. In fact, he believed that it would be best for both strategies to be followed simultaneously, so that it would not look as if the Commission was proposing to create a new supranational policy.

Toulemon acknowledged that the WP 3 under his direction had failed to go further than a synthesis of work carried out elsewhere, namely in the intergovernmental network which constituted the Working Party 29 (WP 29) of the European Commission for Europe of the United Nations (UN), which was outside the

EC system. Composed of members of the national chambers of automobile producers and covering the whole of Europe, WP 29 merely issued non-binding recommendations for adoption by UN member-states in an extremely drawn-out process. Under the pressure of public opinion, national governments thus began taking unilateral action on technical standards, which effectively erected new non-tariff barriers to trade, complicating the exports of automobile products within the EC market and increasing the prices for cars everywhere. Against this background, the Commission officials suggested to Renault to work for the creation of a 'light structure, not within, but outside of the Brussels Commission'.[33] Ouin drafted two alternative institutional blueprints: one for the creation of a European institute or agency for safety inspired by the ECSC experience, the other for an expert group with consultative status vis-à-vis the Commission. The institute accordingly should fulfil the ambitious task of preparing texts to be approved by the Council of Ministers

Eventually, the two state-owned companies Renault and VW decided to utilize close Franco-German co-operation in the Council for advancing Toulemon's suggestions. Renault was in direct touch with the French President Georges Pompidou through his adviser Bernard Esambert, and with the French Minister of Industry, François-Xavier Ortoli. It was during the high level Franco-German meeting of February 1972 that Pompidou suggested to Chancellor Willy Brandt, lobbied by VW via Julius Leber, the social democratic transport minister, to issue a Franco-German initiative for the creation of a European Office for Safety.[34] VW convinced the German government that the safety standards developed by the US would be very different from those to be agreed at the European level. The Americans were about to change their already demanding norms to upgrade their safety requirements, something that would not benefit European carmakers, which had lower demands on safety.[35]

Crucial to the change in the German strategy was Daimler-Benz's decision to support the drafting of European rather than transatlantic safety standards. At the time, Daimler-Benz had agreed an alliance with VW and BMW, which was, somewhat prematurely, interpreted as the draft constitution of a large German automobile holding. According to Dreyfus, he informed the Chairman of Daimler Benz, Joachim Zahn, that 'We are tempted to favour the creation of a European organization in Brussels. Zahn has agreed with great satisfaction (!!)'.[36] This shift in Daimler-Benz's position seems to have occured during the second conference on experimental safety vehicles held in Sindelfingen in October 1971. At that moment, Daimler-Benz stated very clearly that the 'competent American authorities still adhere to their rigid, and partly utopian, conceptions'.[37] Eventually, Zahn publicly voiced at the Geneva Auto Show of March 1972 his new position that the EC and the member-states should declare their support for the unification of safety regulations.

Creation of the CCMC: membership and objectives

On 18 May 1972, the chairmen of the largest automobile multinationals of the EC met, for the first time in many years, in Paris. These business leaders, influential in their respective countries, had decided to take a major step: the creation of a mechanism to co-ordinate their companies' attitudes towards EC institutions and policies. They were the chairmen and CEOs of Fiat (Agnelli), Renault (Dreyfus), Peugeot (François Gautier), VW (Rudolf Leiding), Citroën (François Rollier), British Leyland Motors Corporation (Lord Stokes), and Daimler-Benz (Zahn). Gautier acted as host. In his invitation he had underlined that the meeting was a joint initiative of the state-owned Renault company and the family-owned multinational Peugeot. At that time, both companies were closely linked by an association agreement covering technical standardization. The decision to organize the meeting in Peugeot's and not Renault's headquarters was probably intended not to antagonize the private French carmaker Citroën, which was very hostile to Renault. The aim of the meeting was clear: to discuss EC-level technical regulations on road safety and environmental standards and the creation of the new agency.

Despite the uncertainties of how the EC member-states would elaborate and approve EC safety regulations after the forthcoming enlargement, Gautier insisted for Peugeot that the automobile producers had to shape future co-operation in this policy field. For this purpose, the French automobile producers suggested the creation of a permanent co-ordination between the EC car manufacturers in one of two ways: either through the creation of a specific association made up of national chambers of automobile producers or the formation of 'an association of Common Market producers (or some of them)'.[38] The existing larger Liaision Committee of the Automobile Industry of the Countries of the European Communities demonstrated the lack of efficiency and influence of this association of national trade associations, however, which did not 'enjoy of a privileged relationship with the EC'.[39] In these circumstances, the better solution appeared to be the creation of the new CCMC, an international network endowed with 'moral power' derived from the domestic political clout of the industrial leaders: 'The creation of the CCMC must be considered as a means of psychological action vis-à-vis governments, but also of influencing public opinion'.[40] According to the French diagnosis, the European public held the automobile producers responsible for high rates of accidents and deaths on roads and environmental damages from pollution. The creation of the CCMC would show that the industry cared about these issues. It would be important to ensure that 'it does not look like a "lobby" charged with delaying decisions'.[41]

Concerning the issue of membership, the French invitation built on the established co-operation in the X Group. Those companies already participating in its operation were considered 'founding members' of the new association, and decided the admission rules for new members.[42] The insiders were the leading European producers, Renault with 11 per cent market-share in Western Europe in 1972, Peugeot (5.5 per cent), Fiat (18 per cent), VW (10.4 per cent), BLMC (8.6 per cent) and Daimler-Benz.[43] In the first official meeting, Renault suggested several criteria for accepting additional members: a minimum threshold (volume of production or turnover), manufacturing only cars, and being an EEC-owned company. Such formal criteria remained irrelevant, however, because the chosen method of accepting new members was their informal co-optation.

Thus, Citroën (6.1 per cent) had not been associated with the X Group's work and did not even know of its existence. Yet, Fiat, which was in the process of merging with Citroën, sponsored its inclusion. The other two companies, which were instantly invited to join, were Alfa Romeo and BMW. The former was also brought into the CCMC by Agnelli under pressure from its CEO, Giuseppe Luraghi, whereas the latter profited from its new links with Daimler-Benz and VW.

In the framework of the European common market, these CCMC multinationals agreed to sponsor the creation of an agency which would fix common technical regulations for cars and perhaps deal with other relevant questions. Their interest was that the common European regulations were reasonable, uniform, applied simultaneously in all member-states, and introduced with the necessary delay to allow the producers to adjust their production and marketing. The ideal solution appeared to be a supranational organization, the Technical Bureau for Vehicles (TBV), which would elaborate these regulations. Renault and other companies had already suggested to national governments and senior Commission civil servants to set up such an institution, but with little success. At the CCMC meeting, Renault presented the draft for the TBV to its partners, however, following Toulemon's proposal. This new plan was for an organization dependant on the Council of Ministers, even if staffed by a secretariat assured by the European Commission. Its mission would be to issue recommendations, receive instructions from the Council and transform them into decisions. The TBV Steering Committee would consist of representatives of the member-states. It could also incorporate consultative committees with representatives from automobile multinationals, insurers, and private or public technical organizations, which already had relevant know-how. The multinational corporations would be in charge of carrying out the research and tests necessary for agreeing on European decisions. The TBV would not have its own laboratories or sufficient means to conduct research and tests itself. More specifically, the TBV should fulfil four tasks: suggesting a working programme to the Council of Ministers, carrying out research reports related to this programme, managing agreed common European standards, and supervising the implementation of European regulations. The Renault leadership believed, however, that it would be very difficult to get the EC to accept another possible task, namely to allow this technical agency to negotiate with third countries, particularly the US, Japan and Sweden, in order to defend agreed European standards.[44]

Thus, the two main reasons for creating the CCMC were the objective of setting-up the TBV and in the long-term, defending the public image of European automobile multinationals. Once the first objective was attained, the CCMC could develop into a more stable institution as a consultative body of major multinationals with a crucial role in preparing common EC regulations. Behind these objectives for institutionalized consultation and decision-making were protectionist concerns, however, which partly explain Agnelli's leading role in setting up and heading the CCMC. Together with his brother Umberto, Giovanni Agnelli had launched Fiat into a process of tight association with Citroën and the French truck producer Berliet. As Agnelli represented the largest group of European automobile producers, Dreyfus suggested to him using the CMCC as an instrument of collective defence of the EC markets against what he and others saw as the dual threat of US norms negotiated bilaterally by the Americans with third countries outside of the EC and the progressive loss of European market-share vis-à-vis Japanese producers in the EC and other European countries, which were traditional markets for European-made cars.

Concerning the Japanese challenge, Dreyfus suggested to Agnelli a few days before the CCMC founding meeting to utilize the CCMC as a tool for privately negotiating a voluntary export restraint agreement with Japanese multinationals and the Japanese Ministry for Trade, like those already negotiated by EC companies in the steel and textile sectors, and encouraged by the contacts between UNICE and Japanese business. These protectionist measures would be justified as legitimate responses to the political measures taken by the Japanese government to protect its domestic markets with highly effective non-tariff barriers and to subsidize Japanese exports. For Fiat and Renault in particular, the creation of the CCMC from the beginning appeared mainly designed to facilitate a common European strategy to meet the Japanese challenge. Ouin acknowledged that 'he was aware that the problems of Japanese imports did not have much to do with vehicle safety and pollution standards'.[45] Still, the General Agreement on Tariffs and Trade (GATT) negotiations scheduled for 1973 would make it very difficult for the EC to retain the common external tariff at 11 per cent vis-à-vis Japanese producers. In this case, Ouin argued,

> If the European automobile industry desires fair competition with the Japanese, we must collectively develop a negotiating stance to deal with the cartelized Japanese industry. (. . .) We need an association of European producers to prepare collectively future direct negotiations with the Japanese industry.[46]

As far as the American question was concerned, all European automobile multinationals shared the fear that the US would create and impose progressively their own safety standards everywhere in the world. In his introductory statement during the first meeting of CEOs, Ouin referred to the American standardization threat as the core reason behind the request by European companies for European harmonization. The Americans had already drafted a flurry of regulations for the most important segments of the car market without taking into consideration the heavy costs of these solutions, which could jeopardize the future export of European models produced to European specifications. In the meeting Dreyfus emphasized the need to accelerate the introduction of European safety standards to bring public opinion behind the European producers. It was VW, the main European exporter to the US, however, which most forcefully argued this point: 'American demands are the source of spending billions and could damage European industry.'[47]

The threat of American standards also largely shaped the relationship between the European companies and the European subsidiaries of the big American automobile companies. The latter would have the least problems with adopting American technical standards, which could give them a competitive edge. Not surprisingly, the Germans were hostile to the possible incorporation into the CCMC of General Motors (Opel), with a European market-share of 10.4 per cent, and Ford (12 per cent), which had their European headquarters in Germany and additional production facilities in Belgium and Britain. The Germans were scared to argue this point openly, however. The CCMC had received legal advice that the new association would have to appear open and non-discriminatory to operate without fear of being accused by the European Commission of violating article 85, 3 of the EEC treaty on cartels. Thus, they chose to inform these European subsidiaries of the CCMC proceedings through their representatives in the Chambers of Automobile Producers.

The American threat became very concrete as one important European country, Sweden, was about to approve its national safety regulations transposing directly the new American standards, which confirmed the CCMC's worst fears regarding the knock-on effects of American standardization. Renault managed to incorporate into the CCMC the Swedish company Volvo, however, which owned the Dutch truck-maker DAF and shared one factory with the French company. In this case, the opposition to its incorporation came mainly from Fiat, VW and BLMC on the basis that Volvo had launched an aggressive sales campaign, using its allegedly higher safety standards as the main distinctive argument in its favour compared to continental European producers. Volvo's CEO, Pehr Gyllenhammar, tried hard to achieve Volvo's admission to the new selective club. He pleaded with the Swedish government to hold back its national regulation until the EC produced a proposal for a different set of rules which Sweden could then accept. The Swedish businessman was in a difficult position as his company had two important markets in the US and the EC, but opted for supporting European regulations. Gyllenhammar was ultimately accepted into the CCMC as a representative of DAF.[48] Thus, the CCMC became established as an enlarged high-level policy-making group of European automobile multinationals. In the following years, it tried to influence EC policy-making, especially with regard to creating a European-level industrial policy.

The CCMC and EC industrial policy

On the suggestion of Daimler-Benz, the CCMC board appointed Agnelli as its first president and Ouin as secretary-general. They also decided to open a small office in Brussels with two engineers, one from BLMC and another from VW. These decisions reflected the search for a balance between all major companies and nationalities. In Brussels, Toulemon produced a roadmap for Ouin for putting the newly formed CCMC at the heart of EC policy-making. Instead of insisting on the creation of the envisaged new institute for automobile safety, he advised the CCMC to become from the beginning an informal consultative body for European institutions, particularly his own directorate-general. In particular, the CCMC should develop a list of priorities concerning safety standardization, which the Commission would submit to the Council.[49]

In order to gain public attention, Toulemon also suggested a high-level meeting between Agnelli and Spinelli, which took place on 7 November 1972. It was at this meeting that Spinelli encouraged the CCMC president to broaden the scope of the organization's activities from advice on more strictly technical issues to tackling more general industrial and economic policy problems concerning the automobile industry. Spinelli confirmed that the Commission was also ready to negotiate bilateral agreements with third countries in Europe about the technical standards that they could adopt. Instead of associating countries like Sweden with drafting the future EC regulations, however, he preferred that the EC automobile industry first agree their own preferences. Agnelli should get the CCMC to prepare a memorandum for the European Commission with a set of concrete demands.[50]

The new Danish Commissioner for the internal market in the enlarged European Commission, Finn Olav Gundelach, confirmed in talking to Agnelli that the EC was prepared to defend the interests of the European automobile industry in the forthcoming Nixon Round of the GATT against new non-tariff barriers constituted by the US technical regulations.[51] The CCMC's hopes for greater influence on EC policy reached a new high point in December 1972 when the EC heads of government and the French president appointed Ortoli as the new president of the European Commission. Ortoli in his former role as French minister of industry was already fully informed of the CCMC's objectives. At the first formal meeting of the CCMC in Paris, the host Gautier could thus inform the other members that 'the future President of the European Commission has already shown his interest in the CCMC'.[52] A few months later Ortoli had dinner with the CCMC members at their next meeting.[53] He encouraged the CCMC to continue to co-operate closely with the Commission, emphasizing that the automobile industry was 'at a turning point of its evolution'.[54]

The interest of the new European Commission in the CCMC was clearly enhanced by the crucial role of Ortoli and Spinelli in industrial policy-making, which allowed them to advance their own ideas about positive integration in this policy domain, counting on the active support of business leaders. This informal network-type political alliance had as its major objective the development of a European industrial policy, which was drafted quickly on the basis of Toulemon's preparatory work. Thus, the Spinelli report issued in May 1973 included five major objectives which coincided with the demands of the CCMC: the elimination of technical non-tariff barriers within the common market, the progressive tendering of public contracts, concrete action to facilitate advanced technology development and assist sectors in crisis, the promotion of competitive European enterprises and lastly, the co-ordination of EC regional, social, commercial and competition policies under the umbrella of a new supranational industrial policy. When the Council adopted this general Commission proposal at the end of 1973, which it considered a fundamental dimension of the realization of economic and monetary union set out in the Werner Plan of October 1970, the CCMC appeared to have achieved a major policy breakthrough.[55]

The CCMC's expectations were raised even higher after the oil crisis of October 1973, which temporarily led to drastic reductions in petrol consumption and in some cases, increases in fuel taxes to compensate for loss of tax revenue, creating a situation of great uncertainty for car producers. A structural rise of oil prices created a fundamental problem of how to deal with the safety and environmental constraints combined. Until then the safety concerns had seemed to imply the need to design heavier vehicles with more powerful engines. For Fiat, the oil crisis created an opportunity to restructure the sector on the basis of a genuine European industrial policy, as the national level would be incapable of tackling the research, transport and industrial problems resulting from this epochal change.[56]

Against this background the CCMC leaders articulated their demands in different public gatherings. They advocated the 'pragmatic and functionalist model' of the ECSC over what they regarded as the 'maximalist' model of the EC oriented towards realizing a regime of perfect competition in which goods, capital and people could circulate freely without obstacles. In Agnelli's view, the EEC treaty did not work well in practice and would have to be modified with a new model to actively manage interdependence to secure the survival of European integration. Agnelli advocated 'privileging a social policy closely correlated with the right regional and industrial policies'.[57] He praised the Spinelli report as a step in the right direction and demanded EC assistance towards the industrial development of those companies that gave Europe an edge in advanced technologies like automobile corporations. Ultimately, Agnelli argued, two EC initiatives would have to go hand in hand: the democratization of the EC through the direct election of the European Parliament and the abandonment of improvised national industrial developmental models in favour of 'the conception of a supranational democratically programmed economy'.[58]

The first concrete result of the greater convergence in policy preferences of some CCMC multinationals and sections of the European Commission was the report issued in December 1974 by DG III which went much further than the previously suggested measures of co-ordinating national state aids, harmonizing national regulations, and boosting automobile exports. It included a much more comprehensive use of EC policies such as its Social and Regional Funds, together with loans from the European Investment Bank (EIB), to facilitate the industrial and social restructuring of those automobile companies seriously shaken by the oil shock. Institutionally, this report advocated the creation of a European Automobile Institute.[59]

This internal report opened the way to the subsequent Commission communication concerning the automobile sector issued during the last days of Ortoli's presidency. This European plan for 'the future of the Community's automobile industry' marked the first systematic attempt to introduce neo-corporatist industrial planning involving all stakeholders: the EC, member-states, trade unions and business actors. The European Commission would assess the impact of international economic changes on the competitiveness and employment rates of the whole industry. It would suggest measures to tackle negative effects with the help of an ad hoc working group formed by the Commission itself, representatives of the member-states, trade unions and companies. It was within this neo-corporatist body, and not a European institute, an idea which had been abandoned for this Commission communication, that six central objectives of industrial policy would be pursued: providing an accurate analysis of the evolution of the industry in each member-state, co-ordinating national research programmes, harmonizing them, elaborating European-level research programmes, co-ordinating the national automobile policies, and lastly, deciding, when necessary, on the means to eliminate old and new technical barriers to intra-EC trade. The financial means to support such measures would come from the EIB and the Social and Regional Funds.[60]

Had this Commission communication been fully implemented, the case of industrial policy in the automobile sector would be an excellent example of the effects of close networking in EC policy-making between a transnational business network and European officials from France, a federalist Italian Commissioner, and a Commission President steeped in the tradition of French industrial planning. Yet this first attempt at developing a comprehensive EC-level industrial policy did not gain sufficient support from the member-states in the Council. In a confidential letter to Ortoli, Spinelli identified two political limitations to his approach. Accordingly, to the Italian radical-socialist leader the fragmentation of responsibilities within the Commission presented one major obstacle. The policy instruments for industrial policy were not all in the hands of his DG III, but scattered around different directorate-generals with responsibility for competition rules, state aids, removal of technical barriers, opening of public markets, trade policy, business laws, and the European Social Fund. Spinelli would have encroached upon the competences of other commissioners, creating problems with his colleagues and with member-state governments with an interest in protecting their influence on particular policy fields.

The second limit was the clear lack of political will on the part of the member-state governments at this stage to allow the development a European industrial policy. From the Colonna report onwards, the French government had been the major opponent of the creation of a European industrial policy, preferring inter-governmental co-operation in particular actions without a Commission role. Thus, the French government had vetoed the establishment of a committee on industrial policy, which would bring together the ministers of industry and the Commission. At the same time, the German government had opposed any kind of interventionist measures against American multinationals operating in the common market.[61] This paradox of a member-state defending American multinationals derived from the fact that Germany was receiving the greatest amount of American foreign direct investment in Europe, substituting the United Kingdom as the European basis of the two major American carmakers, General Motors and Ford. Their investments had created thousand of jobs strengthening German exports and its balance of payments.[62] Moreover, any discrimination against American companies in Europe could have provoked retaliation from the American government against German automobile exports to the US. Yet, German cars were the only EC-produced cars sold in significant numbers in the most competitive market of the world. With the Italian and Belgian governments as the only genuine adherents to the Commission approach it was impossible to create a majority in the Council.[63] These member-state preferences persisted when the more pro-European Giscard d'Estaing became French president in May 1974 and Helmut Schmidt was elected German chancellor in the same month. The Council continued to reject a supranational industrial policy to cover ad hoc measures to support sectors like shipbuilding, the computing industry and aerospace.[64]

Spinelli suggested overcoming the resulting policy blockade in the Commission and the Council with three somewhat less ambitious and possibly less controversial measures: the creation of financial instruments to help the expansion of European industry abroad, the Europeanization of state aid, and the creation within the Commission of forecasting instruments in industrial affairs, taking the automobile industry as a pilot sector. Spinelli clearly expressed all his frustration about internal resistance to his plans and lack of support from some member-states in writing to Ortoli:

> After four years of fighting to get everything possible from the existing policy instruments, I must acknowledge that the results are near zero. The lack of political will of member-states and the bad utilization of existing instruments risk putting the burden on the directorate-general in charge of industrial policy, while the Commission does not give the directorate-general the necessary means to do its job. . . . If the Commission does not accept a better distribution of tasks and co-ordination of policy-making, this means that it does not really want an industrial policy. It will confirm the views of those who consider the existence of a directorate-general for industrial policy superfluous.[65]

At the end of the day the joint action of the combined political and business networks working for a stronger role of the European Commission failed to fulfil their initial objectives of EC standardization and a common industrial policy. The member-states in the Council chose to retain power over industry in times of great economic uncertainty. Nonetheless, this direct attempt to overcome the limitations of the European nation-state in order to confront the challenges of economic globalization demonstrates how after the creation of the customs union, the EC was progressively turning into a full-fledged multi-level political system. This system encouraged the formation of transnational networks like the CCMC, and energized them into attempting to influence the inter-institutional, dynamics in the EC to realize their objectives.

Conclusions

Although the CCMC's policy impact was limited in the short-run, it still had long-term consequences. The constitution of the network allowed the most influential automobile businessmen for the first time to get to know each other, to meet on a regular basis and to work closely with the European Commission. When Etienne

Davignon took over DG III in 1977, co-operation with the CCMC intensified. During the Commission presidency of Jacques Delors from 1985 onwards the CCMC became a major actor in EC policy-making. The CCMC not only assisted European business leaders in developing close working links with the European Commission and individual commissioners, but also served as a hub for the setting-up and evolution of other informal transnational business networks. The most important example of this is the ERT created in 1983, which was initially dominated by leaders from the major automobile and other industrial companies. It was through the CCMC that the founder of the ERT, Volvo's CEO Gyllenhammar, first developed his own high-level contacts within the EC. His co-operation with the likes of Ortoli, Davignon and other CCMC members like the new Renault and Fiat chairmen, Bernard Hanon and Umberto Agnelli, encouraged him to pursue his idea to form the ERT, which the latter two joined as founding members.

To some extent, the original CCMC proposals still informed policy-making in the first 'Europeanist' period of the ERT. Its first achievement was after all not the well-known proposal for completing the internal market, but advising the socialist French President François Mitterrand to suggest a European industrial policy to create European 'champions' capable of competing with American and Japanese companies on a global level. Anchored in the proposal to create a truly internal market through the elimination of non-tariff barriers and the adoption of common standards, the French memorandum inspired by the ERT was still coupled with the traditional French preference of high protection towards third countries and European projects for technological research programmes funded by the EC.[66] Converting Mitterrand to this cause was greatly facilitated by the appointment of Dreyfus, the founder of the CCMC, as his minister of industry and later, until his death, adviser for industrial affairs.

Linked through the CCMC, the chairmen and CEOs of some of the major automobile companies, who were members of the ERT in a personal capacity, played a central agenda-setting role in initially advocating a more neo-mercantilist approach to European integration. Dominant under the ERT presidencies of Gyllenhammar and Wisse Dekker from Philips, the CCMC strongly influenced the policy agenda of protectionist regionalism in the face the new challenges of globalization. As several studies from a neo-functionalist and neo-Marxist perspective have shown, the ERT exercised substantial influence on the drafting of the single market programme and the Single European Act of 1986 which included the elimination of technical obstacles to trade in order to create a single market.[67] The original project for European integration based on an interventionist European industrial policy was progressively transformed, with the shift towards more strongly neo-liberal preferences of many member-states and the rise of the neo-liberal influence in the ERT itself. This was clearly reflected in its general report *Reshaping Europe* of 1991, which fed to some extent into the discussions about the Maastricht Treaty.[68] In the automobile sector this shift resulted in the social-liberal European model of automobile policy devised by the German Commissioner for Industry, Martin Bangemann, during the Delors Commission.[69]

In this long-term historical perspective, the CCMC became a solid pillar of the process of Europeanization of large corporations and their political activism as it helped to define their political priorities in relation to European integration issues and to establish high-level direct personal contacts with key decision-makers in European institutions. Up to a point, it allowed them to bypass intermediaries like national governments and the national trade chambers, to build their own networks with no influence of powerful American and Japanese multinationals. In this sense, the creation and activities of the CCMC as a marginally institutionalized transnational network contributed to the evolution of a system of multi-level governance in which these and other societal actors have become increasingly engaged at all levels of policy-making

Notes

1 Eric Bussière, Michel Dumoulin and Sylvain Schirmann (eds.), *Milieux économiques et intégration européenne au XXe siècle: la crise des années 1970, de la Conférence de La Haye à la veille de la relance des années 1980*, Brussels: P.I.E.-Peter Lang, 2006; Eric Bussière, Michel Dumoulin and Sylvain Schirmann (eds.), *Europe organisée, Europe du libre-marché? fin XIX siècle-années 1960*, Brussels: P.I.E.-Peter Lang, 2006; Laurent Badel *et al*.,'Cercles et milieux économiques', in Robert Frank (ed.), *Les identités européennes au XXe siècle*, Paris: Publications de la Sorbonne, 2004, pp.13–48; Michel Dumoulin (ed.), *Economic Networks and European Integration*, Brussels: P.I.E.-Peter Lang, 2004; Eric Bussière and Michel Dumoulin (eds.), *Milieux économiques et intégration européenne en Europe occidentale au XXe siècle*, Arras: Artois Press, 1998; Michel Dumoulin, René Girault and Gilbert Trausch (eds.), *L'Europe du patronat*, Bern: Peter Lang, 1993.
2 Justin Greenwood, *Interest Representation in the European Union*, Basingstoke: Palgrave, 2007; idem. (ed.), *The Effectiveness of Business Associations*, 2nd ed., Basingstoke: Palgrave, 2002.
3 Ernst B. Haas, *The Uniting of Europe. Political, Social and Economic Forces, 1950–1957*, Stanford, CA: Stanford University Press, 1958.
4 Neil Fligstein and Alan Stone Sweet, 'Of Markets and Politics: an Institutionalist Account of European Integration', *American Journal of Sociology*, vol. 107, no. 5 (2003), pp. 5–43; Neil Fligstein, Wayne Sandholz and Alec Stone Sweet (eds.), *The Institutionalisation of Europe*, Oxford: Oxford University Press, 2001.
5 Marine Moguen-Toursel, *L'ouverture des frontières européennes dans les années 50: fruit de la collaboration entre les industriels?* Brussels: P.I.E.-Peter Lang, 2002; Gilbert Noël, 'Le patronat: CNPF et CCI face à l'organisation d'une communauté agricole européenne entre 1950 et 1957', *Journal of European Integration History*, vol. 2, no. 2 (1996), pp. 61–91; Philippe Mioche, 'Le patronat français et le projets d'intégration économique européenne dans les années cinquante', in Gilbert Trausch (ed.), *The European Integration from the Schuman Plan to the Treaties of Rome*, Baden-Baden: Nomos, 1993, pp. 241–59.
6 Werner Bührer, 'The Federation of German Industry and European Integration 1949–60', in Dumoulin, Girault and Trausch (eds.), *L'Europe du patronat*, p.27f.; Thomas Rhenisch, *Europäische Integration und industrielles Interesse. Die deutsche Industrie und die Gründung der Europäischen Wirtschaftsgemeinschaft*, Stuttgart: Steiner, 1999; Markus Schulte, 'Challenging the Common Market Project: German Industry, Britain and Europe, 1957–63', in Anne Deighton and Alan S. Milward (eds.), *Widening, Deepening and Acceleration: the European Economic Community 1957–1963*, Baden-Baden: Nomos, 1999, pp. 167–81.

7 Francesco Petrini, *Il liberismo a una dimensione. La Confindustria e l'integrazione europea 1947–1957*, Milano: Franco Angeli, 2005.

8 Michel Dumoulin, 'Milieux patronaux belges et construction européenne autour de 1960', in Bussière, Dumoulin and Schirmann (eds.), *Europe organisée*, p.149f.; Elisabeth Devos, *Le patronat belge face au Plan Schuman*, Bruxelles: Ciaco, 1989.

9 Thierry Grosbois, 'L'influence des groupes patronaux sur la prise de décision au sein du Benelux (1946–50)', in Dumoulin (ed.), *Réseaux économiques*, pp. 111–59.

10 Alan McKinlay, Helen Mercer, and Neil Rollings, 'Reluctant Europeans? The Federation of British Industries and European Integration 1945–63', *Business History*, vol. 42, no. 4 (2000), pp. 91–116; Jörg Leitolf, *Wirtschaft – Verbände – Integration. Britische Industrie und westeuropäische Integration von 1945 bis 1975*, Bochum: Brockmeyer, 1996.

11 Bo Stråth, *Nordic Industry and Nordic Economic Cooperation: the Nordic Industrial Federations and the Nordic Customs Union Negotiations 1947–1959*, Stockholm: Almqvist and Wiksell International, 1978.

12 Luciano Segreto, 'L'UNICE et la construction européenne (1947–69)', in Antonio Varsori (ed.), *Inside the European Communities. Actors and Policies in the European Integration 1957–1972*, Baden-Baden: Nomos, 2006, pp. 195–208; Neil Rollings and Mathias Kipping, 'Networks of Peak Industrial Federations: the Council of Directors of European Industrial Federations and the Council of European Industrial Federations', in Dumoulin (ed.), *Economic Networks*, pp. 277–300.

13 Michel Dumoulin and Anne-Myriam Dutrieue, *La Ligue Européenne de coopération économique (1946–1981)*, Bern: Peter Lang, 1993.

14 Anne-Myriam Dutrieue, 'Le CEPES, un mouvement patronal européen? (1952–67)', in Dumoulin, Girault and Trausch (eds.), *L'Europe du patronat*, pp. 213–30.

15 Thierry Grosbois, 'L'action de Josef Retinger en faveur de l'idée européenne 1940–46', *Revue européenne d'Histoire*, vol. 6, no. 1 (1999), pp. 59–82.

16 Catherine Hodeir, *Stratégies d'Empire: le grand patronal colonial face à la décolonisation*, Paris: Belin, 2003.

17 Paolo Tedeschi, 'Une nouvelle Europe à construire. La section italienne de la LECE, de 1948 à la creátion du Marché Commun', *Journal of European Integration History*, vol. 12, no. 1 (2006), pp. 87–105.

18 Conversation du Baron Boël, Président de la LECE avec M. Vittorio Valletta, Président du CEPES à Paris le 3 Octobre 1953, 22 October 1953, European League of Economic Cooperation (ELEC) Archives, Université Catholique de Louvain, dossier (d.) 517.

19 Joint comittee CEPES/PEP/SNS, 14 December 1959, ELEC Archives, d. 521.

20 Valerie Aubourg, 'Le groupe de Bilderberg et l'intégration européenne (1952–65)', in Dumoulin (ed.), *Economic Networks*, pp. 411–29.

21 Robert Aldrich, *The Hidden Hand. Britain, America and Cold War Secret Intelligence*, London: John Murray, 2001.

22 Volker R. Berghahn, *America and the Intellectual Cold Wars in Europe. Shepard Stone between Philanthropy, Academy, and Diplomacy*, Princeton: Princeton University Press, 2002.

23 Ernest Mercier, Alberto Pirelli, Georges Theunis, Rolf von Heidenstam and Edmond Giscard d'Estaing.

24 Sigfrido M. Ramírez Pérez, 'Antitrust ou Anti-US? L'industrie automobile européenne et les origines de la politique de la concurrence de la CEE', in Bussière, Dumoulin and Schirmann (eds.), *Europe organisée*, pp. 203–27.

25 The only exception has been the American carmaker Ford. Steven Tolliday, 'The Origins of Ford of Europe. From Multidomestic to Transnational Corporation, 1903–76', in Hubert Bonin, Yannick Lung and Steven Tolliday (eds.), *Ford 1903–2003: The European History*, vol. 1, Paris: ETAI, 2003, pp. 153–242.

26 Valerio Castronovo, *Una certa idea dell'Europa e dell'America: Giovanni Agnelli*, Torino: Einaudi, 2005.

27 Bastian van Apeldoorn, *Transnational Capitalism and the Struggle over European Integration*, London: Routledge, 2002; Maria Green Cowles, *The Politics of Big Business in the European Community: Setting the Agenda for a New Europe*, PhD, Washington: American University, 1994.
28 Thierry Gandillot, *La dernière bataille de l'automobile européenne*, Paris: Fayard, 1992, p. 114; Andrew McLaughlin and Glynn Jordan, 'The Rationality of Lobbying in Europe: Why are Euro-Groups so Numerous and so Weak? Some Evidences from the Car Industry', in Jeremy Richardson and Sonia Mazey (eds.), *Lobbying in the European Community*, Oxford: Oxford University Press, 1993, pp. 122–61.
29 Réunion du "Groupe X" du 10 September 1970, Archives Renault (AR), Rélations extérieures (Rel. ext.), dossier (d.) 973.
30 Compte-rendu de la journée d'information organisée à Paris le 15 Mai 1970 par l' association Europe Université Industrie sur le thème 'La politique industrielle de la Communauté', 15 May 1970, Historical Archives of the European Union (HAEU), Edoardo Martino (EM), dossier (d.) 251.
31 Robert Toulemon and Jean Flory, *Une politique industrielle pour l'Europe*, Paris: Presses Universitaires de France, 1974.
32 Ramírez, 'Anti-trust ou anti-US?'.
33 Lettre de Y. Georges adressée aux Membres du Groupe X. Rapport de M. Ouin sur ses entretiens avec les membres de la Commission de Bruxelles, 27 December 1971, AR, Rel. ext., d. 973.
34 Projet de Note de Ouin pour Fiala et Van Winsen, 17 February 1972, ibid.
35 Réunion du 'Groupe X' du 10 September 1970, ibid.
36 Note de M. Ouin 6.419, 16 February 1972, ibid.
37 Translation from *Handelsblatt*, 'Daimler-Benz demande l'unification des règlements de sécurité', 10 March 1972, ibid.
38 Lettre d'invitation de Fr. Gautier aux Présidents, 12 April 1972, Archivio Storico Fiat (ASF), Capogruppo (CG) 89, busta (b.), 63 (3).
39 CCMC, Réunion des Présidents du 18 Mai 1972, Projet d'ordre du jour annoté, 8 May 1972, ibid.
40 Procès-verbal de la réunion des présidents des principales firmes automobiles du marché commun le jeudi 18 mai 1972, 19 May 1972, ibid.
41 Ibid.
42 Ibid.
43 Unfortunately, market share data was unavailable for Daimler-Benz.
44 Projet de Note de Ouin pour Fiala et Van Winsen, 17 February 1972, ibid.
45 Letter Ouin (Renault) to Montabone (Fiat), 14 April 1972, ibid.
46 Ibid.
47 Ibid.
48 CCMC, Conseil d'administration du 16 Juillet 1973 à l'Hôtel Royal Windsor à Bruxelles, ibid.
49 M. Ouin, Entretiens avec M. Toulemon, Directeur Général des Affaires Industrielles à la Commission des Communautés Européennes, 11 November 1972, AR, Rel. ext., d. 973.
50 Telex, M. Agnelli a parlé le 7 Novembre du CCMC à M. Spinelli, 9 November 1972, ASF, CG 89, b. 63 (3).
51 CCMC, Secrétariat Général, Assemblée générale ordinaire tenue le lundi 16 Juillet 1973 à Bruxelles, 25 July 1973, ibid.
52 CCMC, Conseil d'administration, réunion du 6 December 1972, ibid.
53 CCMC, Telex 218, 9 September 1973, ibid.
54 Lettre de F. X. Ortoli à Agnelli, 2 August 1974, ASF, CG 89, d. 64 (2).
55 Ministero dell'industria, Promemoria e appunto: la politica industriale della CEE, 28 August 1973, ibid.
56 Fiat, *The automotive industry in Western Europe*, 3 November 1974, ibid.

57   Giovanni Agnelli, Un programma per l'Europa, Conferenza all'Istituto Affari Internazionali, 24 November 1973, ASF, CG 89, 131 (1).
58   Ibid.
59   Commission des Communautés Européennes, DG des affaires industrielles, technologiques et scientifiques, *La situation de l'industrie automobile de la Communauté*, 16 December 1974, Archives of the European Commission (AEC), BAC 8/1985, d. 18.
60   *L'avenir de l'industrie automobile dans la Communauté*, Communication de la Commission SEC (76) 4407 du 30 Novembre 1976, *Agence Europe*, 928, 12 January 1977.
61   Eric Bussière, 'L'improbable politique industrielle', in Michel Dumoulin (ed.), *La Commission Européenne, 1958–1972: histoire et mémoires d'une institution*, Luxembourg: Eur-Op., 2007, p. 482.
62   Steven Tolliday, 'The origins of Ford of Europe: from multidomestic to transnational corporation, 1903–76', in Hubert Bonin, Yannick Lung and Steven Tolliday (eds.), *Ford, 1903–2003: The European history*, vol. 2, Paris: Plage, 2003, pp.194–239.
63   Interview with Robert Toulemon, 17 December 2003, p.46, HAEU, Oral History Collection.
64   *M. Spinelli exprime au conseil sa déception sur le manque abasolu du progrès en matière de politique industrielle-Adoption d'une résolution sur l'informatique et prorogation pour six mois de la directive concernant les aides à la construction navale*, Agence Europe, 1547, 27 February 1974.
65   Lettre Confidentiel de A. Spinelli à M. Fr-X. Ortoli, Président de la Commision, 23 September 1974, HAEU, Fondo Altiero Spinelli, b. 270.
66   Keith Middlemas, *Orchestrating Europe*, London: Fontana Press, 1995, p. 139.
67   Maria Green Cowles, 'Setting the Agenda for a New Europe. The ERT and EC 1992', *Journal of Common Market Studies*, vol. 33, no. 4 (1995), pp. 501–26.
68   Apeldoorn, *Transnational Capitalism*, pp. 115–32.
69   Sigfrido M. Ramírez Pérez, 'The European Search for a New Industrial Policy (1968–1992)', in Stefania Baroncelli, Carlo Spagnolo and Leila S. Talani (eds.), *Back to Maastricht: Obstacles to Constitutional Reform within the EU Treaty (1991–2007)*, Newcastle: Cambridge Scholars Publishing, pp. 303–25.

6 Socialist party networks in northern Europe

Moving towards the EEC applications of 1967

Kristian Steinnes

A distinct feature of early European integration was the divide between the original core Europe and other Western European countries, in particular Britain and Scandinavia. While core Europe opted for supranational solutions to postwar challenges, the northern European countries preferred intergovernmental solutions as in the free trade area initiative of 1956–58 and the European Free Trade Association (EFTA) formed in 1959–60. Differences in national European policies persist, although Britain and the Scandinavian countries (except Norway) are now members of the European Union (EU). Even Norway has in many ways become deeply involved in core dimensions of integration by signing and implementing the Schengen and European Economic Area (EEA) agreements.

Studies of postwar European integration have largely focused on core Europe successively widening their scope in line with the EU's progressive geographical expansion. However, interaction between the northern European countries and core Europe was far-reaching long before they joined the EU/EEA. This was already the case in the period up to 1967 when the government of Harold Wilson applied for membership of the European Economic Community (EEC). As Melissa Pine and others have recently demonstrated, the Wilson governments paved the way for British membership, although Labour's defeat at the general election of June 1970 meant that its policy was brought to fruition by the Conservatives under Prime Minister Edward Heath who negotiated the accession conditions.[1] Wilson moreover exercised crucial leadership in getting a divided party and government to support the second EEC application after the first failed bid of 1961. In a less hierarchically structured party compared to the Conservatives, party policy largely shaped government decisions.

The predominant interpretation of the Labour Party's European policies until 1967 tells a story of a reluctant party excluding itself from early core Europe integration in 1950 and subsequently remaining aloof from the process during the 1950s and early 1960s. Profoundly shaken by the prevailing economic and political realities, Labour gradually reassessed its European policies from 1966 onwards. Wilson, too, is believed to have opposed British involvement in the integration process in the mid-1950s.[2] In 1962 he supported party leader Hugh Gaitskell in insisting that Britain could only enter the EEC if certain strict conditions were fulfilled,[3] only to reluctantly realize from 1966 onwards that Britain had to enter core Europe.[4]

Recent archive-based works by historians have largely strengthened this line of reasoning. Anne Deighton refers to Wilson in a debate in the House of Commons in April 1965 in which he 'made it clear that "there is no question whatever of Britain either seeking or being asked to seek entry into the Common Market in the immediately foreseeable future"'. Allegedly, his position was 'consistent with the stance taken by Labour when in opposition'.[5] Helen Parr argues that the decision to develop a new approach to the EEC was pragmatic and a result of the sterling crisis in July 1966.[6] Wolfram Kaiser suggests that Wilson's objectives for launching the application were in part tactical, denying the Conservatives 'one important policy platform on which to attack the government', appeasing the pro-Europeans within the government and the Labour Party and conveying 'the impression of activity and decisiveness to the electorate'.[7] In line with this view, Oliver Daddow claims that the bid can be seen 'as a "successful failure" for the Prime Minister', soothing both the pro- and anti-factions in the Labour Party and the government.[8]

Most historical studies of the Wilson government's application rely heavily on government sources, however. The resulting state-centric focus tends to marginalize other influences of political party policy-making and transnational contacts that often overlap with intergovernmental co-operation. As Wolfram Kaiser shows in his chapter in this book, and argues forcefully in his innovative study of Christian democratic party co-operation,[9] processes of transnationalization formed crucial features of the emerging supranational polity. In this context, transnational party co-operation could impact on domestic European policy-making.

Based on new documents from archives in five countries, this chapter will analyze the contacts and co-operation between leading politicians in the British Labour Party and socialists from the northern European periphery and from core Europe countries in the period leading up to the second membership application in 1967. Some of these contacts were institutionalized, as in the Socialist International (SI) and on the margins of intergovernmental contacts such as in EFTA, while others were of a more informal ad hoc character. Among these settings were the conferences of party leaders, which were set up and subsequently institutionalized during the early 1960s. They were held to deal with current affairs, in part sparked by the first EEC membership bids. It becomes clear that northern European socialists were in close contact throughout the formative years leading up to 1967. Up to a point, their exchanges influenced their perception of, and strategies for, responding to core Europe integration. The analysis of their networking suggests that existing state-centric accounts of Britain's second application have to be modified by taking into account transnational links and influences.

The Labour Party, Britain and Europe

Once the tide in the United Kingdom (UK) had turned towards EEC membership it could not easily be reversed, as writer and United States (US) State Department official Miriam Camps noted in 1966.[10] The Conservative government's decision to apply for EEC membership in 1961 represented a major change of

British foreign policy. Yet, French President Charles de Gaulle vetoed the British application in January 1963. In the aftermath of the French veto, both the Conservatives and Labour temporarily wanted to keep the contested European issue at bay. As long as the Conservatives remained in office the European question was scarcely discussed. In the long run-up to the general election of October 1964, which Labour narrowly won, nobody seriously invoked the issue. The Labour Party merely stated in its general election manifesto that it would seek to achieve closer links with Europe.[11] However, soon after the new government had been installed the Conservative Party front bench openly began to advocate EEC membership, a preference that was strongly reinforced by the election of Edward Heath as party leader. Heath had been Harold Macmillan's chief negotiator from 1961–63. At this point, Labour Party policy was still based on the policy document 'Labour and the Common Market' passed by the National Executive Committee (NEC) in September 1962. Although a vital part of the document consisted of five conditions which had to be met before Britain could join the EEC, it stated that the

> Labour Party regards the European Community as a great and imaginative conception. It believes that the coming together of the six nations which have in the past so often been torn by war and economic rivalry is, in the context of Western Europe, a step of great significance. It is aware that the influence of this new Community on the world will grow. . . . It is these considerations . . . and not the uncertain balance of economic advantage – that constitute the real case for Britain's entry.'[12]

In the light of the more positive tone of the policy document, intra-party and domestic political cleavages and tactical considerations largely account for the more negative character of Hugh Gaitskell's 'end of thousand years of history' speech at the annual conference of 1962. In fact, in a confidential conversation with the Swedish press attaché in March 1961, Gaitskell even referred to the ardent opponents of EEC membership in the party as 'lunatics'.[13] On 11 February 1965, the new Foreign Secretary Michael Stewart took up the more positive policy line by stating in Brussels that there 'is no reason at all to think that we can go less far than the members of the Community together in promoting European unity and common policies'.[14] At the same time, the Swedish Ambassador in London, Gunnar Hägglöf, believed that British attitudes towards the EEC were changing. Market issues were increasingly discussed, he noted, and 'I am convinced that these ideas eventually will result in new attempts at arranging in some way Britain's relationship with the European common market. It may take time, yet my assumption is that it will take place sooner than generally believed.'[15] In April 1965, Wilson admitted to the Danish Prime Minister Jens Otto Krag that resuming membership negotiations with the EEC in the not too distant future was likely.[16] One month later, Barbara Castle, a left-wing member of the cabinet and passionate opponent of EEC membership, recorded in her diary that Douglas Jay, another leading sceptic, warned 'that we must watch the Party's drifting into the

Common Market. The pressures that way were unrelenting.' She also referred to George Brown, the deputy party leader, who in talking to the *Guardian* newspaper had implied 'that revisions of policy were going on.'[17]

Setting out a strategy

From February 1965 Whitehall officials suggested to the Prime Minister to re-evaluate his policies towards core Europe.[18] As the EEC increasingly developed into a more coherent and assertive unit, they emphasized, Britain risked being isolated accelerating its relative decline. In these circumstances, Wilson and his colleagues took initial steps towards clarifying Britain's relationship with core Europe in a transnational political arena. Invited by Wilson in his role as party leader a carefully selected group of socialist leaders held detailed discussions at Chequers on 24 April 1965. After attending a meeting of the SI in London twelve party leaders dined together.[19] The main topic was European integration. The issue was initially discussed in general terms by the whole group. A smaller group of mostly northern European socialist leaders was invited to stay overnight.[20] In addition to Wilson, this group consisted of the Swedish Prime Minister Tage Erlander, the Danish Prime Minister Jens Otto Krag, the former Norwegian Finance Minister, leader of the social democratic parliamentary party and future Prime Minister Trygve Bratteli, the leader of the Austrian Sozialistische Partei (SPÖ) and President of the SI Bruno Pittermann and Mayor of Berlin, leader of the Sozialdemokratische Partei Deutschlands (SPD) and future German Foreign Minister and Chancellor Willy Brandt.[21]

In addressing this selected group the following day, Krag emphasized that 'the full cooperation of the UK in European political and economic integration is as important for Europe as it is for the UK herself'. Limited co-operation in industrial production, patents and standards between EEC and EFTA would not in itself pave the way for the ultimate goal of comprehensive co-operation in Europe. The Danish expected the UK 'to tackle this important problem'. Krag added that Denmark was ready – as in 1961 – to support Britain in ending the split in Western Europe and joining the EEC. This 'should be constantly on our minds', he emphasized. Krag believed that a new bold approach was not doomed, 'as long as it is well prepared and properly timed'. His proposed strategy was to move forward gradually 'through the elimination of restrictions and tariffs, through increasing liberalisation . . . and through frequent political conferences at high level'.[22]

Following Krag's call for a renewed attempt to join the EEC, the SI called the meeting an 'outstanding success'.[23] It received wide attention in the press. Swedish newspapers reported that Wilson was 'cautiously' moving towards closer relations with core Europe.[24] By this time, earlier frictions between social democrats in the EEC and EFTA had been reduced, improving conditions for future relations between the two blocs.[25] These tensions between core Europe integrationists and reluctant northern European intergovernmentalists had run high both at the SI's Congress in Rome in October 1961 and in Brussels in July 1962.

In Rome the French representative and executive member of the Section française de l'internationale ouvrière (SFIO) – the French Socialist Party – Gérard Jaquet, emphasized that the common market was not a commercial arrangement: '[w]e have never tried to hide our political aims. Deep down in our hearts we have always hoped for the creation of a wide and integrated Europe.'[26] In Brussels the former Belgian Foreign Minister Paul-Henri Spaak, who had played a key role in setting up the EEC in the mid-1950s, deeply regretted that no enthusiasm existed for an integrated Europe among the applicant states. Wilson retorted at the time that Britain apparently did not seek to join an economic community, but a church, in which careful theological assessments were required.[27] Moreover, tensions over the illegal imposition in November 1964 of a British tariff surcharge had brought EFTA on the brink of collapse, and several meetings had been summoned in order to sort out the impasse.[28] This surcharge crisis probably induced Wilson to think about closer relations with the EEC as neither EFTA nor the bridge-building initiatives between the blocs were deemed viable long-term solutions.

British newspapers also reported extensively on the meeting at Chequers. The *Sunday Times* argued that such meetings served important purposes. 'In the case of the Chequers meeting, a specific purpose, for if there is one single linking thread running through the ill-knit fabric of European Socialism, it is that of the wish for a more united Europe, and in particular a closer British association with that Europe.'[29] The left-leaning *Guardian* portrayed the meeting as an important factor in Britain's future diplomatic relations with core Europe. One delegate was reported as saying '[m]y cynicism took a beating – this was the kind of frank, practical meeting of mind which I had heard happens at the summits of Commonwealth Prime Ministers, but had never seen myself until now . . . Mr. Wilson's use of the magic of Chequers appears to have been deft and effective.'[30] If Western Europe were to be led by socialists, *The Times* noted, the meeting at Chequers 'may prove to have been a very useful beginning'.[31]

Remarks by the participants confirmed these observations. 'The time for such an initiative seems ripe', Bruno Pittermann concluded on his return to Vienna.[32] Willy Brandt suggested that Germany 'should be ready to make its contribution towards bridging the gap between the Common Market and EFTA'. The British Prime Minister was now, he continued, 'the keenest among the European Socialist leaders'. According to Brandt the British government no longer saw the EEC as 'a barrier to greater unity in Europe'.[33] The EEC no longer 'involves insurmountable problems for Britain', Olof Palme declared in his report from the meeting. The biggest challenge was possibly agricultural policy.[34] Britain 'is now poised to take a new initiative in European economic cooperation', Wilson declared after the meeting, less than six months after becoming Prime Minister.[35] At this time, Wilson was probably thinking about a strategy of gradual rapprochement with the EEC. His ultimate goal was EEC membership, however. Wilson knew that if Britain were to join the EEC, his government would have to accept the legal and political acquis communautaire – the body of EU treaties, legislation, and norms – of the EEC.

Pursuing a strategy of gradual rapprochement

'If we can't build a bridge, we will dig a tunnel', Wilson claimed on his arrival at the EFTA meeting in Vienna in May 1965.[36] He added that Britain saw 'the advantages of joining' the EEC.[37] At Chequers, the socialist leaders had agreed to raise the Vienna talks from ministerial to prime ministerial level, an initiative taken by Krag and supported by Wilson and Erlander. Wilson was strongly supported by the Danes, who alongside Britain wished to approach the EEC, whilst the Swedes and Norwegians feared that the British government was using EFTA as an instrument for getting closer to, or preferably joining, the EEC but leaving other countries in the lurch.[38] Erlander even warned of the dangers of inviting a rebuff from core Europe. All the same, the participants at the Vienna meeting agreed that the EFTA Council should prepare a report on Wilson's proposals to be submitted at a ministerial meeting in Copenhagen in October 1965. Tentative core Europe reactions to Wilson's proposals were cautious and sceptical, however, not least because there were no indications of any change in French policy on British membership.[39]

Erlander and Krag discussed the issue again in June, just after Krag's return from Bonn and discussions with Ludwig Erhard, the Christian democratic chancellor. In his conversations with Erhard, who was traditionally interested in the creation of a larger Western European market, Krag had tried to persuade him to support the Vienna initiative. According to Krag, Erhard had assured him that he would make no further concessions to de Gaulle.[40] Talks continued at Harpsund, the Swedish prime minister's country house outside Stockholm, at the end of July. Like the previous meeting in 1963 and 1964, this meeting resembled the SI party leaders' conferences. It was private in character and thus offered an opportunity for socialist leaders with different political functions to discuss sensitive issues, including European unification, in an open atmosphere. The Harpsund meetings were mainly attended by leading northern European social democrats. Apart from Wilson, who was prevented from attending at the last moment and was replaced by Brown, the participants were largely those of the Chequers meeting, although they also included a British, a German and an American trade union leader. At Harpsund, the northern European social democrats reaffirmed their determination to pursue Wilson's Chequers initiative intended to overcome the European deadlock.[41] The issue was further discussed in September when Brown visited Krag in Denmark.[42] At the EFTA meeting in Copenhagen in October, ministers reaffirmed their intention to work for closer co-operation between EFTA and the EEC.[43] Overcoming the impasse was deemed increasingly urgent, as trade within core Europe would be fully liberalized in less than 18 months completing the customs union and the Common Agricultural Policy (CAP). At the same time, the internal EEC stalemate of the so-called 'empty chair crisis', when France boycotted the Council of Ministers, made it difficult for the EEC to engage in complex external matters. The undecided issue of financing the CAP and de Gaulle's opposition to the introduction of majority voting from 1 January 1966 thus impacted on the Western European periphery, too.

Wilson's strategy of trying in some way to arrange for Britain to accede to the EEC did not pay off during his first year in office. His premiership was dominated by other economic and political issues. Britain suffered from recurring balance of payments deficits, at the same time as the European market fast became more important for British exports. Foreign policy was dominated by the Rhodesian crisis and the conflict between India and Pakistan. The EEC issue was partly overshadowed by these other issues, yet the economic challenges to some extent moved it higher up on the agenda. Wilson did not abandon his long-term strategy, however. As the gradual tactics of 'bridge-building' or 'closing the gap' did not yield results, Wilson soon activated the transnational social democratic network to prepare a British application for EEC membership.

Transnational contacts with core Europe

In early 1966, British Labour Party politicians arranged for contacts with Dutch and German social democrats to discuss Britain's future relations with the EEC. The meeting took place in Amsterdam on 15 January 1966 under the leadership of the Dutch Labour politician, EEC Agriculture Commissioner and Vice-President of the European Commission, Sicco Mansholt. Participants concentrated on two core aspects: first, how to conduct future negotiations between Britain and the EEC and, second, how to deal with the agricultural question.[44] The Partij van de Arbeid, the Dutch Labour Party, was part of the coalition government in The Hague. The SPD was still in opposition but would join the grand coalition led by the Christian democrats later in 1966. Both the Netherlands and Germany were founding member-states of the EEC. While the Netherlands were a major agricultural exporter, Germany was Britain's main European trading partner. As member-states, they had access to Community expertise and policy-making. Mansholt was the leading expert on agricultural issues in the EEC and the Netherlands had vested interests in this field. As agricultural commissioner and vice-president, Mansholt had first hand knowledge of policies, strategies and position papers in this policy area. He had been instrumental in setting up the CAP, and substantially influenced agricultural policy-making. According to the agreed timetable, the CAP would be fully put in place by July 1967. Moreover, as Ann-Christina Knudsen discusses in her chapter in this book, by 1 January 1970 a system of common financing of the CAP would have to be implemented on the basis of 'own resources'.

Although the French socialists, who had no governmental role, were not involved, the transnational framework appeared promising for Wilson. If the British government entered into formal membership negotiations with the EEC, Britain would not only accede to an existing customs union, but also have to subscribe to the CAP set up and institutionalized by the six founding member-states. Yet the informal Luxembourg compromise, which settled the empty chair crisis at the end of January 1966, appeared to imply that each member-state retained the right to exercise a veto on matters, which it claimed, might adversely affect its own vital national interests. Anyhow, it would be necessary to adjust the CAP for an enlarged EEC of ten member-states, as it was considered likely by the British that Denmark, Norway and Ireland would follow Britain into the Community. Thus, there appeared to be scope for modifications and reforms in line with British preferences.

As a result, a core feature of the meeting was dedicated to discussing solutions to the agricultural issues outlined in a detailed memorandum produced by Mansholt.[45] Accordingly, the negotiating procedures would be important 'if not decisive', and had to differ substantially from the failed negotiations in 1962–63.[46] 'When we are all agreed that a great united and integrated Europe is needed', Mansholt emphasized, we 'have to solve' the agricultural problem.[47] Technical arrangements in one policy area, albeit a very important one, should not, according to Mansholt, be allowed to jeopardize other and more important objectives. Over a transition period of five to six years, Mansholt argued, Britain would make budgetary savings through the reduction and abolition of its direct deficiency payments to farmers and by imposing levies on imports from third countries, especially Commonwealth states which until then had enjoyed tariff-free access to the British market. By using these sums for social policy measures, especially for assisting families on lower incomes, Mansholt believed that the British government would largely be able to compensate for the increased costs of living if Britain joined the CAP.[48] Agriculture, he concluded, 'is indeed a knotty problem but, when the political will exists on both sides, it can be solved in the interest of us all'.[49] Yet, evaluating Mansholt's proposals, the British still found the agricultural issue very problematic due to the knock-on effects of CAP participation for the British balance of payments and costs of living, patterns of domestic agriculture and overseas suppliers from the Commonwealth. Besides, Jay and other opponents of British membership within the Labour Party in part based their opposition on arguments about rising food prices. The prospects of resolving these difficulties 'in renewed negotiations' would certainly depend 'on there being on both sides the necessary understanding and political will to succeed', the British emphasized.[50]

Confidential information concerning the meeting was strictly kept within selected socialist circles. The Swedish Ambassador in Brussels, Sten Lindh, was duly informed, and eventually discussed the initiative with Mansholt himself on 27 January 1966.[51] The question was highly sensitive and Lindh's report to Stockholm was classified personal and secret, emphasizing that the 'letter and its enclosures [must not] be distributed outside ministerial circles'.[52] Lindh knew that Mansholt had initiated the talks in a private capacity, not as commissioner. The deliberations had been carried out 'strictly along social democratic party-lines'.[53] Officially, the Commission and its secretariat had no knowledge of the contact and talks. Likewise, no official documents were produced, which under-lines the informal character of this meeting. Mansholt's proposals are the first documented written account of contacts between British Labour politicians and social democratic leaders from EEC countries concerning the highly sensitive issue of how to deal with future British membership negotiations including the agricultural issue.[54] The meeting of January 1966 formed an integral part of

Wilson's strategy for dealing with the EEC issue. One important dimension of this strategy was to take advantage of the transnational party network. State-centric accounts of the Wilson government's European policies based on government records only show that Wilson endorsed independent and secret studies on the possibility of accession on 19 January 1966, suggesting that this step was initiated by 'a group of interested officials'.[55] Instead, the Whitehall initiative has to be seen in the context of the Amsterdam meeting which induced Wilson to instruct officials to look into technical policy issues of EEC accession. In any case, the initiative constituted a crucial turning point after which Wilson 'was willing to begin to address the implications of' EEC membership.[56]

The Socialist International network

Due to his narrow parliamentary majority, reduced to three MPs within three months after the 1964 election as a result of lost by-elections, Wilson called a snap election on 31 March 1966 securing a comfortable majority of 96 seats. The election campaign confirmed his government's European ambitions. It was the first election campaign ever in Britain in which the European issue played an important part. The election manifesto 'Time for Decision' stated that the Labour Party believed that Britain 'should be ready to enter the European Economic Community, provided essential . . . interests are safeguarded'.[57] After the election Wilson stated that the government's intention was 'to probe in a very positive sense the terms on which we would be able to enter the European Economic Community and its related organisations'.[58] This policy was confirmed by the SI's congress in Stockholm in May. Brown, who was to become foreign minister in August, now also declared that Britain was ready to enter the EEC provided that essential interests were safeguarded. The political will to join existed. The five conditions from 1962, Brown maintained, 'never were, and are not now five reasons why we should not join the Community'. We 'want an expanded EEC, we want to be a member of it and we want to find the basis on which this would be possible'. The government 'is determined to play its full part in bringing about' European unity.[59] Brown further argued that a particular concern 'of ours in 1962 was the ability to plan our economy. Fortunately this does not now appear to pose serious problems for us. There is nothing in the Treaty of Rome which inhibits the approach set out in our own National Plan.'[60] In fact, this point had been maintained by core Europe socialists since the creation of the EEC. In their judgement, the EEC did not prevent the implementation of economic planning, full employment and social security policies at national level. Over the years they had sturdily conveyed this message inside the socialist network, especially through the SI.[61]

The northern European socialists welcomed Brown's statement. Krag stressed that the strategy for rapprochement between core Europe and EFTA 'born at Chequers' in April 1965, elaborated in Vienna and Harpsund and adopted in Copenhagen in October 1965, should be pursued energetically. Moreover, negotiations would 'not be very difficult if Britain and other EFTA countries – in one form or another – join the market at the same time.'[62] The Swedish Minister of Trade, Gunnar Lange, acknowledged the rationale behind Brown's and Krag's ambitions. He emphasized that the market division increasingly affected both the EEC and EFTA, 'slowing down progress and the rate of economic growth'. There was only one answer, he maintained: 'we must work to bring Western Europe economically closer together'.[63] In his report from the congress, the Deputy Chairman of Det norske Arbeiderparti (DNA), the Norwegian Labour Party, Reiulf Steen, argued that the British were 'on their way from distant skies to Europe'.[64] He stressed that his report 'could not, of course, reproduce the atmosphere of a Congress'. It could not even give 'an adequate account of all contacts established on a personal level, which in the end might be as important as the formal discussions altogether.'[65] Despite its reluctant attitude in 1961–63, the DNA became more positive towards joining core Europe, especially after it was forced into opposition in October 1965.[66] Swedish newspapers' perceptions of the British position were unambiguous. 'England ready to approach the EEC with a sound economy and strong balance of trade', the *Aftonbladet* noted, corroborated by *Dagens Nyheter* which stated that the United Kingdom 'struggles to join the EEC', yet reckoned that it would take some time until negotiations could start.[67]

On 10 November 1966, Wilson announced to the House of Commons his government's intention to undertake a 'high-level approach' to see whether suitable conditions existed for fruitful discussions on the possibility of joining the EEC.[68] In the following debate in the House of Commons on 16–17 November, Brown, now foreign secretary, echoed Wilson emphasizing: 'We mean business.'[69] During Wilson's and Brown's probing tour to the capitals of core Europe countries in early 1967, even the enthusiastically pro-European Brown was surprised by Wilson's 'firm line in favour of Britain's applying to join.'[70] Back in London, they persuaded the cabinet to recommend to Parliament that a formal application to join the EEC should be submitted. The big question was whether de Gaulle would veto a new application. In Brown's judgement, as he put it to the parliamentary party, the situation in 1967 was markedly different to what it had been in 1963. In their conversations with de Gaulle, he and the Prime Minister had seen 'nothing so far' that would 'make us believe they would resist our entry, and the other Five have a general desire that we should go in.'[71] This is in sharp contrast to most observations by foreign politicians as related to the British government during 1966–67, however, which generally held that de Gaulle's attitude towards British membership was essentially unchanged.[72] Even Brown's adviser asked him to 'clear the exact form of words' in his address to the Labour MPs, recommending that he delete the sentence: 'In any event I do not think France will apply the veto again.'[73]

This might indicate that the EEC application had instrumental objectives. The Labour leadership had to consider possible adverse effects of a renewed veto. Yet, such a veto would also 'make clear where the responsibility for the division' lay, as the *Financial Times* put it.[74] Even if Brown and Wilson sincerely believed the situation in 1967 to be markedly different, and that it would be difficult for de Gaulle to exercise a second veto, they also knew that if the French President did do so, he risked becoming further isolated both internationally and domestically. Putting him under pressure by applying for membership once more could thus facilitate Britain's long-term objective of joining. Similarly, a second veto could strengthen the socialist alliance across the EEC and EFTA divide and thus increase social democratic influence on an enlarged EEC. Indeed, the growing socialist strength and influence in Western Europe had been an important consideration in Labour's European policy-making since 1964. When the EEC Treaty came into force in 1958, Christian democratic parties still dominated government formation. When socialist leaders met at Chequers in April 1965, however, socialist parties were in power alone or in coalitions in five of seven EFTA countries and on the electoral rise in the EEC, too. The Scandinavian countries were social democratic strongholds. Thus, 'speaking as Socialists', Foreign Secretary Brown at the conference of party leaders in Rome in January 1967 maintained that 'it will have tremendous effect on what we want' if Britain, Denmark, and possibly Norway were to join the EEC, and Sweden and Austria were brought into closer association with the Community.[75]

On 2 May 1967 Wilson informed the House of Commons of the British government's decision to submit a formal application to join the EEC according to article 237. Shortly afterwards, on 16 May, de Gaulle declared his negative attitude towards British EEC membership, and his veto in November 1967 put an end to Britain's second attempt to join the EEC. Initially, the British still hoped that the Council of Ministers would save the application, and that 'the Five would be able to take a very tough line with the French . . . and be able to press for the opening of negotiations some time in January'.[76] In this situation, Wilson again looked to the northern European party network, calling for a conference of party leaders at Chequers on 9 December.[77] Brown assured his fellow socialists that the British application was of a long-term nature, an indispensable part of a great and general movement towards European unity. The 'first and most important reasons for our application are political . . . We see the widening of the Common Market to include us and other Western European countries as the means of bringing about . . . closer political unity [in Europe].' The application 'is in and it will remain in. We do not propose to withdraw it.'[78] On 18 December, however, the EEC Council of Ministers was unable to change de Gaulle's attitude. The French general had once more blocked Britain's road to Europe, and its accession had to wait until 1973.

Conclusions

Focussing on transnational party networks on the European periphery, this chapter demonstrates that northern European socialists were in close contact during the process leading up to the applications of 1967, as they were before the actual EC enlargement of 1972–73. Sharing to a large extent common values and political objectives, the partially overlapping networks comprised a relatively stable group of leaders from party elites, eventually incorporating into these networks younger politicians like Olof Palme and Reiulf Steen when they assumed key positions in national parties. These networks had three main functions.

First, they greatly facilitated the exchange of information on the European issue. Prior to 1960, the general level of knowledge on the subject was low, as the long-serving Norwegian Foreign Minister, Halvard Lange, stressed in addressing the Norwegian Parliament in 1966. He could have spoken on behalf of the northern European periphery when emphasizing that 'we have not paid sufficient attention to what has taken place in post-war continental Europe. [Moreover,] we have not kept ourselves adequately informed about the political and economic development, and about the ideological debate which has taken place, and is taking place, in the EEC and throughout continental Europe.'[79] Their transnational networking changed this situation from 1960 onwards. After indications that the British Conservative government was about to review its European policies, both the British Labour Party and its Scandinavian sister parties embarked upon extensive policy-making processes with a view to developing coherent approaches towards core Europe. These deliberations, in turn, were the basis for thorough discussions and further elaboration inside the transnational networks. As demonstrated in this chapter, the increased focus on the European issue coincided with the setting up and subsequent institutionalization of the SI conferences of party leaders and the Harpsund meetings in 1961 and 1963 respectively. The interaction between national and transnational political processes largely provided the participants with new information and policy ideas.

Second, their networking activities changed the participants' perceptions of core Europe, indicating that socialization took place. On the eve of the 1960s, the British and Scandinavian socialist parties were largely unenthusiastic about core Europe, although the Danish Socialdemokratiet (SD), the Social Democratic Party, was about to decide in favour of EEC membership. Only once Britain and Denmark submitted their membership bids in mid-1961, the Norwegian DNA reluctantly supported the application for full membership in 1962. The Swedish Socialdemokratiska Arbetarparti (SAP) in turn opted for applying for association with the EEC according to article 238 of the EEC Treaty, which the EEC sought to reserve for countries willing, but unable to join for economic reasons. By 1967 this situation had changed. The British Labour government, followed by the Danish SD government, applied for membership of the EEC. The Norwegian party, albeit out of power, declared its support for joining and actively pushed the Centre-Right government to submit an application.[80] As opposed to 1961, the Swedish SAP seriously contemplated applying for full membership although it still adhered to the non-alignment policy.[81] On a personal level, Wilson had been reluctant towards deeper involvement with core Europe in the early 1960s. Yet, as he became integrated in the transnational network as party leader, he developed a more positive attitude towards joining core Europe.

These changes in perceptions of, and attitudes to, core Europe were facilitated by at least four factors. First, the internal EEC crisis leading up to the so-called Luxembourg compromise appeared to reduce the supranational implications of membership by allowing governments to veto decisions, which might adversely affect their vital national interests. To reluctant northern European social democrats, this substantially mitigated fears of integration with core Europe. Second, the electoral rise of social democratic parties and politicians at the expense of Christian democratic parties in the EEC promised greater socialist influence. Third, it was widely believed that this influence would be substantially enhanced if social democratic strongholds like Denmark, Norway and possibly Sweden joined the EEC together with a Labour-led Britain. This hope was reinforced by the incorporation into the networks and rise to power in Germany of Brandt. During the national-socialist period from 1933 to 1945 Brandt was in exile first in Norway and then in Sweden. After the war, he initially returned to Germany as a Norwegian citizen. When Brandt, a fellow socialist they knew and trusted, was elected leader of the SPD in 1964 and became foreign minister in 1966, socialist perceptions of Germany and also of core Europe changed. In fact, after EC enlargement in 1973, the enlarged Commission only had two Christian democratic Commissioners, and the Socialist parties formed for the first time a larger parliamentary party in the European Parliament than the Christian democrats. Fourth, since the creation of the EEC core Europe socialists had been in continuous contact with their northern European colleagues in EFTA, especially through the SI. They had repeatedly stated that instead of preventing the implementation of socialist policies the EEC actually contributed to upgrading welfare provisions.

The third function of the transnational party networks was to influence foreign policy-making. The British Labour elite engaged in transnational networking in the hope of influencing reluctant parties with a view to strengthening the socialist alliance across the EEC–EFTA divide in an enlarged EEC. Wilson's preferred strategy for elaborating and advancing his European policies was the use of the transnational socialist network, as the Chequers meeting in April 1965 and the Amsterdam meeting in January 1966, in particular, demonstrate. These venues provided the participants with an arena in which they could deal with sensitive issues in a frank manner and with no resolutions publicly issued. At the same time, socialist leaders were exposed to policy objectives, which were defined by other socialist parties and governments and in turn influenced their own foreign policy-making. The party networks also influenced the agenda of the intergovernmental EFTA. After the Chequers meeting in April 1965 and the Vienna meeting in the following month, the EFTA agenda switched from the surcharge crisis towards how to deal with core Europe. Thus, this case study corroborates what Wolfram Kaiser argues in his chapter in this book about the importance of transnational networks for the transfer of ideas and policy solutions and for cross-border socialization.

In the British context, the policy-making role of the northern European socialist networks necessitates that existing accounts of Britain's second application based exclusively on government records be modified. Wilson's primary objective soon after taking office in 1964 was to arrange in some way Britain's accession to core Europe,[82] while his tactical rhetoric of 'closing the gap' and 'bridge-building' only developed from early 1965. The sterling crisis of July 1966 might have influenced the timing of the announcement, yet he took the decision in principle much earlier. The great challenge was of course how to achieve EEC accession.

Arriving in Vienna in May 1965 Wilson emphasized that he clearly saw the advantage of joining core Europe, but that there was no question of signing the dotted line, 'for there was no dotted line there to sign on. That was why he was proposing bridge building, for the situation was too urgent for sitting down and waiting for the French to change their attitude.'[83] The bridge-building initiative has to be viewed as a first tactical step towards implementing a medium-term strategic objective rather than trying to achieve some undefined closer arrangements between the two blocks. Besides, this strategy was in line with policies elaborated by the Labour Party since 1962, indicating greater continuity in its European policies from 1962 to 1965.

Socialist networks were well-established prior to core European integration, yet subsequently adjusted to the changing institutional context and new policy-making requirements. When EC enlargement materialized in 1973, socialists had forged close bonds across the EEC–EFTA divide. This bonding created social trust between party elites.[84] Still, individual parties or political leaders could change their opinions, tactics and policies. In the British case in particular, the rise of the Left in the Labour Party and its antagonism to the new Conservative government of Margaret Thatcher and the EEC as a capitalist club had profound effects. In 1979, Labour adopted a policy of leaving the EC, splitting and almost destroying the party when the Social Democratic Party was created by Roy Jenkins, David Owen, Bill Rodgers and Shirley Williams in 1981. Transnational networks failed to contain the policy dispute and to keep the Labour Party together, not least because the hard-core Left was not nearly as well networked in European politics as the more mainstream Centre-Right in the Party. The British case thus also demonstrates the limits to the socializing powers of transnational networks if faced with incompatible dramatic domestic political shifts, although the more moderate party leader Neil Kinnock was to reverse the decision of 1979 in the 1980s.

Notes

1   Melissa Pine, *Harold Wilson and Europe: Pursuing Membership of the European Communities 1967–1970*, London: I.B.Tauris, 2007. See also Helen Parr, *Britain's Policy Towards the European Community. Harold Wilson and Britain's World Role, 1964–1967*, Abingdon: Routledge, 2006, p. 202 and Oliver J. Daddow (ed.), *Harold Wilson and European Integration. Britain's Second Application to join the EEC*, London: Frank Cass, 2003, pp. 1–36, here p. 18.
2   Simon Rippingale, *Hugh Gaitskell, the Labour Party and Foreign Affairs 1955–63*, Phd, Plymouth: University of Plymouth, 1996, p. 217.
3   John W. Young, *Britain and European Unity, 1945–1992*, London: Macmillan, 1993, p. 88.
4   Austen Morgan, *Harold Wilson*, London: Pluto Press, 1992, p. 295.
5   Anne Deighton, 'The Second British Application for Membership of the EEC', in Wilfried Loth (ed.), *Crises and Compromises: The European Project 1963–69*, Baden-Baden, Brussels: Nomos Verlag, 2001, p. 392. See also Anne Deighton, 'The Labour Party, Public Opinion and "the Second Try" in 1967', in Daddow (ed.), *Harold Wilson*, pp. 9–55, here pp. 39–41.
6   Parr, *Britain's Policy*, pp. 62–64, 185, 190–94.

7 Wolfram Kaiser, 'Party Games: The British EEC Applications of 1961 and 1967', in Roger Broad and Virginia Preston (eds.), *Moored to the Continent? Britain and European Integration*, London: Institute of Historical Research, University of London, 2001, pp. 55–78, here p. 71f.

8 Oliver Daddow, 'Introduction', in idem. (ed.), *Harold Wilson and European Integration*, p. 71f.

9 Wolfram Kaiser, *Christian Democracy and the Origins of European Union*, Cambridge: Cambridge University Press, 2007.

10 Miriam Camps, *European Unification in the Sixties. From Veto to Crisis*, London: McGraw-Hill Book Company, 1966, p. 157.

11 'The New Britain', the Labour Party manifesto for the 1964 General Election.

12 'Labour and the Common Market', 29 September 1962, p. 1, Labour Party Archives, The Labour History Archive & Study Centre in Manchester (LAM), National Executive Committee (NEC).

13 Conversation Hugh Gaitskell–Gunnar Fagrell, 9 March 1961, The Swedish Labour Movement's Archives and Library, Stockholm (ARAB), Tage Erlander's Papers (TEA), box 075.

14 Quoted from Camps, *European Unification*, p. 166f.

15 Confidential memo from Gunnar Hägglöf to Foreign Secretary Torsten Nilsson, 9 February 1965, p. 9, ARAB, TEA, box 079.

16 Talks Krag–Wilson, 23 April 1965, p. 2, The Danish Labour Movement's Library and Archives, Copenhagen (ABA), Jens Otto Krag's Papers (JOKA), box 76.

17 Barbara Castle, *The Castle Diaries, 1964–70*, London: Weidenfeld & Nicolson, 1984, p. 18; quoted from Stephen George: *An Awkward Partner. Britain in the European Community*, Oxford: Oxford University Press, 1990, p. 36.

18 Parr, *Britain's Policy*, p. 41.

19 Socialist leaders from UK, Sweden, Denmark, Norway, Finland, Iceland, France, Germany, Italy, Netherlands, Belgium and Canada participated in the full meeting. The British delegation was composed of Harold Wilson, Anthony Greenwood, colonial secretary, Walter Padley, minister of state for foreign affairs and Alan Williams, under-secretary of state for economic affairs.

20 ABA, JOKA, box 76, 22 April 1965; Camps, *European Unification*, p. 172; *Dagens Nyheter*, 25 April 1965 and ARAB, Olof Palme's Papers (OPA), box 002, meeting Chequers, 24 April 1965.

21 Meeting Chequers, 24 April 1965, ARAB, OPA, box 002; Camps, *European Unification*, p. 172.

22 Krag's contribution, ABA, JOKA, box 76, 24 April 1965. See also Bo Lidegaard, *Jens Otto Krag 1962–1978*, vol. II, Copenhagen: Gyldendal, 2001, pp. 239–42.

23 SI Circular to member parties 1965, International Institute of Social History, Amsterdam (IISH).

24 *Dagens Nyheter*, 25 April 1965 and *Aftonbladet*, 26 April 1965.

25 *Dagens Nyheter*, 25 April 1965.

26 Speech by Gérard Jaquet, p. 2, SI, 7th Congress, Rome, 23–27 October 1961, IISH, SI, 252.

27 Report from SI Conference in Brussels, 15–16 July 1962, ARAB, TEA, box 038 and Socialist International Information (SII), vol. 12, 1962, p. 326, IISH, SI. The SII was published fortnightly by the SI. It mediated information originating from various sources, for instance member countries, meetings staged by the SI, speeches held by socialists in various member countries, etc., to member parities and other subscribers. The SII also produced its own reports from meetings, speeches, polls, etc.

28 Wolfram Kaiser, 'The Successes and Limits of Industrial Market Integration: The European Free Trade Association 1963–69', in Loth (ed.), *Crises and Compromises*, pp. 371–90, here pp. 387–90.

29 *The Sunday Times*, quoted from IISH, SI, SII, 1965, p. 108.

30 *The Guardian*, quoted from IISH, SI, SII, 1965, p. 108.
31 *The Times*, 26 April 1965.
32 IISH, SI, SII, 1965, p. 120.
33 Ibid.
34 Meeting Chequers, 24 April 1965, ARAB, OPA, box 002.
35 IISH, SI, SII, 1965, p. 134. See also 'When Six into Eight won't go, the Answer is a Summit', *Daily Mail*, 24 May 1965.
36 *Daily Mail*, 24 May 1965.
37 IISH, SI, SII, 1965, p. 134 and *The Guardian*, 25 May 1965.
38 Report EFTA meeting Vienna, 24–25 May 1965, ARAB, TEA, box 080.
39 See *Daily Telegraph*, 28 May 1965 and Parr, *Britain's Policy*, p. 54.
40 Secret summary Krag–Erlander talks, 20 June 1965, p. 2, ARAB, TEA, box 080.
41 IISH, SI, SII, 1965, p. 200.
42 Lidegaard, *Jens Otto Krag*, vol. II, p. 241.
43 Messages from the Swedish foreign ministry to Prime Minister Erlander, 10/1965, pp. 3–4, ARAB, TEA, box 081.
44 Address by Mansholt, 15 January 1966, IISH, Sicco Mansholt papers (SMA), box 121. Memorandum (translated into Swedish) presented to the social democratic parties of Germany and UK, 10 February 1966, ARAB, TEA, box 082.
45 Ibid.
46 Address by Mansholt, 15 January 1966, p. 2.
47 Memorandum presented to the social democratic parties of Germany and UK, 10 February 1966, ARAB, TEA, box 082.
48 Address by Mansholt, 15 January 1966, p. 11f.
49 Ibid., and personal and secret letter from Lindh, Brussels, to Montan, Stockholm, 10 February 1966, ARAB, TEA, box 082.
50 Comments on Mansholt's proposals of 15 January 1966, IISH, SMA, box 166.
51 Secret letter from Lindh to Montan, 10 February 1966.
52 Ibid.
53 Ibid.
54 Address by Mansholt, 15 January 1966; translated memorandum, enclosed in letter from Lindh to Montan, 10 February 1966.
55 Parr, *Britain's Policy*, p. 62.
56 Ibid. p. 64.
57 'Time for Decision', the Labour Party manifesto for the 1966 General Election, IISH, SI, SII, vol. 14, 5/1966.
58 Hansard, 21 April 1966.
59 Speech by Brown, 6 May 1966, SI, 10th Congress, Stockholm, IISH, SI, 256.
60 Ibid.
61 See for instance Resolutions of the 10th Congress of EEC Socialist Parties, 17–18 November 1966, IISH, SI, SII.
62 ABA, JOKA, box 144, 5 May 1966; Krag's speech, May 1966, SI, 10th Congress, Stockholm, IISH, SI, 258.
63 Lange's speech, May 1966, SI, 10th Congress, Stockholm, IISH, SI, 258.
64 Report from SI's 10th Congress, May 1966, 20 July 1966, The Norwegian Labour Movement's Archives and Library (AAB), Finn Moe's papers (FMA), box 008.
65 Ibid.
66 Hans Otto Frøland, 'The Second Norwegian EEC-Application, 1967: Was There a Policy at all?', in Loth (ed.), *Crises and Compromises*, pp. 437–58, here pp. 447–50.
67 *Aftonbladet* and *Dagens Nyheter*, 7 May 1966.
68 Cf. *The Times*, 11 November 1966.
69 Brown's speech to the House of Commons, 16 November 1966, IISH, SI, 589.

70 George Brown, *In My Way. The Political Memoirs of Lord George-Brown*, London: Victor Gollancz, 1971, p. 214.
71 George Brown papers Bodleian Library, Oxford (GBBLO), box c. 5015/161, 6 April 1966.
72 See for instance Kaiser, 'Party Games', pp. 68–72; Deighton, 'The Second British Application', p. 404f.
73 P. M. Kelly, 'Your speech to the PLP on Europe' [on 6 April 1966], GBBLO, box c. 5015/161.
74 *Financial Times*, 25 May 1965.
75 Conference of party leaders, Rome, 4–5 January 1967, IISH, SI, 345.
76 Brief for Bilateral Talks during the Visit of SI Leaders in London, [6 December 1967], GBBLO, box c. 5019/165.
77 The conference was attended by Willy Brandt, Helmut Schmidt, Jens-Otto Krag, Trygve Bratteli, Tage Erlander and Olof Palme.
78 Socialist International conference of party leaders, European Integration, Talking points, [6 December 1967], GBBLO, box c. 5019/165.
79 Halvard Lange to Parliament (Stortinget), 22 February 1966, ARAB, TEA, box 082.
80 Frøland, 'The Second Norwegian EEC-Application', pp. 447–50; idem., 'DNA og Vest-Europa 1945–95: kontakter, samarbeid og utsyn', in Knut Heidar and Lars Svåsand (eds.), *Partier uten grenser?* Oslo: Tano Aschehoug, 1997, pp. 169–201.
81 See for example ARAB, TEA, box 038, 29 June 1967.
82 This view was also expressed by *Financial Times*, 25 May 1965.
83 IISH, SI, SII, 1965, p. 134; *The Guardian*, 25 May 1965.
84 For a discussion of social versus instrumental trust see Roderick M. Kramer and Tom R. Tyler, *Trust in Organizations: Frontiers of Theory and Research*, London: Sage, 1996.

7 Transnational communication in the European public sphere

The summit of The Hague 1969

Jan-Henrik Meyer

Historians have only recently begun to take note of the debate on the European public sphere and have started inquiring into its history. Remarkably, historians from cultural and social history rather than from European integration history proper first devoted attention to this question.[1] Issues of European politics in a broader sense have already been intensely discussed at earlier moments of European crises, when *ad hoc* European public spheres emerged temporarily.[2] In the postwar period, for the first time, there was an institutional addressee for a political public sphere.[3] Such a European public sphere can be characterized as a sphere of communication for mediating between European citizens and the institutions of the European political system, which is a key precondition for democratic governance. It is in the public sphere, and mainly via the media, that citizens learn and form an opinion about the European Union (EU). At the same time, by observing the European public sphere, European policy-makers find out what Europeans think and expect of the EU.[4]

Social science research on the European public sphere has mainly focused on comparative media analyses. These analyses take the synchronous reporting of (European) issues, that is 'the same topics at the same time at the same level of relevance' as an indication of a European public sphere.[5] While this line of research has shown that in recent years Europeans have been discussing the same EU issues,[6] it does not provide direct evidence of transnational communication. Yet, only such evidence has the potential to demonstrate that European affairs are not discussed separately in closed national public spheres. In order to elicit to what extent the European public sphere is in fact integrated across borders, researchers have to devise ways for examining transnational communication.[7] Transnational exchanges are difficult to trace in national media, as journalists usually do not acknowledge their sources. Such exchanges, therefore, remain often invisible, taking place by what Jürgen Habermas calls 'osmotic diffusion'.[8] Analyzing the European summit at The Hague in December 1969, this chapter will inquire into different aspects of transnational interaction in the European public sphere, attempting to make visible what usually goes unnoticed.

First, journalists covering European topics interact and mediate across borders and are pivotal cultural brokers in the transnational integration of the European public sphere. These journalists participate in professional and social networks, which is likely to influence their views and opinions. Second, traces of journalists' interaction in the media can occasionally be made visible as transnational inter-media references or direct transfers of ideas and viewpoints. Third, transnational communication takes place when journalists present views from abroad in their articles, thereby mediating them to their domestic audiences. Thus, the extent to which the views of other Europeans are subjected to discussion provides evidence of the intensity of transnational communication. Finally, as Wolfram Kaiser argues in his chapter, repeated transnational communication in networks influences the participants' perception of Europe and their views on European policy issues. Commentators discursively construct 'transnationality'[9] as a way of conceptualizing the political and social space of an integrating Europe. Combining evidence on these four aspects of transnational communication, I will draw some tentative conclusions about the importance of the summit of The Hague in the historical emergence and evolution of the European public sphere.[10]

The summit of The Hague: a focal point of the European public sphere

The importance of the summit of The Hague in the history of building a European polity has frequently been emphasized. The summit marked the turning point to a new era shaped by 'Europe's second generation'.[11] After French President Charles de Gaulle, who had long opposed further integration, had left office, his successor Georges Pompidou took a new approach. He as well as German Chancellor Willy Brandt were part of this second generation of European leaders who attempted to overcome the integration deadlock of the European Communities (EC) by means of intergovernmental leadership. The summit of The Hague was the first in a series of such meetings that eventually developed into the new European Council institutionalized in the Single European Act of 1987. Crucially, these summits provided a forum for decision-making at the highest political level. Pompidou's programme for the conference at The Hague included three themes that set the agenda for the subsequent decade: first, 'completion' provided the Communities with their own financial resources; second, 'deepening' extended the scope of EC policies, most notably in the fields of monetary and political union. Third, Pompidou lifted de Gaulle's veto imposed in 1961 and again in 1967, and opened the door to the EC's enlargement, which lead to the accession of Britain, Denmark and Ireland.[12]

The historical significance of the summit of The Hague has only become clear in retrospect. The salience of an event in the public sphere is a function of what happened at the event itself, however, and to what extent it was seen to have 'news value' at the time. News values describe journalists' selection criteria, that in turn shape the awareness of the media and the public as a whole.[13] Jürgen Gerhards has argued that attention to the EC has long been low precisely because most news stories about European integration were not regarded to have much news value.[14] The summit of The Hague, however, clearly fulfilled important criteria of newsworthiness, such as conflict, the involvement of central political actors and the relevance of the issues at stake. That the leaders of France and Germany were new in office made the event less predictable and allowed for personification. Even historiography highlights the public attention the summit received, including the European Movement's demonstrations in front of the conference venue, the medieval *Ridderzaal*.[15] From this perspective, it seems likely that this summit was one of the events for which evidence of a European public sphere of the media across Europe can be made visible. Further, the summit may serve as a case study that can be meaningfully juxtaposed to other politically important EC summits or the later European Council meetings.[16]

Journalists and transnational communication

Commentaries in newspapers are a particularly revealing source for the analysis of transnational references and the formation and expression of opinions because they represent the newspapers' own voice.[17] Different types of authors dominated the comment sections in the British, German and French quality newspapers selected for this study.[18] In the British and German newspapers, leader writers, editors and the Brussels correspondents wrote most of the opinion pieces. In the French newspapers, by contrast, external authors contributed a major part of the commentary. However, at the summit of The Hague, there was only one single case in which a foreign external commentator contributed to a transnational exchange of views.[19] Commentaries on the EC were written by a relatively wide group of authors in most of the newspapers. Across all six newspapers there were only ten authors – EC correspondents and columnists – who contributed more than one piece. Only in *Süddeutsche Zeitung* and in the *Guardian*, commentary writing was more concentrated. *Süddeutsche's* EC correspondent Hans-Josef Strick wrote about a quarter and columnist Maxim Fackler one half of *Süddeutsche's* European commentary. The *Guardian's* long-serving columnist Peter Jenkins (1967–85) accounted for a third of the *Guardian's* commentary. Both columnists were professionally involved in transnational networks. Jenkins was a well-known 'Europhile' whose vision for the United Kingdom was that of a social-democratic European country. He could rely on a transnational network of contacts across Europe and the United States. For instance, Jenkins was a regular and prominent participant in the Anglo-German Society's high-level Königswinter conferences that repeatedly dealt with European policy issues.[20] Fackler was a distinguished expert who published in foreign affairs journals in Germany and Britain.[21]

The EC correspondents belong to an 'aristocracy' of journalists, the foreign correspondents,[22] who master foreign languages and professionally engage in transnational interaction. An impressive case, and also one of the few women within a male-dominated elite, is the *Guardian's* European correspondent Hella Pick, whose transnational biography initially was not a deliberate choice. Born in Vienna in 1929, Pick was brought to England as a Jewish refugee child in 1939.[23] After graduating from the London School of Economics and Political Science, she started writing for the *Guardian*. Before and after her assignment as a Geneva-based European correspondent (1968–71), she reported from the United States, but commented again on European affairs at Maastricht in 1991, then as the *Guardian*'s diplomatic editor.[24]

EC correspondents stayed in their job for extensive periods of time. *Frankfurter Allgemeine*'s Brussels correspondent Hans Herbert Götz arrived in 1963 and remained there until 1975. *Süddeutsche Zeitung*'s Strick stayed from the 1960s until the 1980s. Philippe Lemaitre worked for *Le Monde* from the 1960s until the 1990s, but continues to write from Brussels. Such long-term assignments reinforced the development of extensive networks not only among journalists, but also with members of the European Parliament, Commission officials and lobbyists.[25] While the research available focuses on the more recent period since the early 1990s, the findings indicate a continuity of stable structural patterns and recurrent practice. Even though national ties have remained strong,[26] journalists' networks have not remained nationally limited, not least because correspondents rely on each other for information. Thus, at the summit, when journalists are called to 'their' national governments' press conferences, they usually double-check with their European colleagues to get a more complete picture. As they write for different national markets, competition among them is low. Therefore, correspondents generously share information across borders.[27]

Among the pre-1991 generation of European correspondents, Christoph Meyer finds strong attachment to the European cause rather than a more critical journalistic outlook. Some of the correspondents slowly turned into 'fake Eurocrat[s] without the wages'.[28] To what extent this was due to transnational socialization, highlighted by Kaiser in his chapter as one important function of networks, is difficult to decide. Brussels clearly is unique as a posting as it provides everyday experience of Europeans working and living together. However, pro-European attitudes could also result from self-selection. Journalists with earlier affinities to European integration may have decided to go to Brussels, which back then was not necessarily a posting that would advance their careers. Pro-integration attitudes may also have resulted from the generational experience of the Second World War as an adolescent or young adult. In fact, despite his harsh critique of the economics and politics of the Common Agricultural Policy (CAP), Götz from the *Frankfurter Allgemeine* was known to be a fervent pro-European.[29] He assisted former Commission President Walter Hallstein – then head of the European Movement (1968–74) – with writing his book on the 'incomplete federal state' published in 1969,[30] which underlines Götz' intimate involvement with Europe's political elite. Walter Farr from the *Daily Telegraph* also published a book on the EC to inform about, and lobby for, British membership.[31]

In the absence of more detailed historical studies,[32] these somewhat impressionist observations suggest that the commentary and reporting analyzed below was produced in, and shaped by a transnational environment of professional networks. As part of their work journalists engaged in transnational communication as avid readers of other countries' newspapers. In fact, EC correspondents occasionally quoted and referred to their colleagues' articles when commenting on the summit of The Hague.

Transnational references and the transfer of ideas and views

The article 'Le Nerf de l'Europe' by Pierre Drouin in *Le Monde* influenced at least two articles by *Süddeutsche Zeitung*'s EC correspondent Strick.[33] Strick explicitly refers to Drouin who argued that historical progress could only be achieved by overcoming the reservations of hesitant 'experts'.[34] In a second article Strick uses this argument again, and goes on to contend that the CAP should be perceived as a European achievement, because it was the only true common European policy.[35] This argument is borrowed from another piece in the same issue of *Le Monde*.[36] The title of Strick's piece 'In die zweite Generation' is taken from the first paragraph of Drouin's article. Jenkins from the *Guardian* explicitly refers to *Le Monde* and *Le Figaro* and refutes their view that Pompidou was the 'star' of the negotiations.[37] Conversely, *Süddeutsche*'s commentator Hermann Probst presents *Le Figaro*'s opinion that the summit helped overcome mutual distrust.[38] Given that commentators do not usually refer to their colleagues writing, such findings demonstrate a substantial level of transnational communication between the newspapers. However, it is remarkable that only French newspapers are quoted. This asymmetry of attention is probably due to the central role the French government played in the negotiations.

The same asymmetry, a predominant focus on the French governments' views, is also prevalent in transnational references to political and societal actors in the commentary. Although references are made to the views of the European Commission as a supranational institution, the focus is on the intergovernmental bargaining between national governments at the summit. Only scant references are made to societal actors such as the German farmers' union in *Le Figaro* and to the European Movement in the *Frankfurter Allgemeine*.[39] At the same time, not even the views of all participating governments are considered in the commentary. Newspapers concentrate on what they perceive to be core actors, namely the French and the German governments. This asymmetry of attention applies to all newspapers. However, whether the French or the German government dominates the story varies between the newspapers. The British and the German newspapers refer most frequently to the French government. Among these newspapers, the *Guardian* attributes most, while the *Frankfurter Allgemeine* devotes least attention to French views. German positions rank second in importance. However, while the German government features prominently in *Le Monde* and the *Guardian*, they are less important in the *Daily Telegraph* and *Le Figaro*. British views are rarely discussed in the German newspapers, while they meet slightly more interest in the French newspapers. Further, the overall attention to foreign views differs. It is highest in the *Guardian* and lowest in the *Frankfurter Allgemeine* and *Le Figaro*. Apparently, conservative newspapers engage less in a transnational debate of views.

Moreover, commentators discuss views from abroad in different ways. The first and most basic form could be called mutual observation. Journalists only observe and describe the positions of foreign actors without subjecting them to critical evaluation. Second, what could be described as inclusive argument implies that commentators integrate the views of foreign actors into the debate. Commentators strategically include such views in order to buttress their own viewpoint with the profile and status of the foreign actor. Still, this may be interpreted as evidence of a transnational European debate, in which the arguments of actors are transnationally transferable. Third, the most intense level of a veritable transnational debate takes place in discursive references. Here, commentators treat the positions or arguments of other European or EC actors in their own right. They extensively criticize, refute, support or debate them with an inconclusive result.[40] Hence, the latter two modes of argument deserve more comprehensive consideration.

All newspapers contain examples of inclusive arguments. Foreign actors seem to enjoy great persuasiveness in EC affairs. The *Guardian's* leader writer – ever critical of the CAP – quotes French and German actors when stressing the urgency of reform.[41] Similarly, the *Guardian's* columnist Jenkins backs up his own critique by referring to witnesses who are shown to argue against what could be expected to be in their 'national interest'. Jenkins quotes a 'Frenchman at the Commission' who warned that the CAP would be an impediment to French economic modernization. Conversely, he refers to a Commission official from Germany – the EC's major net contributor – who stressed Italy's and France's development problems that are routinely used to justify generous agricultural subsidies.[42] In a similar way, the *Daily Telegraph's* pro-European commentators cite continental actors to criticize British hesitancy towards joining the EC. Farr quotes Jean Monnet: 'You British do not understand ideas. You only understand facts. When these are staring you in the face you will act.'[43] The *Daily Telegraph's* columnist writing under the pseudonym of 'Peterborough' points to a 'Parisian socialist' who supported the newspaper's earlier claim that continental governments had a historical and moral obligation to allow Britain to join the EC. The 'Parisian socialist' is reported to have argued that de Gaulle, who rejected British membership twice, had been the most prominent beneficiary of British hospitality during the Second World War.[44] When pointing to the drawbacks of the CAP, the *Frankfurter Allgemeine's* editor Jürgen Eick finds an ally in Britain. He praises Britain's superior, more transparent and effective system of agriculture as an example the EC should follow.[45] Former French Commissioner Robert Lemaignen writing in *Le Monde* advances his own critique of de Gaulle by citing Adenauer's remarks about de Gaulle's hostility towards the European Commission.[46] *Süddeutsche Zeitung's* commentator Probst quotes Dutch criticism of the lack of progress towards supranationalism in order to substantiate his own disappointment with the summit results.[47]

Commentators do not only rely on personification when selecting news, they also use it to structure the debate. This is most prominent in discursive references of British newspapers to mainly French, but also to German government positions on agricultural policy and enlargement. Journalists speculate whether, and at what cost, enlargement will take place. The 'shadow of de Gaulle' seems to explain Pompidou's hesitancy concerning enlargement. Commentators repeatedly refer to the general's consistently anti-British policy. Expectations of a real policy change are low.[48] Jenkins from the *Guardian* criticizes, for example, what he perceives as a high-handed and self-centred Gaullist policy towards France's European partners: 'Political unity in the French vocabulary still means cooperation between independent sovereign less [sic] Governments; stated bluntly it means agreeing with France.'[49] Also in the German newspapers de Gaulle's policy seems to have eroded trust in the French government. *Süddeutsche Zeitung*'s columnist Maxim Fackler notes that French negotiators are always very skilful at extracting a collateral when giving up a position.[50] While initially the German newspapers are not entirely convinced of Pompidou's willingness to co-operate,[51] at the end of the summit most commentators start to believe that he has overcome de Gaulle's policy.[52] Occasional criticism of Pompidou's alleged preference for an intergovernmental Europe remains, however.[53] Juxtaposing Brandt and Pompidou, the British newspapers celebrate the German chancellor's unexpectedly assertive stance, his pro-enlargement views as well as his critique of the CAP.[54] *Le Monde* also discusses Germany's pro-enlargement position,[55] but criticizes the new government's views on the CAP[56] and its hesitancy concerning the introduction of a common monetary policy.[57]

All in all, the analysis of transnational references shows that commentators engage in a vivid transnational debate. They clearly attribute legitimacy to foreign views, which they use to corroborate their own arguments. In addition to such instrumental usage of inclusive arguments, commentators discuss foreign views in their own right. However, there are limitations. First, the geographical scope of transnational references is narrow and asymmetric. Most observations and debates relate to the position of the French president and government, which reflects the centrality of France in the decision-making process, especially concerning enlargement. Second, criticism often refers to simplified, cliché-like versions of the opinions and behaviour of the European partners. At times, it appears as if the newspapers discuss stereotypes of the European partners and their supposed national characteristics rather than their actual political action. Frequently, arguments are also aligned with the national government's positions on the respective policy. In many cases, commentators seem to defend what they perceive as 'national interest'. Both effects can also be found in national political debates, where the divides of party politics shape perceptions and may encourage alignment. However, while in a national context, such divides are rarely regarded to be problematic for the cohesion of the political system, at the EC level, critics have interpreted the argumentative alignment along the national cleavage as indicating a lack of a European identity. Consequently they argued that the socio-cultural basis for the emerging European polity was deficient.[58] In the face of this view, it is important to explore to what extent a sense of transnational commonality across Europe was constructed in the transnational debate.

Construction of transnationality

Hartmut Kaelble, Martin Kirsch and Alexander Schmidt-Gernig have distinguished between the process of 'transnationalization' as increased transnational interaction and 'transnationality'.[59] The latter concept describes how contemporaries have imagined and understood the (European) political space beyond the nation-state. This collective conception of the transnational political space of the emerging European polity is discursively constructed in relation to the nation, the European partners and the EC. Moreover, transnationality may involve a shift or extension of identification with a (European) political community beyond the nation-state. However, transnationalization is by no means a one-way street to European identity. As Kaiser emphasizes in his chapter, this process is open-ended. It remains an open question to what extent a shared vision for Europe will actually result from transnational interaction. Three aspects of transnationality may be distinguished: first, and most basically, the perception of common or conflicting interests; second, the perception of trust in the European partners; and third, and most elusively, the invocation of a transnational sense of belonging or identification.

The newspapers discuss common and conflicting interests with respect to three main policy areas: agriculture, enlargement and the new policies for Europe's 'relaunch', that is monetary union and foreign policy coordination. Essentially, only the *Guardian* consistently highlights the conflict of national interests about the CAP. Its commentators argue that as a major food-importing country alongside Germany, Britain would have to pay for the EC's agricultural policy after its accession, to the direct benefit of France and the indirect benefit of Germany. They resent the French government's insistence on maintaining the status quo. Further, they point to the dangers for Britain's balance of payments and national competitiveness resulting from higher food prices in the EC.[60] Downplaying the cost of the CAP, the *Daily Telegraph*, at that time a fervently pro-European newspaper, does not construe such a conflict of interests.[61] Although the German newspapers criticize the effects of the CAP, they do not frame the issue as a conflict of national interests. *Süddeutsche Zeitung* instead highlights the reconciliation of interests with France and Italy in this policy area as a positive result of integration.[62] While the *Frankfurter Allgemeine*'s leader writers harshly criticize the rising cost of the CAP, they primarily stress that this policy would work against the interests of consumers and tax-payers, regardless of their nationality.[63] Occasionally, they hint at the fact that it would be in Germany's interest to limit the cost.[64] At the same time, editor Jürgen Tern also mentions that Germany was to blame as the government had insisted on high prices for cereals in the 1960s, for example.[65] The French newspapers' commentary is divided on whether to stress European or national interests in agriculture. Some of *Le Monde*'s commentators concede flaws of the CAP.[66] Similar to *Süddeutsche Zeitung*,[67] *Le Monde* also stresses the reconciliation of national interests as a European achievement that would outweigh the cost of intervention.[68] At the same time, commentators in both French newspapers assert what they perceive as the defence of France's 'legitimate economic interest'.[69]

Particularly for the *Guardian*, the cost of the CAP appears to outweigh the expected long-term benefits of eventual EC membership for Britain, namely invigorating its economy.[70] These are precisely the benefits that the

Daily Telegraph highlights. Along this line of reasoning, even with the additional costs of participating in the CAP, Britain's economy would be better off inside the EC, with its bigger markets allowing for economies of scale. Britain's international role, its security and defence would also be strengthened by EC membership, in particular if monetary and political union were to be achieved.[71] Due to the negative externalities the EC generates, for example for British trade, it would be in Britain's interest to join a community that has proven to be effective.[72] Both British newspapers self-confidently emphasize the interest the EC in turn should have in British membership. The *Guardian* argues that it would politically strengthen the EC vis-à-vis the outside world and balance the growing strength of Germany. British democratic traditions would help the EC. Her industry and technology would reinforce the EC economy.[73] The *Daily Telegraph* and *Süddeutsche Zeitung* point to the expected 'new impetus' the EC would receive from British membership.[74] *Le Monde*'s commentators also argue that integrating Britain would be in Europe's interest. The EC would benefit from British technology and financial markets.[75] However, *Le Figaro* warns that British membership could weaken the political cohesion of the Community. Britain's political and economic interests and what the *Le Figaro* perceives to be those of the EC appeared to diverge.[76]

As on agricultural policy, the German newspapers also downplay potential conflict of interest in the new policy areas of monetary union and foreign policy co-operation. *Süddeutsche Zeitung*'s EC correspondent explains away any notion of diverging interests between France and Germany on monetary union. Rejecting the idea that Germany would have to make sacrifices, he suggests that a European solution would be in Germany's interest. Establishing common monetary institutions would allow Germans to occupy central leadership positions in the new institutions to be set up. Likewise, concerning common foreign policy, the *Frankfurter Allgemeine*'s leader writers stress the convergence of national and European interest in defending Europe's interest vis-à-vis the outside world. Commentator Jan Reifenberg supports French insistence on European technological and industrial independence from the superpowers.[77] It is precisely in this policy area that the French newspapers perceive a common interest between France and the EC as a whole. The Gaullist vision of French independence[78] would only be achievable on a European scale, merging resources in research and industrial production.[79] Monetary union would be an additional tool for gaining strength vis-à-vis the United States.[80] Conversely, the French newspapers suggest a potential conflict of interest between France and Germany. Germany's growing economic power and more assertive European and foreign policy in the context of *Ostpolitik* might lead to a decline in France's role as a political leader. *Le Monde*'s editorialist warns: 'Europe is at a crossroads, but it is less sure now than before that solely France – as we have believed for too long – holds the keys to its future.'[81] However, French commentators do not present French leadership as solely being in the interest of France, but in the interest of the EC as a whole, preventing unacceptable German domination. Hence they present French and European interest not only as overlapping, but, in fact, portray France as the guardian of European interest.[82] The discussion of interests as an aspect of transnationality shows that while the *Guardian* and *Le Figaro* are more aware of conflicting national interests within the EC, most German commentators, the *Daily Telegraph* and to some extent also *Le Monde* are more oriented towards the shared interest of Europe as a transnational political community. In part, this reflects the political affiliations of the newspapers. The *Guardian*[83] is characterized by left-wing Euroscepticism and *Le Figaro* by Gaullist hesitancy concerning British membership.

Are there similar patterns in the discussion about trustworthiness of the European partners? How commentators evaluate the behaviour of the European partners, indicates whether they perceive (and want to present) them as trustworthy. Trust is an important aspect of transnationality and a European sense of community. It is a necessary precondition for continuously successful co-operation.[84] Trust rests on the impression that there is a common ground of fairness, of reliability and honesty, and ideally also of reciprocity and equal burden sharing. The invocation of transnational solidarity reflects a high level of trust, as solidarity is usually limited to clearly bounded communities.[85] Fairness and honesty are central for the *Daily Telegraph* in evaluating the behaviour of the member states vis-à-vis each other and the European institutions. The *Daily Telegraph* stresses the instrumentality of European democratic institutions such as the Parliament and the Court in ensuring compliance within a system of 'checks and balances'.[86] Democracy is understood here as a precondition for trust in common institutions. Moreover, the *Daily Telegraph*'s commentators insist that governments should 'play it straight' rather than being 'out to make more money for France'.[87] Like the *Daily Telegraph*, the *Süddeutsche Zeitung* criticizes the French government's tendency to extract unfair advantages whenever concessions are necessary to reach a compromise.[88] However, *The Guardian*'s columnist Jenkins suspects that this distrust may be mutual and that the French government might wonder, whether 'Britain [was] ready to be a reliable partner for France?'[89]

For the *Daily Telegraph*, supporting French agriculture seems fair because it is based on reciprocal commitments. Given that France bared her markets for industrial products of the previously high tariff protection, the country 'deserved some agricultural recompense'.[90] In a similar way, the German newspapers accept Italy's demand for regulating the fruit market on the grounds of fairness, given that the northern member states achieved more effective protection for their produce.[91] Honesty and fairness through reciprocity are central for the *Daily Telegraph* in evaluating the behaviour of the member states vis-à-vis each other and the European institutions. The *Daily Telegraph* refers to Europe's historical-moral obligation towards Britain. Expecting fair retribution, the commentator highlights that Britain had been a safe haven for many of the current continental European leaders during the Second World War and the sole defender of Europe against national-socialist Germany.[92]

Despite their harsh criticism of the CAP, the *Guardian*'s commentators stress the need to mutually consider important national interests and reach a fair compromise. The commentators even consider the domestic pressures under which the French government operated. The French farmers are understood to be an important constituency, which explained why the French government could not give up the CAP. Similarly, the *Frankfurter Allgemeine* points to domestic pressures on the French government.[93] Finally, the need for transnational solidarity is more explicitly invoked in the *Guardian*, the *Süddeutsche Zeitung* and the French newspapers, although in different ways. The *Guardian*'s columnists express compassion with the poverty of ten million continental farmers, which required and justified EC solidarity: 'The common agricultural policy is not a joke about butter but a problem of people.'[94] In the *Süddeutsche Zeitung* solidarity appears almost as a euphemism for package deals.[95] In the French newspapers, solidarity is not about compassion, but understood as a legal entitlement. Reference is made to the acquis communautaire, the existing body of European law. In the French language, this term carries the connotation of 'achievement'. The common market for agricultural products is not only based on 'single prices' but also on 'community preference' and 'financial solidarity'.[96] The French government had to insist, commentators argue, that these European achievements were to be defended, especially in the face of any free trade-minded accession states.[97]

Finally, with respect to a sense of belonging, the differences between nation and Europe are downplayed in all newspapers that engage in constructing European identification. Commentators uphold two main tenets. First, according to what Hans-Jörg Trenz calls the ideology of 'progressive Europeanism',[98] the nation and Europe are placed in a temporal relationship, Europe as a political community appears not simply as a utopian vision, but as the inevitable result of historical progress.[99] Invoking a strong European sense of belonging, German and French commentators describe a federalist, supranational Europe as the future. The nation-state is denigrated as old-fashioned and of the past.[100] Even if national politicians still refused to realize, the nation-state would inevitably have to give up sovereignty in order to build a strong European Community. Otherwise, Europe would fall apart, and return to its violent past. On the basis of this idea that is near-universal among French and German commentators, politicians' efforts to work for European integration and against nationalism are evaluated.[101] Even the *Guardian*'s commentators suggest the inevitability of ceding sovereignty. The more pro-European *Daily Telegraph* calls for Euro-enthusiasm. Commentators demand greater 'community spirit'[102] as a lesson from the past[103] and as a utopian ideal of eventually overcoming national divides in the transnational European political space: 'Unless we go into it with trust, unless we want to merge our sectional interests in the common interest of Europe, unless we are ready to regard the other countries as partners in a great ideal rather than parties to a bargain . . . '[104]

Second, Europe and the nation are no longer perceived as mutually exclusive. This assumption lies at the heart of the critical evaluation of intergovernmental negotiations. German and French newspapers present intergovernmental bargaining as petty 'horse trading'.[105] National politicians had simply not yet realized that the goal was a common one. Remarkably, in support of British EC membership, both British newspapers suggest that Britain is part of Europe and that

British and European identity could go together. The *Guardian's* commentator William Davis manages to convince his 'Euro-irritated' fictitious interlocutor 'Aunt Bertha' that Europe would be nothing to be afraid of. In fact, she happily accepts that 'to become a European' is easily reconciled with 'stay[ing] British'.[106] Similarly, the *Daily Telegraph's* EC correspondent firmly places Britain in Europe, in 'this part of the world we live in'. Acknowledging the fellow European as a partner who is fundamentally similar, Farr points to the resemblance between the British and the French: 'the pride of the French, perhaps even greater than our own'.[107]

On the whole, common features are more frequently invoked in the construction of transnationality than divisive ones. Most commentators, with the exception of the *Guardian* and *Le Figaro*, point to shared interests. The predominance of 'progressive Europeanism' suggests that commentators worked hard promoting European identification. This may have appeared necessary to them, given the doubts about the trustworthiness of the European partners. Next to continuing suspicions vis-à-vis the European partners, in particular among German and British commentators, there is a strong sense of community, even involving solidarity, within the European political space.

Conclusions

At the time of the summit of The Hague, the level of transnational communication within the European public sphere of leading British, German and French quality newspapers was remarkably high. A variety of indicators support this observation. First, a substantial part of the commentary was produced by EC correspondents whose long-term assignments in Brussels enabled them to establish networks of information exchange that were at least in part transnational. However, such transnational networks of European journalists require more research in a long term perspective covering the entire postwar period. Based on the notions introduced by Kaiser in his chapter, it would be worthwhile inquiring to what extent such networks influenced media reporting and even policy-making in the EC. The example of Götz acting as a co-author for Hallstein, would suggest that he and probably others, too, were part of an advocacy coalition that actively promoted the European cause.

Second, journalists acted as transnational cultural brokers. German and British commentators quoted and borrowed ideas from French newspapers. This may only have been the tip of the iceberg. Still, transnational media interaction was asymmetric and unidirectional. Only French newspapers were quoted.

Third, transnational references to actors from other member-states were similarly asymmetric and mainly discussed the views of the French and German governments. They largely ignored other national and societal actors. This may be deplorable from the normative perspective of deliberative democracy,[108] but is mainly a consequence of journalists selecting whom they regarded as the most relevant and influential actors. In an intensive transnational debate the views of the European partners were critically evaluated. Commentators proved to be remarkably familiar with the arguments of others in the debate. This evidence further points to comprehensive transnational communication. To be sure, the transnational debate of the views and actions of the European partners frequently reproduced national clichés. Commentators' views were often, but not always, aligned with what was perceived as 'national interest'. Still, media's political alignment and also deliberately disparaging representations of political adversaries are familiar from national debates on controversial issues. Europe just adds another conflict dimension.[109] This is an important point to keep in mind when evaluating transnational communication. Moreover, foreign opinions were not only observed, but frequently also included in one's own argument. This shows the shared relevance of these views and suggests that the views of Europeans from other countries enjoyed substantial legitimacy.

Fourth, the analysis gives evidence of how commentators constructed transnationality. We can elicit how the transnational space of the European polity is conceptualized. Commentators from all countries predominantly highlighted the commonality of economic and political interests. Only to the *Guardian* and *Le Figaro* national interests seem to be clashing. In a similar way, while there are doubts about the trustworthiness of the European partners, there is a remarkable propensity for solidarity across the European political space in particular among German and British commentators. While the discussion of interest and trust already suggests an orientation towards the transnational European level, the overwhelming majority of commentators engage in promoting progressive Europeanism and constructing European identification. Commentators' conceptions of transnationality, which are strongly oriented towards the transnational level, are probably at least in part a result of their strong involvement in transnational interaction and communication. At the same time, the strong ideological undertone of the utopian concept of progressive Europeanism and the deliberate construction and invocation of a transnational European sense of community could also be interpreted as a compensatory reaction to the absence of a transnational political space as an everyday reality beyond the long corridors of Brussels offices.[110] However, both interpretations can only be verified by studying changes in transnational communication in the course of the evolution of a European public sphere and concomitant changes in the conception of transnationality. This clearly requires a long-term analysis of later summits and European Council meetings.

Notes

1 Jan-Henrik Meyer, 'Europäische Öffentlichkeit aus historischer Sicht', in Ulrich K. Preuß and Claudio Franzius (eds.), *Europäische* Öffentlichkeit, Baden-Baden: Nomos, 2004, pp. 209–27, here p. 221f.
2 Cf. for example Sören Brinkmann, 'Bilder eines Krieges. Europa und der Bürgerkrieg in Spanien', in Jörg Requate and Martin Schulze-Wessel (eds.), *Europäische* Öffentlichkeit. *Transnationale Kommunikation seit dem 18. Jahrhundert*, Frankfurt: Campus, 2002, pp. 250–72, here p. 271f. See also the results of the EMEDIATE

project directed by Bo Stråth, http://www.iue.it/RSCAS/Research/EMEDIATE/, accessed 6 November 2007.

3 Hartmut Kaelble, *Wege zur Demokratie. Von der Französischen Revolution zur Europäischen Union*, Stuttgart: Deutsche Verlagsanstalt, 2001, p. 171.

4 Cf. Klaus Eder, 'Öffentlichkeit und Demokratie', in Markus Jachtenfuchs and Beate Kohler-Koch (eds.), *Europäische Integration*, Opladen: UTB, 2003, pp. 85–120, here p. 85f.

5 Klaus Eder and Cathleen Kantner, 'Transnationale Resonanzstrukturen in Europa. Eine Kritik der Rede vom Öffentlichkeitsdefizit', in Maurizio Bach (ed.), *Die Europäisierung nationaler Gesellschaften*, Opladen: Westdeutscher Verlag, 2000, pp. 306–31, here p. 315.

6 See, for example, Marianne van de Steeg, 'Does a Public Sphere Exist in the EU? An Analysis of the Content of the Debate on the Haider Case?', *European Journal for Political Research*, vol. 45, no.4 (2006), pp. 609–34, here p. 627f.; Hans-Jörg Trenz, *Europa in den Medien. Die europäische Integration im Spiegel nationaler Öffentlichkeit*, Frankfurt: Campus, 2005, pp. 282–88.

7 Kaelble, *Wege zur Demokratie*, p. 161; Bernhard Peters *et al.*, 'National and Transnational Public Spheres. The Case of the EU', in Stephan Leibfried and Michael Zürn (eds.), *Transformations of the State*, Cambridge: Cambridge University Press, 2005, pp. 139–60, here p. 153.

8 Jürgen Habermas, 'Braucht Europa eine Verfassung?', in Jürgen Habermas (ed.), *Zeit der Übergänge*, Frankfurt: Suhrkamp, 2001, pp. 104–29, here p. 120.

9 Hartmut Kaelble, Martin Kirsch and Alexander Schmidt-Gernig, 'Zur Entwicklung Transnationaler Öffentlichkeiten und Identitäten im 20. Jahrhundert. Eine Einleitung', in Hartmut Kaelble, Martin Kirsch and Alexander Schmidt-Gernig (eds.), *Transnationale* Öffentlichkei*ten und Identitäten*, Frankfurt: Campus, 2002, pp. 7–33, here p. 10.

10 This research is part of a larger project. Jan-Henrik Meyer, *Tracing the European Public Sphere 1969–1991. A Comparative Analysis of British, French and German Quality Newspapers Covering European Summits*, PhD, Berlin: Free University, 2008.

11 Franz Knipping and Matthias Schönwald (eds.), *Aufbruch zum Europa der Zweiten Generation: die Europäische Einigung 1969–1984*, Trier: Wissenschaftlicher Verlag Trier, 2004, p. ix. They quote a speech by Gaston Thorn in 1981 for this expression. However, the idea of the second generation was coined by contemporaries. Cf. Pierre Drouin, 'Le Nerf de l'Europe', *Le Monde*, 27 November 1969; Hans-Josef Strick, 'In die zweite Generation', *Süddeutsche Zeitung*, 29 November 1969.

12 See, for example, Jan van der Harst, 'The 1969 Hague Summit: a new Start for Europe?', *Journal of European Integration History*, vol. 9, no. 2, (2003), pp. 5–9, here p. 5; Jürgen Mittag and Wolfgang Wessels, 'Die Gipfelkonferenzen von Den Haag (1969) und Paris (1972): Meilensteine für Entwicklungstrends der Europäischen Union?', in Knipping and Schönwald (eds.), *Aufbruch zum Europa*, pp. 3–27, here p. 4.

13 For an overview of these criteria see Christiane Eilders, 'News Factors and News Decisions. Theoretical and Methodological Advances in Germany', *Communications. The European Journal of Communication Research*, vol. 31, no. 1 (2006), pp. 5–24, here p. 8.

14 Jürgen Gerhards, 'Westeuropäische Integration und die Schwierigkeiten der Entstehung einer Europäischen Öffentlichkeit', *Zeitschrift für Soziologie*, vol. 22, no. 2 (1993), pp. 96–110, here p. 103.

15 Desmond Dinan, *Europe Recast: a History of European Union*, Boulder: Lynne Rienner, 2004, p. 129; van der Harst, 'The 1969 Hague Summit', p. 5.

16 Jan-Henrik Meyer, 'A European Public Sphere at the Summits of The Hague (1969) and Paris (1974)? Common Issues and Frames in British, French and German Newspapers', in Jan van der Harst (ed.), *Beyond the Customs Union: The European*

124 *Jan-Henrik Meyer*

Community's Quest for Completion, Deepening and Enlargement, 1969–1975, Bruxelles: Bruylant, 2007, pp. 341–57.

17 Friedhelm Neidhardt, Christiane Eilders and Katrin Voltmer, 'Einleitung. Die Stimme der Medien – Pressekommentare als Gegenstand der Öffentlichkeitsforschung', in Christiane Eilders, Friedhelm Neidhardt and Barbara Pfetsch (eds.), *Die Stimme der Medien. Pressekommentare und politische Öffentlichkeit in der Bundesrepublik Deutschland*, Wiesbaden: Verlag für Sozialwissenschaften, 2004, pp. 11–38, here p. 11.

18 Editorials and other comment-style articles on EC politics from British, German and French quality newspapers were chosen for the analysis, as they best reflect how the journalists discuss the opinions of actors from other member-states and European relations. For each country, a left-leaning and a conservative paper were selected: *The Guardian* and *The Daily Telegraph; Süddeutsche Zeitung* and *Frankfurter Allgemeine Zeitung;* and *Le Monde* and *Le Figaro*. The summit was covered during a two-week period around the event from 24 November–6 December 1969. The summit took place from 2–3 November 1969.

19 In *Le Figaro*, British *Financial Times* journalist Reginald Dale discusses the EC's competition policy. This is made explicit to the readers as the *Financial Times'* logo is placed in the text. Reginald Dale, 'La CEE s'en prend', *Le Figaro*, 6 December 1969.

20 Brian Brivati and Richard Cockett, 'Profile of Peter Jenkins', in Brian Brivati and Richard Cockett (eds.), *Anatomy of Decline: the Political Journalism of Peter Jenkins. Introduction by Polly Toynbee*, London: Cassell, 1995, pp. 15–22, here pp. 17 and 21. For the Königswinter conferences see: http://www.debrige.de/documents/Konigswinter Konferenzenseit1950.pdf (1 October 2007).

21 E.g. Maxim Fackler, 'Die italienischen Parteien', *Politische Studien*, vol. 5, no. 59 (1955), pp. 30–38, Maxim Fackler, 'The French-German Treaty: The End of Hereditary Enmity', *The World Today*, vol. 21, no. 1 (1965), pp. 24–33.

22 Andrew Marr, *My Trade. A Short History of British Journalism*, London: Pan MacMillan, 2005, p. 374f.

23 Cf. for these measures that saved Jewish children: Wolfgang Benz, Claudia Curio, and Andrea Hammel, 'Special Issue: Kindertransporte 1938/39 – Rescue and Integration', *Shofar: An Interdisciplinary Journal of Jewish Studies*, vol. 23, no. 1 (2004), pp. 1–131.

24 A series of biographical and historical interviews with Hella Pick is available at: http://www.londonmet.ac.uk/genesis/search/$-search-results.cfm?CCODE = 690 (1 October 2007).

25 Olivier Baisnée, 'Can Political Journalism exist at the EU level', in Raymond Kuhn and Erik Neveu (eds.), *Political Journalism: New Challenges, New Practices*, London: Routledge, 2002, pp. 108–28, here p. 111.

26 Gerhards, 'Westeuropäische Integration', p. 107.

27 In July 2004, I conducted interviews with the Brussels correspondents of all of the newspapers used in this study, as well as the French, British and German permanent representations' spokespersons. See also Christoph O. Meyer, *Europäische Öffentlichkeit als Kontrollsphäre. Die Europäische Kommission, die Medien und politische Verantwortung*, Berlin: Vistas, 2002. p. 122.

28 Ibid.

29 Cf. Jürgen Eick, 'Hans Herbert Götz 60', *Frankfurter Allgemeine Zeitung*, 29 January 1981.

30 Walter Hallstein, Hans Herbert Götz and Karl-Heinz Narjes, *Der unvollendete Bundesstaat: Europäische Erfahrungen und Erkenntnisse*, Düsseldorf: Econ, 1969.

31 Walter Farr, *Daily Telegraph Guide to the Common Market*, London: Collins, 1972.

32 Studies available focus on recent developments, for example Olivier Baisnée, 'Le corps de presse accrédité auprès de l'Union européenne: une comparaison franco-britannique', in Dominique Marchetti (ed.), *En quête d'Europe: médias*

européens et médiatisation de l'Europe, Rennes: Presses Université de Rennes, 2004, pp. 153–75.

33 Drouin, 'Le Nerf de l'Europe'; Strick, 'In die zweite Generation'; idem., 'Ursachen der Hoffnung für die Haager Gipfelkonferenz', *Süddeutsche Zeitung*, 28 November 1969.

34 Strick, 'In die zweite Generation'.

35 Idem., 'Ursachen der Hoffnung für die Haager Gipfelkonferenz'.

36 'L'Europe en mal de relance', *Le Monde*, 27 November 1969.

37 Peter Jenkins, 'Still Vague in the Hague', *The Guardian*, 3 December 1969.

38 Hermann Probst, 'Von Gipfel zu Gipfel', *Süddeutsche Zeitung*, 6 December 1969.

39 Jean Domenge, 'De laborieuses négociations', *Le Figaro*, 5 December 1969; NB, 'Im Rittersaal und draußen', *Frankfurter Allgemeine Zeitung*, 2 December 1969.

40 For a similar specification see Stefanie Sifft *et al.*, 'Segmented Europeanization: Exploring the Legitimacy of the European Union from a Public Discourse Perspective', *Journal of Common Market Studies*, vol. 45, no. 1 (2007), pp. 127–55, here p. 142.

41 'The Makings of a Welcome', *The Guardian*, 3 December 1969; 'To pay for France's Farmers', *The Guardian*, 25 November 1969.

42 Peter Jenkins, 'Operation Verité', *The Guardian*, 25 November 1969.

43 Walter Farr, 'Single European Foreign policy', *The Daily Telegraph*, 24 November 1969.

44 Peterborough, 'As You Were', *The Daily Telegraph*, 2 December 1969.

45 Jürgen Eick, 'Die teuflische Doppelfunktion', *Frankfurter Allgemeine Zeitung*, 25 November 1969.

46 Robert Lemaignen, 'La Commission de Bruxelles doit-elle rester serve', *Le Monde*, 27 November 1969.

47 Probst, 'Von Gipfel zu Gipfel'.

48 For example Farr, 'Single European Foreign policy'; 'Sacred Cows Among the Six', *The Guardian*, 1 December 1969; 'Europe's Door Ajar', *The Daily Telegraph*, 3 December 1969.

49 Peter Jenkins, 'The Rhetoric Lingers on', *The Guardian*, 5 December 1969.

50 Maxim Fackler, 'Vor dem Ende der WEU-Krise', *Süddeutsche Zeitung*, 6 December 1969.

51 Idem., 'Europäische Fanfarenstöße', *Süddeutsche Zeitung*, 1 December 1969; Jürgen Tern, 'Warten auf Pompidou', *Frankfurter Allgemeine Zeitung*, 1 December 1969.

52 See, for example, Maxim Fackler, 'Gefestigte Gemeinschaft', *Süddeutsche Zeitung*, 3 December 1969; Hans Herbert Götz, 'Neues Vertrauen in Europa', *Frankfurter Allgemeine Zeitung*, 4 December 1969.

53 Probst, 'Von Gipfel zu Gipfel'.

54 *Guardian*, 'The Makings of a Welcome'; Jenkins, 'Still Vague in The Hague'; *Telegraph*, 'Europe's Door Ajar'.

55 Le Monde, 'L'Europe en mal de relance', *Le Monde*, 27 November 1969.

56 Pierre Uri, 'Recettes pour la Haye', *Le Monde*, 29 November 1969.

57 Paul Fabra, 'Les six et la monnaie', *Le Monde*, 4 December 1969; Lemaignen, 'La Commission'; 'Un compromis', *Le Monde*, 4 December 1969.

58 See, for example, Gerhards, 'Westeuropäische Integration', p. 106f. For a critique of this notion cf. Cathleen Kantner, *Kein modernes Babel: kommunikative Voraussetzungen europäischer Öffentlichkeit*, Wiesbaden: Verlag für Sozialwissenschaften, 2004, pp. 118–20.

59 Kaelble, Kirsch and Schmidt-Gernig, 'Zur Entwicklung transnationaler Öffentlichkeiten', p. 10. For a similar distinction see Peter Friedemann and Lucian Hölscher, 'Internationale, International, Internationalismus', in Otto Brunner, Werner Conze, and Reinhardt Koselleck (eds.), *Geschichtliche Grundbegriffe. Historisches Lexikon zur Geschichte der politisch-sozialen Sprache in Deutschland*, Stuttgart: Klett-Cotta, 1982, pp. 367–97, here pp. 392–97.

60 See, for example, 'To pay for France's Farmers'; Hella Pick, 'The Farmers and Their Surplus of Sacred Cows'; *The Guardian*, 29 November 1969.

61 Walter Farr, 'European Notebook', *The Daily Telegraph*, 25 November 1969; Maurice Green, 'The Heartfelt Road to Europe', *The Daily Telegraph*, 25 November 1969.

62 Maxim Fackler, 'Europa – am Tag danach', *Süddeutsche Zeitung*, 4 December 1969; Strick, 'In die zweite Generation'.

63 For example Eick, 'Die teuflische Doppelfunktion'; Hans Herbert Götz, 'Die Agrarpreise senken', *Frankfurter Allgemeine Zeitung*, 24 November 1969.

64 For example Eick, 'Die teuflische Doppelfunktion'; Jürgen Tern, 'Den Haag zweiter Teil', *Frankfurter Allgemeine Zeitung*, 28 November 1969.

65 Tern, 'Den Haag zweiter Teil'; cf. Ann-Christina Lauring Knudsen, 'Creating the Common Agricultural Policy. Story of Cereals Prices', in Wilfried Loth (ed.) *Crises and Compromises: the European Project 1963–1969*, Baden-Baden: Nomos, 2001, pp. 131–54, here p. 131.

66 Cf. Henri Frénay, 'Pour un référendum', *Le Monde*, 2 December 1969; 'L'Europe en mal de relance'; Uri, 'Recettes pour la Haye'.

67 This overlap of arguments is most likely a result of transnational communication, see discussion in the previous section.

68 'L'Europe en mal de relance'.

69 'L'Heure de l'audace', *Le Monde*, 29 November 1969; Roger Massip, 'Un nouveau départ', *Le Figaro*, 4 December 1969.

70 William Davis, '"Let's get Blowing" Suggests Aunt Bertha', *The Guardian*, 24 November 1969.

71 See, for example, Green, 'The Heartfelt Road to Europe'; Roland Gribben, 'Into Europe - if the Price is Right', *The Daily Telegraph*, 4 December 1969.

72 Farr, 'Single European Foreign policy'.

73 See, for example, Mark Arnold-Forster, 'What the Ministers Want', *The Guardian*, 29 November 1969; Jenkins, 'Operation Verité'.

74 Fackler, 'Europäische Fanfarenstöße'; Farr, 'Single European Foreign policy'.

75 Pierre Fauchon, 'Sommets européens', *Le Monde*, 1 December 1969; Uri, 'Recettes pour la Haye'.

76 Massip, 'Un nouveau départ'; Jean-Pierre Soisson, 'Décembre à Courbevoie', *Le Figaro*, 2 December 1969.

77 Jan Reifenberg, 'Pompidous europäischer Realismus', *Frankfurter Allgemeine Zeitung*, 6 December 1969; Strick, 'In die zweite Generation'; Tern, 'Den Haag zweiter Teil'; Adelbert Weinstein, 'Nato und Entspannungspolitik', *Frankfurter Allgemeine Zeitung*, 2 December 1969.

78 See, for example, Robert Gildea, 'Myth, Memory and Policy in France', in Jan-Werner Müller (ed.), *Memory and Power in Post-War Europe. Studies in the Presence of the Past*, Cambridge: Cambridge University Press, 2002, pp. 59–75, here p. 62.

79 For example Louis Cartou, 'Crise monétaire et faillite de l'Europe à la carte', *Le Monde*, 2 December 1969; Paul Fabra, 'Créer la base industrielle nécessaire à l'indépendance du vieux continent', *Le Monde*, 2 December 1969; 'L'Heure de l'audace'; Soisson, 'Décembre à Courbevoie'.

80 For example Drouin, 'Le Nerf de l'Europe'; Alain Vernay, 'Fiançailles monétaires', *Le Figaro*, 4 December 1969.

81 'Un manque de souffle', *Le Monde*, 3 December 1969.

82 Roger Massip, 'L'enjeu de La Haye', *Le Figaro*, 27 November 1969; 'Un compromis'; 'Une cathédrale gothique', *Le Monde*, 5 December 1969.

83 Clemens A. Wurm, 'Sozialisten und europäische Integration. Die britische Labour Party 1945–84', *Geschichte in Wissenschaft und Unterricht*, vol. 38, no. 5 (1987), pp. 280–95, here p. 290f.

84 Karl Wolfgang Deutsch *et al.*, *Political Community and the North Atlantic Area. International Organization in the Light of Historical Experience*, Princeton: Princeton University Press, 1957, p. 36.

85 Jens Beckert *et al.*, 'Einleitung', in Jens Beckert, *et al.* (eds.), *Transnationale Solidarität. Chancen und Grenzen*, Frankfurt: Campus, 2004, pp. 9–14, here p. 9.

86 Farr, 'Single European Foreign policy'; Green, 'The Heartfelt Road to Europe'.

87 Green, 'The Heartfelt Road to Europe'; 'Europe Meets', *The Daily Telegraph*, 1 December 1969.

88 Fackler, 'Vor dem Ende der WEU-Krise'.

89 Jenkins, 'The Rhetoric Lingers on'.

90 Green, 'The Heartfelt Road to Europe'. Cf. Ann-Christina Lauring Knudsen, 'Le mythe de l'accord franco-allemand: retour sur les origines de la politique agricole commune', in Éric Bussière, Michel Dumoulin and Sylvain Schirmann (eds.), *Milieux économiques et intégration européenne au XXe siècle*, Paris: Ministère de l'économie des finances et de l'industrie, 2005, pp. 218–38.

91 kpk, 'Noch mehr Obstüberschüsse', *Frankfurter Allgemeine Zeitung*, 28 November 1969; Hans-Josef Strick, 'Der Filz der Vorbehalte,' *Süddeutsche Zeitung*, 25 November 1969.

92 Peterborough, 'As You Were'; idem., 'Six who Found in Britain a Friend', *The Daily Telegraph*, 1 December 1969. For this motif in British collective memory ('having held out alone') cf. Tony Judt, *Postwar: A History of Europe since 1945*, London: Penguin Press, 2005, p. 163f., N. Piers Ludlow, 'Us or Them? The meanings of 'Europe' in British political discourse', in Mikael af Malmborg and Bo Stråth (eds.), *The Meaning of Europe: Variety and Contention within and among Nations*, Oxford: Oxford University Press, 2002, pp. 101–24, here p. 111.

93 Bruno Dechamps, 'Neue gute Chance', *Frankfurter Allgemeine Zeitung*, 3 December 1969; 'Sacred Cows Among the Six'; Margot Lyon, 'Fear and Fury on the Farm', *The Guardian*, 26 November 1969; Hella Pick, 'The Snares and the Delusions', *The Guardian*, 29 November 1969.

94 Peter Jenkins, 'Flesh on old Bones', *The Guardian*, 2 December 1969. Similar is Lyon, 'Fear and Fury on the Farm'.

95 Strick, 'Der Filz der Vorbehalte'.

96 Cf. Pierre Gerbet, *La construction de l'Europe*, Paris: Imprimerie Nationale, 1999, p. 216; Franz Knipping, *Rom, 25. März 1957: die Einigung Europas*, Munich: Deutscher Taschenbuchverlag, 2004, p. 113f.

97 Cartou, 'Crise monétaire'; Massip, 'L'enjeu de La Haye'; Jean Schwoebel, 'Le chef de l'état veut amener les Six à affirmer leur solidarité', *Le Monde*, 2 December 1969.

98 Trenz, *Europa in den Medien*, p. 361.

99 Cf. Bo Stråth, 'A European Identity. To the Historical Limits of a Concept', *European Journal of Social Theory*, vol. 5, no. 4 (2002), pp. 387–401, here p. 396.

100 On the use of progress as a political argument that has enjoyed legitimacy since the age of enlightenment see Reinhart Koselleck, '"Erfahrungsraum" und"Erwartungshorizont" – zwei historische Kategorien', in Reinhart Koselleck (ed.), *Vergangene Zukunft: Zur Semantik geschichtlicher Zeiten*, Frankfurt: Suhrkamp, 1979, pp. 349–75, here p. 363. (English translation: Reinhart Koselleck, *Futures Past. On the Semantics of Historical Time*, New York: Columbia University Press, 2004 [1985].)

101 For example Fauchon, 'Sommets européens'; Jean Lecerf, 'Trois objectifs majeurs', *Le Figaro*, 27 November 1969; Strick, 'Ursachen der Hoffnung für die Haager Gipfelkonferenz'; Tern, 'Warten auf Pompidou'.

102 Farr, 'Single European Foreign policy'; *Telegraph*, 'Europe Meets'.

103 Peterborough, 'Six who Found in Britain a Friend'.

104 Green, 'The Heartfelt Road to Europe'.

105 See, for example, Drouin, 'Le Nerf de l'Europe'; Massip, 'L'enjeu de La Haye'; NB, 'Im Rittersaal und draußen'; Strick, 'Der Filz der Vorbehalte'.

106 Davis, '"Let's get Blowing" suggests Aunt Bertha'.

107 Farr, 'Single European Foreign policy'.

108 Cf. for example Jürgen Habermas, 'Remarks on Dieter Grimm's 'Does Europe Need a Constitution?" *European Law Journal*, vol. 1, no. 3 (1995), pp. 303–7, here p. 306.

109 Ruud Koopmans and Paul Statham, 'The Transformation of Political Mobilisation and Communication in European Public Spheres. A Research Outline', europub.com project, 2002, http://www.leeds.ac.uk/ics/euro/europub.pdf. (1 October 2007), p. 11f.
110 This argument is borrowed from Koselleck, '"Erfahrungsraum" und "Erwartungshorizont" – zwei historische Kategorien', p. 374.

8 DG IV and the origins of a supranational competition policy

Establishing an economic constitution for Europe

Katja Seidel

Political scientists Michelle Cini and Lee McGowan state that 'Competition policy is one of the least understood of all the European Union's policies. [I]t has only recently been subjected to systematic scrutiny from a political and public administration perspective'[1] and – one could add – from a historian's perspective.[2] However, this lack of attention does not reflect the importance of this policy. Also referred to as 'the first supranational policy in the European Union',[3] competition policy is a field where the European Commission has acquired extensive powers that can have direct impact on enterprises and individuals in the member-states.

This chapter analyses the formative years of the Directorate-General for Competition (DG IV) in the Commission of the European Economic Community (EEC), focusing in particular on institutionalization and socialization processes within this organization. It will demonstrate how DG IV's evolving institutional culture and its particular outlook were decisive for the policy eventually adopted by the EEC. Discussing institutional theory, Morten Rasmussen highlights in his chapter how rational and historical institutionalist approaches completely over-look the importance of institutional and administrative cultures of European institutions for policy-making. Several sociologically inspired studies have demonstrated, however, that such cultures play a fundamental role in institutional preference formation and policy-making. Hence, institutional culture is important for understanding the relationship between the institution, the policy and the context in which this policy was created.[4] The success of institutionalization depends on the ability of the organization to develop certain values and a mission and to convince actors that pursuing the goals derived from this mission are legitimate and worthwhile. The actors' adoption and internalization of these norms, rules, values and aims could be called socialization. According to Jarle Trondal, '[a]ctors become norm- and rule-driven as a result of the internalization of roles and identities'.[5] The formative years of an institution are crucial with regard to institutionalization and actor socialization. Cini has shown, for exam-ple, that original institutional structures, norms and values in DG IV persisted into the 1990s.[6]

Hans von der Groeben, the first Commissioner responsible for competition policy between 1958 and 1967, had a holistic understanding of competition. Under his leadership competition came to be, and still is considered, one of the central means to promote European integration and to realize the goals laid out in the treaty establishing the EEC. These are the establishment of a common market, the approximation of economic policies, the promotion of harmonious development between the member-states, economic expansion and a higher standard of living for individuals. During von der Groeben's term of office, important groundwork was accomplished and the powers of the Commission in competition policy were established. In 1962, for instance, Regulation 17 entered into force, implementing articles 85 and 86 of the EEC treaty concerned with restrictive practices and monopolies. This regulation, also known as the 'procedural bible',[7] attributed substantial powers to the Commission in cartel policy. It was only replaced in 2003, with Regulation 1/2003.

The first section of this chapter examines how and why the articles dealing with competition were introduced in the EEC treaty. The institutionalization of DG IV and of a certain competition concept developed by von der Groeben and his collaborators will be dealt with in the second section. The third section investigates the recruitment patterns and the biographical background of DG IV's high officials, while the fourth section analyses working methods introduced in DG IV and, linked to this, possible factors of socialization such as expertise, role models, participation and autonomy. These factors induced the officials to adopt DG IV's norms, values and aims. With the establishment of Regulation 17, the fifth section scrutinizes the first tangible result of the Commission's competition policy, attempting to link institutional culture to a particular policy outcome.

Origins of a European competition policy

Competition law in Western Europe is mostly a post-1945 phenomenon.[8] Until 1958 only the French and the German governments had adopted national competition laws, the Dutch government introducing a cartel law only in July 1958.[9] At the European level, the treaty establishing the European Coal and Steel Community (ECSC), 1951, comprised anti-trust rules with articles 65 and 66 that were introduced under the influence of transatlantic networks, as Brigitte Leucht demonstrates in her chapter. Contrary to other policy areas covered by the EEC treaty, competition policy was thus a comparably recent field in which the administrations of member-states had little experience.

During the intergovernmental deliberations in the summer and autumn of 1955, resulting in the so-called Spaak report, it was generally agreed that rules were necessary to prevent competition in the future common market from being distorted.[10] The experts participating in the negotiations, however, showed little inclination to introduce a uniform anti-trust and competition law in all the member-states.[11] During the Val Duchesse negotiations in 1956–57 leading to the signing of the EEC treaty, the delegations could not agree on the nature of competition rules. The opposing positions were represented by the French and the German delegations.[12] The German delegation was in favour of a liberal market economy with competition rules to guarantee fair competition in the common market. The French negotiators were also in favour of a market economy in principle but with an element of planning and greater state intervention.[13] However, the French negotiation position on a European competition policy was not clearly developed. On the one hand there were those who hoped for a modernization boost for the French industry through competition policy, a standpoint defended by leading French civil servants such as Robert Marjolin, Jacques Donnedieu de Vabres and Jean-François Deniau.[14] French industrialists, on the other hand, feared that some sectors of the French economy would not be able to survive increasing competition in a common market.[15] As a result, the French position was not cohesive. It is likely, however, that the more competition-friendly French negotiators were able to use German pressure to override domestic protectionist opposition. In his autobiography, Alfred Müller-Armack, the state secretary in the German economics ministry, describes how the competition rules entered the treaty:

> We had to go to Brussels three times in order to push through a version corresponding to our demands. In particular the French delegation put up fierce resistance until I asked them to present a draft of their own. To our surprise their draft hardly deviated from our ideas and the text codified later on. Without hesitating, I instantly adopted the French proposal.[16]

The main difficulties, however, were to agree upon concrete measures on how to realize a common competition policy and to decide on the distribution of competencies between national governments and community institutions. Hence, the treaty only comprised some basic principles, which were to be fleshed out later on. According to Cini, the EEC competition rules were similar to the first draft for a German competition law, the so-called Josten draft,[17] while Laurent Warlouzet argues that article 85 of the EEC treaty resembled the French law of 1953.[18] These differing interpretations in the literature show that the competition articles were broadly formulated and left room for interpretation. Each negotiation team was therefore able to sell them as a success of their respective government. It was thus up to the Commission, and in particular DG IV, to define a competition policy and to submit proposals to the Council of Ministers. The only target date set by the treaty, in article 87, concerned articles 85 and 86, for which a regulation had to be elaborated within three years of the treaty entering into force.

Institutionalizing DG IV and a certain concept of competition

Nowadays the existence of a directorate-general for competition in the European Commission is taken for granted. However, the following incident shows how a small episode determined future developments in European competition policy. In a first draft of the Commission's organizational scheme, dating from January 1958, Vice-President Marjolin subsumed responsibility for the treaty's competition rules under a large department for political economy and finance. President Walter Hallstein and Commissioner von der Groeben presented this scheme to leading government officials of the ministries of economics and foreign affairs in Bonn.[19] In the meeting, the participants underlined that competition should become an independent unit, reflecting the importance the German government attributed to competition policy. Competition thus became a directorate-general in its own right, led by von der Groeben, a former senior civil servant in Ludwig Erhard's economics ministry. The ground was laid for DG IV to become the 'German' DG in the Commission.[20] Social market economy, a term coined by Müller-Armack, and the ordo-liberalism of the Freiburg School, framed the economics ministry's policy-making[21] and they were no less important for policy-making in DG IV. It is therefore necessary to briefly evoke some of the protagonists and basic principles of this school.

The ordo-liberal Freiburg School was developed in Germany in the early 1930s by an interdisciplinary group of academics at the University of Freiburg, its protagonists being the lawyers Franz Böhm and Hans Großmann-Doerth and the economist Walter Eucken. Having witnessed the downfall of the Weimar Republic and the rise of National Socialism these scholars were convinced that the main problem had been the failure of the legal system to prevent the rise and subsequent abuse of private economic power.[22] Competition was at the heart of their economic and political programme, providing the key to the two goals of economic prosperity and political stability, which in their view were complementary.

Von der Groeben shared this outlook of competition being central to the smooth functioning of an economy. DG IV was attributed responsibility for four sectors: restrictive practices and monopoly policy, state aids, approximation of laws and taxation (articles 85 to 99, EEC treaty). Starting from there, von der Groeben and his collaborators developed a holistic competition concept, corresponding to the ordo-liberal notion of an economic constitution, or *Wirtschaftsverfassung*; that is, an 'economic order based on competition.'[23] They considered that all possible distortions to free competition were interdependent, and therefore these had to be seen in their overall context. Von der Groeben thus conceptualized the common competition policy with the aim of creating a European competition order, or *Wettbewerbsordnung*.[24] Competition policy was seen as *the* co-ordinating instrument in the common market.[25] Following this integral view, DG IV officials considered competition policy as being at the basis of a legally protected common market governed by a regime of fair competition.[26] The dominant idea in DG IV was that conditions of free competition had to be created. With national agencies not being able to cope, it was the Commission's task to use its competencies laid out in the EEC treaty accordingly and, if possible, to extend them. All in all, as in the American anti-trust legislation, the Commission's competition policy had a strong socio-political dimension. Competition had to be protected to keep the market mechanisms operating smoothly but also to protect the individual consumer.[27] The officials of DG IV had to work their way forward in this relatively new policy area. Young officials such as the Italian Aurelio Pappalardo had to familiarize themselves with this concept of competition and in particular with the ordo-liberal Freiburg School and its protagonists such as Eucken and Böhm. Their writings were part of the underlying conception in DG IV. According to Pappalardo, this was: 'cartels are bad, state intervention is bad.'[28]

'Europe's sanguine young men':[29] high officials' recruitment and background

The Commission recruited a Dutch cartel expert as director-general of DG IV. Pieter VerLoren van Themaat studied law at Leiden University where he completed a thesis in anti-trust law. He had extensive experience in Dutch and international cartel policy. Since 1945 VerLoren van Themaat had been first a senior official in and later the director of the directorate 'regulatory questions' in the Dutch ministry of economics. He had worked closely on Dutch cartel policy with the Dutch Minister of Economics, Jelle Zijlstra. As a cartel expert, he had collaborated in the negotiation and completion of the Benelux customs union.[30] Moreover, he had headed a delegation of European cartel experts to the United States, organized by the OEEC, where they visited Harvard University and different governmental organizations concerned with anti-trust policy.[31] VerLoren van Themaat did not participate in the Val Duchesse negotiations, but was consulted as an expert in questions related to competition.[32] As to his recruitment to the EEC Commission, VerLoren van Themaat recalls that he was a candidate of the Dutch government, presented to von der Groeben by Sicco Mansholt.[33] It is not certain whether von der Groeben knew VerLoren van Themaat beforehand. It is likely, though, that he was appointed because of his expertise. His party affiliation possibly played a role too. VerLoren van Themaat was close to the Dutch social democratic Partij van de Arbeid[34] and may have been recruited to counterbalance von der Groeben, a Christian democrat. Nevertheless, collaboration between him and von der Groeben was good, not least because VerLoren van Themaat was fluent in German. Moreover, Dutch cartel policy corresponded more to the German conception of competition than the French, for instance. In a memorandum dating from before the signing of the EEC treaty, VerLoren van Themaat expressed his views on the future European cartel policy. In the Netherlands, cartels were not considered harmful under all circumstances and could even have a useful function. Hence, VerLoren van Themaat hoped that the Commission would follow the Dutch 'medium course in cartelpolicy.'[35] In May 1958, after VerLoren van Themaat was appointed director-general, he put down his first thoughts for von der Groeben.[36] These reflect his particular interest in and his experience with the Dutch, the ECSC and the American competition experiences. For instance, VerLoren van Themaat was in favour of a close dialogue with representatives of consumers, trade unions and industry. This corresponded to the Dutch corporatist tradition as was reflected, for instance, in the Sociaal-Economische Raad (SER), or Socio-Economic Council, introduced in 1950, which was composed of these groups and had advisory functions.[37] VerLoren van Themaat doubted that, considering the different national economic policies in the member-states, a purely 'neo-liberal political philosophy of the Commission'[38] would be acceptable in the Community. At the same time, a policy in favour of restricting competition would also not go down well. He thus suggested the following 'political philosophy' of the Commission in competition policy: DG IV should not advocate a 'total' competition but economic freedom should only be restricted where this was in the interest of the Community. He advocated a 'genuine performance-based competition [. . . and] a more effective division of labour.'[39] These aims could not only be achieved by free competition but should also be facilitated through industry co-operation or public measures.[40]

VerLoren van Themaat was clearly influenced by more socialist-inspired competition conceptions. His emphasis on the possibility of public intervention, the social responsibility of competition policy as well as his rather tolerant attitude vis-à-vis industrial collaboration differed from the German position. Taking this into account, Hallstein wrote to Erhard asking him to nominate a director for the 'cartels and monopolies' directorate in DG IV as a counterweight to Dutch influence.[41] He thought it important to appoint a German for this directorate who would be able to shape this area decisively, which he considered very 'important for European integration'.[42] Hallstein would have liked to appoint Eberhard Günther, head of the German cartel office, for this post. However, Günther was not prepared to enter the Commission as director, a position which would not have been an improvement compared to his independent status as head of the German cartel office. Thus, the directorate A, 'cartels and monopolies', went to Hermann Schumacher who von der Groeben already knew beforehand. Schumacher was the son of the economist Hermann Schumacher who had been the mentor of Eucken.[43]

Directorate A comprised 20 A officials in 1960. By 1963, the number had increased to 34 A officials.[44] It was the largest directorate within DG IV, thus reflecting the importance of cartel policy during the first years of European competition policy. Directorate B, 'approximation of laws', was led by Jean Dieu, a former chef de cabinet of the Belgian minister of justice.[45] The Italian Pietro Nasini headed directorate C, 'tax policy'. Directorate D 'state aid policy' was under the leadership of the Frenchman Armand Saclé, who had worked at the directorate for external economic relations of the French economics ministry. Marjolin had recommended him for a post in the Commission.[46] However, VerLoren van Themaat also knew Saclé from the OEEC trip to the United States.[47] A couple of leading competition experts who shared the experience of having participated in attempts by the Americans to familiarize European experts with the American anti-trust legislation thus entered the Commission. Recruitment of leading officials was based either on recommendations of national governments, as in the case of Dieu and Nasini, or on previous contacts or on both in the case of Saclé. As I will demonstrate below, other, mainly German officials in DG IV shared this American anti-trust experience while also having an educational background in ordo-liberalism. As Wolfram Kaiser argues in his chapter, networks are important for the wider acceptance of policy solutions by social actors. In this case, a small competition community already existed in Western Europe. Other leading officials in DG IV did not have this kind of background, however. They had to familiarize themselves with competition policy after coming to Brussels. This is not surprising, as some

EEC countries had no national competition legislation. Moreover, there were few international negotiations dealing with competition in postwar Europe. In contrast, the case of agricultural policy was quite different. Mansholt, the Commissioner responsible, was able to recruit from a community of internationally experienced and networked agricultural experts when building his Directorate-General for Agriculture.

The average age of DG IV officials entering the Commission's service was 34.7 years.[48] This average confirms the image of the Commission as a young administration.[49] DG IV is usually regarded as a DG controlled by lawyers. However, the ratio of lawyers and economists was equal. Apart from lawyers, VerLoren van Themaat sought to also recruit political economists as he had made the experience in the Dutch economics ministry that these could make a useful contribution to cartel policy.[50] While ten DG IV officials were law graduates, an additional six held a combined degree in law and economics and a further ten officials had a background in economics or political economy. One official had a degree in agriculture combined with a postgraduate degree from the College of Europe in Bruges.

As to previous professional experience, the national civil service clearly dominated with 16 officials having this kind of background. Some of them had worked for agencies such as the German cartel office or the Dutch cartel commission before going to Brussels. Another four officials had been employed in academia. Three came from the ECSC, five from interest groups and unions, one had worked in private business and one had been a barrister. Before entering the Commission, 13 officials had international experience of some kind, including studies abroad, service in international organizations or participation in international negotiations. DG IV's administration was thus composed mainly of young lawyers and economists ready to familiarize themselves with a new policy area with a few having previous experience in the matter. These officials spent an average of 25.2 years in the Commission's administration, and not only in DG IV. VerLoren van Themaat encouraged officials to move into other DGs to constitute a network of allies throughout the Commission.[51] This intensive long-term exposure of the officials to institutional structures is important as it increases the likelihood of their being affected by institutional dynamics and, as a consequence, developing strong loyalties with the institution.[52] Likewise, their relatively young age and their inexperience with competition law made the officials more open and ready to take on and internalize the dominant competition conception in DG IV.

Together with Commissioner von der Groeben and his cabinet these officials set off to develop a European competition policy. Initially, von der Groeben, VerLoren van Themaat and Ernst Albrecht, von der Groeben's chef de cabinet, were most influential in formulating the basic ideas of the Commission's competition policy. Having studied philosophy, theology and political economy, Albrecht wrote his PhD thesis under the supervision of Fritz W. Meyer, one of the leading German neo-liberals. At the age of 23, Albrecht commenced working for the secretariat of the ECSC Council of Ministers in Luxembourg. At the Val Duchesse negotiations he was the secretary of the 'internal market' working group, chaired by von der Groeben. In spite of being the youngest chef de cabinet in the Commission, Albrecht was already an experienced European civil servant when he entered the Commission in 1958. Fluent in French, he served as an intermediary between von der Groeben and those Commissioners and officials with a Romanic background.[53] For Albrecht the American influence on European competition policy was limited. In retrospect, he emphasized that it was due to Germany and its experience with the social market economy that Europe ended up with a common competition policy.[54] Ivo Schwartz was another influential official and later cabinet member in DG IV. He graduated with a degree in law from the University of Freiburg, where one of his teachers was Walter Eucken. He also studied anti-trust law at Harvard law school, and was an assistant to Heinrich Kronstein, a German emigrant professor and cartel expert at the Institute for Foreign and International Trade Law at Georgetown University in Washington. In March 1961, Schwartz drafted an overall concept of European competition policy for von der Groeben which served as a basis for DG IV's activities.[55]

Working methods and other socialization factors

Policy-making in DG IV was essentially academic and expert based.[56] This has to be seen in connection with von der Groeben's ideas regarding a modern and efficient administration. Accordingly, a classical nineteenth and early twentieth century administration, fragmented and hierarchically organized, could not satisfy the needs of the contemporary world where the economy occupied an increasingly important role. A modern administration required new working methods and clear aims.[57] For example, von der Groeben was keen to involve experts and academics in policy-making. Because competition law was a rather recent area of economic policy in Europe, he thought consultation and advice of external experts were all the more important. He recruited Ernst-Joachim Mestmäcker, a pupil of Böhm.[58] A professor at the University of Saarbrücken, Mestmäcker had been familiarized with cartel law of the 1920s, American anti-trust and allied deconcentration law during his studies in Frankfurt.[59] At first, Mestmäcker advised von der Groeben informally. In 1962, this consultancy was institutionalized and he became a special adviser to DG IV.[60] Other advisers to von der Groeben were the German economist Hans Möller, the agriculture expert Hermann Priebe and Jacques Houssiaux, a young economist at Nancy University. Houssiaux had published on competition policy in the common market[61] but, being a younger and less experienced man, he did not have the same impact as Mestmäcker, not least because of the language barrier between him and von der Groeben. Houssiaux was probably appointed out of considerations of national balance. These experts mostly met with von der Groeben and his cabinet, partly also with DG IV officials. In Germany, experts and academics have traditionally served as advisers to political bodies. Von der Groeben even sought to introduce the German tradition into the Commission as a whole. For instance, he sought – in vain – to convince his colleagues to institutionalize a board of economic advisers to the Commission, consisting of external academics and experts and modelled after the Academic Advisory Board, Wissenschaftlicher Beirat, of the German economics ministry.[62] The Academic Advisory Board, founded in January 1948, with Böhm as one of the founders and Mestmäcker becoming a member in 1960, was initially dominated by the Freiburg School.[63]

With his insistence on close and institutionalized contacts with the academic community and experts, von der Groeben was the exception in the Commission in the 1960s.[64] DG IV, like any newly founded institution, had to acquire a good reputation. In the long-term this was facilitated by collaborating with leading experts in the field. Initially, however, DG IV's exclusive focus on mainly German academics was criticized not only externally, but also internally. In one internal paper, the (anonymous) authors deplored the lack of transparency of the decision-making process and of the Commission's competition policy as a whole and the insufficient information policy of DG IV towards what are now often described as societal 'stakeholders'. DG IV officials were accused of a tendency to secrecy as they would only organize meetings, or so-called hearings, with representatives of national administrations and interest groups when a draft or a decision was already finalized. The hearings, the authors deplored, appeared more like gestures of politeness than a mechanism for real consultation.[65]

Especially for the cartel policy sector, Lawrence Scheinman confirms this criticism. 'Some Community pundits have dubbed the cartel sector as "l'Université", especially in view of its tendency to draw heavily on independent experts in the academic community.'[66] It seems that the academic discussions in DG IV left the officials with the impression that they were *the* experts in the matter in the Community. This resulted in the development and the nurturing of a culture of expertise within DG IV, which then became part of the officials' self-perception. The situation seems to have changed during the 1970s. In the late 1970s DG IV officials appear to have become more accessible and they consulted more broadly with (external) professionals concerned with competition policy.[67] The reason for this could be that by then a community of competition experts, consisting of national civil servants, lawyers and academics, had formed with which DG IV collaborated closely, not least because competition policy was beginning to have a tangible impact. From 1958 onwards DG IV organized so-called cartel conferences with representatives of national administrations and Regulation 17 provided for a committee for cartel and monopoly questions. It is likely that these forums have facilitated the incremental formation of a transnational competition network. The participants were socialized into this competition community and developed 'shared causal beliefs and policy aims',[68] which eventually resulted in their backing of the Commission's competition policy. It is thus plausible that the socialization of DG IV officials into a certain concept of competition was followed by the constitution of an expert network transcending the Commission.

Leadership is important for assessing the effectiveness of a directorate-general on the one hand and for facilitating socialization processes on the other. In contemporary interviews, officials emphasized 'the importance of leadership in the early EEC phases for the subsequent patterns of policy development in the various DGs'.[69] In DG IV, von der Groeben and VerLoren van Themaat had an excellent reputation as the founders of the European competition policy.[70] Because they were regarded as successful leaders, they served as role-models for their employees. Their success triggered processes of imitation and social learning. Moreover, frequent and direct contact with these European role models was crucial for motivating DG IV officials. Von der Groeben's working methods facilitated such contacts. He created an atmosphere of open-mindedness and discussion.[71] At least during the first and crucial years, when competition policy was shaped, even younger lower-ranking officials were received and heard by the Commissioner. Von der Groeben organized regular meetings with DG IV officials and members of his cabinet where current topics and problems of competition policy were freely discussed.[72] These meetings resembled the so-called *table ronde* organized by Vice-President Mansholt in the Directorate-General for Agriculture: first one or several officials of DG IV competent in the matter to be discussed gave an introduction and that was followed by an open discussion.[73] Von der Groeben promoted teamwork and discussion even if this meant a 'loosening of hierarchies'.[74] He was particularly in favour of involving younger officials in the policy-making process and to assign them their own areas of responsibility, thus fighting not only the 'horizontal but also the vertical isolation'.[75] For von der Groeben, Mansholt's round table model was an ideal mechanism for excluding secretiveness and avoiding lack of co-operation. To him, teamwork was particularly important in a multinational administration because the different economic and political developments in the member-states and the resulting repercussions for EEC-level policy-making would require a constant collaboration between Commission officials of several nationalities.[76] VerLoren van Themaat had similar working methods. He held regular meetings at DG IV level and weekly meetings with the directors[77] and he also created ad hoc working groups.[78] The feeling of being able to contribute to the decision-making process was important and created a strong sense of solidarity with the aims and values of DG IV. According to the available eyewitness evidence, this facilitated the formation of an *esprit de corps* among the civil servants, especially during the founding period when the Commission was still a rather small administration.[79]

Compared to other DGs in the Commission, DG IV stands out because of its autonomy and the direct influence it can exert on the economy in the common market. For von der Groeben, the Common Agricultural Policy (CAP) has always been in the hands of the member-states whereas in competition policy the Commission was autonomous in the implementation of regulations. Furthermore, the Commission's autonomy in this sector was subsequently extended with the help of Court rulings strengthening the Commission's position.[80] This autonomy and a sense of 'being different' were deeply engrained in the self-perception of DG IV officials. Pappalardo believes, for example, that competition was different from other services in the Commission: 'DG Competition is an exception in this "mega-mechanism" still today. The competition regulations are to a large extent applicable without consent of the Council.'[81] DG IV 'celebrates its autonomy from the council' as Michelmann put it.[82] The officials took pride in their effective and important policy sector. Similarly, the idea of being the 'judges' of the Commission was propagated by some officials.[83] After all, DG IV has judicial functions and its rulings affect enterprises and the governments themselves. Their judge-like task had an influence on the officials and their relation with the outside world. DG IV officials nurtured an image of the incorruptibles of the Commission,[84] or the Commission's watchdog.

Expertise, leadership, participation and autonomy were perceived in a positive way by DG IV officials. These factors contributed to creating loyalties and facilitated the adoption and internalization of DG IV's aims, values and norms. The next section will investigate if institutional values influenced the policy-making process in DG IV.

Regulation 17: policy-making at the supranational level

Within the field of competition policy, the Commission first focused on cartel policy, as article 87 decreed that a regulation implementing articles 85 and 86 had to be established within three years. With article 88, however, the EEC treaty provided for local authorities in the member-states to take over responsibility for the application of articles 85 and 86 until the EEC passed a regulation. The Commission tried to enforce this and asked the member-states to co-operate.[85] This turned out to be difficult as only France, Germany and the Netherlands had appropriate legislations. Hence, a regulation providing a European solution in cartel policy became a pressing need. The Commission's proposal, submitted to the Council on 31 October 1960, envisaged a notification system and the general prohibition of restrictive practices and agreements with the possibility of applying for an exemption (article 85, 3). In this draft, the Commission was the only instance authorized to grant permission of an agreement. In spite of vehement protests against this draft of industrialists in Germany, France and Belgium and of member-state governments such as France, these three crucial elements of the initial draft – prohibition of restrictive practices, obligatory notification of agreements to the Commission and the Commission as the only instance to grant an exemption – made it into the final version of Regulation 17, adopted in late December 1961.

In possession of the right of initiative in the Community, the Commission was able to shape the draft in conformity with its ordo-liberal outlook. The most important aim for DG IV was to realize a common line in European cartel policy. This was the lesson the Commission had drawn from the first three years of experience in competition policy, in particular with the unsatisfactory application of article 88 by national agencies. During the process of formulating the regulation, von der Groeben maintained close contact with member-states' politicians and civil servants, members of the European Parliament, the Economic and Social Committee, and the permanent representatives of the member-states. Also, frequent trips to the European capitals by von der Groeben and his collaborators were designed to prepare the ground for the Commission's competition policy.[86] Moreover, in the preparatory phase of the regulation, the Commission convened so-called cartel conferences with experts of the administrations of the member-states as well as working group meetings, which should facilitate reaching a consensus. The Commission sought to avoid the institutionalization of these conferences, however. They were only intended as an informal forum for the exchange of ideas since the Commission wanted to maintain its independence.[87]

A Commission document shows that while it was in favour of organizing regular meetings with experts, presumably from member-states' administrations, it was hesitant when it came to organizing similar meetings with representatives from industry. On the one hand, such meetings were seen as necessary because of the Commission's policy of informing and consulting with interested groups. On the other hand, the Commission did not want to take on an air of exclusiveness. Therefore, it organized similar meetings with trade unions, agricultural and trade interest groups.[88] Not least, business representatives, being among the most critical of the Commission's proposal, should be kept at bay as the Commission's aim was to impose a strict cartel policy. DG IV officials perceived the cartel conferences more as a forum to inform about policy rather than to discuss it. Or, as Scheinman put it, '[t]here does exist a Conference des Ententes which serves as a meeting ground for national Community experts, but this organ has never been turned into a consensus-building body for cartel policy.'[89]

Von der Groeben had achieved that the Council of Ministers would not comment on the Commission's draft regulation but that it was immediately forwarded to the European Parliament.[90] The contribution of the European Parliament, and of its internal market committee in particular, was very useful for the Commission. The committee was chaired by the German lawyer Arved Deringer, a Christian democrat, who shared the Commission's ordo-liberal attitude towards competition.[91] The report of this committee, discussed and adopted by the European Parliament on 19 October 1961, not only backed the Commission's proposal in its general principles but improved it considerably.[92] Crucially, the well argued and balanced report of the internal market committee was an important source of arguments for the Commission in the subsequent Council negotiations on Regulation 17. With the opinion of the European Parliament supporting the Commission's draft, it would have been difficult for the Council to dramatically alter the Commission's proposal. Likewise, the trade unions, who were traditionally opposed to cartels as encroaching on the interests of workers as consumers, backed the Commission in its attempt to achieve a European solution.[93] As to the positions of the different member-states, the German, Dutch and also the Italian governments supported the Commission's proposal.[94] The French government, however, favoured a system of legal exemption instead of the notification regime proposed by the Commission which would empower the Commission to decide on an exemption.[95] In the domestic context, the French administration had traditionally been rather tolerant towards cartels.[96] The French employers' organization, the Conseil National du Patronat Français (CNPF), was also in favour of a lenient competition policy and of integration through industrial agreements. Instead of prohibiting cartels, competition rules should encourage this sort of collaboration between enterprises.[97]

There are three main reasons why, in spite of this opposition, the Commission's view prevailed. First, the French negotiation position was not clearly developed, a situation comparable to the Val Duchesse negotiations. While the French government criticized the Commission's proposal, it did not come up with a convincing alternative suggestion.[98] Instead of lobbying the Commission, and DG IV in particular, French business representatives relied on the, in this case, passive French government officials to push through their views.[99] Second, a coalition formed in favour of the Commission's proposal composed of the internal market committee of the European Parliament, trade unions, the German government and its federal cartel office and the Dutch government. The Italian, Luxembourg and, finally, the Belgian governments also rallied to the Commission's standpoint. Third, Regulation 17 was not a priority for the French government.[100] When it secured major gains in agriculture in the Council negotiations on the CAP of December 1961 and January 1962, it was in return prepared to vote for the regulation after a prohibition of vertical agreements, on which the French government insisted, had been incorporated in the proposal.[101] The CAP and Regulation 17 were tied together in a package-deal and the Council unanimously adopted the regulation on 5 February 1962.

Under Regulation 17, which entered into force on 13 March 1962, the Commission and thus DG IV acquired substantial powers. As Cini and McGowan have put it, 'Regulation 17, based on a German model of notification, evaluation, and exemption, effectively centralized enforcement and marginalized the national authorities.'[102] The Council adopted the initial Commission proposal with relatively little modifications, the main adjustments were made to accommodate suggestions from the report of the internal market committee of the European Parliament.[103] The regulation stipulated that only the Commission was authorized to grant permission for any agreement formed after 13 March 1962. A Court ruling could of course modify or nullify the Commission's decision. Also, the Commission was now in a position to impose fines in cases of abuse, to request information from enterprises and to lead an enquiry in a particular sector.[104] While a committee for cartel and monopoly questions was established on the request of the French government, this merely had to be consulted by DG IV before passing on a decision to the college of Commissioners for approval. Regulation 17 is thus at the heart of the autonomy of DG IV officials.

Conclusions

It is a paradox that, while most German social market and ordo-liberal economists initially opposed regional integration out of fear that it might impede rather than facilitate global trade liberalization as their core objective, their ideas were nevertheless spread through the EEC Commission and in particular DG IV. The French director in DG IV, Saclé, qualified competition as a mind-set or *Geisteshaltung*.[105] This statement coming from a leading French official in DG IV who did not have a background in ordo-liberalism is an indicator for the successful adoption of DG IV's competition ideology by its officials.

Saclé's statement was directed against economic planning, something Marjolin attempted to introduce into the Commission. It is important to emphasize once more the haphazard nature of the creation of a directorate-general for competition, going back to a decision of Hallstein and von der Groeben backed by the German government. This episode shows how a single decision at an early point in time can determine the path for future developments, thus confirming historical institutionalists' claims that small and often unintended events can have a disproportionate effect on policy outcome. In this respect it needs to be underlined that it is most unlikely that, had Marjolin been responsible for competition policy, he would have come up with a similar proposal for what has become Regulation 17. DG IV subsequently defended the principle of competition as the basis of the common market. Von der Groeben and DG IV were considered a fortress against French dirigisme and planning.[106] When in 1966 the renewal of the Commissioners' term of office was discussed, Karl-Heinz Narjes, Hallstein's chef de cabinet, wrote to the Commission president that von der Groeben was an important figure in the Commission because he was 'an effective barrier against the dissemination of economic planning and other ideas of statism in Germany and the Benelux countries'.[107] Narjes was concerned that if after the merger of the executives in 1967, DG IV was to be reorganized and von der Groeben was to leave, it might be impossible to maintain this barrier.

The institutionalization of DG IV as the Commission's bulwark of economic liberalism clearly had an impact on the shape of the common competition policy. The Commission's proposal for Regulation 17 was in line with the ordo-liberal preferences of von der Groeben and leading DG IV officials. It was equally in line with the institutional and policy culture of DG IV reflected in the aim of realizing a European competition policy following the ordo-liberal concept of an economic constitution. Lastly, the Commission benefitted from its right of initiative and could define the principles of its proposal for Regulation 17. In this chapter, I demonstrated how a particular path and institutional culture can impact on preference formation in institutions and ultimately influence the shape of a Community policy. Narrowly conceptualized rational choice approaches such as Liberal Intergovernmentalism which exclude factors such as ideas as embedded in institutional cultures from the analysis of decision-making fail to give convincing explanations for policy formation.

When it came to putting its preferences into practice, however, the Commission had to rely on external factors such as a strong coalition in favour of the Commission's proposal. These are the limits to the influence an organization such as DG IV can have on policy outcomes in a multi-level political system such as the EEC. While this chapter demonstrates that DG IV officials were socialized into DG IV's institutional culture through mechanisms such as leadership, expertise and autonomy, it is difficult to measure the direct impact of socialization on Regulation 17. The regulation was elaborated only three years after the EEC was founded. Socialization appears to be a long-term process, which is reinforced over time. It is likely that the powers DG IV obtained through Regulation 17 triggered new, or intensified the impact of, certain socialization factors. For instance, the factor of autonomy certainly gained momentum only *after* Regulation 17 entered into force as this regulation constituted the basis of DG IV's independence. Hence, a policy and its effects in turn also impact on institutionalization and can fuel socialization processes. These processes do not only affect actors within the Commission. As I have demonstrated, a network of competition experts, consisting of academics, lawyers, judges and national civil servants that were socialized into the Commission's competition concept, emerged in the 1970s.

The downside of the Commission's success to concentrate decisions in competition policy at the supranational level became evident in the aftermath of the implementation of Regulation 17. DG IV received more than 34,000 notifications of bilateral and multilateral agreements, but only had some 40 people in directorate A dealing with this flood. DG IV was paralyzed. In 1965 the Council adopted a block exemptions regulation, the practical solution to the problem. The first major decisions in monopoly cases were taken in 1968–69 and a first fine was imposed on an enterprise. The court rulings of the 1970s solidified competition jurisdiction and practice and strengthened the Commission's role.[108] Moreover, three of the first officials of DG IV, Ernst Albrecht, Manfred Caspari and Willy Schlieder, became director-general for competition in the 1960s and 1970s,[109] thus assuring continuity in European competition policy. The initial competition concept of DG IV was perpetuated.

Notes

1 Michelle Cini, Lee McGowan, *Competition Policy in the European Union*, Basingstoke: Macmillan, 1998, p. 1.
2 Notable exceptions are Sibylle Hambloch, 'Die Entstehung der Verordnung 17 von 1962 im Rahmen der EWG-Wettbewerbsordnung', *Europarecht*, vol. 37, no. 6 (2002), pp. 877–97; Laurent Warlouzet, 'La France et la mise en place de la politique de la concurrence communautaire (1957–64)', in Eric Bussière, Michel Dumoulin and Sylvain Schirmann (eds.), *Europe organisée, Europe du libre-échange. Fin XIXe siècle – Années 1960*, Brussels: P.I.E.-Peter Lang, 2006, pp. 175–201. I am grateful to Sibylle Hambloch for kindly making some of the interviews she conducted with DG IV officials available to me.
3 Lee McGowan and Stephen Wilks, 'The First Supranational Policy in the European Union: Competition Policy', *European Journal of Political Research*, vol. 28, no. 2 (1995), pp. 141–69.
4 For a definition of (institutional) culture see Michelle Cini, 'La Commission européenne: lieu d'émergence de cultures administratives. L'exemple de la DG IV et de la DG XI', *Revue française de science politique*, vol. 46, no. 3 (1996), pp. 457–72, here p. 458. See also Michelle Cini, *Policing the Internal Market: the Regulation of Competition in the European Commission*, PhD, Exeter: Exeter University, 1994, p. 33.
5 Jarle Trondal, 'Political Dynamics of the Parallel Administration of the European Commission', in Andy Smith (ed.), *Politics and the European Commission: Actors, Interdependence, Legitimacy*, London: Routledge, 2004, pp. 67–82, here p. 74.
6 Cf. Cini 'La Commission'.
7 Cini and McGowan, *Competition Policy*, p. 13.
8 See David J. Gerber, *Law and Competition in Twentieth Century Europe: Protecting Prometheus*, Oxford: Clarendon Press, 1998, for early twentieth century attempts to realize competition legislation in Europe.

9   The German Gesetz gegen Wettbewerbsbeschränkung (GWB), 27 July 1957; in France
    the Ordonnance No. 45–1483, 30 June 1945 and the law of 1953; and the Dutch cartel
    law, 16 July 1958. The Italian *Codice Civile* only included a couple of vague articles
    on competition.
10 Rapport des chefs de delegation aux ministres des Affaires étrangères, Bruxelles,
    21 avril 1956, esp. Title II, chapter I, published on European Navigator, http://www.
    ena.lu?lang=1&doc=13904 (accessed 4 November 2007).
11 Hanns Jürgen Küsters, *Die Gründung der Europäischen Wirtschaftsgemeinschaft*,
    Baden-Baden: Nomos, 1982, p. 180.
12 Ibid., p. 364.
13 Warlouzet, 'La France', p. 179.
14 Küsters, *Die Gründung*, p. 366.
15 Hans von der Groeben, *Aufbaujahre der Europäischen Gemeinschaft. Das Ringen um
    den Gemeinsamen Markt und die Politische Union (1958–1966)*, Baden-Baden: Nomos,
    1982, p. 80, footnote 51.
16 Alfred Müller-Armack, *Auf dem Weg nach Europa. Erinnerungen und Ausblicke*,
    Tübingen: Rainer Wunderlich, Stuttgart: C. E. Poeschel, 1971, p. 114.
17 Cini, *Policing*, p. 44.
18 Warlouzet, 'La France', p. 179.
19 Aufzeichnung betr. Besprechung über Organisations-und Personalfragen von EWG
    am 26. Januar 1958, 27 January 1958, Deutsches Bundesarchiv, Koblenz (BA),
    Personal papers Walter Hallstein (N 1266), 1092.
20 Cini, 'La Commission', p. 466.
21 Bernhard Löffler, *Soziale Marktwirtschaft und administrative Praxis: das
    Bundeswirtschaftsministerium unter Ludwig Erhard*, Stuttgart: Steiner, 2002, see
    especially chapter B.3.
22 Gerber, *Protecting*, p. 235.
23 Ibid., p. 241.
24 Hans von der Groeben, 'Wettbewerbspolitik in der europäischen Gemeinschaft',
    Bulletin der EWG, No. 7/8 (1961), pp. 3–31, here p. 10.
25 Ibid., p. 12.
26 Ibid., p. 5.
27 Ivo Schwartz interviewed by Sibylle Hambloch, Brussels, 2 May 2002.
28 Interview with Aurelio Pappalardo, Brussels, 8 March 2005.
29 'The Eurocrats', *The Economist*, 29 July 1961, p. 449
30 Interview with VerLoren van Themaat, Bilthoven, 29 April 2004; see also
    VerLoren van Themaat interviewed by Sibylle Hambloch and Gerold Ambrosius,
    Bilthoven, 26 February 2002.
31 See VerLoren van Themaat, interviewed by Sibylle Hambloch and Gerold Ambrosius.
    See also Brigitte Leucht, 'Tracing European Mentalities: Free competition in post-
    WW II transatlantic Europe', in Marie-Thérèse Bitsch, Wilfried Loth, Charles Barthel
    (eds.), *Cultures politiques, opinions publiques et integration européenne*, Brussels:
    Bruylant, 2007, pp. 337–53, here p. 343f., mentioning a similar case of a journey
    organized by the US European Cooperation Administration (ECA) for German
    anti-trust experts to the US.
32 Interview with Pieter VerLoren van Themaat.
33 Ibid.
34 Ibid. See also the interview with Ernst Albrecht, Burgdorf/Beinhorn, 27 April 2005.
35 Dr. Pieter VerLoren van Themaat, Cartelpolicy in the Netherlands, undated,
    074/1, Archiv für Christlich-Demokratische Politik (ACDP), Personal papers
    Hans von der Groeben (I-659).
36 P. VerLoren van Themaat, Wettbewerbspolitik (Erste Diskussionsgrundlage),
    23 May 1958, 001/2, ACDP, I-659.

37 Johan de Vries, *The Netherlands Economy in the Twentieth Century*, Assen: Van Gorcum & Comp. B.V., 1978, p. 103.
38 P. VerLoren van Themaat, Wettbewerbspolitik (Erste Diskussionsgrundlage), 23 May 1958, 001/2, ACDP, I-659.
39 Ibid.
40 Ibid.
41 President Hallstein to Professor Ludwig Erhard, 11 April 1958, BA, N 1266, 1113.
42 Ibid.
43 http://www-wiwi.uni-muenster.de/~09/ecochron/personen/pm_eucken1.pdf (accessed 27 September 2007).
44 Staff numbers from European Commission, Historical Archives, (ECHA), Folder 'Organigramme'.
45 Information provided by Franz Froschmaier. Interview with Franz Froschmaier, Brussels, 15 April 2004.
46 INT-ECH 718, Armand Saclé, Historical Archives of the European Union (HAEU).
47 VerLoren van Themaat interviewed by Sibylle Hambloch and Gerold Ambrosius.
48 For this chapter, I analyzed the social, educational and professional background of approximately 40 officials of the A career. However, the number of officials working in DG IV surpassed this number already in 1960 when DG IV counted 70 A officials, excluding Commissioner von der Groeben's personal cabinet staff. The figures in the following paragraph are the author's own calculations based on information derived from interviews, curriculum vitaes and memoirs.
49 See for example 'The Eurocrats', *The Economist*, 29 July 1961, p. 449.
50 VerLoren van Themaat interviewed by Sibylle Hambloch and Gerold Ambrosius.
51 Interview with Eduard Brackeniers, Brussels, 10 March 2005.
52 Trondal, 'Political dynamics', p. 79f.
53 Ivo Schwartz interviewed by Sibylle Hambloch.
54 Interview with Ernst Albrecht.
55 This was published under von der Groeben's name in the EC Bulletin. Von der Groeben, 'Wettbewerbspolitik'.
56 The argument in this section is based on primary sources from von der Groeben's private papers, interviews with former DG IV officials, and social science literature on the EEC Commission of the 1970s, which I utilize as a source.
57 Hans von der Groeben, Vermerk für die Herren Mitglieder der Kommission, Betr: Arbeitsmethoden der Kommission, 29 June 1962, 058/1, ACDP, I-659.
58 Between 1925 and 1931 Böhm had worked in the cartel department of the Reichswirtschaftsministerium in the Weimar Republic.
59 Erich Mestmäcker interviewed by Sibylle Hambloch, Hamburg, 4 October 2002.
60 Ivo Schwartz, 'Ernst-Joachim Mestmäcker als "stiller Europäer"', in Christoph Engel, Wernhard Möschel (eds.), *Recht und spontane Ordnung. Festschrift für Ernst-Joachim Mestmäcker zum achtzigsten Geburtstag*, Baden-Baden: Nomos, 2006, pp. 459–86, here p. 461.
61 Jacques Houssiaux, *Concurrence et Marché commun* (Collection d'économie moderne), Paris: M. Th. Génin, 1960.
62 von der Groeben, Vermerk für die Herren Mitglieder.
63 Löffler, *Soziale Marktwirtschaft*, p. 72. Löffler calls Böhm and Eucken 'political professors'.
64 While in 1958 Robert Marjolin appointed the Belgian economist Robert Triffin as adviser, he does not even mention Triffin in his biography, *Le travail d'une vie. Mémoires 1911–1986*, Paris: Laffont, 1986.
65 No author, Wettbewerbspolitik der EWG, 2 July 1963, 001/3, ACDP, I-659.
66 Lawrence Scheinman, 'Economic Regionalism and International Administration: The European Community Experience', in Robert S. Jordan (ed.), *International*

Administration: Its Evolution and Contemporary Applications, Oxford: Oxford University Press, 1971, pp. 187–227, here p. 212f.

67 Hans J. Michelmann, *Organizational Effectiveness in a Multinational Bureaucracy*, New York: Praeger, 1978, p. 63.

68 Wolfram Kaiser, 'Transnational Western Europe since 1945. Integration as political society formation', in Wolfram Kaiser, Peter Starie (eds.), *Transnational European Union: Towards a Political Space*, London: Routledge, 2005, pp. 17–33, here p. 22.

69 Michelmann, *Organizational Effectiveness*, p. 170.

70 Cf. the author's eye-witness interviews but also Michelmann, *Organizational Effectiveness* and Cini, *Policing*.

71 See for example the summary of a discussion in DG IV in P. VerLoren van Themaat, Entwurf, Zusammenstellung der wichtigsten Diskussionspunkte im Rahmen der Besprechung mit Herrn von der Groeben über die Wettbewerbspolitik, 20 March 1961, 001/1, ACDP, I-659.

72 Schwartz, 'Ernst-Joachim Mestmäcker', p. 473f.; Interview with Aurelio Pappalardo.

73 See for example Zusammenfassung der Besprechung am 21.6.1962 bei Herrn von der Groeben, 21 June 1962, 001/1, ACDP, I-659.

74 von der Groeben, Vermerk für die Herren Mitglieder.

75 Ibid.

76 Ibid.

77 Interview with the assistant to Director-General VerLoren van Themaat, Brussels, 14 April 2004.

78 Vermerk VerLoren van Themaat an von der Groeben, Zusammenfassender Bericht des Gedankenaustausches zwischen dem Generaldirektor und den Direktoren hinsichtlich der Bildung einer beratenden internen Arbeitsgruppe zur Unterstützung des Generaldirektors bei seinen Koordinierungsaufgaben, 4 November 1964, 002/1, ACDP, I-659.

79 See the author's interviews with former DG IV officials.

80 Hans von der Groeben, *Deutschland und Europa in einem unruhigen Jahrhundert*, Baden-Baden: Nomos, 1995, p. 346.

81 Interview with Aurelio Pappalardo.

82 Michelmann, *Organizational Effectiveness*, p. 78.

83 Interview with Kurt Ritter, Brussels, 3 March 2005.

84 Ibid.

85 PV of the EEC Commission, 25 session, 15–16 July 1958, pt. 23, ECHA, BAC 209.80.

86 Von der Groeben, *Deutschland und Europa*, p. 309.

87 Hambloch, 'Verordnung 17', p. 880f.

88 See the discussion in PV of the EEC Commission, 25 session, 15–16 July 1958, pt. 23, ECHA, BAC 209.80. See also, for instance, the sections on competition policy in the Bulletins of the EEC Commission.

89 Scheinman, 'Economic Regionalism', p. 199, footnote 15.

90 See Pieter VerLoren van Themaat, 'Einige Betrachtungen über die Entwicklung der Wettbewerbspolitik in Europa vor und seit dem Zustandekommen der Verordnung 17/62', in Ulrich Everling, Karl-Heinz Narjes, Joachim Sedemund (eds.), *Europarecht, Kartellrecht, Wirtschaftsrecht. Festschrift für Arved Deringer*, Baden-Baden: Nomos, 1993, pp. 398–415, here, p. 398.

91 On the role of Deringer in the development of Regulation 17 see ibid.

92 Ibid., p. 399.

93 Hambloch, 'Verordnung 17', pp. 888–90.

94 Von der Groeben, *Deutschland und Europa*, p. 309.

95 Hambloch, 'Verordnung 17', p. 891.

96 Warlouzet, 'La France', p. 179.

97 Ibid., p. 180.

98   This is explained in detail in Laurent Warlouzet, *Quelle Europe économique pour la France? La France et le Marché commun industriel, 1956–1969*, PhD, Paris: University of Paris IV, 2007, chapter VI-2.
99   Warlouzet, 'La France', p. 191.
100 Ibid.
101 Hambloch, 'Verordnung 17', p. 895.
102 Cini and McGowan, *Competition Policy*, p. 19.
103 VerLoren van Themaat, 'Einige Betrachtungen', p. 399. A detailed analysis of the initial proposal of Regulation 17 and the modifications it underwent in the negotiation process is beyond the scope of this chapter. Some of the documents leading to Regulation 17 are published in Reiner Schulze, Thomas Hoeren (eds.), *Dokumente zum Europäischen Recht*, Band 3: Kartellrecht, Berlin, Heidelberg: Springer, 2000. These documents are also accessible at http://www.eu-history.info/ (accessed 28 September 2007).
104 Cini, *Policing*, p. 133.
105 Aufgaben der Wettbewerbspolitik in der EWG, Niederschrift über die Besprechung bei Herrn von der Groeben am 12.6.64, 001/1, ACDP, I-659.
106 Ivo Schwartz, Kurzprotokoll, Besprechung von der Groeben, Mestmäcker, Möller, Priebe (zeitweise), Steffe, Wirsing (zeitweise), Schwartz über Wettbewerb und Programmierung, 22 January 1963, 001/1, ACDP, I-659.
107 Karl-Heinz Narjes to President Hallstein, 10 June 1966, BA, N 1266, 1119.
108 Two landmark decisions were: Commission vs Grundig & Consten, Cases 58/64 and 56 [1966] European Court Reports (ECR) 299; Case 6/72, Europemballage Corporation vs Commission [1973] ECR 215 (Continental Can).
109 Willy Schlieder entered the Commission in July 1958 as an A5 official in the Cartels and Monopolies Directorate.

9 The origins of Community information policy

Educating Europeans

Lise Rye

Spurred by negative votes on a European Constitution in France and the Netherlands as well as by a widely recognized gap between the European Union (EU) and its citizens, the European Commission decided in 2005 to make communication one of its strategic objectives.[1] Lack of enthusiasm for the process of integration in general and the proposed constitution in particular was linked to the claim that EU citizens had been kept at a distance from the process of integration for too long and that the result of this was a lack of socialization into the Community.[2] This chapter focuses on early efforts to familiarize Europeans with the process of integration.[3] It deals with the period 1958 to 1967, when the forerunner of today's communication policy, the common information policy of the European Communities (EC), was developed and carried into effect.

Like today, the activity in the field of information in the 1950s and 1960s was marked by the awareness of lack of public support for the European construction. The chapter shows how administrative and political actors within the three executives, that is the executives of the European Coal and Steel Community (ECSC), the European Economic Community (EEC) and the European Atomic Energy Community (Euratom), tried to bring people closer to the process of integration by informing as well as educating nationals of the participating member-states into European citizens. Gradually, and through increasing interaction with other actors, these efforts became a defined policy of information.

On a more general level, the emergence of information policy illustrates relations between the executives as well as relations between the representatives of supranational institutions and the representatives of the member-states. The central argument of the chapter is that information policy developed as a result of the supranational executives' independent action, outside the constitutional framework of the treaties, and that the executives managed to stay in control of the field against the will of member-state representatives. Thus, this account touches upon several of the institutional approaches discussed by Morten Rasmussen in his chapter. Most importantly, however, it illustrates the complexity of the European political system in its early phase as well as the often accidental nature of historical developments, also in EU history.

The legacy of the ECSC

The decision to create a joint service for press and information for the European communities was taken on 31 January 1958, when the executives of the three communities held their first meeting in Luxembourg. The formal initiative came from Jacques-René Rabier, who since 1955 had directed the Press and Information Service of the High Authority. This service constituted an important basis for the development of the Joint Service as its setting up in Brussels required the transfer of staff, ideas and working methods from Luxembourg. Research on the ECSC service has not yet been published. Testimonies from its director indicate, however, that aspects regarding its origins and established views may shed light on some of the questions that the history of the common policy of information raises. One of these questions regards the independence with which the executives were able to operate within the field of information. The second concerns the relationship between the executives and member-state representatives. If we believe Rabier, the views regarding the purpose of information that later would become a source of disagreement between the Hallstein Commission and the French government were not conceived within the Joint Service. Rather, these were long-standing ideas developed within the ECSC Information Service and later transferred from Luxembourg to Brussels, where they would steadily gain support.

On 10 August 1952 the High Authority of the ECSC installed itself in Luxembourg. The ECSC treaty of 1951 contained no dispositions regarding external information. The Press and Information Service of the High Authority can therefore hardly be considered the result of a formal demand from the member-states. In January 1953, Rabier, who in the period of 1946 to 1952 had been the director of Jean Monnet's private office at the French Planning Commission, came to Luxembourg to take up the position as head of Monnet's private office at the ECSC. This marked the beginning of a long career in the field of European information. In both oral and written testimonies, Rabier has later traced the gradual development of an information service to the importance attached by Monnet to public information.[4] Rabier claims that Monnet had always been concerned about the need to make the activity of the institutions in which he worked transparent and traces this to Monnet's experience in the United States. Strongly concerned about the need to clarify and explain the actions of the new community to the public, Monnet's initiatives gradually grew into a service of its own. While Monnet's fellow members in the High Authority took little interest in public information to begin with, at the time of the 1955 Messina conference, both members of the High Authority as well as members of the European Parliament (EP) had realized the importance of an active policy of information.

Rabier's testimonies make clear that the ECSC Information Service had developed clear ideas about the purpose of external information. The service differentiated between two sorts of information. On one hand, there was information of economic and technical nature. Typical recipients were the industrial and commercial communities as well as the EP, who needed to be kept up to date about the workings of the ECSC. On the other hand, the service had from the very beginning concerned itself with the importance of communicating the ideas that had been formulated in the Schuman declaration and that reflected Monnet's ideas about the ultimate purpose of European integration. In keeping with these conceptions, the service was concerned with the need to demonstrate that the process of integration was an essentially political project, the finality of which was the union of the European people. The purpose of information was therefore not only to inform, but to contribute to the education of European citizens. The people of Europe had to be told that the reason behind the setting up of new and complex institutional structures was to create a sort of European patriotism that the uniting of the European people in turn would demand.[5]

The Hallstein Commission, in office from 1958 to 1967, communicated similar views on the purpose of integration. Walter Hallstein himself used numerous occasions to stress the political nature of economic integration. The three communities were, he said, 'aspects of a process of development which in the end should lead to a politically united Europe in a more comprehensive sense'.[6] Social integration was presented as a condition upon which successful political integration would depend. And, while admitting that people's loyalty towards their respective nation-states was strong, Hallstein left no doubt about the fact that it was the purpose of the EEC to eliminate peoples' habits of regarding the nation-state as the normal unit of social and economic development.[7]

The emphasis on the need to change the minds and habits of the people of Europe was expressed in even stronger terms within the EP. The inability of the executives to agree on the organization of the Joint Service caused from 1959 onwards a parliamentary commission, the Commission of Political Affairs, to keep a close eye on developments in the field of information. The scrutiny resulted in a rather harsh report from November 1960. The views presented in it were in perfect accordance with the ones prevailing within the Joint Service and the EEC Commission: Information had a twofold purpose. Its immediate objective was to make the activities of the European Communities known to the public, and to awake their interest and improve their understanding. Its ultimate objective was the European political community, the realization of which would demand a new European spirit, new ways to think and act. A new European public opinion would have to be forged, that would fill the same autonomous and democratic function that national public opinions did within the frontiers of the different countries.[8]

Dispute between the executives

The January 1958 decision to develop the ECSC information service into a Joint Service marked the beginning of a turbulent period that would last for more than two years. The EEC and Euratom treaties of 1957, like the ECSC treaty before them, contained no dispositions regarding external information. This made the early years of the Joint Service a period in which the executives had the field to themselves, unrestrained by intervention from other institutional actors.

What, then, did they disagree about, and what consequences did their inability to reach agreement have?

The dispute between the executives concerned the question of whether priority should be given to the information resources of the respective executives or to their new Joint Service. The EEC Commission claimed an increase in its personal information resources, arguing that this was necessitated by the diversity and extent of its tasks as well as by specific events, like the competition between the EEC and the European Free Trade Association for the favour of American public opinion.[9] The other executives insisted that as long as the contributions of the executives to the overall budget of information remained unchanged, personal information resources ought to stay comparable.[10] The failure to agree had noticeable effects. One was that it caused the Council of Ministers and the EP to intervene in the field of information. Another was that the disagreement on organization distorted the focus on content, and thereby delayed the development of a common policy.

Co-operation in the field of information was to begin with co-ordinated by an inter-executive working-group, comprising Roger Reynaud, a former French civil servant, for the High Authority, and the former Dutch politicians, Sicco Mansholt and Emmanuel Sassen, for the EEC Commission and the Euratom Commission respectively.[11] It was this group that provided the Joint Service with instructions and received its reports. Within the group, the diverging prioritizations regarding the organization of information soon became evident.

The three executives had agreed to keep the ECSC Information Service and develop it into a joint functional, administrative and budgetary unit. This was partly an economic decision, as one joint service would allow for better use of resources than three separate ones. It was at the same time a political decision, reflecting the executives' concern with the need to present the three communities as parts of one process.[12] Since some of the information activity was closely related to the policies of each community, the executives also agreed on each having their own spokespersons vis-à-vis the press. The original understanding was that these spokespersons should form limited groups for immediate and daily action. In the period that followed, the EEC Commission departed from this agreement and sought to prioritize its spokespersons' service at the expense of the joint resources.

In a situation with more generous funding, the actions of the EEC Commission might have been unproblematic. In a time where the economic resources devoted to community information by most comparisons were limited, they were not.[13] This became evident in the course of 1959 as the working-group struggled to agree on the organization and budget of the Joint Service for the following year. The group did agree on a 1960 budget of 85 million Belgian francs, of which the EEC and the ECSC was to provide 40 per cent each and Euratom 20. However, Sassen and Reynaud were not ready to accept demands from the EEC Commission destined to strengthen the spokespersons' service of this institution. This could only happen they said, if the services of the other executives were strengthened in a proportional manner, something which in turn would imply profound changes in the Joint Service to the detriment of the joint sections.[14] In the months that followed the EEC Commission sustained its demand. The representatives of the High Authority and Euratom held their ground as well, arguing that an increase of the kind envisaged by the EEC Commission was an attack on the principle of a joint service. Following the working-group's inability to agree, Mansholt declared the EEC Commission unable to pronounce itself in detail on the organization and budget of the Joint Service for 1960.[15]

Through the financial provisions of the EEC treaty, the Council of Ministers had the power to exert economic pressure on the executives. The 1959 deadlock caused the Council to make use of this power – an effort that in the end was crowned with success. Through the EEC treaty, the Commission was instructed to deliver a preliminary draft budget to the Council no later than 30 September of the year preceding that in which the budget would be implemented. The Council would then forward a draft established by qualified majority to the EP until 31 October. Before doing so, the Council was entitled to make changes to the Commission's draft budget. The EP, in turn, had the right to propose modifications to the Council's draft. If this happened, the Council was obliged to discuss the modified draft with the Commission and other institutions concerned. In the end, though, formal power was in the hands of the Council, which had the right to pass the budget by qualified majority.[16]

In mid-November the executives were aware of the fact that the Council intended to use its budgetary powers to enforce detailed information from the executives on how the amount demanded for information purposes would be spent. The Council had at this point in time signalled a reduction in the financing demanded by the inter-executive working-group for 1960 from 85 to 75 million Belgian francs. While this caused the executives to agree on common action, their first move fell short of what the Council was after. To secure the financing originally asked for, the parties simply decided to send a document to the EP and the Council of Ministers containing what they described as 'sufficient explanations of the organization of the service, its overall need for personnel as well as major activities envisaged', but not the details on budget and organization demanded by the Council.[17]

The executives knew that their response fell short of what the Council of Ministers expected, and the only way to explain this is that both parties, the EEC Commission on the one hand and the Euratom Commission and the High Authority on the other, refused to compromise. The Euratom Commission had already elaborated a document with the information demanded by the Council and had proposed to hand this over to the Council until 15 December.[18] The EEC Commission refused, however, to accept the proposals regarding the size of the spokespersons' groups and continued, in the period that followed, to argue for a strengthening of its own group.

The events in the field of information mobilized the EP, who sided with the three executives in the matter of financing. During the budgetary debate at the end of November 1959, the Parliament passed a resolution asking for an increase in the financing of the Joint Service from 75 to 85 million Belgian francs.

This had, however, no substantial effect on the Council of Ministers, who, as its president Italian Minister of Foreign Affairs Giuseppe Pella made clear, would not give in as long as it was not presented with a precise programme and a budget in which personnel expenses were kept at a reasonable level.[19]

In March 1960, the Council's continued pressure produced the intended effect. The price for the agreement was that the spokespersons' services now became detached from the Joint Service and administratively linked to their respective executives. The long-awaited accord was awarded in the supplementary budget, in which the Council accepted the EP's November 1959 proposition, albeit limiting the increase to 5 million Belgian francs, as several months of 1960 already had passed. On 18 May 1960, the EP approved the supplementary budget.[20]

Part of the March 1960 agreement was a decision to transfer the prerogatives of the inter-executive working-group to a new body, the Administrative Council, the Conseil d'administration, consisting of one member from each executive. The Luxembourg diplomat Albert Wehrer now joined on behalf of the High Authority.[21] Sassen still represented Euratom. According to its statutes, the presidency of the new body was to be held permanently by the EEC Commission. Its first president, Mansholt, resigned after a month, however, to concentrate on his work in the Commission's agricultural section. He was replaced by one of his Italian colleagues, the Christian democratic politician Giuseppe Caron, who headed the new group until May 1963. Caron, who was a member of the European federalist movement, presented ideas about the ultimate purpose of integration and the role of information that were in perfect accordance with the ones first formulated within the ECSC information service. European economic integration was the first step towards more comprehensive integration, he explained to the Belgian Centre for Public Relations in October 1960. Due to this, special attention would have to be given to the education of public opinion.[22]

A new policy takes shape

The inter-executive dispute had caused the EP to follow developments in the field of information closely from 1959 onwards. The report presented by the Commission of Political Affairs in November 1960 left no doubt about the fact that the definition and development of a common policy had been seriously hampered by the executives themselves. The Commission of Political Affairs expressed concern with the fact that the Community remained ignored by the general public in the member-countries. It accused the executives, who, while declaring themselves in favour of a joint information service, had proved unwilling to give up personal instruments of information. Priority had as a consequence been given to the spokespersons' services of each executive at the expense of the new Joint Service that was supposed to present information about the process of integration as a whole. In the light of the coming fusion of the three communities, the Commission of Political Affairs denounced any action contributing to costly rivalry between the executives on the budgetary level as well as inopportune rivalry on the political level. If a common policy was to take shape, every executive would have to renounce on the sort of absolute sovereignty which, in international relations, Community institutions had caused the retreat of. The time was now ripe for considering how Europe and the European Communities ought to be presented to the various segments of public opinion.[23]

Following the March 1960 agreement, the focus shifted from organization to content. The effort resulted in a 'Memorandum on Community Information Policy for the attention of the Councils' presented by the EEC Commission in June 1963 that remained the basis for the communities' policy of information throughout the period treated in this chapter.[24] The policy fleshed out in the 1963 memorandum gave priority to what was referred to as 'leaders of opinion' rather than the wider public. This was partly a result of the fact that a situation with limited resources demanded prioritization, partly an expression of the belief that these leaders of opinion would be able to exercise effective influence on the public at large.

A first attempt to sketch out a coherent policy had been edited by Rabier in 1959.[25] Its starting point was the demand to which information of public opinion ought to respond: daily updates as well as in-depth information, general as well as specialized information would have to be provided. Finally, while information on each community was needed, so was information on the achievements and significance of the European Communities as a unitary process. Small and medium-size firms, organizations of engineers and technicians, trade unions, agricultural communities, universities, organizations for popular culture and youth were identified as target audiences. The service expressed a preference for written and audio-visual information, joint participation on fairs and expositions as well as internships, conferences and information visits.[26] These priorities were in accordance with the way in which the resources of the Joint Service had been disposed previously, as these four techniques accounted for 91 per cent of the resources spent on information activities in 1957–58.[27] The stated purpose was not only to inform, put to provide the various segments of public opinion with a European education.

In the 1963 memorandum, the executives sustained the belief that a continued effort towards the public opinion in the communities would be necessary. The year before, a European opinion poll, the first community wide survey of this kind and the result of an EP resolution, had been undertaken. This survey demonstrated that a large majority of the public opinion in the member-states, between six and eight citizens out of ten, favoured European unification. At the same time, the answers provided by those interviewed indicated growing permissive consensus, as the European public showed little passion and curiosity for the process of integration. This lack of engagement was considered the result of a feeling that the process was inevitable,[28] something that must have worried the executives, who themselves asserted the opposite view, namely that nothing could be accomplished without the conscious political action of the European institutions.[29]

The 1962 opinion poll had revealed considerable, but probably unsurprising variations in knowledge about the communities: men were better informed than women, industrialists were better informed than workers, and educated people were better informed than the uneducated. The memorandum established that continued effort would have to be made towards both leaders of opinion and mass opinion. It did, however, indicate a clearer division of labour between the various actors involved than had been the case in 1959. The services of Community institutions would reinforce their direct action towards leaders of opinion. The actions of Community services, in contrast, would be indirect towards public opinion in general, as governmental services or other national actors would play an important role towards this group.

The 1963 community information budget demonstrates to what degree the group 'leaders of opinion' was a main target. That year 78 per cent of the resources spent on information were directed towards this group. Clear priority was given to internal information, which accounted for 57 per cent of the total budget. Compared to 1957–58, a considerable reduction in resources used on audio-visual techniques had taken place. While audio-visual information (radio, TV, cinema and photos) had occupied 20 per cent of the 1957–58 budget, the corresponding percentage in the 1963 budget was down to 7 per cent. This suggests less focus on mass opinion, women and people without higher education – the groups to whom audio-visual techniques were considered to have the highest appeal. Written information, more appreciated by people with higher education and considered to have a more lasting effect on attitudes, accounted in contrast for one third of the expenses on activities. A sizeable reduction had taken place here as well, as 36 per cent of the total 1957–58 budget had been spent on written information.[30] The figures for written information as well as representations at fairs and exhibitions on the 1957–58 budget is, however, not representative for average spending on these items, as the 1958 world exhibition in Brussels had caused much higher expenses on brochures and stands than what would be the case in the following years.[31]

The executives gave priority to a group of already convinced Europeans because they believed this group was able to exercise decisive influence on the dissemination of information and the shaping of attitudes – a belief that remained unwavering throughout the period treated here. In 1964, however, changing attitudes towards the process of integration began to concern the Joint Service. The opinion was that the political and slightly romantic Europeanists of the 1950s had been replaced by a new generation of leaders, inspired by domestic political objectives and more concerned with economic aspects than the political aspects that the executives from the very beginning had set out to spread. 'Leaders of opinion' still remained target group number one. From now on, however, this group too, was considered one that, just like others, would have to be educated about the general principles that had inspired and given significance to the process of integration.[32]

In retrospect, there is reason to question the executives' unshakable faith in the ability of elites to influence mass public opinion in the wanted direction. One reason for this is the above-mentioned emergence of a new generation of leaders, less concerned with the political aspects of integration. Research into the attitudes of elites versus public opinion on European integration has also demonstrated considerable differences between the preferences of these groups. While elites favour a large competitive market with political muscle, mass opinion prefers policies that protect them from the vagaries of capitalist markets.[33] The belief in the ability of elites to influence mass opinion in a desired direction might thus have been exaggerated.

Relations between the EEC institutions in information policy

The 1963 memorandum launched an up to then non-existent dialogue between the institutions on the policy of information. The Council's interest had previously been restricted to the financial aspects of information, and its intervention had been limited to the yearly budgetary debates. When this changed, and information policy became the object of political discussions in the Council, it did so as a result of the executives' initiative, who now asked the Council to engage in the field.

It was Caron, in his capacity as president of the Administrative Council, who at the Council's meeting in October 1962 asked that the problems related to the Communities' policy of information were discussed in the Council before its discussion of the 1964 budget.[34] The EP promptly gave their support to the proposal. So did the Committee of Permanent Representatives (Coreper), who in March of the following year pointed to Caron's request, and asked for a discussion on problems regarding the organization of the Joint Service and the Communities' policy in the field of information in general. The Coreper also asked that this discussion should be based on a document unrelated to the budget. The resulting document was the EEC Commission's June 1963 memorandum on information in the European Communities.

Why would the executives call for Council involvement in a field where they enjoyed considerable discretion? While the executives were able to make decisions regarding programme and organization of the Joint Service in relative freedom, the Council's budgetary control constituted an effective hindrance to the executives' ability to implement their decisions. The Council had often refused to grant the financing for which the executives had asked, and this was now traced to unfamiliarity with the objectives and means of the policy of information. The opinion was that if a policy was formally defined, the Council's understanding for the challenges facing this sector would increase and unfortunate effects of ignorance on the yearly budgetary debates could be avoided.[35] Indirectly, the demand for increased Council involvement may thus be read as an attempt of the executives to maintain their influence on information policy, as an expanded financial basis would increase their ability to put policy decisions into practice.

The most noticeable consequence of the entry of member-state representatives into the field of information was the introduction of new measures destined to increase their control with developments in the field. In the beginning of July 1963, the Coreper decided to set up an ad hoc working-group consisting of member-state representatives, charged with preparing a report based on the EEC Commission's memorandum, on which following discussions in the Coreper and the Council were to take place. Rabier had been invited to the first meeting in this group to comment upon the Commission's memorandum. His intervention gave the impression that the Joint Service opted for constructive co-operation with the member-states, as he stressed the need to make sure that the Joint Service's objectives corresponded with the common view of the member-states and community institutions.[36] Rabier further made clear that the wish for an exchange of views with the member-states had a double purpose. Partly motivated by the need to inform about developments in the field, the initiative was also an attempt to circumvent a number of problems and to focus on problems that had not yet been solved. In order to achieve this, he suggested institutionalizing a dialogue that would allow regular confrontations on technical and political aspects of the action undertaken.

In accordance with the suggestions of the Joint Service, the working-group recommended in its September 1963 report the establishment of a group of national experts on information that would meet regularly with the Joint Service and the spokespersons.[37] The Coreper supported the proposal,[38] as did the Council, who decided on the establishment of this group in its discussion on information policy in September 1963.[39] Its mandate was to study problems related to Community information policy in a regular manner and without regard to their budgetary aspects.[40] Its reports would, in turn, serve as basis for the Council's yearly discussions on information policy.

This is probably the point at which the relations between the institutions began to deteriorate, as the member-states used the entry of national experts to tighten their grip on Community information policy. One indication of deteriorating relations is found in the executives' reaction to the formulation of the mandate of the national experts. The executives had first been given the impression that the national experts would have a consultative role only, which was something to which they attached considerable importance.[41] The working-group had, however, left the executives with little influence on this matter, as it had decided to leave the definition of the group's mandate to the Coreper. While the Coreper had produced a draft in which the consultative role of the expert-group had been established, its final text had left this formulation out. The Administrative Council reacted strongly to what they considered an attempt to weaken the executives' responsibility with regard to management of the Joint Service, and described this as something that would have to be avoided.[42] As it turned out, nothing indicates that the expert-group ever had anything but advisory power. Its setting up still led to an increase in member-state influence on information policy, as the Coreper was empowered to go through the expert-group's reports and select the elements it gathered needed Council approval. The Council would then decide on these elements, and its decisions would, in turn, be taken into account by the budgetary committee in its studies of the budgetary proposals presented by the Joint Service.[43]

On a general level, and rather unsurprisingly, the member-states represented an approach to information policy that was less supranational than the one advocated by the executives. The September 1963 report from the working-group is illustrative of this tendency, as it recommended a strengthening of the spread of community information by means of increased use of the services of member-state embassies.[44]

It did so in spite of the objections raised by the German representative, who argued that since member-state interests would not always be consistent with community interests, the activity of national embassies could not replace the one of community offices.[45]

On a more specific level, the member-state representatives expressed opposing preferences regarding the level of independence that ought to be accorded to the Joint Service, the setting up of new offices and the balance between external and internal information. The dividing lines differed from one case to another, and give no grounds to identify one country as more or less in favour of the policy of the executives than any other. It is worth noting that several countries spoke up in favour of increased member-state control with the Joint Service. This was particularly true for the Luxembourg representative, according to whom the role of information was to support the Community in its undertakings, which was a far more limited role than the one hitherto played by the Joint Service. The French and Italian representatives expressed themselves in similar but more modest terms, arguing for increased co-operation between community information services and the services of the member-states.[46]

In the question of whether priority should be given to external or internal information, the German, Luxembourg and Dutch representatives favoured an increase in external information. The opposite view was advocated by the Italian representative, who, possibly inspired by the result of the 1962 opinion poll, which had revealed that knowledge about the Community was particularly low in Italy, insisted on the need to maintain the existing balance between external and internal information.[47] It is worth noting that the executives argued for continued effort towards the public opinion within the Communities. Information on European problems within the Communities was considered very superficial, and great variations in levels of knowledge existed between various segments of the public, with particularly low awareness of European institutions and ideals in the countryside.[48] However, a majority of member-states had already decided in favour of an increased effort towards external information.[49] The issue is thus an illustration of how the entry of the member-states not only influenced relations between the institutions, but also shaped the actual content of the common policy of information.

The politicization of information

While dividing lines between the member-states were weak and impossible to generalize upon to begin with, this changed towards the mid-1960s, when the escalating conflict between the French government and the European Commission reached the field of information. The view on the purpose of information advocated by the Joint Service collided with the view now expressed by the French government, which was that the Joint Service should restrict itself to factual information about the activity of the institutions and refrain from anything likely to be described as "education des citoyens".[50] Perhaps the change in the French position was the result of a more visible and thus more provocative information policy. Given the remarkable stability in the policy promoted by the Joint Service, it is, however, just as likely that information policy simply became victim of the French president's strong dismay with Community developments in general. What is certain is that the situation spurred the government in Paris to present new demands for more member-state control with the Joint Service – a project which eventually failed.

On 25 June 1965 the Secrétariat Général du Comité Interministériel pour les Questions de Coopération Économique Européenne (SGCI) sent a letter to the French ministries. According to the SGCI, unfortunate transgressions had been committed by the Joint Service which needed to be remedied. One way to do this would be by redefining the workings of this service in a way that would impose respect for good behaviour in delicate matters that affected activities of political or cultural character not part of the domains of the ECSC, EEC and Euratom treaties. As part of this plan, the SGCI asked the ministries involved to report about events omitted in the annual reports.[51]

That same day in June, the French government's representative used a meeting in the expert-group on information to announce his government's dissatisfaction with developments in the field of Community information. The minutes of this meeting reveal that while the underlying reason for the harsh critique of the Joint Service was its focus on integration as a political and cultural process,[52] the triggering cause was an article in the April number of *European Communities*, a newspaper published by the executives. In this article, Alfred Mozer, Mansholt's chef de cabinet, argued, amongst other things, against a political union in Europe, which lacked a democratic structure, sought a place for Europe between east and west, was militarily independent and loosened or finally broke the Atlantic link. The time was now ripe, Mozer wrote, for the launching of 'a clear political plan for Europe' that was 'opposed to the Paris view'.[53]

The French government's response to what it described as a vigorous attack on its policy was to provide its information advisors on duty in third countries with new instructions. These advisors should no longer participate in co-ordinating meetings with information advisors from other member-states. Nor should they continue their distribution of readings of political character coming from the services of the executives. The French government made it clear that the Joint Service ought to restrict itself to subjects of economic nature, and announced upcoming proposals for more effective control with this service.[54] While the French government was ready to assume its responsibility with regard to the presidency of the expert-group, the French delegation would not take any active part in the workings of this group.[55]

This was not the first time that the French government had levelled criticism against the Joint Service. What was new was that criticism was now levelled against the content and purpose of information, and thus towards completely different aspects than what had previously been the case. The French delegation had in a meeting in the expert-group in October 1963 launched a number of objections against the Joint Service. These objections had, however, mainly dwelled on the organization of information. The French view anno 1963 had been that the Joint Service was sufficiently financed, but that organizational changes, for instance in the form of letting national information bureaus distribute Community publications, could improve the efficiency of the service. In 1963, the French delegation had even encouraged the service to make an effort in the political field, in order to explain and defend the policy of the EEC.[56] The change in the French behaviour towards the Joint Service supports the argument recently made by Piers Ludlow, namely that France before 1965 accepted and contributed to most community policies in a positive manner, but that this changed with the crises, when Charles de Gaulle made French diplomats politicize issues that previously had functioned with French acquiescence.[57] One could, of course, object that the views of a group of national experts not necessarily represented the views of the French government. The fact that the objections presented by these experts later were summed up in writing and passed on to the Secretary General of the Council by the French government's permanent representative in Brussels indicate, however, that they did.

The French reactions did not have the intended effect, neither at home, or in Brussels. The SGCI failed to receive the answers it had hoped for from the French ministries. In fact, the few that responded reported about excellent connections with the Joint Service.[58] As for the French boycott of various committee meetings, it seems to have produced the opposite effect of what the government in Paris initially may have hoped for. The French government forbade French civil servants on several occasions to participate in committees whose activities were initiated by the Joint Service. Far from paralyzing activities in the field of information, the immediate result of these moves was that the executives gave priority to co-operation with independent experts rather than civil servants.[59] It is reasonable to assume that this, over some time, weakened the influence of the member-states on the policies initiated by the executives. One illustration of the shift from governmental to independent experts is found in a meeting between European experts on cinema, arranged by the Joint Service in December 1965. The representative of the Centre National de la Cinématographie in Paris had not obtained permission to participate in this meeting. His absence was then compensated for by the presence of Louis Terrenoire, former French minister of information and then a member of the EP, who stepped in and took great interest in the initiative.[60] A report from the programme on information destined towards youth and adult education in 1965 points in the same direction. According to this report, 1965 was a year in which co-operation between the Joint Service and a number of important French institutions for adult education grew better and better.[61]

More than a year after the Luxembourg compromise, French representatives still failed to attend meetings initiated by the Joint Service. This might be explained with dismay with the actual results of the compromise. While the French government, at Luxembourg, had gained acceptance for a statement on information that indicated increased Council control with the definition and implementation of the programme of the Joint Service, new mechanisms for member-state control failed to materialize.[62] Nothing indicates, however, that the absence of the French representatives constituted an obstacle to work in the various committees. Illustrative of this are the minutes of a meeting between high civil servants that met in February 1967 to discuss information directed towards youth. According to the minutes, the meeting took place 'in the French represen- tatives' absence, but in an environment of excellent co-operation'.[63]

Other indications on a loosening of the member-states' grip on information policy in this period also exist. One is the halt in the activity of the expert-group on information. After the before mentioned meeting on 25 June 1965, no further meetings took place during the rest of the period that the Joint Service existed.[64] In fact, it was the Commission that after the 1967 merger demanded in front of the Coreper that the group resumed its activity. The Commission used the same occasion to establish that the purpose of this group ought to be to prepare the yearly debates between the Council and the Commission on information policy, and not to control the activity of the Commission in this field.[65] Another indication is an increase in the 1967 information budget – interpreted by the Joint Service as an expression of faith from the other institutions in the policy of information conducted by the Administrative Council and the executives.[66]

Conclusions

The emergence of a common policy of information demonstrates how the supranational executives were able to create a policy field outside the treaties and to stay in control of it against the will of member-state representatives. What made this possible? The fact that no basis for this policy had been spelled out in the treaties is part of the explanation. If the executives had been obliged to imple- ment a policy defined by the member-states, there would have been less room left in which to pursue their own preferences. Another aspect that should be kept in mind is that the activity in the field of information was carried out within a service that in every respect was small and by many probably considered as insignificant. That the development towards a common policy was a very gradual process probably added to its inability to engage member-state representatives. Its non-provocative nature is illustrated by the fact that more than five years passed before information policy became the object of political discussions in the Council.

What enabled the executives to remain in control of community information policy in spite of repeated attempts from member-state representatives to gain it? On more than one occasion, member-states managed to control the executives. This happened in 1960, when the Council enforced executive agreement by use of its budgetary powers. It was also the case in 1963, when the Council strength- ened the role of the expert committee against the executives' wish. In spite of these and other episodes, though, the period as a whole appears as an illustration of a policy that, over time, gained sufficient strength and support to resist attempts from its opponents to control it.

One reason for this was that the member-states were disadvantaged by their late arrival. The entry of the member-states in 1963 was preceded by a ten year period in which the executives had the field to themselves. During this decade, knowledge was acquired, contacts established, and a steady increase in the service's activity took place. When the French government tried to paralyze the Joint Service through the withdrawal from committees initiated by it, its activities were left unaffected because the Joint Service was able to replace governmental experts with independent contacts.

Another explanatory factor is that the member-states drifted apart. As long as their front was united the member-states were quite successful in their attempts to structure and control the activity in the field of information. From the mid-1960s onwards, critique against the Joint Service no longer came from the Council, but from the French government alone. It was no longer levelled against organizational and budgetary aspects, but against the view on information as education that had been a consistent feature of Community information policy since the early 1950s. Thus, it was not the policy of the executives that had changed but the policy of the French government. Maybe this was because Community information policy had become more visible, maybe it was because the French government now used every opportunity to attack the Hallstein Commission. In any event, the French government's isolated position prevented it from enforcing its views, and in the end both proposals for increased control and outright obstructionism proved fruitless.

What are the theoretical lessons that may be drawn from this? First, this account refutes the rational institutionalist claim that member-states over time control the Community they have established. Second, regarding the principal-agent model's emphasis on how the agent's inherent urge to increase its powers necessitates control mechanisms, the events in the field of information illustrate how budgetary powers enabled the Council to dictate the executives and how more active member-state involvement in information policy was followed by the introduction of new measures designed to increase member-state-control. The executives were, in turn, and in accordance with the assumption of the agent's innate interest in self-empowerment, unwilling to give up management of the Joint Service. Still, the executives' behaviour does not fully fit the description of an agent incessantly struggling to increase his powers. The most important reason for this is that while the formal definition of information policy in 1963 came about as a result of a demand from the Council to the executives, the initial activity in this field was not the result of delegation but of the executive's independent action. The events in the field of information also show that the supranational institutions were able to bypass governmental representatives for the benefit of co-operation with independent national experts, and that these actors together pursued policies that the member-states in turn were forced to relate to. The role of the executives in this matter thereby exceeds general descriptions of both principals and agents. Finally, and in accordance with a central tenet of historical institutionalism, the narrative of the development of community information policy shows how small, initial events, like the inter-executive dispute on the role of the spokespersons, may influence outcomes in a disproportionate manner.

More than an account that confirms or disproves general theories, this is one that illustrates the complexity of the European political system in its early phase as well as the complex and often accidental nature of history: Without Jean

Monnet's American experience, the ECSC information service would perhaps not have seen the day. If the Commission of the EEC had been more flexible when negotiating with the other executives, member-state intervention in the field could perhaps have been avoided or delayed. And, if the 1965 conflict between the Hallstein Commission and the French government had not politicized information policy, member-state representatives might have had a greater say in its formulation. It is thereby an illustration of one of the advantages of historical narratives, namely their ability to capture the details that sometimes have decisive impact.

Notes

1 Action plan to improve communicating Europe by the Commission, 20 July 2005, documents that do not belong to other categories of Commission documents (SEC), (2005) 985 final; Communication from the Commission to the Council, the European Parliament, the European Economic and Social Committee and the Committee of the Regions, 13 October 2005, propositions and other communications from the Commission to the Council and/or other institutions (COM), (2005) 494 final; White Paper on a European Communication Policy, 1 February 2006, COM (2006) 35 final. The documents were accessed on the website of the Directorate-General for Communication: http://ec.europa.eu/dgs/communication/index_en.htm (16 October 2007).

2 Isabelle Petit refers to this interpretation in 'Dispelling a Myth? The Fathers of Europe and the Construction of a Euro-Identity', *European Law Journal*, vol. 12, no. 5 (2006), pp. 661–79.

3 For other dealings with this topic, see Piers N. Ludlow, 'Frustrated ambitions. The European Commission and the Formation of a European Identity, 1958–67', in Marie-Thérèse Bitsch, Wilfried Loth and Raymond Poidevin (eds.), *Institutions européennes et identités européennes*, Brussels: Emile Bruylant, 1999, pp. 307–26; Alexander Reinfeldt, 'Jean Monnet und die Informationsnetzwerke der EGKS in den USA', in Jürgen Elvert und Michael Salewski (eds.), *Historische Mitteilungen*, vol. 18, no. 1 (2005), pp. 175–86; Petit, 'Dispelling a Myth?'; Michel Dumoulin, 'What Information Policy?', in idem. and Marie-Thérèse Bitsch (eds.), *The European Commission, 1958–72: History and Memories*, Luxembourg: Office for Official Publications of the European Communities, 2007, pp. 507–31.

4 Jacques-René Rabier, 'La naissance d'une politique d'information sur la Communauté européenne (1952–67)', in Felice Dassetto et Michel Dumoulin (eds.), *Naissance et développement de l'information européenne*, Berne: Peter Lang, 1993, pp. 21–32; Jacques-René Rabier interviewed by Gerard Bossuat, June 1998, European University Institute, Oral History Project, http://wwwarc.eui.eu/oh/bin/CreaInt.asp?rc=INT609 (accessed 4 November 2007); Jacques-René Rabier interviewed by Étienne Deschamps, 8 February 2002, http://www.ena.lu/mce.cfm (accessed 4 November 2007).

5 Rabier interviewed by Deschamps.

6 Statement by Walter Hallstein to the European Parliamentary Assembly, 20 March 1958, European Commission, Historical Archives (ECHA), Speeches collection, Walter Hallstein (WH).

7 Ibid.

8 Assemblée Parlementaire Européenne, Documents de séance, Rapport fait au nom de la Commission des affaires politiques et des questions institutionelles sur les problèmes de l'information dans les Communautés européennes, 18 November 1960, ECHA, High Authority of the European Coal and Steel Community – Administration et finances (CEAB 12), No. 715.

9 Letter from Wehrer to Sassen, 5 December 1959, ECHA, Notes d'information sur les travaux du Conseil (SI), 1960, No. 689; letter from Hallstein to the president of the Council of Ministers, 22 December 1959, ECHA, EEC and ECSC Commissions (BAC) 3/1978, No. 664.

10 Letter from Hallstein to the president of the Council of Ministers, 22 December 1959; letter from Wehrer to Mansholt, 3 February 1960, ECHA, SI/1960, No. 689.

11 Projet de procès-verbal de la 1ère séance du Groupe de Travail le 9 mai 1958 à 16 h, 9 May 1958, ECHA, BAC 118/1986, No. 875.

12 Éléments de réponse au questionnaire de la Commission des affaires politiques au sujet du service commun d'information, 23 July 1959, ECHA, CEAB 1 (Service Juridique), No. 687.

13 Ludlow, 'Frustrated ambitions', p. 320.

14 Projet de procès-verbal da la réunion du groupe interexécutifs de presse et d' information du mardi 15 septembre 1959, 23 September 1959, ECHA, CEAB 1, No. 344.

15 Projet de procès-verbal de la réunion du groupe interexécutif de presse et d'information du lundi 9 novembre 1959, 13 November 1959, ECHA, CEAB 5 (Division relations extérieures), No. 671.

16 Treaty of Rome, article 203.

17 Projet de procès-verbal, 13 November 1959.

18 Propositions de la commission d'Euratom relatives au programme, à l'organization et au budget du service commun d'information, 1 December 1959, ECHA, CEAB 12, No. 715.

19 Letter from Sassen to Malvestiti (President of the High Authority), 30 November 1959, ECHA, CEAB 1, No. 344.

20 Assemblée Parlementaire Européenne, Documents de séance, Rapport, 18 November 1960.

21 Note sur l'organization et l'activité en 1960 du service commun de presse et d' information, April 1960, ECHA, CEAB 12, No. 715.

22 Communication à la presse, speech held by Caron to the Belgian Centre for Public Relations, 6 October 1960, ECHA, BAC 3/1978, No. 664.

23 Assemblée Parlementaire Européenne, Documents de séance, Rapport, 18 November 1960.

24 Memorandum sur la politique des communautés en matière d'information à l'attention des conseils, 26 June 1963, ECHA, BAC 25/1980, No. 475.

25 Note préparatoire à un échange de vues sur la politique d'information des communautes, 12 May 1959, ECHA, CEAB 1, No. 687.

26 Ibid.

27 Note historique et critique sur le service d'information, 12 May 1959, ECHA, CEAB 2 (Secrétariat general), No. 597.

28 Memorandum sur la politique, 26 June 1963.

29 Petit, 'Dispelling a Myth?'.

30 Memorandum sur la politique, 26 June 1963.

31 Note historique et critique, 12 May 1959.

32 Service de Presse et d'Information des Communautés Européennes, Programme d'activité pour 1965, undated, ECHA, BAC 38/1984, No. 131.

33 Liesbeth Hooghe, 'Europe Divided? Elites vs. Public Opinion on European Integration', *European Union Politics*, vol. 4, no. 3 (2003), pp. 281–304.

34 Memorandum sur la politique, 26 June 1963.

35 Extrait du procès-verbal da la 66ème session du Conseil de la CEEA tenue à Bruxelles, les 10 et 11 juillet 1963, ECHA, Council of Ministers of the EEC and Euratom (CM2)/1963, No. 0178.

36 Réunion le 10 juillet 1963 du Groupe de travail "ad hoc" sur la politique des Communautés en matière d'information, 19 July 1963, ECHA, CM 2/1963, No. 0178.

37 Politique des Communautés en matière d'information, Rapport du Groupe de travail "ad hoc" au Comité des Représentants permanents, 12 September 1963, ECHA, CM 2/1963, No. 0178.
38 Extrait du compte rendu de la réunion du comité des représentants permanents, tenue à Bruxelles, les 17, 18, 19 et 23 septembre 1963, ECHA, CM 2/1963, No. 0178.
39 Procés-verbal de la 110ème session du Conseil de la CEE tenue à Bruxelles, les lundi 23 et mardi 24 septembre 1963, 14 November 1963, ECHA, CM 2/1963, No. 51.
40 Politique des Communautés en matière d'information, 2 July 1964, ECHA, CM 2/1964, No. 869.
41 Telex from Rochereau to Wehrer, 24 September 1963, ECHA, CEAB 2, No. 2886.
42 Procès-verbal de la quatorzième réunion du conseil d'administration du Service de presse et d'information des Communautés européennes, 12 November 1963, ECHA, CEAB 2, No. 2886.
43 Politique des Communautés en matière d'information, 2 July 1964, ECHA, CM 2/1964, No. 869.
44 Politique des Communautés en matière d'information. Rapport du Groupe de travail "ad hoc" au Comité des Représentants permanents, 12 September 1963, ECHA, CM 2/1963, No. 0178.
45 Politique des Communautés en matière d'information. Projet de rapport au Conseil, 1 August 1963, ECHA, BAC 3/1978, No. 829.
46 Réunion le 10 juillet 1963 du Groupe de travail "ad hoc", 19 July 1963.
47 Politique des Communautés en matière d'information, Rapport du Groupe de travail "ad hoc", 12 September 1963.
48 Memorandum complementaire sur les developments des activités d'information en 1964, 2 October 1963, ECHA, BAC 14/1967, No. 9.
49 Procès-verbal de la 110ème session du Conseil de la CEE tenue à Bruxelles, les lundi 23 et mardi 24 septembre 1963, 14 November 1963, ECHA, CM 2/1963, No. 51.
50 Rabier interviewed by Deschamps.
51 The letter from the SGCI to the French ministries is reproduced in Edmond Jouve, *Le général de Gaulle et la construction de l'Europe*, vol. II, Paris: Europe, 1967, pp. 516–20.
52 Compte-rendu de la réunion du groupe de l'information du 25 juin 1965, 5 July 1965, ECHA, CM 2/1965, No. 238.
53 Albert Mozer, 'Capitulation is no Policy', *European Community*, vol. 3, no. 4 (1965), p. 9.
54 Somer à Fourier-Ruelle. Réunion du Groupe de l'Information en date du 28 juin 1965, 28 June 1965, ECHA, BAC 118/1986, No. 312.
55 Compte-rendu de la réunion du groupe de l'information du 25 juin 1965.
56 Texte reprenant les considérations developpées oralement par la délégation française lors de la réunion du groupe d'experts de l'information à Bruxelles le 7 octobre 1963, Boegner to Calmes on 20 December 1963, 9 January 1964, ECHA, BAC 25/1980, No. 475.
57 N. Piers Ludlow, *The European Community and the Crises of the 1960s. Negotiating the Gaullist challenge*, Oxon: Routledge, 2006.
58 Rabier interviewd by Deschamps.
59 Note aux membres du groupe de preparation, 8 February 1967, ECHA, CEAB 2, No. 2914.
60 Communication de Monsieur J. R. Rabier à messieurs les membres du Groupe de préparation "presse-information", 4 July 1966, ECHA, CEAB 2, No. 2914.
61 Rapport sur la réalisation du programme d'information europénne des milieux de jeunesse et d'éducation des adultes pour l'année 1965, ECHA, CEAB 2, No. 2913.
62 Ludlow, 'Frustrated ambitions', p. 324f.
63 Communication de Monsieur J.R. Rabier à messieurs les membres du Conseil d'Administration, 22 February 1967, ECHA, CEAB 2, No. 2914.

64 Politique d'information de la Commission, Communication de la Commission au Conseil, 14 May 1968, ECHA, CEAB 2, No. 2914.
65 La politique d'information de la Communauté, 12 November 1968, ECHA, BAC 28/1980, No. 602.
66 Avant-projet de programme d'activité pour 1967, 31 January 1967, ECHA, CEAB 2, No. 2913.

10 Delegation as a political process

The case of the inter-institutional debate over the Budget Treaty

Ann-Christina L. Knudsen

The role of the European Parliament (EP) has changed remarkably over time, from being an international assembly with weak oversight and advisory powers, to becoming one of the more powerful elected chambers in the world today.[1] The revision of the EP's position began when in 1970 it was granted certain budgetary powers. Subsequently, in 1979 the Members of the EP (MEPs) became directly elected, and since the mid-1980s their legislative powers have gradually been strengthened. This chronology seems to be in accordance with the democratic traditions of the member-states. The trajectory for these acts of delegation to the EP, however, could not have been foretold, as I show in this chapter that examines the decade-long debate among the Community's institutions over how and what to finally delegate in the so-called 'Budget Treaty' on 22 April 1970.[2]

Democratization, institutional architecture, and the financing of public policies are all central issues to politicians, but are also quite technical matters. The Budget Treaty connected the introduction of certain budgetary powers of the EP with a new model of financing the Community, passed by the Council in Luxembourg the day prior to the new treaty.[3] The Community had originally been financed through direct member-state contributions, like other international institutions where the member-states retain full responsibility over budgetary decisions. The treaty establishing the European Economic Community (EEC) had foreseen the introduction of so-called own resources, borrowing from the terminology of financing the European Coal and Steel Community. The Commission was mandated by the EEC treaty to launch an enquiry into how a new model for establishing financial autonomy to the Community institutions could be introduced. In addition to the classical consultation procedure, the EEC treaty stipulated that after the unanimous agreement of the Council, the new financial model would need to be submitted 'to the Member States for adoption in accordance with their respective constitutional provisions.'[4] Hence, national parliaments were included in the procedure for establishing own resources, but the EEC treaty did not anticipate the budgetary empowering of the EP, although it did foresee the creation of direct elections.[5] The fact that the EP was empowered with budgetary powers before it became directly elected was therefore not in accordance with the EEC treaty. Nevertheless, the Budget Treaty granted the indirectly elected EP an active role in the revised budgetary procedure, while also delimiting its powers to only being part of allocating around 3 per cent of the total budget.[6] This model essentially kept the EP away from influence over funding to politically highly salient areas such as the Common Agricultural Policy (CAP).

Recent studies of delegation in the Budget Treaty by Berthold Rittberger and Mark Pollack reflect these two readings; their theoretical contributions are outlined in Morten Rasmussen's chapter. More specifically, Rittberger argues that what needs to be explained is the fact that delegation to the EP took place at all.[7] He shows that national political elites widely agreed that a link existed between the introduction of financial independence to the Community and the empowering of the EP in budgetary matters. However, whereas some – especially political elites in the Netherlands, Germany and Italy – argued that the granting of budgetary powers to the EP could balance out the so-called legitimacy deficit created by own resources, others refused to acknowledge that legitimacy could be created outside national parliaments. The latter view was advocated by French Gaullists in particular. Against this well-known positioning of the principal political actors, Rittberger argues that pro-delegation national elites were able to employ their arguments strategically in support of supranational parliamentary legitimacy. The second reading of the Budget Treaty focuses mainly on the limits to delegation. Pollack accepts that normative motives can play a role in delegation to majoritarian institutions, but insists that member-states will only empower the EP when they expect an efficiency gain.[8] Pollack's study primarily examines the final rounds of inter-governmental negotiations from the time of The Hague summit in December 1969 when the French demands for delimitations were brought in. Pollack additionally points out that the reluctance of the French government was further fuelled because under the constitution of the Fifth Republic, the National Assembly was only second tier to the strong executive in the domestic French budgetary process.

Both have made important contributions towards explaining delegation in the Budget Treaty. Yet, it seems evident that the empirical evidence behind these studies has been selected to support rather than problematize their theoretical frameworks. The desire to mainly explain one side of the act of delegation – the active powers for the EP, or the delimitations – meets strong challenges from available primary sources. Thus, the intimate link between the EP's position in the Community's budgetary procedure and the creation of own supranational resources – based on as many as three different sources of revenue, namely the common external agricultural levies and customs duties, and a fixed percentage of national value added tax (VAT) – meant that it was often practically impossible to separate the different financial and normative positions of the political actors involved. This is especially the case in the later stages of these negotiations, when the political solution was bound to include multiple issues. Second, both scholars focus on national political elites. It is certainly true that the road towards empowering the EP was paved with the persistent influence by national governments, from the notorious French hick-up that triggered the so-called 'empty chair crisis' in 1965–66 to the final signing of the Budget Treaty. At the same time, both studies tend to ignore that other types of actors, such as commissioners or MEPs, could have played a role in selecting the powers for delegation. Third, both operate with a view of the policy process confined mainly to formal politics around the Council, and clearly marked history-making moments.

This chapter tells another story, namely of a decade-long debate among the Community's institutions about own resources and the empowerment of the EP. It shows that it can be a somewhat more complicated task to determine exactly when some of the decisions about delegation were made. In order to nuance our understanding of how powers were selected for delegation it is necessary to look beyond the rigid dichotomies and temporal perspectives advocated by the approaches above. Historical institutionalism, as outlined in Rasmussen's chapter, explains why it is necessary to trace the steps of the policy process over time. Accordingly, delegation can be regarded as a policy process that includes formal decision-making moments as well as informal debates, that is, times when competition of ideas and preferences is likely to have taken place among the multiple actors involved. Over time the alternative path for policy options became narrowed down by actors who were in a position to do so. Thus, timing and sequencing matter because identifying how and when such choices were made, and alternative options for policy design were discarded, helps us to identify how delegation to the EP was formulated in a policy process over time.[9] While scholars have recently called the study of the period in between the major rounds of member-state negotiations the interregnum, it is difficult to see how it differs essentially from the assumptions laid out by historical institutionalism.[10] This chapter examines more specifically the continuous inter-institutional debate that took place among the Commission, the EP, and the Council throughout the 1960s about the introduction of own resources and delegation to the EP.[11] Before embarking upon the new historical narrative, the following section reviews the relevant budgetary provisions.

The power of the purse

The so-called power of the purse is at the core of modern democratic systems.[12] Along with direct representation, democratically elected parliaments hold the power to decide over raising state revenue, allocating public spending, passing public budgets, and overseeing the executive. In practice, the exact role of national parliaments in the budgetary process varies from one constitution to another, and the power of the purse usually does not mean that national parliaments have complete freedom over public finances. Constitutions also constrain the parliamentary room to manoeuvre due to the wish to assure a degree of financial autonomy to the executive, and the stable functioning of public infrastructure.

The Budget Treaty may be said to constitute a supranational interpretation of the power of the purse.[13] The EP's role in the budgetary procedure was originally confined to consultation at the second reading of the draft budget, and the Council could overrule amendments proposed by the EP without any justification.[14] The active powers for the EP introduced in the Budget Treaty centred on the EP's right to amend the draft budget. The treaty introduced a five-stage procedure, starting with the Commission establishing the preliminary draft budget that would have to be accepted by the Council by qualified majority. The draft budget would subsequently be transmitted to the EP that could propose amendments. The Council became obliged to deliberate over these amendments in consultation with the Commission, and to vote on each of these with qualified majority. In case the Council was unable to agree to the proposed amendments in this way, it would have to re-submit the draft budget to the EP, explaining why the amendments were unacceptable. The EP would then need to muster a majority of its members, as well as three-fifths of the votes cast, to modify the Council's counter-amendments. If this succeeded, the EP would indeed have the 'final word' in settling the budget, just as it would have in case the Council failed to respond to the EP's initial amendments within a certain period. If, however, the EP would fail to mobilize the votes needed to counter the Council's objections, it would lose the opportunity to influence that year's budget on any given issue. In any event, the president of the EP would declare the annual budget finally settled, even if this was a symbolic function.

The new procedure also contained limitations to the EP's power of the purse. First, the involvement of the Commission throughout the budgetary process remained much more prominent than that of the EP, which would only be involved at the second reading. Second, the double-condition for the Council's input constituted a relatively high threshold for parliamentary influence, in fact just as high as for the censuring of the whole Commission.[15] Third, a division was created between 'compulsory' and 'non-compulsory' expenditures arising from the activities of the EEC treaty. The EP's right to amend concerned only compulsory expenditure such as Community spending on staff and buildings. This effectively barred the EP from decisions pertaining to most of the Community's budget. A window of opportunity for further EP involvement was opened in relation to setting the maximum rate of increase of the budget. The Commission would have to be consulted over this with the EP's committees for budget and economic policy, and follow key indicators of the general economic development. While this procedure did not give the EP any direct power to decide over the allocation of funds, it was bound to result in more transparency over how decisions with budgetary implications were made in the Commission, thus further enhancing the parliamentary legitimacy of the Community's budgetary procedure.

The peculiar entry of own resources

Already in late 1958, several draft proposals for own resources appeared inside the Commission. It was, however, in the context of designing the CAP that the question first gained prominence.[16] Importantly, a Council resolution passed in December 1960 established that the revenue generated from common external agricultural levies should flow to the Community rather than to the importing member-state.[17] The initial debate about own resources was therefore limited to the emerging discussions over how to finance the CAP, and it did not anticipate revising the status of the EP.[18] Resolutions are not legally binding, but may be seen as political commitments. Thus, the resolution of December 1960 had not required the consultation of the EP, and several member-state administrations proved to be unprepared for this potentially wide-reaching political commitment. Own resources based on agricultural import levies meant that a gross calculation of financial winners and losers was relatively straightforward – net agricultural importers would 'win', and net exporters would 'lose' – which seemed to be the first calculations made in national economics and finance ministries.[19] Although the political commitment of the December 1960 resolution did become disputed within some governments, the integral connection to the CAP ensured that own resources remained firmly on the political agenda.

Towards the end of December 1961, the debate re-surfaced in the context of the discussions about financing the CAP that followed the notorious Council 'marathon' for finalizing the first stage of the common market. Own resources became one of the central elements of the financing agreement passed in the early morning hours of 14 January 1962. The ensuing regulation 25 became hailed by Community fanfare as the 'financial solidarity' underlying the CAP.[20] Accordingly, at the end of the transition period, agricultural levies accrued from imports from third countries would go to finance the CAP. Regulation 25 was, however, merely a temporary agreement terminating on 30 June 1965. Moreover, it had been conceived under somewhat unusual political circumstances, just as its wording was ambiguous. First, the procedure under which this regulation had been created actually violated the consultation procedure of the EEC treaty. It had been drawn up during the heat of the marathon meeting to disconnect the financing of the CAP from the political substance of this policy. Consequently, regulation 25 had not been on the usual journey from draft to final, thus avoiding the scrutiny of national administrations and parliaments as well as the consultation procedure with the EP. Second, own resources introduced through regulation 25 circumvented article 201 EEC treaty, which demanded explicitly consultation with the EP, and the final approval by national parliaments. The EP subsequently refused to acknowledge that own resources had been tabled in any legal form, though it did not call for cancellation of regulation 25, as later happened in the iso-glucose case in 1979. Third, the legal ambiguity of regulation 25 also concerned whether it was at all possible to make binding provisions for a period after which this act had expired. Finally, regulation 25 made no mention of the EP, or linked own resources to (supranational) parliamentary legitimacy.

Linking supranational parliamentary legitimacy to own resources

The EP did not fail to mention the procedural flaws behind regulation 25 when discussing the Commission's annual report in October 1962. But rather than rejecting own resources altogether, MEPs eyed an opportunity to use the issue as a lever to enhance their own role.[21] The EP's Deringer report argued that national parliaments had lost legislative and budgetary powers with the institution of Community policies and own resources and thus addressed the so-called legitimacy deficit.

By including the EP in the decision-making process, the democratic balance of the Community could allegedly be restored. From this point onwards, the Community saw a steadily growing number of resolutions and reports issued by the EP about the legitimacy deficit, and how to solve it. Notably the subsequent Furler report of July 1963 drew up a detailed catalogue aiming to ensure 'the democratic principle of the separation of powers'.[22] Along with other positive legislative powers, it demanded that the EP should have the power of decision over budgetary matters once the Community would possess own resources. While these demands may have seemed idealistic, they always had the potential of being drawn into national political debates due to the double parliamentary member-ships and transnational political networks of the MEPs.

The Commission's initial response to the Furler report was supportive. At the EP's plenary session towards the end of the July, however, Commission President Walter Hallstein argued that the widening of the EP's powers should only extend to the establishment of the budget, and it should have no part in the execution of the budget.[23] Hallstein thus put a fence around the Commission's powers to execute the budget. Shortly thereafter, the Council began responding positively to the EP's request. By December, it mandated the Committee of Permanent Representatives (Coreper) to study all available positions of the member govern-ments 'in view of the reinforcement of the role of the Assembly', particularly referring to the budgetary powers of the EP.[24] The Council considered revising the budgetary procedure in the context of the fusion of the institutions of the Communities. This latter discussion had recently been revamped in the Action Programme, launched by the German government and intended to bring new momentum to the European integration process after the failed accession negoti-ations with Britain January 1963. Although it was supported with more or less enthusiasm by the other key political actors, the Action Programme came to live a relatively subdued life in the shadow of the parallel discussions over designing the CAP. Yet, while the Council had only taken a short debate about linking own resources and the strengthening of the budgetary position of the EP – what Rittberger has called the 'logical link'[25] – in this context, the result was that all the Community's three institutions now de facto accepted it.

The Council's acceptance of the logical link made it complicated for any government to change position in this respect. Moreover, it encouraged MEPs to go even further with their visions for future empowerment. The Kreissig report of October 1963 also insisted that consultations with the EP should happen at all stages of the policy process.[26] For example, at what point a revised Commission proposal would trigger a new consultation procedure with the EP was currently a grey area, just as certain developments during the first enlargement negotiations where own resources had been discussed.[27] But while Hallstein in his October address to the EP again claimed to support the EP's demands, he also cautioned the MEPs. Hallstein emphasized that he was constrained by what was 'realizable', and estimated that the problem of the financing of the CAP and 'budgetary inde-pendence' would have to be solved before further parliamentary powers could be installed.[28] Hallstein thereby made a subtle attempt to deconstruct the logical link, fearing that it could otherwise complicate the passing of the common grain price, the centre-piece of the CAP. These CAP negotiations remained deadlocked until December 1964, as the German government let itself be taken hostage by the country's powerful farm group.[29]

Although Hallstein had attempted to put a lid on this debate, it actually intensified towards the end of 1963 in anticipation of the Coreper report commissioned by the Council in July. Hallstein therefore decided to open the discussion within the Commission in early November.[30] This discussion showed that most commissioners actually wanted an EP that in certain cases could overrule the Council. Agreement was therefore made to try to push for an institutional reform focusing on strengthening the EP's budgetary powers. The commissioners' ideal model was one where the EP should enter the procedure in the second reading of the draft budget, amendments to the draft budget would have to be agreed by two-thirds of all MEPs, and these could only be overruled by unanimity in the Council. This was one of the most ambitious plans for empowering the EP to be sketched by the Hallstein Commission, and the commissioners expressed that they were aware that it may prove to be indigestible for some member governments.

The discussions at Community level transgressed into national politics as at least three member governments during 1963 threw their support behind a revision of the EP's role. The Dutch government had already in late February proposed to reinforce the powers of the EP in connection with the fusion. This opinion also echoed the EP's reactions to regulation 25 in the autumn 1962 about the legitimacy deficit being worsened with the introduction of own resources.[31] This position was at different times supported by representatives of the Italian government. Towards the end of the year, the Luxembourg and German governments advanced further suggestions.[32] These were remarkably similar in terms of assigning positive powers to the EP, as well as delimiting these. Both argued that the EP should be able to amend the draft budget up to the total amount of expenditure agreed by the Council. To settle the budget, the EP should muster a double-majority consisting of two-thirds majority of the votes cast among a majority of the MEPs. The two proposals only deviated over the threshold in the Council for overturning the amendments made by the EP which at this stage most likely was not politically significant. The positions of these governments mostly drew on declarations made in their national parliaments.

In short, there was certainly a sense of a broad political will to continue the debate over the link between own resources and supranational parliamentary legitimacy, confirmed also in the Coreper report towards the end of the year. Though the Council had not really had the opportunity to discuss this report in detail, it passed a declaration on 23 December emphasizing the connection between the specific model for financing the CAP and reinforcing the budgetary powers of the EP. The general conclusions from the Council's session in February also re-stated its intentions to strengthen the budgetary powers at the same time as the fusion.[33] This became the first time that the topic was allowed to generate real debate in the Council, and for the first time a certain hesitance began to transpire, especially from French representatives. The debate had largely been provoked by a highly sceptical French foreign minister, Maurice Couve de Murville. While he had strongly supported own resources in regulation 25, he now made clear that the French government was reluctant to accept any modifications of the budgetary procedure that could affect the financing of the CAP.[34] The Council's declaration was therefore, in his view, not a green light for institutionalizing the logical link. Several options for the empowering of the EP were discussed in the Council at meetings in March, June, July and September 1964. Meanwhile, the EP passed no less than 16 resolutions towards this purpose during 1964, keeping the dialogue with the other institutions alive.[35] And in October, the Commission promised the EP that it would incorporate the revised budgetary procedure into the proposal for financing the CAP replacing regulation 25.[36]

The Commission's internal agreement over the future powers of the EP coincided with the most far-reaching initiative in this area to date, promoted by the German government in November 1964. The 'European Initiative' argued among other things for making the competences of the EP 'comparable to those of the national parliaments in the areas where the Community has subtracted from the national parliaments.'[37] It specified both budgetary and legislative powers for the EP. This German initiative stood in contrast to the stubbornness with which this government still allowed its powerful farm lobby to block the CAP negotiations. But once the common grain price was finally settled in mid December – against a lump-sum pay-off to German grain farmers – a more concentrated focus on the issues of the logical link began. The grain price decision was followed by a Council request to the Commission for drawing up a proposal for replacing regulation 25.

Questioning delegation

In the light of the debate that had been developing within the Community for several years now, the Commission's March 1965 proposal integrating financing of the CAP, own resources, and the strengthening of the EP's budgetary powers does not seem quite as radical as it has sometimes been judged. A week before transmitting the proposal to the Council, Hallstein presented it to the EP.[38] The political drama that began when the French government withdrew high-level representation from the Community for about eight months, the empty chair crisis, only began about two months after the Commission had submitted its proposal. What exactly provoked President Charles de Gaulle to go to such extreme still remains disputed, most likely a series of domestic and Community affairs in combination with his particular sense of drama.[39] He certainly took a dislike to the notion of a supranational parliament, which at the press conference on 9 September he described with contempt as 'a technocratic embryo, in large part foreign, that has been destined to impact on the French democracy . . . '.[40]

Here, it is worth taking a closer look at the Commission's proposal concerning the EP and the budgetary procedure, as well as the subsequent reactions to this part of the proposal.[41] The basic argument of the Commission's proposal was that the introduction of own resources for financing the CAP would change the balance of power among the political actors of the Community. As the national parliaments' ability to control Community financing would wither away, the Commission called for further budgetary powers to the EP. Indeed, the active powers to the EP laid out in the Commission's proposal are the ones most often cited, but it is interesting to note that it also delimited the EP's role already at this point. Most importantly, the Commission argued that it was not appropriate to give the EP full powers before it was elected by universal suffrage. Once direct elections were in sight – which they were not in this proposal – the Commission promised that it would revise the budgetary procedure again to enhance the EP's standing. The Commission would, however, remain central to the budgetary procedure at any time. In short, those wishing for further budgetary powers to the EP were kept waiting for the introduction of direct elections in some distant future.

Although the Commission has often been seen as having 'gone beyond the mandate which had been given to it',[42] as expressed by French government representatives, Hallstein had all along been aware not to stray too far away from what he estimated to be politically feasible. At an internal Commission meeting in early June 1965, for instance, Hallstein was quoted for saying that 'it seemed to him to be premature to modify substantially the distribution of powers and competences between the institutions of the Community. This distribution of powers and competences will in effect be modified if, as the resolution of the Parliament demanded, the power of decision ("the final word") in budgetary matters will be transferred to the Parliament'.[43] Hallstein also tried to assure the French delegation by the middle of June that 'the Council continues to be the supreme authority in budgetary matters'.[44]

The EP certainly noticed the limitations to its powers imposed by the Commission, and expressed discontent with the condition of direct elections in the future. In response, the EP issued a report in May demanding further budgetary powers as soon as own resources were introduced, and that it should be more difficult for the Council to disregard EP proposals for amendments.[45] The EP also demanded direct elections from September 1971, at which time the Community budget should be passed by majority voting of the MEPs. Hallstein responded in an address to the EP on 11 May that as far as he could see, the only difference of disagreement was the moment when the EP's powers would be increased.[46] In practice, however, it was clear that as long as the Commission had *not* proposed a date for direct elections to the EP, this might been postponed. In the Council, the Dutch and Italian delegations pointed out that there should be an extension of the EP's powers in legislative matters, while the German and Luxembourg delegations specifically wanted the EP's budgetary powers to be gradually extended to give it the final say over the budget.[47]

As the 30 June deadline for renewing the financial regulation was approaching, practically no progress had been made in the Council negotiations. In early June, one internal Commission document noted that further negotiations seemed practically impossible, and that '[t]he ambassadors were extremely cautious'.[48] Another document noted that the Commission was now 'without many illusions' that its proposal would pass in the Council.[49] Indeed, the French government left the negotiations entirely on 30 June. Meanwhile, the Merger Treaty had been signed in April 1965, stripped of any elements pertaining to the strengthening of the powers of the EP that the fusion of the Communities' institutions was once intended by the Council to have. When governments resumed negotiations in January 1966, the Commission's proposal from March 1965 was dissected into its main elements. Own resources and the empowering of the EP became detached from the financial regulation for the CAP.[50] The negotiators aimed for an agreement over the latter to cover the remaining transition period of the EEC, an agreement that could inject a sense of success and progress without causing political controversy. It became a new temporary agreement, set to expire at the end of 1969 in which the gradual surrendering of own resources to the Community was continued. A final legal status for own resources was however still to be found.

For a while thereafter, the debate between the Community's actors over the reform of the budgetary procedure was kept on the back-burner, but especially the Dutch, German and Luxembourg delegations made clear on several occasions that this was still their aim. In the context of the Coreper, the Dutch representative in particular tried pushing for a renewed discussion over the logical link, while the French insisted that 'all that needed to be said about that topic had already been said in regulation 25'.[51] The EP joined into the debate, for example with the Illerhaus report from October 1966 that reiterated the problem of the legitimacy deficit resulting from the gradual loss of control of CAP expenditure by national parliaments. This report concluded that '[a]ll efforts for a reform of the communautarian constitution should be centred on the budgetary procedure.'[52] Hence, the EP still expected that own resources would be the lever for further empowerment, while accepting that direct elections and legislative powers would have secondary priority for now.

In short, the empty chair crisis and its relatively peaceful ending did not result in delegation to the EP. Meanwhile, own resources were in fact being partially implemented as an integral part of the temporary budgetary agreements, making it more difficult for sceptics to reject it entirely, and for advocates of institutional reform to set further conditions. The Commission's position, however, was a good example of the complexity of a situation that could not be rigidly divided into supporters and opponents. While its proposal was often seen as a strong support of supranationalism, it also delimited the EP's powers in several decisive ways. Hence, it relegated the EP to the second reading of the budgetary process, and removed any alternative options for the EP to participate in the execution of the budget. The subsequent debate over the budgetary empowerment of the EP essentially stayed on the path laid out by the Hallstein Commission regarding these points. Moreover, the EP's road to influence was further delayed by the condition of direct elections laid out in the proposal, which were not resolved until the end of the 1970s. It is thus crucial to recognize that these early choices made by the Commission came to have decisive influence over the future chronology of delegation to the EP.

Rebooting the debate

The question of delegation of budgetary powers regained prominence in a highly ambitious communication from the Commission to the Council in April 1968.[53] The document had been drawn up under the new Commission President Jean Rey in the run-up to the administrative reform following the Merger Treaty. Its vision was that the fusion of the institutions of the Community should provide the departure towards political union, direct election of the EP, and the creation of financial autonomy for the Community. The Commission's initiative prompted the Council to renew its commitment to reinforcing the budgetary powers of the EP. The ensuing Council resolution referred back to various Community documents prior to 1965–66, as well as the most recent resolution by the EP.[54] This was evidence that the Council saw the dialogue as being continued, as if the empty chair crisis had not happened; why the French government – still led by de Gaulle – now accepted this, calls for further research. Subsequently, the Commission joined in with a declaration on 1 July 1968.[55] It here argued further that the progression of creating the Community – especially with the Merger Treaty, the finalizing of the common market, and the end of the veto right in the Council – necessitated further supranational parliamentary legitimacy through the strengthening of the budgetary and legislative authority of the EP, and the institution of direct elections. Needless to say, the EP met these new developments from both the Commission and the Council with open arms.[56]

From the spring of 1968 to the summit in The Hague in December 1969, the Community saw a series of similar general statements from all its institutions about the need for strengthening the (budgetary) powers of the EP. Meanwhile, at the time the common market and the CAP were nearly implemented, the Community witnessed significant changes in the economic and political climates throughout Western Europe, the advent of monetary turbulence, and mounting costs of the CAP. There was also a gradual change in certain forms of co-operation within the Community, such as the beginning of summitry, and more frequent meetings of the finance ministers. The latter meant that financing problems of the Community began to be discussed outside the context of the CAP, and the finance ministers were certainly keen to solve the recurrent problems. They discussed the establishment of own resources in Rotterdam on 9 September 1968, which led to a widening of the definition of own resources to include not only agricultural levies, but also customs tariffs and possibly other sources of revenue too.[57] Most notably, the German representative made a long intervention arguing that own resources were producing a legitimacy deficit which could only be balanced out by strengthening the EP's budgetary powers, as well as the Commission's role in executing the budget.[58] The conclusions of the meeting did not go this far, but produced another Council commitment to reinforcing supranational parliamentary legitimacy as a pre-condition for creating own resources.[59]

In response, the Commission created an internal ad hoc working group of high-ranking officials mandated to study further options for creating own resources. Towards the end of March 1969, the Commission completed a working programme for the creation of the new financial model, and in mid-July a new proposal was born.[60] The proposal specifically departed in the continuous dialogue in the Community since 1963.[61] It argued that strengthening the budgetary powers of the EP would be a condition for introducing own resources. This was justified through the logic of market integration, the subsequent loss of budgetary control by national parliaments in the financing of Community activities, as well as the ever increasing total of Community expenditure. The Commission proposed a highly complicated new budgetary procedure. The first novelty was a conciliation committee to mediate in the event that the Council would reject the EP's amendment proposals. The Commission would participate throughout the procedure, and the EP and the European Court of Justice would also be brought in. This procedure bore the hallmark of the strongly partisan officials from the working group, keener on strengthening the Commission's own role than that of the EP. This part of the proposal provoked resistance from most governments and the EP, and simply delayed the Council's work for a while. The second novelty of the proposal was a gradual introduction of own resources by January 1974. Only then would the EP be given the final word over the budget. The proposal was at this point incomplete as to how this procedure would be finalized, and the Commission promised a complementary proposal after the summer holidays. In short, this was a far cry from the enthusiastic signals given by the Commission in April 1968. The general mood in the Community had certainly changed, and the question of empowering the EP had become divisive also inside the Commission, as some high-level officials within criticized the turn away from a genuine strengthening of the EP's budgetary and legislative powers.[62]

The EP's response came with the second Furler report from early October, and was a predictably harsh critique.[63] It concluded that the proposal did not at all correspond to the demands or promises of real budgetary powers which could only be defined as the EP having the last word over the budget. It criticized the bias of the conciliation procedure towards the Council and the Commission, and the omission of direct elections for the EP. The Commission responded partly to this in the complementary proposal issued at the end of October.[64] Here it explained the turn-around since April 1968 with reference to the disappointing lessons drawn from the 1965 proposal. The complementary proposal therefore in fact amounted to a further delimitation of the EP's powers in relation to the Commission, namely that the EP's amendments could not exceed the total amount of expenditures set by the Commission in the preliminary draft budget. For the final phase, the Commission proposed a double voting condition for the EP over final amendments.

The complementary proposal was discussed by the Coreper at least once before it was temporarily shelved due to the preparations of the summit that would take place in early December 1969 in The Hague.[65] Originally a French initiative, the summit was given the headings of completion of the Community's original agenda, deepening of the scope of co-operation, and enlargement with the renewed possibility of British accession.[66] The form of a summit, instead of an ordinary Council meeting, allowed for new political linkages to be made between these long- and medium-term plans for the Community. The agenda was supported by all the member governments, though each of them emphasized different issues. Financing fitted under the agenda heading of completion, but there seemed to be no consensus as to where, if at all, the strengthening of the EP's budgetary powers belonged. As earlier, the issue was carried forward by especially the Netherlands, Germany, and Luxembourg, but it ultimately resumed second rank at the summit.[67]

The institutional reform discussion at The Hague was additionally complicated by these new possible linkages. On the one hand, the broader basis for collecting own resources, agreed at Rotterdam, meant that several of those member-states who originally had promoted the EP's empowerment based on normative arguments now had to revise their cost-benefit analyses.[68] Inside the Dutch administration, for example, budgetary restraints had already weakened the internal support for the logical link.[69] On the other hand, the fact that enlargement had entered the equation further complicated the scheme of things as the member governments saw differently upon this. In an address to the French National Assembly in November 1969, for example, French foreign minister Maurice Schumann now argued that it would be crucial to cement a permanent financing agreement before embarking upon the accession negotiations with Britain.[70] Schumann did not, however, mention the possible institutional reform in the Community as a consequence of the new financial model. Inside the French administration this point was still contested, as parts of the governing party were working to find arguments denying that own resources could cause a legitimacy deficit, which in fact was an acknowledgment of the existence of the logical link. Schumann subsequently downplayed the logical link in public.

Finding a solution to financing the CAP and the Community was a very tangible challenge in The Hague, as leaders had to face mounting costs of agricultural surpluses and currency instability.[71] The current financing regulation would expire at the end of the year, and nobody wished to repeat the provisional financial government during the empty chair crisis. Hence, financing was discussed on the first day, and broad agreement was reached among the governments. The Commission had not been invited to the first day of the summit, and was surprised to discover that financing had already been dealt with when it arrived.[72] The final communiqué from the summit has by some been described as a 'watershed', and by others as 'vague and evasive'.[73] It was both, in terms of linking the financing of the CAP with own resources and the EP's integration into the budgetary process.[74] Article 5 of the communiqué essentially reiterated the logical link, yet the summit agreed to separate the subsequent negotiations for the financing solution and delegation to the EP. This advance had been engineered, as new historical research has shown, by the German government, and meant that the EP's new role could be negotiated in a new way.[75] The French government had at the summit rejected any talk about direct elections of the EP, but had accepted that from now on there was no turning back on negotiating the strengthening of the EP's role in budgetary matters. After the summit, therefore, there was no rejection of the logical link by anyone. The negotiations between December 1969 and

April 1970 were not concerned with the basic principle, but rather with the degree to which delegation and institutional reform should happen.[76] Most of these provisions would have to be in place by the early spring before the opening of the accession negotiations with Britain.

Strengthening whose powers?

Immediately after the summit the Commission was summoned by the Coreper to face extensive questioning over the July and October proposals. While accepting these proposals as a point of departure, the Coreper questioned the resulting balance of power within the Community, summed up as a 'substantial limitation of the powers of the Council', 'a limited strengthening of the powers of the Assembly', and an 'award of powers to the Commission'.[77] The national representatives criticized especially the Commission's attempt at strengthening its own role by proposing that only it could set limits to the estimates for expenditure made by other institutions, just as it would be solely responsible for both the revenue-side of own resources and the execution of the budget. The Commission defended this provision partly with reference to article 199 EEC treaty – according to which the Community's budget should always be in balance, – and partly as a procedure to avoid that the Community's expenses could be augmented excessively by an institution that was not actually responsible for the execution of the budget, that is, the EP.

The Council meeting did not produce any clear conclusions. Given that the national parliaments were scrutinizing the movements of the Council very closely at this point, most government representatives now looked to the EP for an opinion before developing more detailed positions. These came with the Spénale report in early December. Just like the Furler report, it was critical of the Commission's proposal.[78] The report insisted that the balance of power should be reversed: the role of the Commission should be 'limited', the Council's 'important', and that of the EP 'essential'. The conciliation procedure was believed to make decision-making inefficient. The report also pointed out that the double condition imposed on the EP for agreeing to the budget was excessive. It argued that in practice this provision could make it impossible for the EP to function. If for instance one of the large national delegations of 36 MEPs would be forced to stay in their national parliaments due to domestic political circumstances at the time of voting in the EP, the two-thirds rule would obstruct the passing of the budget even if a very strong majority of the MEPs present were in favour. Interestingly, the report also seemed to accept a number of other proposed limitations to its powers, particularly that the total amount of expenditure could not be augmented apart from in agreement with the Commission, and a limit to the overall rate of increase of own resources. Finally, the Spénale report suggested a further own resource based on national VAT.

The Council took up several of these points on 8 and 9 December, particularly VAT as an own resource, and the rejection of the conciliation procedure.[79] Although the Commission in an internal note prided itself with the fact that no member-government had presented counter-proposals, it subsequently moved to revise its 1969 proposal.[80] Most importantly it removed the conciliation procedure, and modified the double-condition for the MEPs to settle the budget by two-thirds majority of the votes cast at the final stage.[81] The revised proposal also incorporated VAT as an own resource, something which had often been mentioned internally in the Commission and by certain member-states, but which had so far not been thoroughly debated in the Council. Importantly, the introduction of VAT as a source for financing the Community opened a new set of issues in the final discussions towards completing the revision of the budget procedure. While government representatives were content with the fact that the Commission had eliminated the conciliation procedure, they criticized the continued prominent role given to the Commission in the revised budgetary procedure.[82] Moreover, the question of direct elections to the EP now divided those member-states that so far had been in support of widening supranational parliamentary powers. The Italian delegation continued to insist that direct elections was the preferred solution. The Dutch and Luxembourg representatives, however, disputed that this was a valid pre-condition for granting budgetary powers to the EP, especially as the national parliaments would still control the VAT-based own resource. Moreover, despite the fact that the Commission was now being overruled and forced to revise its proposal, several of its earlier inputs regarding the delimitation of the role of the EP were now taken for granted in the debate.[83]

Degrees of parliamentary legitimacy

Subsequently, discussion over the degree of delegation of budgetary authority to the EP, and the resulting balance of institutional reform, characterized the Council meeting from 17 to 21 December.[84] On the question of the VAT-based revenue, the French government had reserved its position prior to the meeting. The French representatives – Schumann and permanent representative Jean-Marc Boegner – arrived with an argument that insisted on the need to respect the multiple layers of parliamentary legitimacy in the Community, both national and supranational.[85] Their worries concerned above all the procedure for deciding over own resources originating from national VAT. VAT was a key domain and responsibility of the French National Assembly, and it would not be possible for this government to bestow equal powers to the EP, not least as the EP was not directly elected by the peoples of Europe. Moreover, they argued that if the Community was given access to up to 1 per cent of national VAT, it would essentially add up to much more than was needed for covering the costs of the CAP, and also therefore it was necessary to limit the EP's direct access to this national tax source.[86]

Although some delegations reacted to the first point by re-emphasizing the need for direct elections and further legislative powers, a more substantial discussion developed over how to separate the budgetary procedure for own resources that could be considered as supranational – customs duties and agricultural levies – and the share of national VAT.[87] The respect for parliamentary legitimacy now became linked not only to supranational legitimacy, but also to the potential problem of undermining national parliamentary control over public finances. It was not an argument easily accepted by all government representatives, yet it followed a similar logic of parliamentary legitimacy as applied to the EP, and the critics were forced to consider it too.[88] It was also closely related to the question of who should be empowered to set limits to revenue and expenditure in the Community.[89] In the current proposal, the Commission occupied a prominent role, but the French delegation – supported by others – now questioned whether any of the two supranational institutions should actually hold this authority, or be allowed to create budgetary frames constraining the possibility of the Council to act. While all actors, including the Commission and EP, agreed to uphold the balanced budget rule enshrined in article 199 EEC treaty, these discussions led to the invention of the distinction between compulsory and non-compulsory expenditure. The resulting agreement, as mentioned above, left the EP to legislate over merely a small fraction of the Community's budget. By the end of December, the Commission had to see its part of its attempt at strengthening its own role in the budgetary process questioned. Meanwhile, the EP's future position had become strongly delimited, first as a result of the Commission's earlier proposals, and further due to the new categorization of Community expenditures.

In-between these developments in the Council, Schumann had decided to invite a select group of MEPs – including Mario Scelba, who was the president of the EP and a prominent Italian Christian democrat, as well as Georges Spénale, the French socialist MEP who was the chairman of the EP's budget committee from 1967 to 1975 – for a meeting. Hence, right after his appearance in the Council on 17 December, Schumann told the MEPs of the turn of tides in relation to the new budgetary procedure and categorization.[90] The MEPs left the meeting deeply frustrated, as they had also just learned of the Commission's revised proposal that had not been presented to the EP for consultation prior to the Council negotiations.[91] Being now disillusioned with both the Commission and the member governments, Spénale and Scelba decided to each write a letter to the president of the Council pointing to the 'extremely serious consequences'[92] that could arise if there was no true reinforcement of the budgetary powers of the EP. They pointed out that 'a majority of the members of the European Parliament will react in the same ways in the national parliaments that have to approve the creation of own resources', thus threatening to draw on their political networks to reject the national passing of the Budget Treaty.[93]

Council agreement on the degree of delegation of budgetary powers to the EP was practically complete by the turn of the year: the EP would enter the budgetary procedure at the second reading of the draft budget, and it would be excluded from drawing up revenue for the Community. The latter agreement seemed to satisfy the concerns of certain member governments about retaining national control over the VAT based own resource.[94] Subsequently, further negotiations over delegation to the EP in budgetary matters were met with less hostility from particularly the French government. The Coreper now began working on outstanding issues such as how to set limits to spending.[95] The Dutch and Italian delegations teamed up behind a German proposal to involve the EP's Budget Committee. The Commission did try to prevent this, but to no avail. In a slightly modified form, the member-states agreed in early February that the Commission would make such previsions of limits to the budgetary increases in consultation with the relevant EP committees.[96] While this in no way created a genuine supranational power of the purse, opponents to this 'tight circumscription' of the EP's role seemed to accept that this was the best deal available at the time.[97] This essentially settled the degree of delegation of budgetary powers for the EP written into the Budget Treaty, and which is still basic to the institutional balance for budgetary decision-making in the EU today.

In the run-up to April 1970, MEPs continued to protest loudly that these agreements were 'intolerable' and 'unacceptable', particularly the distinction between compulsory and non-compulsory expenditure, and the fact that no direct elections were in sight.[98] They continued to threaten to use their extensive political networks to make national parliaments to prevent national ratification of the Budget Treaty.[99] There is little evidence, however, that these MEPs seriously turned their threat into actions, as it was in any case a considerable enhancement of the supranational power of the purse. The final meeting of the Council to sign the agreement on own resources and the Budget Treaty in April 1970 had more the character of a ceremonial closure than intergovernmental bargaining because the final budgetary model, and the institutional architecture related to it, had been settled gradually in the inter-institutional dialogue during the 1960s.

Conclusion

This chapter offers a fresh understanding of delegation to supranational institutions. Current studies of delegation to the EP in the Budget Treaty are complementary from an empirical point of view though their different theoretical departures offer different readings of how and why delegation took place. Further, advancing historical institutionalist assumptions about the temporal dimension of politics and change by tracing the policy process over time and by identifying the actors involved in shaping the formulation of what was to be delegated, further nuances our insights into the political mechanisms behind delegation.

The EP in the 1960s is often assumed to have been inefficient because it had no formal powers. The narrative above, however, revealed that this is only partially true, yet it is necessary to identify more precisely how it was efficient in designing delegation. The EP was above all instrumental as an agenda-setter in constructing the logical link between the introduction of own resources and the budgetary empowerment of the EP. This was an important pre-condition for delegation because it did not exist in the EEC treaty. By the time the EP brought the logical link to the political agenda, own resources were already on their way to becoming reality, but without (supranational) parliamentary involvement. Own resources had been part of the technical discussions inside the Commission for financing the Community, and the member-states had in fact passed a declaration towards this end already in December 1960, and a regulation in January 1962 without discussing delegation at all. Yet, MEPs used own resources to point to the legitimacy deficit, and subsequently produced a stream of reports and declarations about it, and used any opportunity to question commissioners about it. Moreover, the political networks of the MEPs obviously extended into national parliaments, and most likely served to mobilize national political parties and leaders. Hence, by pulling multiple strings, MEPs managed to maintain the issue of delegation on the political agenda of the Community over time.

The Commission also acted as agenda-setter in this matter, but in a different way. The degrees of enthusiasm over proposing delegation to the EP varied over time along with fears of losing its exclusive competencies in budgetary matters. While it was difficult for the Commission to deny the logical link, we saw several instances where Hallstein or commission officials treated the EP as a rival that could encroach upon the Commission's sole right to execute the budget. Its proposals therefore put fences up around the Commission's territory in budgetary matters, and it continuously placed the EP in a secondary position in the budgetary process. The idea that there could be limits to the EP's room for amending expenditure was also first brought up by the Commission, though someone else would probably also have come up with a version of this in the economically gloomy days when the Budget Treaty was finalized. The Commission's imprint on delimiting delegation to the EP is not immediately obvious if the empirical investigation begins towards the final intergovernmental deliberations. Hence, although the Commission had out-played its role in this matter towards the end of 1969, it should nevertheless be clear that the delimitations to delegation to the EP that it had proposed earlier left a significant mark on the final version of delegation.

The role of the member-states also varied over time. The Council's acceptance of the logical link was important in legitimizing the EP's continuous call for delegation at an early stage. It was however mainly towards the end of the policy process that the member-states provided significant input to the debate. From the perspective of delegation over time, the empty chair crisis caused some confusion about delegation, but it also helped confirm the path of delimitations to the role of the EP selected by the Commission in its March 1965 proposal. The French government did not reject the logical link after The Hague, but it did try to find a model whereby the EP's privileges would not encroach upon the right of its own national parliament regarding the VAT. This exact demand cannot have been part of a long-term strategy by the French government of delimiting delegation to the EP, as the VAT based own resource only entered the picture at this late stage. While intergovernmental negotiations settled the final degrees of delegation to the EP, they did not provide most of the input into the long-lasting debate that modelled the delegation of the budgetary powers. The nuances brought to the understanding of European integration history by extensive historical narratives, in short, are necessary because they can challenge assumptions brought about by theoretical dichotomies, just as they reveal new political mechanisms in the emerging European political system.

Notes

1 So characterized by Simon Hix, Tapio Raunio, and Roger Scully, 'Fifty years on: Research on the European Parliament', *Journal of Common Market Studies*, vol. 39, no. 2 (1999), pp. 191–202, here p. 192.

2 Treaty amending certain budgetary provisions of the treaties establishing the European Communities and of the treaty establishing a Single Council and a Single Commission of the European Communities, *Journal Officiel des Communautés Européennes*, 2 January 1971, L/2–12.

3 Council Decision, 28 April 1970, *Journal Officiel des Communautés Européennes*, 28 April 1970, L94, pp. 19–22.

4 Article 201 of the 'Treaty Establishing the European Economic Community', in *Treaties Establishing the European Communities. Treaties Amending these Treaties*, Luxembourg: Office of Official Publications of the European Communities, 1987.

5 Article 138, 3 EEC treaty.

6 Figure from EP, Draft Report, PE 23.807, 23 January 1970, Historical Archives of the European Communities (HAEC), Brussels Archives Commission (BAC), 51/1986, 833.

7 Berthold Rittberger, 'The Creation and Empowerment of the European Parliament', *Journal of Common Market Studies*, vol. 41, no. 2 (2003), pp. 203–25.

8 Mark Pollack, *The Engines of European Integration. Delegation, Agency, and Agenda Setting in the EU*, Oxford, New York: Oxford University Press, 2003, pp. 256–59.

9 Paul Pierson, *Politics in Time. History, Institutions and Social Analysis*, Princeton: Princeton University Press, 2004, p. 64.

10 Jeffrey Stacey and Berthold Rittberger, 'Dynamics of Formal and Informal Institutional Change in the EU', *Journal of European Public Policy*, vol. 10, no. 6 (2003), pp. 858–83.

11 Among others, references will be made to three documents composed by the Secretariat General, collecting a very extensive range of legal documents and minutes from the Commission, Council and EP over time in this matter: SEC(69)1250, 25 March 1969, and SEC(69) 1250/2, 31 March 1969, both HAEC/BAC, 187/1995, 11; and SEC(69) 1250/3, 28 March 1969, HAEC/BAC, 187/1995, 12. Commission documents found in the consecutive series of 'COM' documents will be referred to by HAEC/BAC.

12 David Coombes, *The Power of the Purse in the European Communities*, London: Chatham House, 1972, p. 5.

13 Brigid Laffan, 'Auditing and Accountability in the European Union', *Journal of European Public Policy*, vol. 10, no. 5 (2003), pp. 762–77.

14 Article 203 EEC treaty.

15 Article 144 EEC treaty.

16 Ann-Christina L. Knudsen, *Defining the Policies of the Common Agricultural Policy. A Historical Study*, PhD, Florence: European University Institute, 2001, chapter 8.

17 EEC Council Resolution, 20 December 1960, annexed to Report, Ministry for Agriculture and Fishery (the Netherlands), 15 Febuary 1961, Ministerie Buitenlandse Zaken (MBZ), Code 996 EEC/1955–65, 1145.

18 EP, Report, Doc. 102, 3 October 1969, HAEC/BAC, 20/1973, 3.

19 For details see Ann-Christina L. Knudsen, 'The Politics of Financing the Community and the Fate of the First British Membership Application', *Journal of European Integration History*, vol. 11, no. 2 (2005), pp. 11–30.

20 Regulation 25, *Journal Officiel des Communautés Européennes*, 20 April 1962 (5), 30, pp. 991–93.

21 EP, Resolution, 74/62, 18 October 1962, SEC(69) 1250/2, p. 1.

22 EP, Doc. 102.

23 EP, Minutes, 27 June 1963, SEC(69) 1250/3, p. 6f.
24 SEC(69)1250, p. 2.
25 Berthold Rittberger, *Building Europe's Parliament. Democratic Representation Beyond the Nation State*, Oxford, New York: Oxford University Press, 2005, p. 122.
26 EP, Resolution, 16 October 1963, SEC(69) 1250/2, p. 2.
27 Knudsen, 'The Politics of Financing'.
28 SEC(69) 1250/3, p. 5f.
29 Ann-Christina L. Knudsen, 'Creating the Common Agricultural Policy. The Story of Cereals Prices', in Wilfried Loth (ed.), *Crisis and Compromises. The European Project 1963–1969*, Baden-Baden: Nomos Verlag, 2001, pp. 131–54.
30 SEC(69) 1250/3, pp. 7–9.
31 Johan H. Molegraaf, *Boeren in Brussel. Nederland en het Gemeenschappelijk Europees Landbouwbeleid 1958–1971*, PhD, Utrecht: University of Utrecht, 1999, chapter 8.
32 SEC(69)1250, p. 2; EP, Doc. 102.
33 SEC(69)1250, p. 4 f.
34 Rittberger, *Building Europe's Parliament*, p. 122.
35 Secretariat General (SecGen), Note, SEC(69)2786, 11 July 1969, HAEC/BAC, 51/1986, 832.
36 SEC(69) 1250/3, p. 9.
37 EP, Doc. 102.
38 EP, Minutes, 24 March 1965, SEC(69) 1250/3, p. 10.
39 Jean-Marie Palayret, Helen Wallace, and Pascaline Winand (eds.), *Visions, Votes and Vetoes. The Empty Chair Crisis and the Luxembourg Compromise Forty Years On*, Brussels: P.I.E.-Peter Lang, 2006; N. Piers Ludlow, *The European Community and the Crisis of the 1960s. Negotiating the Gaullist Challenge.* London: Routledge, 2006, pp. 71–93.
40 Supplement, Quotidien 'Europe', 9 September 1965, HAEC/BAC, 187/1995, 11.
41 Commission, Proposal, COM(65)150, 31 March 1965, HAEC/BAC.
42 SEC(69)1250, p. 8
43 Communication Hallstein, G(65)280, quote, SEC(69) 1250/3, p. 13.
44 Council, Minutes, 14–15 June 1965, quote, SEC(69) 1250/3, p. 14.
45 EP, Resolution, 14 May 1965, Council of Ministers (CM2), 1965, 474.
46 SEC(69) 1250/3, p. 12.
47 Council, Rapport, R/622/65 (AGRI 254) (FIN 51) (ASS 250), 9 June 1965, HAEC/BAC, Cabinet Marjolin, 1965, 285.
48 SEC(69)1250, p. 10.
49 Ibid., p. 12.
50 For example, Council, Press statement, 29 January 1966, CM2, 1966, 476.
51 Various documents from the first months of 1966, HAEC/BAC, Cabinet Marjolin, 1966/1036P.
52 EP, Resolution, 20 October 1966, quote, SEC(69) 1250/2, p. 7.
53 Extract, SEC(69) 1250/3, p. 21.
54 SEC(69)1250, p. 16f.
55 COM(68)550, 1 July 1968, SEC(69) 1250/3, p. 23f.
56 For example, EP, Report, 3 July 1968, SEC(69) 1250/2, p. 9.
57 SEC(69) 1250/3, p. 25.
58 Communication, M. Grund, 9 September 1968, SEC(68)3201, HAEC/BAC, Cabinet Mansholt, 38/1984, 18.
59 For example, Comité de politique budgétaire, Report, 12 December 1968, HAEC/BAC, 20/1973, 1.
60 SecGen, Report, SEC(69)1071, 14 March 1969, HAEC/BAC, 7/1973, 28/1; SEC(69) 1250/3, p. 31.
61 SecGen, Draft proposal, SEC(69)1071/9, 14 July 1969, HAEC/BAC, Bxl, 20/1973, 2.
62 SecGen, Report, SEK(69)1071/4, 23 June1969, HAEC/BAC, Cabinet Mansholt, 38/1984, 18.

63 EP, Draft advice, PE 23.263, 11 November 1969, HAEC/BAC, 187/1995, 13; EP, Doc. 102.
64 Commission, Communication, COM(69)1020final, 30 October 1969, HAEC/BAC, 207/1996, 29.
65 Council, Note, R/2077/69 (AGRI 622) (FIN 378), 7 November 1969, ibid.
66 N. Piers Ludlow, *The European Community*, chapter 7.
67 Rittberger, *Building Europe's Parliament*, p. 126.
68 For example, SecGen, Note, 5 December 1969, SEC(69) 4638/2, HAEC/BAC, 20/1973, 3.
69 Molegraaf, *Boeren in Brussel*, chapter 8.
70 Berthold Rittberger, 'The Creation', p. 215.
71 For example, Commission, Bulletin, no. 305, 4 December 1969, CM2, 1969, 1271 (temp).
72 N. Piers Ludlow, 'An Opportunity or a Threat. The European Commission and the Hague Council of December 1969', *Journal of European Integration History*, vol. 9, no. 2 (2003), pp. 11–26.
73 Jan van der Harst, 'The 1969 Hague Summit: a New Start for Europe?', *Journal of European Integration History*, vol. 9, no. 2 (2003), pp. 5–10, here p. 7.
74 Communiqué of the meeting of Heads of State or Government of the Member States at The Hague on 1 and 2 December 1969. Reproduced: http://www.ena.lu/mce.swf?doc=1565%lang=2 (accessed February 2007).
75 Claudia Hiepel, 'In Search of the Greatest Common Denominator. Germany and The Hague Summit Conference 1969', *Journal of European Integration History*, vol. 9, no. 2 (2003), pp. 63–82, here p. 79.
76 Rittberger, *Building Europe's Parliament*, p. 124.
77 Council, Note, R/2340/69 (ASS 1223, FIN 449), 3 December 1969, HAEC/BAC, 207/1996, 29.
78 EP, Report, Doc. 174, 8 December 1969, HAEC/BAC, 207/1996, 29.
79 SecGen, Note, SEC(69)4729, 14 December 1969. HAEC/BAC, 187/1995, 15.
80 SecGen, Note, SEC(69)4710, 8–9 December 1969, ibid.
81 Commission, Communication complementaire, COM(69)1020 final 2, 11 December 1969, HAEC/BAC, 20/1973, 3.
82 SecGen, Note, SEC(69)4769, 13 December 1969, HAEC/BAC, 187/1995, 15.
83 For example, Council, Questions à examiner, R/2520/69 (ASS 1246), 16 December 1969, HAEC/BAC, Cabinet Coppé, 74/1985, 648.
84 PE 23.807.
85 Council, Minutes, extract, 17 and 19–21 December 1969, HAEC/BAC, 51/1986, 833; SecGen, Note and Annex II, SEC(69)6989, 19 December 1969, HAEC/BAC, 187/1995, 15.
86 Pollack, *The Engines*, p. 212.
87 SEC(69)6989.
88 Rittberger, *Building Europe's Parliament*, pp. 133–35.
89 SecGen, Note, SEC(69)4769, 13 December 1969, HAEC/BAC, 187/1995, 15; Council, R/2520/69 (ASS 1246).
90 PE 23.807.
91 SecGen, Minutes, Commission des finances et des budgets, 27 December 1969, SEC(69)5047, HAEC/BAC, 51/1986, 833.
92 EP, Letter, *Bulletin*, 1969–70, no. 49, 9 January 1970, HAEC/BAC, 20/1973, 4.
93 EP, Note, ibid.
94 EP, Communication, 22 December 1969, ibid.
95 Council, Note, R/14/70 (AGRI 6) (FIN 2), 7 January 1970, HAEC/BAC, 207/1996, 29; Minutes, COREPER, 15–16 January 1970, HAEC/BAC, 187/1995, 15.
96 Council, Minutes, 19–20 January 1970, HAEC/BAC, 51/1986, 833.

97 Anjo Harryvan and Jan van der Harst, 'Swan Song or Cock Crow? The Netherlands and The Hague Conference of December 1969', *Journal of European Integration History*, vol. 9, no. 2 (2003), pp. 27–40.
98 PE 23.807, HAEC/BAC, 51/1986, 833; Also, Letter Rey/Scelba/Harmel, 13–15 December 1970, HAEC/BAC, 187/1995, 16; Council, Note, C/6/70 (ASS 3), 26 January 1970, CM2, 1969, 1270 (temp).
99 Letter, Scelba to Rey, 15 April 1970, HAEC/BAC, 187/1995, 16.

11 The European Commission and the rise of Coreper

A controlled experiment

N. Piers Ludlow

In late April 1965 the six permanent representatives of the founding member-states of the European Economic Community (EEC) gathered in Brussels to hear a serious complaint from one of their number, Jean-Marc Boegner, about the behaviour of the European Commission. The French government, Boegner explained, was growing ever unhappier with the work of the Press and Information Service of the European Communities. In the most serious of a number of recent abuses of its power, the Commission Service had assisted an American academic, Professor Daniel Lerner, to circulate to around one thousand Europeans of note, a questionnaire, which invited participants to give their opinions of the policies of Charles de Gaulle, the French President. This was not appropriate behaviour for a Community institution. Boegner had thus written to Walter Hallstein, the President of the European Commission, raising this issue but had yet to receive a reply. The French government had therefore decided to demonstrate its disapproval by cancelling the planned visit to Brussels of its representative on the 'Information' working group, with the result that the scheduled April 28 meeting of this committee would not go ahead.[1]

A little over a week later, Boegner himself visited Hallstein, to remonstrate further and to broaden the list of complaints to include the invitation to visit Brussels which the Press and Information Service had issued to a delegation of members of the French *Conseil d'Etat*. Such invitations, the permanent representative asserted, should only be transmitted via the Permanent Representation so that the French foreign ministry could remain aware of which Frenchmen were visiting the Community institutions. And once more French displeasure was not limited to verbal complaints. Boegner also informed the Commission President that the *Conseil d'Etat* delegation would not be visiting Belgium at all.[2]

While Lise Rye demonstrates in her chapter in this book that member-state influence over the Commission's incipient information activities remained limited, both of these incidents could be regarded merely as preliminary skirmishes between France and the European Commission in the months that preceded the outbreak of the 'empty chair crisis'. By early July 1965 indeed with a French boycott of most Community meetings underway and rumours circulating around Europe about De Gaulle's intention of seeking a radical alteration of the whole Community system and a drastic reduction in the European Commission's prerogatives, the cancellation of a working group meeting and a relatively low-level fact-finding trip to Brussels can appear of little intrinsic importance.[3] But if one looks less at the substance of dispute between Boegner and Hallstein and more at the manner in which French displeasure was made known to the Commission and to France's Community partners, these two minor spats may be of rather greater interest. For they serve to underline how important the permanent representatives had become, both individually and collectively through the Committee of Permanent Representatives (Coreper), in policing the activities of the European Commission and trying to ensure that the self-styled European 'executive' did not escape from tight member-state control.

Few member-states admittedly were quite as aggressive in their critique of the Commission as were the French especially immediately prior to and during the empty chair crisis. The unprecedented ferocity of Boegner's assault in the Lerner case provoked an anxious discussion amongst the Commissioners about what procedure should be followed were the institution ever again to be given a dressing down of this sort in the Permanent Representatives Committee.[4] Several of Boegner's fellow Coreper members, moreover, while recognizing some of the substance of the French complaints, appeared reluctant to become embroiled in the wider dispute between Gaullist France and the European Commission.[5]

While extreme, however, this use by France of the permanent representatives to check the increase in Commission power could be seen as part of a wider trend. In part this involved an attempt to monitor and oversee the increasingly intense dialogue between the EEC's self-styled 'executive' and member-state bureaucracies. The steady increase in the level of Community activity during the EEC's early years had been accompanied by an ever greater flow of national civil servants to Brussels. Commission figures suggest that between 14,000 and 15,000 national experts per annum were brought in to serve on the multiple committees designed to guide the preparation of draft legislation. The Commissioners themselves, moreover, spent on average 100 days a year travelling – most often to their own member-state of origin, where they would consult extensively about what the Commission ought to be doing. The member-states had however shown some indication of discomfort about this trend and a desire closely to monitor its development. Commission requests for additional funding to cover the travel costs of those it invited had for instance been turned down. The Council of Ministers had furthermore insisted that complex rules be drawn up between itself and the European Commission limiting the size of such expert gatherings, requiring a long period of notice before any such meeting could be called and insisting on prior written consultation of the member-states via the Council before national experts became involved. Commission invitations to national experts were to be issued via the permanent representatives, with each member-state free to decide which civil servants would be included in each national delegation. And all correspondence between the Commission and national civil servants was sent through the Permanent Representations, allowing Coreper members to keep a close watch on all interchange between member-state and European level bureaucracies.[6] The insertion into the Heptalogue – the document about Council/Commission relations which was to emerge from the Luxembourg meetings of January 1966 – of a German drafting amendment, which spoke of all pre-consultation between the Commission and the member-states being organized 'with the permanent representatives acting as intermediaries', was thus an acknowledgment of established practice more than a genuine suggestion of change.[7]

Another aspect of the control over the Commission exercised by and through the permanent representatives was the limitation of Hallstein and his colleagues' international diplomatic ambitions. The level of international reaction and interest generated by the early successes of European integration was one of the greatest surprises in the EEC of the 1960s. No sooner had the Community begun its own internal development than it found itself inundated by requests from third countries to open representative missions in Brussels, suggestions for the negotiation of special economic arrangements between the Six and countries both within Europe and without, and invitations from multiple international organizations for Community Europe in some shape or form to participate in their deliberations. The EEC treaty contained few specific provisions covering the EEC's international profile and there was hence little direct legal guidance as to the division of labour between the Commission and the member-states in this area. And Hallstein made no secret of his ambitions in this area and of his belief that a high international profile would increase the power and prestige of both the Community in general and the institution over which he presided. In early 1965 he told a German audience that:

> It is said that a man is defined by what others expect him to be. This certainly applies to the Community: to the extent that it is perceived as unified by those who surround it, so it will be obliged to sharpen its unity. [8]

None of the member-states were content to allow the Commission's ambitions to develop unchecked in this field. In 1960 the negotiations surrounding Greece's association to the European Community were nearly derailed by a serious dispute between the Commission and the member-states over the extent to which Jean Rey as the chief Commission negotiator had exceeded the mandate which he had been given by the Council.[9] A year later, the governments of both the Netherlands and France launched a serious if ultimately unsuccessful bid to deny the Commission any significant role in the first round of enlargement negotiations with the British, Irish, Danes and Norwegians.[10] In the aftermath of the 1963 failure of the first negotiations, neither the applicants nor any of the member-states reacted favourably to Hallstein's suggestion that the task of maintaining a close link between the Six and those states whose ambition to join the EEC had just been frustrated should be primarily left to the Commission's representative office in London.[11] And throughout the period there were periodic tussles between the Commission and the permanent representatives about the day-to-day interaction between the Community and the outside world: it was for instance a dispute over the Commission and the member-states' roles in a proposed trade negotiation with Iran which signalled Coreper's return to effective operation after the paralysis induced by de Gaulle's first veto.[12]

It would be the French, however, who would escalate tension over this question in the course of the 1965–66 period. In May 1965, the French were well to the fore in a Coreper discussion which questioned the appropriateness of the Commission participating in the deliberations of the Organization for Economic Co-operation and Development's agricultural policy committee.[13] In October 1965, during the period when France had absented itself from most Community meeting, Maurice Ulrich, the French Deputy Permanent Representative contacted the Secretary General of the Council of Ministers in order to complain about the Commission's efforts to establish a dialogue about trade with the government of Afghanistan.[14] And most famously of all, the overly grandiose ceremonial which the Commission President had devised to receive diplomats presenting their credentials to the EEC was one of the ten French grievances enumerated in the Decalogue, the *cahier de doleances*, about Commission behaviour drawn up by the French in January 1966.[15] But significantly, while most of the member-states rejected the more extreme positions adopted by the French they did prove willing to go much further towards de Gaulle's position on this issue than they did over several of the other matters in dispute between France and its partners in the course of the empty chair crisis. The Heptalogue did thus include the suggestion that the procedure for the accreditation of foreign representatives to the European Community (EC) be revised.[16] And almost uniquely amongst the provisions of this document, most of which were set out in writing but never again officially revisited by either the Council or the Commission, there were follow up negotiations in the course of 1966 to ensure that a new procedure for receiving foreign emissaries was put in place. France was not alone, it would appear, in feeling somewhat affronted by Hallstein's diplomatic delusions of grandeur.

Even more revealingly than these periodic disputes between the member-states and the Commission was the way in which the whole institutional structure of the Community tilted towards ever greater member-state control of the Commission's actions. This trend long pre-dated the empty chair crisis or the Luxembourg compromise which brought the French boycott of Brussels meetings to an end. As early as 1962, the Deringer report drawn up by the European Parliament on the Community's Fifth Activity Report contained a lengthy denunciation of the trend away from Commission power.

> Current practice gives the impression that the Council always succeeds in gaining a role in the management of the Community's current affairs, which, under the Treaty, ought to be the sole responsibility of the Commission, the Council's task being that of deliberating on the Commission's proposals. The collaboration foreseen by article 162 as being between two legally equal but distinct entities, has taken on the form of an intergovernmental conference in permanent session at various levels (ministers, permanent representatives, experts from national ministries) in which three secretariats participate: the European Commission with its 2000 staff, the Council secretariat which numbers several hundred civil servants, and the delegations to the Community of the different member states, not to mention the numerous

national civil servants who periodically take part in the meetings. Thus is born a mixed administration the work of which cannot be identified as being the outcome of the efforts of any individual participant but only of the whole, since it is impossible to identify the role of any single player.[17]

Concrete examples of this tendency are not difficult to find in the course of the EEC's early development. One clear case in point was the emergence of the Special Committee on Agriculture – a member-state dominated entity – as one of the key structures determining the evolution of the increasingly complex Common Agricultural Policy (CAP).[18] Another would be the way in which the member-states gradually devised a series of structures designed to oversee and control the Commission's information and press strategy.[19] And a third example would be the centrality of the Article 111 Committee, composed primarily of national trade experts, to the Community's involvement in the Kennedy Round negotiations in the General Agreement on Tariffs and Trade (GATT) between 1963 and 1967.[20] Each of these would, however, be no more than part of a much wider pattern of increased member-state control which extended from the ever more central activities of Coreper itself – given belated recognition in the Merger Treaty of 1965 – to the proliferation of Council committees devoted to virtually every aspect of Community activity.[21] As the clearly alarmed European Parliament rapporteur summed it up: 'In multiple parts of the general report [on the activities of the EEC], the unwary reader would gain the impression that the work of the executive had been to a large extent handed over to experts or to committees of experts.'[22] The independence of the Commission – to say nothing of the ambition of the European Parliament to become the principal body responsible for overseeing the activities of the Community's self-styled 'executive' – was decisively reduced by these developments.

This pattern could be seen as at least partial evidence for Mark Pollack's recent attempts to apply 'principal agent' theory to the development of the EC/European Union (EU).[23] Agriculture and commercial negotiations were both fields in which substantial powers had been delegated to the agent – the European Commission. The Brussels institution had moreover shown great dynamism in exploiting to the full the room for manoeuvre, which it had been granted – greater dynamism than many had perhaps expected.[24] As a result, the principals – the member-states – had been obliged to reinforce their mechanisms of control so as to avoid a situation in which an energetic and power-hungry European Commission moved further and faster towards centralized European governance than they were prepared to allow. The reinforcement of Coreper and the emergence of member-state dominated oversight bodies such as the Special Committee for Agriculture or the Article 111 Committee could thus be seen as a reaction to the Commission's early successes and an attempt to bolster the treaty-given powers of the member-states with a new range of provisions more suited to the full range of delegation involved in the EEC. How effective a means of control such structures proved to be would of course vary significantly according to the policy area involved. But it would not be at all surprising were this development to have been regarded with some suspicion, annoyance or even alarm both by the European Commission itself and, perhaps still more, by a European Parliament which saw one of its key rationales – the control of the European 'executive' – in danger of being usurped by the member-states.[25] Pollack's analysis could therefore go some way towards explaining the frustration and consternation apparent in the wording of the Deringer report.

It would however be too much of a simplification to explain the increased role of the Council of Ministers and its multiple subordinate bodies purely or even mainly in terms of the member-states' desire to curtail or control the amount of power delegated to the European Commission. After all, in the EEC of the 1960s, the member-states still retained multiple other, equally effective means of holding Commission power in check, not least their total control of the Community's purse strings. This meant for instance that the ambitions of the early Commission were very effectively curtailed by the impossibility of engaging more staff.[26] Had the object of the exercise therefore been to clip the wings of the European Commission there were multiple other, less bureaucratically complex, easier and more effective means of doing so. Indeed as the collapse of the Commission's morale in the aftermath of the empty chair crisis would illustrate, both the ambitions and hopes of the Brussels body were much more deeply affected by the extent to which member-states allowed it to pursue its overarching political dreams, than by the presence or otherwise of oversight structures such as Coreper.[27] A full explanation of why the Council of Ministers and its multiple off-shoots developed so precipitously during the Community's first decade of operation therefore needs to go beyond the principal agent theory and the emphasis on member-state control of the European Commission as 'agent'.

Controlling the Community, not controlling the Commission

The real motivation behind the emerging importance of Coreper and the other subordinate bodies of the Council of Ministers was the member-states' collective need to control the whole integration process – not just the activities of the European Commission. In order to do so, the six founding members of the EEC had to cope with a level of governance which both expanded in policy scope with unexpected rapidity and which became more central to the priorities and political success of the countries involved than had been initially anticipated. The only previous encounter which the Six had had with the operation of supranational integration had been the establishment of the European Coal and Steel Community (ECSC) in the early to mid-1950s.[28] The ECSC, however, had been a highly specialized body, exclusively concerned with the control of two vital, but limited, sectors of the economy: the coal and steel industries. In the light of this narrow scope, the Six had felt able to permit the institutions of the ECSC to exercise a very high degree of direct control over their areas of responsibility – hence the far-reaching powers given to the High Authority. In practice, of course, member-state supervision had gone rather further than a strict reading of the

ECSC treaty would have implied. Despite the theoretical extent of its powers, the High Authority had seldom felt able to take important decisions without obtaining the prior consent of the member-states, either through the ECSC Council of Ministers or the precursor to Coreper in the form of the Coordination Committee (Cocor).[29] Yet despite this gradual slippage from the degree of supranationality seemingly established by the ECSC treaty, the ECSC model was still based on a relatively low degree of direct member-state involvement and control within the policy process. It would hence take a while for the Six fully to establish how much more member-state involvement and control were necessary in the significantly broader range of activities possible under the EEC treaty. But once the EEC began its very rapid initial development, it quickly became apparent that the Community was involved in too much, and was too central for each of the member-state's economic and foreign policy success, for the central institutions to be permitted the type of latitude afforded to the High Authority of the ECSC.

The rise of Coreper and other similar entities were thus in part a reflection of the fact that the new Communities – even in the 1960s, let alone more recently – were doing too much for their activities to be adequately supervised merely by means of periodic ministerial meetings. Monthly get-togethers amongst the six foreign ministers were in no sense sufficient to keep member-state capitals informed about the integration process, to take the multiple decisions, legislative and administrative, which the EEC's development involved, or to guide the fledgling Community in the policy directions desired. Instead, the foreign ministers soon found themselves flanked by multiple other ministerial level encounters in the form of specialist agricultural Councils, trade Councils, or finance Councils. Each of these ministerial gatherings, moreover, was prepared, assisted and followed up by official level activity. In the ECSC, Cocor had met sufficiently infrequently for its members still to be based in the member-state capitals, travelling to Luxembourg only as and when a need arose.[30] Within the EEC by contrast not only were the permanent representatives Brussels-based, but they soon found themselves at the head of sizeable representative offices staffed with the plethora of specialists required to engage with the Community's ever-growing policy range.[31] At its most basic, this proliferation of national officials could be described as a reaction to the much greater scale of EEC activity when compared with other international or supranational structures.

It was also, however, a reflection of how important the EEC had become to each of the member-states involved. With so much at stake in Brussels, none of the Six were willing to run the risk of the integration process developing in ways contrary to their national interests. They thus each spent much of the EEC's formative decade devising ever more complex administrative structures to ensure that they were both as well informed as possible about the way in which policy debates within the Community were evolving and could maximize the impact of their desiderata within EEC debates.[32] The permanent representatives were central to both of these ambitions.

The roles of the permanent representatives

One aspect of their role was to provide early information about the trend of discussions in Brussels and the positions adopted by each of the Community member-states. The archives of each foreign ministry of the founding member-states thus abound in detailed reports, despatched from Brussels, about the way each Coreper meeting had developed and about the stance assumed by every participant. Such official reports are often flanked by dispatches outlining information gleaned about the various national positions from more informal conversations between individual permanent representatives. And this reconnaissance role of the permanent representatives provided the logical starting point for their advisory function also. For it was on the basis of their unrivalled knowledge of what was going on in Brussels and of the likely behaviour of each of their Community partners, that the permanent representatives were so often able to play a key role within the domestic policy debate of each member-state. In the autumn of 1964, for instance, it was largely due to the line taken by Antonio Venturini, the Italian Permanent Representative, that the initial Italian critique of the evolution of the CAP was presented in a highly *communautaire* and non-confrontational manner, thereby facilitating the December 1964 accord on cereal prices. Within the key policy-making committee in the Italian capital, Venturini's insistence that the Italians should present their discontent as being soluble 'within the system' and not as misgivings 'with the system' had a decisive effect on the stance subsequently adopted by Italian ministerial representatives.[33] The permanent representative's judgement about how best to play the Brussels game was, in other words, a crucial factor as national policy was established in Rome.

Equally vital was the permanent representatives' role in the Community's legislative process. The EC/EU has always been a system grounded in law and exercising many of its key functions through the establishment of an ever-growing corpus of European law. Its formative decade was therefore a time when the EEC had to extend the body of European law from the narrow domain of the coal and steel industries to a much wider range of economic activities, including of course both a functioning customs union and the highly complex CAP. Doing this required a great deal of legislation. For instance, according to Hallstein's figures between 1962 and 1965 the Commission issued on average 80 regulations and 50 directives per annum.[34] Each of these needed to be approved by the Council of Ministers before becoming law. And this process of Council approval would not have been conceivable without the permanent representatives.

For a start, there was a great deal of Community law which ministers neither saw nor discussed. From 1962 onwards a significant proportion of the EEC's legislative output – 138 out of 192 decisions in 1964 for instance – was agreed by Coreper and passed onto the Council of Ministers as 'A Points' which required no further deliberation.[35] Ministers thus sanctioned such law in an entirely automatic fashion, leaving the permanent representatives as the most senior national representatives to have debated and examined it in any detail. But even for those more important issues that were discussed in some depth at the full Council of Ministers, the ability of ministers to reach effective decisions within the limited time for which they could be present in Brussels was almost entirely dependent on the lengthy pre-negotiations held amongst the permanent representatives.

At this level, individual permanent representatives could have a significant impact on the final legislation approved. The European Commission, after all, although still theoretically in charge of each legislative proposal and able to modify or withdraw it as appropriate, was normally more concerned about obtaining national approval for its legislative suggestions than about the finer details of individual points. As a result, its representatives had every incentive to heed strong arguments advanced in the course of Coreper meetings and to alter the proposal to take these points into account. On April 27, 1966, for instance, the Commission responded to the detailed consideration by Coreper of its latest proposal on CAP finance by dropping a number of provisions and substantially altering the wording of others.[36] A determined permanent representative, moreover, especially if representing the country holding the rotating presidency of the Council of Ministers, could have an even more direct impact on the wording of Community legislation by putting forward drafting suggestions and technical amendments designed to bridge the gap between divergent national positions. At an earlier point of those same negotiations over CAP finance in the spring of 1966, for example, the wily and highly experienced Luxembourg Permanent Representative, Albert Borschette, had used his position as chair of Coreper to advance a number of compromise formulas which succeeded in narrowing substantially the gap between the member-states on several sub-issues.[37] Several of the ideas outlined in Borschette's compromise document found their way into the final Community legislation on this subject agreed in May 1966.

The permanent representatives' role continued even when the ministers themselves joined the negotiations. Many Council meetings thus began with a detailed briefing from the permanent representative of the country holding the presidency about the state of play in discussions and the key issues, which ministers needed to decide.[38] On ministers' desks moreover there was normally a copy of the permanent representatives' collective report, outlining which parts of the legislative text had been agreed, and where, by contrast, divergent opinions persisted. Many of the ministers would, furthermore, have benefited from a detailed briefing from their own permanent representative, often over dinner the evening before.[39] And the permanent representatives were nearly always on hand throughout the talks, ready either to advise the minister on points of detail, or, at times to step in and resume their representative role were the minister unable to remain in Brussels for the whole duration of the Council – a not infrequent occurrence for foreign ministers as busy as Maurice Couve de Murville of France or his German counterpart Gerhard Schröder.

Alongside this legislative role, the permanent representatives also acted as more general trouble-shooters, able quickly to respond to the multiple frictions, tensions and incidents that institutionalized co-operation produced. Coreper and the individual permanent representatives were for instance vital ingredients in the EEC's ability to overcome the multiple crises, which beset its first decade.

In the aftermath of episodes such as de Gaulle's 1963 veto of British membership, which had severely strained relations between France and its fellow member-states, it was at the level of committee of permanent representatives that the Community first began to pick up the pieces and resume normal co-operation.[40] Likewise, throughout the 1965–66 empty chair crisis, the five states who sought to resist the French boycott carried out much of their internal co-ordination and tactical discussion through Coreper, while at the same time using the fact that France retained a deputy permanent representative in Brussels throughout the crisis months to ensure that communications with Paris could continue.[41] At such moments of difficulty, the professionalism, the knowledge of the Community system and the discretion of the permanent representatives proved vital for all of the states involved. And even at less problematic times, the permanent representatives could be used quickly to devise a collective response to an unexpected situation whenever the need arose. In the field of external relations in particular, the EEC frequently found itself needing rapidly to devise an answer to approaches, questions and invitations reaching it from would-be commercial partners, international organizations, and aspirant members. As discreet, Brussels-based experts, well versed in both national sensitivities and some of the Community's general needs, the permanent representatives became central actors in improvising a collective response.[42]

The growing importance of the permanent representatives was therefore much more than just a reaction to the activism and dynamism of the European Commission. The permanent representatives did play an over-sight role vis-à-vis the European Commission, whether individually or collectively. And they were used as a channel for some of the member-state frustration at the behaviour of Hallstein and his colleagues. But this was just one of their many functions and does not deserve to be turned into the primary explanation of their rise. Indeed, it is interesting to note that the Six were to devise a very similar mechanism to that of Coreper, in the form of the so-called 'deputies', to handle the 1961–63 enlargement negotiations, despite the fact that hardly any powers had been delegated to the Commission over the question of enlargement.[43] The need for an official level complement to ministerial negotiation and a largely Brussels-based body able to cope with many of the day-to-day problems which arose in a complex negotiation, was in other words the key to explaining why the 'deputies' were given their role in 1961–63 and was almost certainly also the prime determinant of Coreper's rise. 'Principle-agent theory' may offer some insights into the Community's early development but needs to be flanked by multiple other explanations.

Undermining the Community?

In reaching a balanced assessment of the rise of Council control, it is also necessary to move beyond some of the more simplistic or knee-jerk denunciations which the trend received from partisans of the 'Community method'. It is certainly the case that the emergence of the Council and its various subordinate bodies as the hub of the entire Community system constituted a major departure from the original vision of Jean Monnet. The original institutional vision which underpinned the Schuman Plan, after all, had not included any form of member-state check on the actions of the planned supranational executive. That an ECSC Council of Ministers had come into existence at all was a result of Benelux misgivings about the untrammelled powers foreseen for the High Authority. The extent to which this belated addition and its subordinate bodies had gone on to become the hub of Community decision-making was therefore a sign of significant divergence from at least some of the founders' vision. It is also true that the Deringer report cited above was not the only expression of discontent about Council power to emerge in the course of the EEC's initial development. The memoirs of an early Commissioner, Robert Lemaignen, contain a similar lament about the emergence of Coreper, for example:

> In reality, the creation of the permanent representatives was one of the first attempts to realize the dream secretly cherished by national administrations: to see this body, which was tightly controlled by the governments, progressively displace the Commission, the treaty of Rome become mummified, and its development discreetly turn towards the resumption of ineffective but traditional international meetings.[44]

And it is also the case that in certain countries – especially the Benelux states – Coreper's very existence remained politically controversial and seen by many as representative of the Community's slide into unaccountable technocracy. For this reason, those permanent representatives eager to see an increase in their committee's role, recognized that such a change would have to be carried out in as low a profile fashion as possible.[45] But such dismay at the growing role of the permanent representatives, while undoubtedly sincere, should not be allowed to obscure the fact that parts of the Commission adapted well to the new realities of the EEC system and came to perceive bodies such as Coreper as a tool which could favour integration rather than as a symbol of sterile intergovernmentalism.

The Commission thus came to recognize that the permanent representatives could be as useful a channel for the communication of their needs and aspirations to national governments as they could be to the flow of information or invocation in the other direction. In late 1966, for instance, as Britain once more began an approach to the Community about the possibility of membership, it was to the President of Coreper that Hallstein turned in order to make clear the Commission's desire to be adequately represented in any co-ordinating meetings which the Six might plan prior to encountering the United Kingdom representatives.[46] Dirk Spierenburg, the Netherlands' permanent representative, duly promised to relay this request to Joseph Luns, the Dutch foreign minister and holder of the Council Presidency in the latter half of 1966.[47] And as a result, Hallstein and Rey were both invited to the working lunch held amongst the foreign ministers of the Six in order to discuss Britain's approach on December 22.[48] Even more revealingly, the permanent representatives could be used as vital sounding boards as the Commission explored the possibilities of action in under-explored areas of the

EEC's activity. In 1963, for example, as Lionello Levi-Sandri contemplated how to follow up the Commission's first communication in the field of social harmonization, he actively sought a meeting with the permanent representatives so as to establish what the next steps might be.[49] It was perhaps significant that in this case several of the permanent representatives were somewhat reluctant to sanction such a meeting, clearly aware that once begun a process of consultation of this sort might develop a momentum of its own which could carry the EEC further and faster than they or their governments were yet ready to contemplate.[50] The Commission also had ample opportunity to explain and defend its point of view at Coreper meetings, where it was normally represented by its deputy secretary general. The ability to lay out its thinking away from the tension inherent in many of the more important ministerial meetings and to gauge member-state views at a stage of the legislative process where there was still time to alter the proposal were both of considerable value to the Commission. It is also very apparent from the recollections of Michel Cointat, who served for several years in the 1960s as one of the agricultural experts in the French permanent representation to Brussels, that staff in each of these delegations was almost as susceptible to waves of collective enthusiasm for the EEC project as were the staff of the Commission.[51] To put in the terms employed in the current political science debate, the permanent representatives were as susceptible to effects of European 'socialization' as those employed in any other part of the Community bureaucracy.[52] Coreper was not therefore necessarily a sceptical and hostile body, intent on emasculating as many Commission proposals as possible so as to protect national sovereignty. Instead it was an entity which shared many of the same assumptions and enthusiasms as the European Commission itself. As a result, it is perhaps unsurprising that Emile Noël, the Executive Secretary of the Commission from 1958 onwards, should react in so sanguine a fashion to French insistence in the final stages of the empty chair crisis on even greater centrality being given to the permanent representatives, noting that

> [t]he permanent representatives naturally defend the interests of their member-state at a Community level, but at the same time they are, like all good ambassadors, the best advocates of the Community [at a national level]. An effort to establish better collaboration between the permanent representatives and the members of the Commission could be made.[53]

To this end, Noël was ready to envisage the institutionalization of a monthly lunch between the Commission and all of the members of Coreper and appeared to regard any increase in co-ordination between the Commission and the permanent representatives as little more than the generalization of previous best practice.[54]

Even more fundamentally, it is possible to argue that the whole expansion of the Community's agenda, from a customs union and an agricultural policy, to the much wider array of policy fields in which the EU of today operates would not have come about without a set of mechanisms which enabled the member-states to feel that they retained an adequate degree of control over the development of the overall European integration process. The member-states have never viewed the European integration process as being about giving up national power. Instead, they have recognized that the gains in effectiveness of collective action outweigh the frustrations and limitations inherent in joint rather than national decision-making. Naturally involvement in a system such as the early EEC did necessitate some sacrifices in terms of total national autonomy. By joining the Community, each member-state bound itself within a system of laws, which would never be solely of its own making. It also handed a number of important powers and responsibilities to institutions such as the European Commission and the European Court of Justice (ECJ) that could only be effective were they vested with a degree of independence and freedom of action.[55] This in turn opened up the possibility of each of these institutions taking steps and making rulings, which would surprise and displease individual member-states. The obvious consternation of some within the French government at the directions in which European law had evolved in the mid-1960s is a case in point.[56] And most fundamentally, involvement in an EEC which so quickly became central to both the foreign and economic policies of all of the member-states involved locked each of the participants into the Community with little realistic possibility of withdrawal. Again the period of French self-reflection induced by the empty chair crisis of 1965–66 is instructive, since the outcome of the multiple ministerial studies carried out in the autumn of 1965 was to highlight how well France did out of the integration process and how impossible it would be to replicate these benefits elsewhere.[57] The costs of 'non-Europe' would in other words be unacceptably high. But despite all of these qualifications, the early integration process remained one which the national governments believed that they could control and steer in directions compatible with their own national interests, both political and economic. The power they gained by operating together within a supranational system, outweighed the power that they lost by committing themselves more or less irrevocably to such a system.

Such a calculation would, however, have been very different and much less likely to have gone in the direction of European integration, had the European structures to which policy responsibilities could be handed over been dominated completely by supranational entities that entirely escaped the control of national governments. This has never proved to be the case. Instead, the European policy-making framework has always been one where the influence and power of institutions such as the European Commission or the ECJ which are not meant to be unduly swayed by national considerations has been counter-balanced by bodies such as the Council of Ministers and, since 1974 the European Council, which ensure that the member-states retain enough leverage and control to direct the overall evolution of the integration process. The EEC was – and the EU of more recent times still is – a system of 'mixed government' to use Majone's term; or a 'hybrid system' neither fully federal nor wholly intergovernmental as I have argued elsewhere.[58] This mixed or hybrid nature has helped maintain a situation in which the member-states have gone on feeling able to suggest new areas into which European co-operation might expand, without fearing that they were entirely undermining their right to self-determination by so doing.

Conclusions

The unexpected and still under-explored expansion of the role of the Council of Ministers, Coreper, and the other committees within the so-called Council pyramid is arguably the single most important institutional change which the European Community underwent during its initial stage of development. It is a change which began from 1958 onwards and continued to 1974–75 and the institutionalization of the European Council at least, if not much later. It is not therefore something confined to, or even particularly deeply affected by, the institutional ructions of the 1965–66 crisis, but instead a transformation spread across all of the EEC's formative years. It is not therefore associated with a single 'grand bargain' of the sort discussed by rational institutionalists, but is instead a set of arrangements that emerged piecemeal across the Community's first decade of operation. It is also something which ran in parallel to and was entirely compatible with the much more publicized increase during the 1958–65 period of the European Commission's powers, prerogatives and range of activity. But despite the superficial appeal of the principal agent theory, it is too much of an over-simplification to describe the rise of Council control simply or even primarily as an attempt by the member-states to rein in a European Commission intent on making the most of the powers which it had been delegated. For, in devoting so much effort and attention to increasing the number and the effectiveness of their representatives in Brussels, the member-states were trying to maximize their hold over the integration process as a whole, rather than simply over the European Commission. More frequent meetings of the Council, the rise of Coreper and similar specialized structures for agriculture, commerce or the enlargement talks, the proliferation of expert committees, and finally the birth of the European Council all reflect the realization by each of the states participating in the early integration process that they needed to engage that much more closely with what was going on in Brussels so as to be able to steer the decision-making process in directions compatible with their national interest.

European integration, most historians now agree, was something which emerged because a sufficient number of European governments decided that it was in their national interest, as they chose to define it, to co-operate more closely with one another. Such calculations of interest did not vanish, however, as soon as the process was under way. On the contrary, throughout the subsequent six decades, all of the countries involved have sought to balance their desire for an effective and dynamic set of European institutions able to take decisions and to implement them, with an equally strong determination to retain a strong hand on the tiller. The Council pyramid was a central – indeed arguably *the* central – response to this dilemma. But while certainly a departure from Monnet's original vision and as such a development decried by some, it has in fact been a vital element in the Community's success and one which the Commission as much as the member-states has learnt to live with and exploit.

Notes

1 For the Commission's anxious discussion of the incident, see European Commission, Historical Archives, (ECHA), COM (65) PV 316, 2ème partie, 5 May 1965; for the Commission's record of the Coreper meeting: Sigrist note to Commission on Coreper meeting, 27–29 April 1965, ECHA, BDT 214/80, G (65) 227.

2 For the French record, Boegner to Quai, 7 May 1965, Ministère des Affaires Etrangères (MAEF), Europe 1961–65, Serie 38, SS 2, Dossier 3, tel. 530/35.

3 The best way into the extensive literature on the empty chair crisis is Jean-Marie Palayret, Helen Wallace and Pascaline Winand (eds.), *Visions, Votes and Vetoes. The Empty Chair Crisis and the Luxembourg Compromise Forty Years On*, Brussels: Peter Lang, 2006.

4 ECHA, COM (65) 320, 2ème partie, 1 June 1965.

5 Sigrist note to Commission on Coreper meeting, 27–29 April 1965.

6 Secrétariat executif analysis of the Decalogue, 23.1.1965 (sic), Historical Archives of the European Communities (HAEC), Fonds Emile Noël (EN), 377.

7 Sigrist note to Commission, 1 February 1966, HAEC, EN, 343, G (66) 65. The text of the Heptalogue can be found on http://www.ena.lu?lang=1&doc=19632 (last accessed 8 November 2007).

8 Walter Hallstein, Speech to the Institut für Weltwirtschaft an der Universität Kiel, 19 February 1965, ECHA, Speeches collection.

9 Elena Calandri, 'La CEE et les relations extérieures 1958–60', in Antonio Varsori (ed.), *Inside the European Community: Actors and Policies in European Integration*, Baden-Baden: Nomos, 2006, pp. 399–431, here p. 425f.

10 N. Piers Ludlow, *Dealing With Britain: The Six and the First UK Application to the EEC*, Cambridge: Cambridge University Press, 1997, p. 58f.

11 Hallstein advanced the idea at 8–9 May 1963 Council meeting: Council minutes, 8–9 May 1963, Council of Ministers Archives (CMA), S/346/1/63. The lack of enthusiasm was clear from the way in which attention quickly turned instead to either a Coreper or Western European Union centred solution. See N. Piers Ludlow, *The European Community and the Crises of the 1960s: Negotiating the Gaullist Challenge*, London: Routledge, 2006, p. 27f.

12 Noël report to Commission on Coreper meeting, 8 February 1963, ECHA, BDT 214/1980, G/122/63.

13 Sigrist note to Rabot on Coreper meeting, 4–6 May 1965, ECHA, BDT 214/80, S/022959/65.

14 Sigrist note to the Commission on the Coreper meeting, 28 October 1965, ECHA, BDT 214/80, G (65) 529.

15 This was point 5 of the decalogue: see http://www.ena.lu?lang=1&doc=1457 (accessed 8 November 2007).

16 http://www.ena.lu?lang=1&doc=19632 (accessed 8 November 2007).

17 Deringer report, Document 74, *European Parliament Reports 1962–3*, p. 36.

18 See Ann-Christina Lauring Knudsen, *Defining the Policies of the Common Agricultural Policy: A Historical Study*, PhD, Florence: European University Institute, 2001, p. 241f.

19 See N. Piers Ludlow, 'Frustrated Ambitions. The European Commission and the Formation of a European Identity, 1958–67', in Marie-Thérèse Bitsch, Wilfried Loth and Raymond Poidevin (eds.), *Institutions européennes et identités européennes*, Brussels: Bruylant, 1998, pp. 307–26, here pp. 322–24.

20 Lucia Coppolaro, *Trade and Politics across the Atlantic: the European Economic Community (EEC) and the United States of America in the GATT Negotiations of the Kennedy Round (1962–1967)*, PhD, Florence: European University Institute, 2006, p. 123f.

21 See Ludlow, *The European Community*, pp. 122f. and 210–14.
22 Deringer report, Document 74, *European Parliament Reports 1962–3*, p. 37.
23 Mark A. Pollack, *The Engines of European Integration – Delegation, Agency, and Agenda Setting in the EU*, New York: Oxford University Press, 2003. For a wider discussion of delegation theory see also Morten Rasmussen's chapter in this volume.
24 The dynamism of the early European Commission is well captured – if over-stated – by its first serious analysts, the neo-functionalists. See Leon Lindberg, *The Political Dynamics of European Economic Integration*, Stanford: Stanford University Press, 1963.
25 Evidence of Commission annoyance can be found in some of the early memoir literature: for example Robert Lemaignen, *L'Europe au Berceau. Souvenirs d'un technocrate*, Paris: Plon, 1964, pp. 85–8.
26 The Commission's repeated attempts to escape from this financial hold are explored in Ludlow, 'A Supranational Icarus? Hallstein, the early Commission and the search for an independent role' in Varsori, *Inside the European Community*, pp. 37–53, here pp. 48–50.
27 Ibid., pp. 50–3.
28 The defining work on this remains Dirk Spierenburg and Raymond Poidevin, *Histoire de la Haute Autorité de la Communauté Européenne du Charbon et de l'Acier: une expérience supranationale*, Brussels: Bruylant, 1993.
29 Ibid.
30 Jean Salmon, 'Les représentations et missions permanents auprès de la CEE et de l'EURATOM' in Michel Virally, Pierre Gerbet and Jean Salmon (eds.), *Les Missions Permanentes auprès des Organisations Internationales*, Brussels: Bruylant, 1971, p. 609f.
31 Ibid. for a detailed description of the sizes of permanent representations.
32 See Laurence Badel, Stanislas Jeannesson and N. Piers Ludlow (eds.), *Les administrations nationales et la construction européenne. Une approche historique (1919–1975)*, Brussels: Peter Lang, 2005, especially parts II and III.
33 Resoconto sommario della XXXIV riunione del comitato ristretto dei direttori generali dei ministeri tecnici incaricati delle questioni CEE e dei rapporti con i paesi terzi, 20 November 1964, Archivio Centrale di Stato (ACS), Ministero del Bilancio e della Programmazione Economica (MBPE), vol. 93.
34 Hallstein speech, 'The Commission, a New Factor in International Life', London, 25 March 1965, ECHA, Speeches collection.
35 Salmon, 'Les repésentations et missions permanentes', pp. 684–87.
36 Item F, 27 April 1966, ECHA, PV COM (65) 357, 2ème partie.
37 Sigrist report on the 31.3.1966 Coreper meeting, ECHA, BDT 144/92, SEC (66) 1013.
38 See, for example, Boegner's report at the start of the ill-fated 1965 CAP negotiations: Council minutes, 28 June–1 July 1965, CMA, R/850/65.
39 For a reference to one such dinner, Yann l'Ecotais, *L'Europe sabotée*, Brussels: Rossel Edition, 1976, p. 19f.
40 Noël report to Commission on Coreper meeting, 8 February 1963, ECHA, BDT 214/1980, G/122/63.
41 For more detail see N. Piers Ludlow, 'Mieux que six ambassadeurs: l'emergence de COREPER durant les premières années de la CEE' in Badel, Jeannesson and Ludlow (eds.), *Les administrations nationales*, pp. 337–55, here p. 349f.
42 Ibid., pp. 346–48.
43 Ludlow, *Dealing With Britain*, p. 68.
44 Lemaignen, *L'Europe au berceau*, p. 87.
45 Harkort to Neef, 3 May 1965, Deutsches Bundesarchiv, Bundeskanzleramt
46 30 November 1966, ECHA, COM (66) PV 382, 2ème partie.
47 6 December 1966, ECHA, COM (66) PV 383, 2ème partie.
48 21 December 1966, ECHA, COM (66) PV 385, 2ème partie.

49 Herbst report to the Commission on the Coreper meeting of 27.2.1963, ECHA, BDT 214/1980, S/0657/63.
50 Ibid.
51 Michel Cointat, *Les couloirs de l'Europe*, Paris: L'Harmattan, 2001, especially pp. 105–7.
52 See Morten Rasmussen's chapter for a discussion of the idea of socialization.
53 Analysis of decalogue, 23.1.1965 (sic.), HAEC, EN-377.
54 Ibid.
55 That even the French recognized this point is clear from the fact that they did not seek to install a weak Commission President as a replacement to Walter Hallstein. See Ludlow, *The European Community*, p. 130f.
56 Ibid., p. 77f.
57 Ibid., p. 91f.
58 Giandomenico Majone, *Dilemmas of European integration: The Ambiguities and Pitfalls of Integration by Stealth*, Oxford: Oxford University Press, 2005, pp. 46–51. Whether the analogy with medieval and early-modern governance, which accompanies this description, is useful or a pointless distraction, is rather more open to debate; my own description of the system was first advanced in Ludlow, 'The Eclipse of the Extremes: Demythologising the Luxembourg Compromise' in Wilfried Loth, *Crises and Compromises: The European Project, 1963–1969*, Baden-Baden: Nomos, 2001, pp. 247–64, here p. 257f. and was amplified in *The European Community*, pp. 118–24.

12 Interdisciplinarity in research on the EU

Politics, history and prospects for collaboration

Alex Warleigh-Lack

European Union (EU) studies is going through a period of self-examination and change. From a political science perspective,[1] the boundaries between the 'European', the 'national' and indeed the 'global' are increasingly blurred, meaning that the separation of the study of politics into separate boxes labelled with such titles as 'comparative politics', 'public administration', or 'International Relations' is decreasingly viable. For political science scholars of the EU, this is generating new opportunities as well as fresh challenges: equipped for many years now to examine the politics of transnational and supranational spaces and processes, we are in a position to contribute positively to the debates around global governance in International Relations (IR) scholarship – a reversal of the traditional hierarchy.[2] And yet, political science studies of the EU are also lacking in certain respects. As political science scholars of the EU we have often shut ourselves away from colleagues in other areas of politics, and our engagement with salient material from other disciplines inside the domain of EU studies is not always as deep or as insightful as it might be.[3] Furthermore, there is an ongoing debate in the field regarding the best way of going beyond the orthodox focus: a 'normal science' movement seeks to replicate in EU political studies the norms of positivist United States (US) political science, whereas an interdisciplinary movement seeks to reach out to a range of disciplines and sub-disciplines in order to generate a holistic perspective.[4]

In this chapter I want to contribute to this debate by examining the potential for interdisciplinary cooperation between historians and political scientists in EU studies, a kind of partnership which could be far more fruitful than has so far been the case.[5] My default position is that this would be very productive for scholars in both disciplines, even if it is likely to be difficult and to generate risks as well as benefits. The chapters included in this volume serve to demonstrate that such collaboration can be very fruitful. They also remind us of the usefulness of qualitative forms of research – a helpful corrective to the Americanisation of political studies in the United Kingdom (UK) and elsewhere in Europe.

An engagement by political scientists with such EU historiography as that to be found here – theoretically informed, source-rich and analytical, aiming for the middle-range rather than the particular – would help us ensure our theoretical claims are sufficiently grounded in evidence and not faddish expressions of 'presentism'. From a positivist perspective – such as Andrew Moravcsik's – it could potentially help develop the evidence to reinforce claims of theoretical generalisability (but see Morten Rasmussen's warning in his chapter in this volume regarding Moravcsik's own skills in this regard).[6] From a constructivist or post-positivist perspective, such engagement with history and historians would reinforce claims about the significance of individuals' behaviour, culture, networks and ideas in determining political outcomes. From any political science perspective, a thorough understanding of this kind of EU historiography would also facilitate an understanding of the essence of our subject: what is the EU? How did it become so? Are our beliefs that certain changes in the EU political system and 'constitution' result from particular Treaty changes (e.g. the Maastricht Treaty and differentiated integration) or policy reform (e.g. the adaptations to the structural funds and their link to the creation of multi-level governance) solid when looked at in historical perspective? Many of the chapters in this volume give pause for thought on this head.

Moreover, those in political science – such as myself – who see potential benefit in transcending the methodological assumption of the non-porous nation state will benefit from the reinforcement of our efforts by such historiography as that contained in this book: if supra- or transnational approaches to EU history are required, might they not also be of use in investigating other political histories, at least in the post-1945 period? Do they not reinforce claims that EU studies is an over-looked and potentially crucial body of literature for those seeking to revise IR scholarship in an era of globalisation?[7] I also think they oblige both political scientists and lawyers to ask searching questions about the onset of the transnational 'new world order' devined relatively recently by Anne-Marie Slaughter.[8]

In fact, scholars have long debated whether there is anything but a temporal divide between politics and history as fields of enquiry, a question which is reinforced by the evidence that the subjects were often considered virtually synonymous in the nineteenth century.[9] Even today it is often difficult to establish when 'contemporary history' ends and 'politics' begins. Many historians might argue that the thirty-year rule regarding access to government archives sets the changing boundary between history and politics, but this is at best an instrumental rather than a substantive way of dividing the two fields of enquiry, particularly given that some states impose longer, or shorter, waiting periods before opening up their archives. It also implies that all history is state-based or diplomatic.

As self-conscious 'disciplines', history and politics parted company gradually, with a decisive caesura in the middle of the twentieth century as a function of the dominance of the US academy and its search to replicate the norms of behaviouralist natural science in social science, with politics in particular seeking to reflect this orientation.[10] Consequently, scholars in both fields can caricature each other with the following result: political scholars are peddlers of hopelessly jargonistic and overly general 'theory'; historians are antiquarian detail-addicts who cannot see the general wood for the particular trees. As with all caricatures, there is an element of truth here. But both fields of enquiry are also internally diverse, with their own (sometimes parallel) debates regarding the nature and purpose of good scholarly work, in particular regarding the extent to which they can, or should, be 'scientific' and, more latterly, regarding the extent to which they can use traditional methods and concepts in an age of transnationalism.[11] This diversity and simultaneous parallel challenge may offer opportunities to reach across the disciplinary divide.

The chapter proceeds as follows. First, I set out how I understand politics and history as fields of academic endeavour. Next, I discuss what I mean by inter-disciplinarity and how it relates to other forms of cross-disciplinary work. Subsequently, I sketch how scholars from the two disciplines of politics and history might collaborate in the specific field of EU studies, and investigate the contri-butions to this volume through the eyes of a political scientist to assess what they indicate for the process of history-politics collaboration in the study of the EU. I conclude the chapter by suggesting some ideas which may help in taking such collaboration forward.

Defining politics and history

It is not easy to define politics exactly as an academic subject because its very essence is open to question. Although it might be agreed that politics as a 'real-world' enterprise is about the use of power – to paraphrase Harold Lasswell, who gets what, how, when, and why – this can be interpreted and studied in a variety of ways.[12] If politics is about the use of power, how is that to be defined? As the use of force and coercion? The making and amending of the rules of social life? As the process of conflict resolution? And on whom should scholars focus: the state or the citizen? Should we emphasise competition, or cooperation, between actors? Should politics be studied normatively (that is, as a quest to uncover how political life might best be organised, however we define that), or 'scientifically'? Should political studies seek to generate a profound understanding of one state or phenomenon, or aim to develop universalistic and generalisable explanations of phenomena and processes in the form of theories and laws?

In fact, different scholars and different sub-disciplines within political science have tended to reach different conclusions to all these questions – and also to revise their conclusions, not necessarily in the same direction, at various junctures.[13] The understanding of politics as an academic subject that I adopt here is therefore somewhat imprecise, but can be summed up as follows: politics is the study of how both public and private sphere conflicts of interest over scarce resources are, or should be, resolved. While a little vague, this definition helpfully focuses on power and its uses, and acts as a reminder that political life is both social and personal, private and public, with potential for collaboration as well as competi-tion and coercion, and with normative as well as empirical concerns the proper subject of study.

Just like politics, history as an academic subject can be understood in different ways, with the *Zeitgeist* having an important bearing on such evolution.[14] It also has a variety of sub-fields like military history, diplomatic history, social history, economic history etc. with their own conventions and emphases. There are certain elements of the subject, however, which seem to me to be common across these understandings. First, history is the search to understand the diversity and richness of human experience as evidenced by historical record. It is thus the search for the particular and the distinct rather than the general, placing emphasis on the differences between human societies and cultures and their respective evolutions.[15] Second, history focuses on evolution over time, seeing events not just in their own right but as part of a continuum. Third, as a result, some structuralist and neo-Marxist historians claim the ability to predict the future based on an understanding of past events of a similar kind.[16] Fourth – and perhaps in contradiction – history is about the interrogation of sources, which are often physically incomplete or, if they are written or oral sources, the products of an author or authors with their own purposes in mind. Hence, sources can be partial in more than one sense, and require careful questioning not only of their author's intention and use, but of why the analyst reaches this conclusion.

Moreover, the decision by any scholar regarding which sources to interrogate, and how this will be done, is not neutral: methodology is politics.[17] Thus, historians are often caught in a trap: understanding the past requires critical knowledge of the sources and sufficient certainty to claim plausible interpretation, but if facts do not speak for themselves there must be much room for error on the part of their interpreters. Hence, claims to speak to the present and/or the future on the basis of what may be a misunderstood past may be questionable.[18] In sum, I understand history as 'the stories we tell about our prior selves or that others tell about us'.[19]

The interdisciplinarity continuum

To understand interdisciplinarity, it is first of all necessary to delve into epistemology. Advocates of interdisciplinary work argue that it is necessitated by the shifting patterns in the way we consider knowledge to be most effectively generated, away from linear models and towards 'a *network* or a *web* with multiple nodes of connection . . . a *dynamic system*'.[20] In other words, interdisciplinarity makes a break with the idea that the best way to understand social reality is to break that reality down into separate small chunks which can then be neutrally observed.[21] Instead, the emphasis should be placed on understanding the issue at hand, and solving the problems it presents, in their entirety. It is thus wrongheaded to privilege a method or set of variables simply because they govern the self-understanding of a particular discipline, as we risk ending up with an incomplete if 'rigorous' set of findings. Many interdisciplinary scholars therefore make an overt connection between interdisciplinarity and complexity.[22] If real-world problems are too multi-faceted for one discipline (or scholar) to address, then the toolkit we use must be correspondingly deep and broad, and the lone scholar model may require reappraisal.

This does not mean, of course, that there are no conditions which interdisciplinary research must fulfil.[23] Newell argues that interdisciplinary work is only required if two basic conditions are met.[24] First, the issue to be studied must have complex and multiple, but coherent, components. If it is a simple problem, or if the links between its various facets are insufficiently robust, then work within a given discipline or which draws only in passing on a range of disciplines is likely to be more effective. Second, to qualify for the label 'interdisciplinary', research must fully integrate insights generated from different disciplinary perspectives into a new perspective.

Further light can be shed on the concept of interdisciplinarity by contrasting it with two related, but separate, concepts – multi-disciplinarity and transdisciplinarity. Although all three concepts refer to 'non-disciplinary' work, they can be distinguished according to one main criterion: the extent to which they integrate insights from the various disciplines on which they draw. Work 'beyond' or 'across' disciplines can be undertaken in a variety of ways.[25] Multidisciplinary research requires scholars to be aware of salient contributions from other disciplines, and to draw on them in useful but limited ways. For example, scholars trying to understand the politics of the European Court of Justice (ECJ) are likely to deliver incomplete findings if they cannot, for example, understand and address legal logics and reasoning, and ECJ case law, in addition to the application of political science theories of European integration or domestic politics of executive-judiciary relations in the member states of the EU. However, in such studies, legal scholarship is likely to be used as a resource or illustration rather than harnessed in a new synthesis.

Interdisciplinary work would take that step, via a sustained process of dialogue, joint problem-definition, and methodology devising by a team of scholars from the salient disciplines or areas. To keep the same example for reasons of clarity, this might involve iterated dialogue between scholars of EU politics, International Relations, international law and EC law. Transdisciplinary work would go one step further, adding an overarching common meta-theoretical perspective to the common definition of the problem and methods. Thus, the imaginary team of scholars investigating the politics of the ECJ might be further united by a shared belief in, say, Marxism.

Thus, non-disciplinary work can usefully be understood as a continuum, and one which includes a range of modes. It should also be understood as a way of working which can create new structures as well as new dynamics: if scholarly collaboration across disciplines to solve a given problem endures, this can eventually replace disciplinarity as the dominant mode of work in that issue area, but the resulting new common structures (scholarly journals, conferences, etc.) may reify new boundaries even as they cut outgrown links to particular disciplines.[26] Interdisciplinary work is therefore no more value neutral or incapable of hegemonic tendencies than disciplinary studies – a note of caution that it is worthwhile to remember even if the critical element of interdisciplinary work provides some degree of alleviation.

Prospects for interdisciplinarity I: collaboration between politics and history[27]

There are certain generalisable benefits and risks of engaging in interdisciplinary work. On the positive side, such collaboration can help scholars escape fragmentation of (sub-)disciplines, foster intellectual creativity and reflexivity, and generate both new understandings and methodological refinements. Problems of such work include difficulties of commensurability between disciplines, technical barriers to cooperation such as academic structures (universities, learned societies, journals) which promote disciplinarity, and the risk of sacrificing depth for the sake of breadth.[28] In the specific context of collaboration between historians and political scientists in the field of EU studies, several more particular issues must be addressed.

The first issue to address here is whether there is sufficient critical mass for such cooperation to be undertaken. The EU history scholarly community is small, if growing.[29] Are enough EU historians willing and able to cooperate with enough political science scholars to generate new understandings that are not reducible to the idiosyncracies of the few scholars concerned? Beyond the crude issue of numbers, there are matters of rival calls to interdisciplinarity to consider. As several scholars point out, in recent years historians have generally been better-disposed to cooperate with anthropologists and sociologists than with political scientists, seeing in such collaboration greater likely methodological synergies and epistemological harmonies.[30] In political science work on the EU, scholars have primarily been influenced by economics and law, if they engage with other disciplines at all.[31] Moreover, in an age of globalisation, it cannot be right to focus on the EU in isolation from other regions in the global political economy[32] or the emerging global polity itself – issues which call political science scholars of the EU to work with those of International Relations, economics and sociology.[33] Thus, an interest in interdisciplinarity may not necessarily translate into concrete history-political science collaboration.

A second, related problem is the often inadequate degree of knowledge of the other discipline possessed by scholars in the two fields of enquiry. In addition to increasing susceptibility to caricature, this relative ignorance of the 'other' literature can make even well-intentioned scholars reinvent the wheel. The editors of this volume note the challenge by historians to Moravcsik's work in political science as one example. In the opposite direction, Alan S. Milward and Vibeke Sørensen's critique of neofunctionalism, supposedly devastating, in fact simply rehashed several points made by Charles Pentland and Reginald Harrison twenty years previously.[34] A third problem is that both history and politics, as disciplinary approaches to the study of the EU, are internally diverse, and their respective various sub-disciplines may not share the same willingness or capacity to collaborate across the disciplinary frontier. For example, comparative political study of EU member states has been slow to integrate the EU as a core aspect of its work rather than an add-on. National historical studies have been similarly slow to embrace the transnational, an argument made forcefully by the editors of this book. This provides evidence of ontological similarity in the two disciplines, but by the same token it demonstrates that certain parts of each of them may resist the opportunity provided by the novelty of the EU context to grow through interdisciplinarity. It also suggests that we may end up with multiple interdisciplinarities, each shaped by pathologies of sub-disciplinary culture, rather than one way of 'doing interdisciplinarity' between politics and history.

A fourth problem follows on from this. Are historians by definition predisposed to deny the novel, rather than the historically-specific? For example, Wolfram Kaiser has argued that many historians will fail to appreciate the post-Westphalian state features of the EU because these have become much clearer only in the post-Single European Act period.[35] As a result, certain theoretical approaches and concepts such as multilevel governance, which are mainstays of political science work on the EU, may seem alien. Coupled with a general distrust of 'theory' (usually understood in a very positivist manner that is by no means universally accepted in political science), and an apparent lack of understanding of its finer points, as in Milward's repeated conflation of functionalism and neofunctionalism,[36] historians may not be able to engage with a fundamental aspect of political science work on the EU, in which theory explicitly shapes research design and execution. The obverse case is also worth discussing: are political scientists too ready to apply generalised concepts to particular historical events, seeing them lazily as proof rather than appreciating the context and specificities? As the editors argue in their introduction to this book, this is certainly true of much IR scholarship,[37] and given the key role of IR scholars in founding EU studies, such possibilities cannot be ruled out. Contemporary EU scholars from more positivist schools of political science may be particularly susceptible to this fault – as the remarks by the editors of this volume rightly remind us.

Finally, whatever the scope for collaboration between historians and political scientists in EU studies, such collaboration cannot be simply the triumph of one discipline over the other. Historians wishing to adopt political science methods may well also have to adapt them to avoid anachronism and over-generalisation.[38] Political scientists will have to accept certain limitations to generalisable theory and methods if they wish to embrace the diachronic as well as the synchronic. This seemingly obvious point matters because the resultant hybridity may not be convincing to defenders of disciplinary norms in either field.

Perhaps the main benefit of such collaboration is that it would help both disciplines – or at least certain parts of them – in their internal ontological and epistemological debates with other scholars in their own fields. Ben Rosamond argues that in EU political science there is an ongoing debate between the 'normal science' scholars and advocates of pluralism.[39] Collaboration with historians would certainly help reinforce such scholars' claims of the validity of normative, qualitative and interpretative approaches to study against the onslaught of positivism, which, as Robert Cox pithily remarks, 'knows only the synchronic'.[40]

In terms of EU history, engagement with political scientists could reinforce the benefits of shifting to a transnational, or even supranational, focus by supplying methods and concepts to help with this. It could also help reinforce historians' appreciation of the fact that they already use models and concepts, often without thinking, and that as a result some forms of political science may not be so alien after all. As Peter Burke points out, 'class' and 'revolution', for example, are concepts, not brute facts.[41] This could help historians deepen their scholarly reflexivity. Moreover, there are various kinds of theory. Rejecting 'grand theory' or the attempt to generate universal laws on the model of Newtonian physics does not translate into a rejection of all kinds of political theory. In fact, political science theoretical approaches to the EU are increasingly diverse,[42] and range from both meta-theoretical jousting (rationalists versus constructivists, with a nascent contribution from complexity theorists) to careful middle-range work aiming at the slow build-up of an holistic understanding.[43]

A further benefit could be reinforcement of the trend away from seeing political history as the study of 'great events' and 'great men'.[44] Although many political scientists in EU studies have focused on intergovernmental conferences (IGCs), seeing them as defining moments of system change and state power use, legion others have also focused on the day-to-day process of legislation, generating a wealth of evidence regarding the role of both state and non-state actors in EU politics, and an understanding that worthwhile study of the EU cannot simply focus on moments of Treaty change.[45]

History-political science collaboration in EU studies can also help both sets of scholars escape their parochial limits. Historians can thereby add a focus on the present to those foci they have on the past and the future.[46] Political scientists can free themselves from present-ism by developing an understanding of historical process and the broader context of the present, which may in turn both generate new theories or fresh evidence of pertinence in theory-testing. This is not a small advantage. For example, scholars of historical cases of confederation in Europe have generated useful insights for the present-day EU[47] which have in turn helped generate new theoretical models.[48] At the very least, such work calls upon political science scholars to broaden their imaginaries and lexicons.

Furthermore, by collaborating, political scientists and historians interested in the EU can test particular methods and assumptions which are commonplace in one or both fields. Do concepts such as 'rational choice' travel well to other times and cultures, or do the specificities of such new locations require reappraisal? Is the evolution of the EU really a steadily unfolding process incapable of rude jolts and directional changes? What are the links between current policies or problems and the EU's past?

Prospects for interdisciplinarity II: history meets politics in practice

The various chapters in this volume shed interesting light on the prospects for cooperation between historians and political scientists in EU studies. No single book could be the ultimate test of such possibilities, and certainly an examination of many political science books in EU studies might make for very cautionary conclusions – particularly if it were a book from the 'normal science' wing of the discipline. Nonetheless, although all the other chapters in this volume are written by historians trying to convince others in that discipline about how to rework the undertaking of EU history as an academic endeavour, and this is of course the primary basis on which their work should be assessed, their collective focus on institutionalist approaches, policy networks and the EU as a transnational entity generates potential intersections and possibilities for cross-fertilisation between political scientists and historians. Indeed, if such a collection of chapters offers no meaningful scope for collaboration across the history-politics frontier, where could it be found?

As a first comment, I think the papers here show that political science concepts *can* be used successfully to inform historical work on the EU. Both path-dependency and policy networks concepts are deployed to useful effect in order to help explain how actors in EU history have both collaborated and competed, and been subject to (as well as co-creating) ideational pressures and institutional patholo-gies which constrained their choices and actions. This is a positive addition to the political science work in new institutionalism and EU governance, and shows how political science concepts can usefully be employed to help historians think more carefully about their definitions of key terms. They also show how political scientists could benefit from engagement with scholars of EU history and their careful piecing together of chains events – an activity which should remind polit-ical scientists of the importance of the actor, the context, and the coincidental in explaining events. For example, the demonstration by Ann-Christina Lauring Knudsen that the EU political system existed long before the Maastricht Treaty challenges the orthodox view in political science and is very interesting for theoretical debates concerning the nature and evolution of the EU.[49] Moreover, Brigitte Leucht's chapter on the ideational contestation and complementarity between different forms of antitrust law sheds interesting light on the role of key actors (both American and European) and influences in the formation of both the EU itself – or at least, its predecessor, the European Coal and Steel Community (ECSC) and its particular competition policy regime. This contribution is rein-forced by Katja Seidel's chapter, which shows how organizational (sub-)cultures can form and, together with the key actors involved, shape the development of policy pathways – and even policy communities.

Sigfrido Ramirez' contribution to this book demonstrates how policy networks, which spanned not only the Atlantic but the Right/Left divide, were significant in the establishment of what is now the EU, a finding which is interesting in at least three ways. First, it asks EU studies political scientists to explore whether this kind of causal mechanism gives the EU rather more in common with such organi-sations as Asia-Pacific Economic Cooperation (APEC) than they usually consider. Second, it asks us to question whether at least some forms of policy network might have been active in shaping EU policy development rather earlier than we often believe – if so, this might challenge the influential typology of EU decision making set out by John Peterson.[50] Third, it points out the active role of transna-tional capitalists in the formation of the EU and determining its key policy areas – a subject which has only recently returned to the fore in EU studies political science.[51] Piers Ludlow's chapter offers evidence to both support and critique a 'principal-agent' approach in EU institutional analysis, and in uncovering evidence to explain the rise of Coreper as a collective means for the member states to retain control of the integration process he reinforces the confederal approaches to understanding the EU which have not always received their due in the mainstream of political science work.

Furthermore, Jan-Henrik Meyer's contribution to the volume shows that at least one method often used in political science can be used by historians in EU studies – discourse analysis. The study here offers many possibilities for collaboration with political scientists interested in public opinion or normative approaches to the construction of EU citizenship and the EU public sphere. Taken together, the chapters in this volume also demonstrate that to argue historians cannot understand the novel is misplaced. The present chapters demonstrate an understanding of the transnational aspects of European integration which is more profound than that of many IR scholars.

The introductory chapter of this volume also makes a convincing case for the role of history in deepening political science understandings of social, cultural and temporal contexts of actor behaviour, a point further demonstrated by the volume as a whole. The editors' argument that holistic analysis requires attention to the singular and accidental, as well as the general and the planned, is well-made. This could, in addition, provide useful support for the claims of political scientists of the same disposition. The claim that the European level has a fundamental impact on decisions at the national level, as well as the reverse, is in keeping with recent political science scholarship, but, as in the chapters by Ludlow and Seidel, this book adds weight to such work by demonstrating that similar links were apparent even before the post-Maastricht political science focus on 'Europeanisation'[52] and 'fusion'.[53] This has potentially significant implications for the development of these theoretical perspectives, and asks their proponents to look again at causal factors and processes. Is 'Europeanisation' inherent in the nature of the integration process rather than an indication of its recent transformation and possible down-grading? Moreover, the transnational perspective deployed here makes clear the links between the failures of state-centric EU history and intergovernmental approaches in EU political science – an intriguing parallel which sheds much potential light on the sociology of knowledge of both disciplines.

Some of the chapters also demonstrate the need for care when approaching the work of another discipline, and hence that interdisciplinarity really does require collective rather than lone scholar modes of research. This is by no means unique for historians embracing political science, or indeed for political scientists embracing history. It simply reflects the simple but challenging fact that holistic and synthetic approaches to studying a given problem require genuine collaboration. Thus, and as an indicator of what might be fruitful subsequent research, it would be intriguing to build on the respective chapters by Rasmussen, Ludlow and Kaiser by exploring how other contributions to integration theory than those scope permits them to address here – such as confederalism – might fare against their robust, and convincing, critiques of principal-agent approaches and Liberal Intergovernmentalism (LI).

Although it is essential for holistic understanding of the EU that scholars from different disciplines bring the benefits of their academic 'home' to bear on the study of the problematic, this must be balanced against a full appreciation of why the scholarship under the microscope has been elaborated in a particular way.

Thus, Rasmussen's chapter in this volume rightly takes Andrew Moravcsik to task for ignoring the impact of time on politics and policy, but political science critiques of Moravcsik's LI focus on its assumption of non-changing state preferences and its inability to explain either the autonomy of the EU institutions or the de facto use of power in day-to-day EU politics.[54] Rasmussen's claim is by no means wrong, and is in fact a useful addition to these political science critiques. However, the simple fact that both Rasmussen's core concern, and the motivation of his critique, are different from those of Moravcsik's critics inside political science demonstrates both the fruitfulness for political scientists of engaging with EU historians and that in order for such cross-disciplinary potential to be harnessed, an explicit process of project definition between teams of scholars from both disciplines would be beneficial. Without taking such a step, chapters written primarily for a mono-disciplinary audience will concentrate on the task of persuading that audience of their argument. Kristian Steinnes' interesting contribution to this volume is a case in point. Building on such a careful construction of the past as is achieved in his chapter, to think about its implications for the present, and how historians and political scientists could explore the salience of transnational networks among EU 'outsiders' raised by Steinnes would make for a fascinating project in the context of EU enlargement and/or differentiated integration.

Perhaps the main conclusion on the issue of interdisciplinarity to be drawn from this volume, then, is how difficult it is to harness its potential from within the confines of one discipline without explicit effort and collaboration between scholars from either side of the disciplinary fence. The essays here provide much evidence that supranational and transnational approaches to EU history are not only possible, but necessary. As a result, it makes a significant contribution to the study not only of EU history, but of the EU in general, and is to be welcomed by political scientists as well as historians. Optimal capitalisation on this development, however, is likely to require sustained cross-disciplinary partnership, and in the final section of the chapter I reflect on how that might be undertaken.

Conclusions: suggestions for future interdisciplinary research

In order to harness the full potential of collaboration between historians and political scientists in EU studies, I take as a departure point the continuum of interdisciplinarity and argue that we need to aim at a stage beyond multidisciplinarity in order to ensure that a shared research agenda can be generated. Following or adapting Newell's seven-step procedure would be a useful guide here.[55] This process sets out a complex but productive process of integration between disciplinary perspectives: conflict-identification (whereby different disciplinary perspectives are compared); evaluation (applying each perspective to the problem at hand); resolution (disciplinary differences are bridged as a result of the evaluation process); creation of a common vocabulary and perspective; constructing a new understanding of the problem on that basis; producing a model of the problem that works out of this new understanding; and testing the model.

To reach this point, a clear audit of collaboration to date and suitable issues for joint research would need to be undertaken by scholars from both disciplines. How much EU history has 'travelled' to political science (and vice versa), and why? How should this double exchange be supplemented? This would require attention to sociology of knowledge issues as well as individual themes and approaches.

A subsequent step would be to agree priority issues for collaborative research. Jensen argued some time ago that collaboration between historians and political scientists could focus on analysis of particularly important events, trends or institutions.[56] In the particular case of the EU, how exactly would this be cashed out – focusing on IGCs and the EU institutions? And should it be an alternative to, or a complement of, research into broader processes? Are there, for instance, poverties in political science accounts of the EU's early days in the 1950s and the run-up to the ECSC in the late 1940s which historians could fill? Might Lise Rye's contribution to this volume serve to generate collaboration with constructivist political scientists on the generation of EU values and identity? Could historians work with political economy scholars and political theorists to explore interesting potential analogies for the present-day EU, such as the 'mixed commonwealth' or 'neo-mediaevalism', and even for other forms of regional polity in the contemporary political economy?[57] Can the relationship between IR and political science as expressed in EU studies yield any useful lessons for the relationship between EU and global histories – and vice versa?

Finally, at the epistemological level, historians and political scientists in EU studies could cooperate in re-thinking area studies for a post- or interdisciplinary, rather than non-disciplinary, age.[58] This ambitious programme should produce extremely fertile research, but requires the sustained will of scholars from both disciplines if it is to be accomplished. The chapters in this volume indicate that the potential for collaboration is both demonstrable and under-exploited. In making the case for a combined supranational and transnational approach to EU history, it therefore also makes the case for a historically-literate approach to EU politics.

Notes

1 I use the terms 'political science' and 'political scientist' with some reservation, and primarily because I cannot find a better term in English. This should not be taken to connote acceptance of the idea that the study of politics can be undertaken as the search for universally applicable laws in the spirit of positivist natural science.

2 Alex Warleigh, 'Learning From Europe? EU Studies and the Rethinking of "International Relations"', *European Journal of International Relations*, vol. 12, no. 1 (2006), pp. 31–51.

3 Ben Rosamond, 'Globalization, the Ambivalence of European Integration and the Possibilities for a Post-Disciplinary EU Studies', *Innovations*, vol. 18, no. 1 (2005), pp. 23–43; Angela Bourne and Michelle Cini 'Introduction: Defining Boundaries and Identifying Trends in European Union Studies', in idem (eds.) *Palgrave Advances in EU Studies*, Basingstoke: Palgrave, 2006, pp. 1–18.

4 Rosamond, 'Globalization'; idem., 'The Political Sciences of European Integration: Disciplinary History and EU Studies', in Knud Erik Jørgensen, Mark Pollack and

Ben Rosamond (eds.) *Handbook of European Union Politics*, London: Sage, 2007, pp. 7–30; Alex Warleigh, 'In Defence of Intra-disciplinarity: "European Studies", the "New Regionalism" and the Issue of Democratisation' *Cambridge Review of International* Affairs, vol. 17, no. 2 (2004), pp. 301–18.

5 Wolfram Kaiser, 'From State to Society? The Historiography of European Integration', in Cini and Bourne (eds.) *Palgrave Advances in EU Studies*, pp. 190–208.

6 Andrew Moravcsik, *The Choice for Europe: Social Purpose and State Power from Messina to Maastricht*, London: UCL Press, 1999.

7 Warleigh, 'Learning from Europe'; Jeffrey Haynes, *Comparative Politics in a Globalizing World*, Cambridge: Polity, 2005.

8 Anne-Marie Slaughter, *A New World Order*, Princeton: Princeton University Press, 2004.

9 Mark Bevir, 'Political Studies as Narrative and Science, 1880–2000', *Political Studies*, vol. 54, no. 3 (2006), pp. 583–606; Peter Burnell, 'Perspectives', in idem. (ed.) *Democratization Through the Looking Glass*, Manchester: Manchester University Press, 2003, pp. 1–19.

10 Richard Jensen, 'History and the Political Scientist', in Seymour M. Lipset (ed.) *Politics and the Social Sciences*, London: Oxford University Press, 1969, pp. 1–28.

11 Jensen, 'History and the Political Scientist'; Haynes, *Comparative Politics*; Kaiser, 'From State to Society'.

12 Harold Lasswell, *Politics: Who Gets What, When, How?*, New York: McGraw-Hill, 1936. For contemporary introductions to the study of politics, see Stephen Tansey, *Politics – The Basics*, London: Routledge, 2000, and Andrew Heywood, *Politics*, 2nd ed., Basingstoke: Palgrave, 2002.

13 Alex Warleigh-Lack and Michelle Cini, 'Interdisciplinarity and the Study of Politics: Conclusions', *European Political Science*, vol. 8, no. 1, forthcoming.

14 Edward H. Carr, *What Is History?* Harmondsworth: Pelican, 1961.

15 Peter Burke, *History and Social Theory*, Cambridge: Polity, 2005.

16 Carr, *What is History?* Eric Hobsbawm, *On History*, London: Weidenfeld and Nicholson, 1997.

17 Martha Howell and Walter Prevenier, *From Reliable Sources: An Introduction to Historical Methods*, Ithaca: Cornell University Press, 2001.

18 For example, in *On History* Hobsbawm writes that 'human beings stay much the same and human situations recur' (p. 27), but also that 'the beginning of historical understanding is an appreciation of the *otherness* of the past' (p. 233; italics in original) – a paradox, if not a contradiction, with which historians must grapple.

19 Howell and Prevenier, *From Reliable Sources*, p. 1.

20 Julie Thompson Klein, 'Interdisciplinarity and Complexity: An Evolving Relationship', *E:CO*, vol. 6, nos. 1–2 (2004), pp. 2–10, here p. 3; emphasis in original.

21 Joe Moran, *Interdisciplinarity*, London: Routledge, 2002.

22 Klein, 'Interdisciplinariy and Complexity'; William Newell, 'A Theory of Interdisciplinary Studies', *Issues in Integrative Studies*, vol. 19 (2001), pp. 1–25; Julie Thompson Klein, *Interdisciplinarity: History, Theory and Practice*, Detroit: Wayne State University Press, 1990.

23 However, post-modern scholars argue that the very utility of interdisciplinarity is its ambiguity and residence at the interstices of discipline boundaries, and that imposing a methodological or theoretical orthodoxy on it would be self-defeating. See Moran, *Interdisciplinarity*.

24 Newell, *A Theory of Interdisciplinary Studies*.

25 Peter Van den Besselaar and Gaston Heimericks, 'Disciplinarity, Multidisciplinarity, Interdisciplinarity – Concepts and Indicators', paper to 8th Conference on Scientometrics and Infometrics (ISSI 2001), Sydney, Australia, 16–20 July 2001.

26 Van de Besselaar and Heimericks, 'Disciplinarity, Multidisciplinarity, Interdisciplinarity'.

27 I here use the term 'interdisciplinarity' to refer to the two more demanding forms of non-disciplinary work, i.e. interdisciplinarity and transdisciplinarity.
28 Warleigh-Lack and Cini, 'Interdisciplinarity and the Study of Politics'.
29 Kaiser, 'From State to Society?'.
30 Burke, *History and Social Theory*; Howell and Prevenier, *From Reliable Sources*.
31 Bourne and Cini, 'Introduction: Defining Boundaries and Indentifying Trends'.
32 Alex Warleigh, 'In Defence of Intra-disciplinarity'.
33 Chris Rumford and Philomena Murray, 'Globalization and The Limitations of European Integration Studies: Interdisciplinary Considerations', *Journal of Contemporary European Studies* vol. 11, no. 1 (2003), pp. 85–93.
34 Alan S. Milward and Vibeke Sørensen, 'Interdependence or Integration? A National Choice', in Alan S. Milward *et al.*, *The Frontier of National Sovereignty: History and Theory 1945–1992*, London: Routledge, 1993, pp. 1–32; Charles Pentland, *International Theory and European Integration*, London: Faber and Faber, 1973; Reginald J. Harrison, *Europe in Question. Theories of Regional International Integration*, London: Allen and Unwin, 1974.
35 Wolfram Kaiser, 'Transnational Western Europe Since 1945: Integration as Political Society Formation', in idem and Peter Starie (eds.) *Transnational European Union: Towards a Common Political Space*, London: Routledge, 2005, pp. 17–35.
36 Alan S. Milward, 'History, Political Science and European Integration', in Jørgensen, Pollack and Rosamond (eds.), *Handbook of European Union Politics*, pp. 99–103.
37 Luke Ashworth, 'Interdisciplinarity and International Relations', *European Political Science*, vol. 8, no. 1, forthcoming.
38 This point is made by Howell and Prevenier, *From Reliable Sources*. However, it should be noted that without such adaptation scholars produce not just bad history but also bad political science.
39 Ben Rosamond, 'The Political Sciences of European Integration: Disciplinary History and EU Studies', in Jørgensen, Pollack and Rosamond (eds.), *Handbook of European Union Politics*, pp. 7–30.
40 Robert W. Cox, 'Foreword: International Organization in an Era of Changing Historical Structures', in Bob Reinalda and Bertjan Verbeek (eds.), *Decision Making Within International Organizations*, London: Routledge, 2004, pp. 3–8, here p. 5.
41 Burke, *History and Social Theory*.
42 See Ben Rosamond, *Theories of European Integration*, Basingstoke: Macmillan, 2000; Antje Wiener and Thomas Diez (eds.) *European Integration Theories*, Oxford: Oxford University Press, 2004.
43 On complexity theory and EU studies, see Robert Geyer 'European Integration, the Problem of Complexity and the Revision of Theory', *Journal of Common Market Studies*, vol. 41, no. 1 (2003), pp. 15–35.
44 See Fernand Braudel, *On History*, Chicago: Chicago University Press, 1980.
45 For a very impressive survey of the state of the art, see Jørgensen, Pollack and Rosamond (eds.), *Handbook of European Union Politics*.
46 Carr, *What is History?*
47 Murray Forsyth, *Unions of States: The Theory and Practice of Confederation*, Leicester: Leicester University Press, 1981.
48 Dimitris Chryssochoou, 'Democracy and Symbiosis in the EU: Towards a Confederal Consociation', *West European Politics*, vol. 17, no. 4 (1994), pp. 1–14; Alex Warleigh, 'History Repeating? Framework Theory and Europe's Multi-level Confederation', *Journal of European Integration*, vol. 22, no. 2 (2000), pp. 173–200.
49 Explicit focus on the EU as a political system has been a feature of recent literature. Arguably, the idea of the EU as a nascent political system was present in neofunctionalism, and certainly the myriad explorations of EU governance and policy making using tools such as policy networks, which can be traced back to the 1970s, assumed

the existence of a system in which such networks can operate. However, only after the debates in integration theory widened out from the intergovernmentalism – neofunctionalism continuum did it become commonplace to acknowledge the EU political system as such. On developments in integration theory, see Rosamond, *Theories of European Integration*. On the EU as a political system, see Simon Hix, *The Political System of the European Union*, 2nd ed., Basingstoke: Palgrave, 2005.

50 John Peterson, 'Decision-making in the European Union: Towards a Framework for Analysis', *Journal of European Public Policy*, vol. 2, no. 1 (1995), pp. 69–93.

51 Alan Cafruny and Magnus Ryner (eds.), *A Ruined Fortress? Neoliberal Hegemony and Transformation in Europe*, Lanham: Rowman and Littlefield, 2003.

52 See Claudio Radaelli, 'Europeanization: Solution or Problem?', in Cini and Bourne (eds.), *Palgrave Advances in European Union Studies*, pp. 56–76.

53 Wolfgang Wessels, 'An Ever Closer Fusion? A Dynamic Macropolitical View on Integration Processes', *Journal of Common Market Studies*, vol. 35, no. 2 (1997), pp. 267–99.

54 Daniel Wincott, 'Institutional Interaction and European Integration: Towards an Everyday Critique of Liberal Intergovernmentalism', *Journal of Common Market Studies*, vol. 33, no. 4, (1995), pp. 597–609.

55 Newell, 'A Theory of Interdisciplinary Studies'.

56 Jensen, 'History and the Political Scientist'.

57 See John Ravenhill (ed.) *Global Political Economy*, Oxford: Oxford University Press, 2005.

58 On the distinction between interdisciplinarity and a-theoretical study, see Michelle Cini, 'The State of the Art in EU Studies: From Politics to Interdisciplinarity (and Back Again?)', *Politics*, vol. 26, no. 1 (2006), pp. 38–46.

Index

ACEA (European Automobile Manufactures
 Association) 76
Acheson, Dean 60-2, 65
acquis communautaire 18, 42, 97, 120
Action Programme in the Field of Technology and
 Industrial Policy 78
Adenauer, Konrad 2-3, 21-3, 60, 62, 66, 68, 115
Administration for the Economy of the Bi-zone 63
administrative culture 38, 43-4, 47-8, 129
advocacy coalitions 15-16, 23, 27, 121
Advocates General 43
Aftonbladet 102
agenda setting 36-7, 88
Agnelli 76, 80-5; Foundation 76; Giovanni 75-6,
 81-5; Umberto 81, 88
agricultural: experts 47, 135, 200; levies 168, 170-1,
 177, 181; policy 16, 32, 39, 97-9, 113, 115-6,
 118, 120, 135, 138, 192-3, 200
Albrecht, Ernst 135-6, 143
Alfa Romeo 81
allegiance 13, 18, 20
Almond, Gabriel 34
American Committee for a United Europe 27, 76
American Committee for a National Trade Policy 76
American Committee for Economic Development
 (CED) 75
American empire 56-7
American organizational sociology 40
Americanization 25, 57, 62
Anaya, Pilar Ortuño 26
Anglo-French Coordinating Committee 59
Anglo-German Society 112
anti-trust: American anti-trust law 57, 61, 63, 66-8,
 132, 134; European anti-trust law 56, 69; German
 anti-trust law 59, 66-7; law 59, 61, 63, 66-9,
 132-3, 136; policy 22, 57, 67, 133; provisions
 56-9, 62-4, 66-9;
APEC (Asia-Pacific Economic Cooperation) 214
appointment of commissioners 37
article 111 Committee 193
article 41 ECSC treaty 64, 66-8
article 42 ECSC treaty 64, 66-7
article 60 ECSC treaty 67
article 61 ECSC treaty 68
article 65 ECSC treaty 56, 67, 130
article 66 ECSC treaty 56, 68, 130
article 85 EEC treaty 83, 130-1, 139
article 86 EEC treaty 130-1, 139
article 87 EEC treaty 131, 139
article 88 EEC treaty 139

article 177 EEC treaty 46
article 199 EEC treaty 180,182
article 201 EEC treaty 171
article 235 EEC treaty 49
Asia-Pacific Economic Cooperation (APEC) 214
Association for European Monetary Union 76
audio-visual: information 154-5; techniques 155
Austria 4, 20, 26, 75, 96, 103
Austrian People's Party 26
Austrian Socialist Party (SPÖ) 96

Ball, George 58-9, 65, 67
Bangemann, Martin 88
Belgian Centre for Public Relations 153
Belgian government 86, 141
Belgium 59, 75, 78, 83, 139, 189
Benelux: 200, countries 56, 142, customs union 133,
 states 200
Berghahn, Volker 25, 66
Berliet (firm) 81
Bidault, Georges 21-2, 60
Bilderberg Group 75-6
BLMC (British Leyland Motors Corporation) 80, 83
BMW (Bayrische Motorenwerke) 79, 81
Boegner, Jean-Marc 181, 189-90
Boël, Baron René 75
Borschette, Albert 197
Bourdieu, Pierre 40-1 43-4
Bowie, Robert 57-9, 62, 65-8
Brandt, Willy 79, 96-7, 105, 111, 116
Bratteli, Trygve 96
Britain 1, 26-7, 48, 75, 83, 93-105, 111-12, 115,
 117-21, 172, 179-80, 199
British Leyland Motors Corporation 77, 80
British Supply Council 59
Brown, George 96, 98, 101-3
Bruce, David 60
Budget treaty 167-9, 182-4
budgetary controls 37
budgetary powers 37, 152, 161-2, 167-8, 171-5,
 177-9, 181-4
budgetary procedure 167-70, 172, 174-6, 178, 181-2
Bundesverband der Deutschen Industrie 74
Burke, Peter 212
Burroughs (firm) 76
Business Europe 75
Böhm, Franz 23, 63, 66-7, 132, 136-7

cahier de doleances 192
Camps, Miriam 94

Lightning Source UK Ltd.
Milton Keynes UK
14 March 2011